The Short
of Nelson Algren

The Short Writings of Nelson Algren

A Study of His Stories, Essays, Articles, Reviews, Poems and Other Literature

RICHARD F. BALES

Foreword by Kenneth G. McCollum

McFarland & Company, Inc., Publishers

Jefferson, North Carolina

ISBN (print) 978-1-4766-8132-0
ISBN (ebook) 978-1-4766-4709-8

LIBRARY OF CONGRESS AND BRITISH LIBRARY
CATALOGUING DATA ARE AVAILABLE

Library of Congress Control Number 2022034674

Front cover: Drawing by Marshall Philyaw based
on a photograph by Art Shay

Printed in the United States of America

*McFarland & Company, Inc., Publishers
Box 611, Jefferson, North Carolina 28640
www.mcfarlandpub.com*

For Joanne, Mike, and Tom
Phyllis, R.J., Beth, Kate, Peggy, David, Jane, and Robert
and for Jack, naturally.

Table of Contents

Acknowledgments

Although I alone am responsible for any of this book's shortcomings, the credit for any of its strengths belongs to the people who have assisted me over the years. My twin brother, Jack Bales, was always there for me, as he has been my entire life, helping me with all of the problems and issues that arise when one is writing a book. He was a reference librarian at the University of Mary Washington in Fredericksburg, Virginia. He is now retired, but while he was at the library, he and his always resourceful co-worker, Carla Bailey, would obtain copies of dozens of items via inter-library loan for me.

Ken McCollum, who contributed the foreword, was one of the first Nelson Algren scholars. His book, *Nelson Algren: A Checklist*, was published in 1973. Throughout my years of research and writing, he offered me constant support and advice. He read and critiqued each essay as I wrote it. Bettina Drew was also the first, with her full-length 1989 biography of Algren. She guided me past several research obstacles.

Rose Appel, Tammy Freese, Catherine Gruber, Jeni LaCalamita, Cheryl Mahony, and Stacy Teegardin, helped me obtain copies of Algren materials, as did Regina Remson of Benedictine University and Ikumi Crocoll, formerly of the Newberry Library. I obtained original Algren books and periodicals from many sources, but book dealers Robert S. Brooks, James J. Conway, Tom Davidson, Tom Joyce, Carlos Martinez, Lynn Roundtree, and Pete Schmidt were especially helpful.

Over the years, countless Chicago researchers have expressed their gratitude to the staff of the Research Center of the Chicago History Museum. I am just one more to add to a very long list. Michael Featherstone, Ellen Keith, and Lesley Martin were always available for me, whether they were getting me needed reference material or listening patiently while I talked enthusiastically about my progress. Thanks also to Peter T. Alter, the museum's Chief Historian and Director of the Studs Terkel Center for Oral History, for his support, and Katie Levi of the museum's Rights and Reproductions Department for her help in getting me

Algren images. Juan Molina Hernández of the Newberry Library helped me obtain a needed photograph. Several miles to the south, Glenn Humphreys of the Chicago Public Library provided me access to the library's extensive Algren collection. I spent many hours at both the Chicago History Museum and the Chicago Public Library, going through endless reels of microfilm. Hundreds of miles to the east, Isabel Planton of the Lilly Library at Indiana University and Jolie Braun and Rebecca Jewett of the Rare Books and Manuscripts Library at Ohio State University helped me obtain materials from their libraries' respective Nelson Algren collections. Even farther eastward, researcher Peggy Brown sent me WPA records from the Library of Congress, and Laurie Longfield of the New York Folklore Society sent me materials concerning the Federal Writers' Project.

I am indebted to Jeff McMahon for his groundbreaking *Chicago: City on the Make* scholarship. George Rogge and Sue Rutsen, founders of the Nelson Algren Museum of Miller Beach, provided me with information about Algren's years in Indiana. Brian Boyer gave me material concerning Algren and his writing for the *Chicago Free Press.*

The employees of OfficeMax, Batavia, Illinois, were consistently gracious as they processed TIF files of the illustrations that fill this book. My sister, Kate Bales, was able to take these images, clean them up, and magically enhance their quality. Marshall Philyaw also created magic with his Nelson Algren artwork.

Thanks also to Victor Armendariz, Peggy Bales, Heidi Beazley, Sabrina Bier, Nina Burke, Karen Carpenter, Mark Eleveld, Brian Harty, Richard Hein, Mary Hricko, Scott K. Kellar, Rick Kogan, Gary Leavitt, Amber Marro, Mark Moran, Deanna Nole, Don Nole, Nate Parker, Kim Reis, Daniel Romo, Richard Shay, Greg Spalenka, Micaela Rae Terronez, Daniel Trujillo, Daryl Van Fleet, Jean Van Fleet, and Anson Whaley.

I could not have written this book without the cooperation, enthusiasm, and kindness of Bernice S. Behar of the Nelson Algren estate. I owe her much.

Finally, thanks to my wife, Joanne, and my two sons, Mike and Tom, for putting up with this project for the past ten years. I owe them, too.

Foreword

by Kenneth G. McCollum

Dick Bales' volume presents considerable new commentary and documentation on Nelson Algren, as well as showing the researcher's genuine appreciation and affection for Algren's work. Although Nelson will be remembered for his novels, primarily, he had a vast amount of other published work, such as book reviews and critical essays, and Mr. Bales has done a masterful job in locating and commenting on these works.

When asked, I told Dick that I would provide some commentary on how the literary research on Nelson Algren started. Mine began after a 1970 dinner with Matthew Bruccoli and family. Matt, a professor at the University of South Carolina who died in 2008, was a prolific publisher of educational volumes. After dinner, Matt and I were in his study, where he showed me his latest biography/bibliography. I said I'd like to do one of those, and Matt replied, "Who would you do?" I offered, "Maybe Nelson Algren." Matt jumped up, pounded the table next to his chair, and said, "Start tonight!" I didn't start then but did soon after and was fortunate to meet Nelson, Jack Conroy, and Studs Terkel along the way.

I remember answering the phone in early 1973 to a voice saying, "This is Studs Terkel." I had written to Studs, a Chicago celebrity and Algren friend, and asked if he would consider writing front matter for a book on Nelson Algren. He wanted to know why Algren, and I responded that I thought his writing deserved attention, I had an interested publisher, and Nelson was the funniest guy around. Studs grabbed the lead and provided the most poignant appreciation of Algren to date, almost 50 years ago.

Jack Conroy, Nelson's close friend and writer during the 1930s, was still distanced from Algren when I was working on the book. Originally, I asked Jack to do an introduction, but he declined graciously. The Conroy-Algren separation, initiated by Algren, continued until Algren's death in 1981.[1]

On one occasion, I went to a book signing and ceremony for Jack's *Writers in Revolt*, hosted by Studs, and had tried to get Nelson to go. He and

1

I had been watching TV at his place. He was close to agreeing, but at the last moment just couldn't do it. This reunion would have been a moment in literary history, but it didn't happen. Jack was very disappointed.

Matt Bruccoli published my Algren compilation, *Nelson Algren: A Checklist*, in the Gale Research series. Martha Heasley Cox and Wayne Chatterton were also collaborating on an Algren effort that would come out in 1975. Matt followed with a then comprehensive bibliography of Nelson's works. Subsequently, Bettina Drew did the Algren biography that needed to be done. Others have followed.

Dick Bales has done the most extensive research on Nelson Algren's "lost" works to date and compiled an impressive study of Nelson and his work in general. I applaud this fine effort and hope the educational community and reading public will do the same.

> Kenneth G. McCollum published numerous scholastic contributions on American authors, including a book on Nelson Algren. He taught American literature at several colleges and universities, while working in defense-related government and industry. He is retired and lives with his wife Tamar in Johnson City, Tennessee.

NOTE

1. Author's note: In 1959 editor and author David Ray interviewed Algren in his Chicago apartment. During the interview, Algren referred to "J. C. Kornpoën" from Groveling, Missouri. Algren told Ray that "Kornpoën occupied the Chair of Make-Believe Literature at Alcoholics Anonymous." Algren's description of Conroy as a rube and a drunk hurt Conroy deeply. Douglas Wixson writes in his 1994 biography of Conroy that "the rift became a kind of legend in Chicago and among Conroy's friends. It continues to be debated today." David Ray, "A Talk on the Wild Side," *The Reporter*, 11 June 1959, 31–33; reprint, "A Talk on the Wild Side," *Cavalcade*, July 1964, 52–55; Douglas Wixson, *Worker-Writer in America: Jack Conroy and the Tradition of Midwestern Literary Radicalism, 1898–1990* (Urbana: University of Illinois Press, 1994), 470–72, 576n67, 577n76.

Introduction

Think that Nelson Algren is probably the best writer
under 50, and name your own figure, writing today.
—Ernest Hemingway to Malcolm Cowley,
11 October 1949.[1]

* * *

Figure 1: This photograph of Nelson Algren
is circa 1968. Chicago's Marina City is visible
in the background. In the movie *The Hunter*
(1980), bounty hunter Steve McQueen pursued
a bail jumper in a car chase through Marina
City's parking garage. The suspect eventually
lost control of his car and drove off one of the
upper floors of the garage and plunged into
the Chicago River (Chicago History Museum,
ICHi-023627; Stephen Deutch, photographer).

For years I have
been interested in Chi-
cago history. My library of
Chicago-related books is
fairly extensive, much to the
dismay of my long-suffering
wife. I would regularly buy
either out-of-print books
from Internet book deal-
ers or new books from
bricks-and-mortar book
stores. Using my Chi-
cago books, ante-fire land
records, and other primary
sources, I wrote a book on
the cause of the Great Chicago Fire of 1871 entitled *The
Great Chicago Fire and the
Myth of Mrs. O'Leary's Cow.*
McFarland published this
book in 2002.

About twelve years
ago I brought home Art
Shay's book, *Chicago's Nelson Algren* (2007). Both the

3

pictures and the text fascinated me. Curious about Algren, I began to read more about the man.

I discovered that during his lifetime and after he died, Chicago author Nelson Algren (1909–1981) has been traditionally thought of and remembered as a writer of novels. He wrote five of them: *Somebody in Boots* (1935), *Never Come Morning* (1942), *The Man with the Golden Arm* (1949), *A Walk on the Wild Side* (1956), and *The Devil's Stocking* (1983). In 1950 his third novel, *The Man with the Golden Arm*, was awarded the first National Book Award for Fiction. Seven years later George Bluestone wrote an essay for *The Western Review* that began with the words, "Nelson Algren is known as a Chicago novelist."[2]

In 1989 James R. Giles published a book entitled *Confronting the Horror: The Novels of Nelson Algren*. Brooke Horvath followed a few years later with his book, *Understanding Nelson Algren* (2005). Horvath's book is about all of Algren's works, not just his novels. Nonetheless, the first sentence on the front flap of the dust jacket of Horvath's book contains the statement that Algren was "a writer best known for his novels *The Man with the Golden Arm* and *A Walk on the Wild Side*."[3]

Algren was obviously a novelist, and so I started buying and reading Algren's novels. But I didn't stop there. I began to purchase books about Algren and his works, such as Bettina Drew's biography, *Nelson Algren: A Life on the Wild Side* (1989) and Kenneth G. McCollum's bibliography, *Nelson Algren: A Checklist* (1973). As I read, I began to realize that there was more to Nelson Algren than his novels. A lot more. I bought Matthew J. Bruccoli's, *Nelson Algren: A Descriptive Bibliography* (1985), and using that as a guide, I started buying the magazines that featured his stories and articles. By then I was obsessed, and I regularly trolled both eBay.com and Abebooks.com, looking for new items. Again to the dismay of my wife, I started attending the Windy City Pulp and Paper Convention in suburban Chicago, where once a year I would spend hours kneeling on the concrete floor of a hotel convention hall, looking through cardboard boxes of men's magazines. I discovered periodicals like *Stag* and *Swank* that featured Algren's work that were not listed in Matthew Bruccoli's bibliography.

Algren wrote hundreds of short stories, book reviews, poems, and magazine and newspaper articles, and much of what he wrote was good, really good. Although James R. Giles discusses Algren's novels in *Confronting the Horror*, no one has written a book devoted solely to Algren's "other" literature—that is, everything but his novels, like his short stories, poetry, and essays. I decided to change that.

Many of Algren's stories and articles were republished in Algren's four collections—*The Neon Wilderness* (1947), *Who Lost an American?* (1963), *Notes from a Sea Diary: Hemingway All the Way* (1965), and *The*

Last Carousel (1973)—but many items were not. Dan Simon and Brooke Horvath, editors of the Algren compilation, *Entrapment and Other Writings* (2009), comment that "some of Algren's finest stories and essays were published once, either in obscure or major magazines, then weren't collected in book form, and so were lost."[4]

"And so were lost." I decided to expand on Dan Simon's and Brooke Horvath's use of the word "lost" in describing Algren's writing. Algren was known as a novelist. But after *A Walk on the Wild Side* was released in 1956, he never wrote and published another novel during his lifetime. Although he continued to write, that did not matter to some people, who would ask him when he was going to write his next novel—what they called the "Big One." Author Meyer Levin commented in 1973 that "Nelson Algren seems to be identified as *the* Chicago writer but—perhaps symbolically—doesn't write." It seems that anything that Algren wrote that wasn't a novel—which would be all of his stories and articles and poems and book reviews—might as well not exist, that these works might as well all be "lost." Thus, this book is a look at that segment of Algren's writing that Meyer Levin and others had ignored—everything but his novels.[5]

What did Meyer Levin ignore? Only three years before Levin claimed that Algren did not write, Algren took "God Bless the Lonesome Gas Man," a 1962 short story he wrote for a men's magazine, and revised it into a story he called "Seven Feet Down and Creeping," which he published in a 1970 issue of *The New Orleans Review*, a university literary journal. This story, as revised, begins with five wonderfully descriptive paragraphs. Although Algren rewrote the story again and published it three years later in his collection, *The Last Carousel*, as "The Leak That Defied the Books," these paragraphs disappeared from the revision. The following memorable lines were published only once; after that, they never appeared in print again:

> The hard-time houses of Moorman Street abide in a brown, old-fashioned light. Smoke holds onto their eaves in winter: the chimneys of Moorman Street take no chances of being billed by some utility company for sending smoke too high.
>
> The windows of Moorman Street never look up lest a meter-man be looking in. Anyhow, why look up? Everything that happens happens on the ground.
>
> The iron fences of Moorman Street have a watchful air; and the grass behind them has a hard time of it all year round.
>
> In this block-long row of low-built houses bearing low-hanging porches under a smoke pall that prefers sidewalks to skies, one house is missing—as if it had sunk. Yet under the nameless weeds and the rubble of the changeful years, the arteried stone remains; where once stood a house that sank, burned or simply fell in. Children of Moorman Street go there to play catch. "I'll meet you at the house that came down," the kid with the ball tells the other kids.

I am the only one who remembers the couple who lived in The House That Came Down.[6]

I originally planned for this book to be a study of Nelson Algren's "non-novels," with separate chapters on the 1930s, the 1940s, the 1950s, and the later years. But I eventually realized that not only would the book be massive, it would be more in the nature of a biography, albeit a literary biography, and three biographies of Algren have already been published. It was clear that because Algren wrote so much, I could not write about everything he wrote.

Chicago writer Rick Kogan is the son of Herman and Marilew Kogan, who were friends of Algren. Kogan believes that Algren's "literary genius" lies in his short stories rather than his novels. Kogan is correct; Algren won three O. Henry Memorial Awards for his stories. Nonetheless, I chose to not write a general essay about his short stories. Algren wrote so many of them, I was afraid that this would result in a "cherry-picking" of only his greatest hits. Many of his articles were as good as the best of his stories, but again, for the same reason, I have not included an essay about his articles in this book.[7]

Instead, I wanted to be both myopic and balanced in my selections, and so I decided to cover eleven very specific subjects. By doing so, I could be comprehensive without being partisan or voluminous.

After Algren's fourth novel, *A Walk on the Wild Side*, was published in 1956, he began writing for a variety of men's magazines with forgettable names like *Rogue* and *Scamp*. His "men's magazines era" covered about eighteen years (1956–1974) and a wide breadth of his writing—short stories, articles, and poems. I decided to write an essay on Algren's men's magazine writing. Algren often revised and reissued his stories, and so I placed a special emphasis on those works that he published only once and then were never seen again.

In 1970 Algren was hired as a contributing writer for the *Chicago Free Press*, a short-lived Chicago newsmagazine. His job description was simple—he could "write about whatever he wants to." Unfortunately, "short-lived" meant only nine issues, but within those issues Algren wrote seven articles, one story, and one book review. The "*Chicago Free Press* era" lasted less than a year, but it nonetheless covered an impressive range of writing.[8]

In 1956 *Chicago* magazine reprinted his 1942 prose poem, "The Swede Was a Hard Guy." Years later, between 1975 and 1981, the magazine published five original and varied articles and stories. *Chicago* may be unique in that it published Algren material both at the beginning and at the end of his writing career—it published one of his earlier works and some of his last works. These contributions also deserve discussion.[9]

Some of Algren's "lost literature" include book reviews and book introductions, and these are discussed in this book. He wrote poetry throughout his life, and although people have tried cataloguing his poetry, no one until now has both catalogued and discussed every known Algren poem. He wrote five poems in the 1930s and five poems in the 1940s, and so the early years of his writing career are well represented in this essay on his poetry.

Nelson Algren wrote about the Chicago White Sox from 1942 to 1981 (the year he died), and I have included a separate essay on his Chicago White Sox baseball literature. *Chicago: City on the Make* is a book-length prose poem that has been reprinted six times since its 1951 publication. I have written a comprehensive analysis and discussion of this major work. Algren enjoyed (and wrote about) horse racing, boxing, and gambling, and I examine these passions in three separate essays. Each of these essays includes a list of Algren's writings relating to each respective interest.

I have divided these eleven subjects into three broad groups. The first group is "Literary Eras," consisting of what I call the men's magazines era, the *Chicago Free Press* era, and the *Chicago* magazine era. (Algren wrote short stories and articles for men's magazines, the *Chicago Free Press*, and *Chicago* magazine, and I discuss his stories and articles in each essay. This is one more reason why I decided to not write essays about just his stories and articles.) The second group is "Specific Genres," which are his poetry, book reviews, and book introductions. The third group is "Special Interests"; this group is composed of his Chicago White Sox Literature, his prose poem, *Chicago: City on the Make*, and works relating to boxing, gambling, and horse racing.

I have catalogued every known anthology in which Algren's work appears, and this chronological study appears in an appendix.

Some of Algren's most memorable work was truly lost, and I have spent years tracking it down. Algren had a "transatlantic love affair" with Simone de Beauvoir from 1947 to 1964. One of my discoveries was a poem about Beauvoir called, "Goodbye Lilies Hello Spring." This poem was published in a 1966 issue of *Zeitgeist*, an East Lansing, Michigan, literary journal, and it appears that it has been unknown to Algren scholars. The relationship between Algren and Beauvoir had ended badly two years earlier, and Algren's poem is quite vitriolic. With the permission of Bernice S. Behar and the Nelson Algren estate, I have included this poem in the essay on Algren's poetry.[10]

Another discovery was the article, "The World's Busiest Police Station," which was published in a 1950 issue of *Negro Digest*. Written more than sixty years before the creation of the Black Lives Matter movement, it is a race relations masterpiece. This article appears in this book in a second appendix, again with the permission of Bernice S. Behar and the Nelson Algren estate.[11]

Notes

1. Ernest Hemingway to Malcolm Cowley, 11 October 1949, in *Ernest Hemingway Selected Letters 1917–1961*, ed. Carlos Baker (New York: Charles Scribner's Sons, 1981), 681; see also Nelson Algren, "A Few Rounds with Papa and a Bottle of Scotch," *Chicago Tribune Book World*, 29 March 1981, 1, 6.

2. George Bluestone, "Nelson Algren," *Western Review*, Autumn 1957, 27.

3. Brooke Horvath, *Understanding Nelson Algren* (Columbia: University of South Carolina Press, 2005), dust jacket.

4. Nelson Algren, *Entrapment and Other Writings*, eds. Brooke Horvath and Dan Simon (New York: Seven Stories Press, 2009), 15.

5. Henry Kisor, "Nelson Algren, Hale and Salty at 64," *Chicago Daily News Panorama*, 27–28 October 1973, 2; Cleveland Amory, "Could It Be That Midwesterners Are the Only Ones Alive?" *Chicago Tribune Book World*, 10 June 1973, 4; Jimmy Breslin, "The Man in a $20 Hotel Room," in *The World According to Breslin* (New York: Ticknor & Fields, 1984), 271.

6. Nelson Algren, "Seven Feet Down and Creeping," *The New Orleans Review* 2, no. 1 (1970): 3.

7. Mary Wisniewski, *Algren: A Life* (Chicago: Chicago Review Press, 2017), 196; Nelson Algren, "The Brothers' House," in *O. Henry Memorial Award Prize Stories of 1935*, ed. Harry Hansen (Garden City, N.Y.: Doubleday, Doran, & Co., 1935), 63–67; Nelson Algren, "A Bottle of Milk for Mother," in *O. Henry Memorial Award Prize Stories of 1941*, ed. Herschel Brickell (New York: The Book League of America, 1941), 69–89; Nelson Algren, "The

Figure 2: In 1972 Nelson Algren was asked to comment on twelve paintings by the artist Edward Hopper. Algren's remarks, together with the paintings, were featured in the February 13, 1972, Sunday magazine of the *Chicago Tribune*. Figure 2 is one of the paintings, "Dawn Before Gettysburg." (© 2021 Heirs of Josephine N. Hopper/Licensed by Artists Rights Society [ARS], NY).

Captain is Impaled," in *Prize Stories of 1950: The O. Henry Awards*, ed. Herschel Brickell (Garden City, N.Y.: Doubleday, 1950), 52–67.

    8. "Editorial," *Chicago Free Press* 1, no. 1 (28 September 1970): 5.

    9. Nelson Algren, "The Swede Was a Hard Guy," *Chicago*, June 1956, 30–34.

    10. Simone de Beauvoir, *A Transatlantic Love Affair: Letters to Nelson Algren*, comp. and annot. by Sylvie Le Bon de Beauvoir (New York: New Press, 1998), 9–10; Nelson Algren, "Goodbye Lilies Hello Spring," *Zeitgeist* 1, no. 4 (Summer 1966): 50–51.

    11. Nelson Algren, "The World's Busiest Police Station," *Negro Digest*, January 1950, 3–8. As noted in the text, Rick Kogan believes that Algren's "literary genius" lies in his short stories rather than his novels. After reading "The World's Busiest Police Station," one might argue that Algren's literary genius lies in his articles as well. Besides this *Negro Digest* article, consider his 1972 essay, "Where Did Everybody Go?," in which Algren was asked to comment on twelve paintings by Edward Hopper. One of the paintings is "Dawn Before Gettysburg." (Figure 2) It shows a group of nine soldiers, sitting wearily on an embankment beside a dirt road. They are in front of a white building (probably a house) and a matching white picket fence. A tenth soldier, probably an officer, is standing in front of them, but looking away. All are lost in thought. Algren writes: "Hopper's soldiers appear to be right out of [Stephen Crane's book] *The Red Badge of Courage*. Each man, isolated within himself by the realization that this dawn may be his last, seems trapped, like Piranesi's prisoners, in a colossal pointlessness. It is the kind of dawn when men do not look into one another's eyes." Nelson Algren, "Where Did Everybody Go?" *Chicago Tribune Magazine*, 13 February 1972, 23. ("Piranesi's prisoners" is a reference to the Italian artist Giovanni Battista Piranesi (1720–1778) and his series of prints called *Imaginary Prisons*. The etchings show complex scenes of vast prison rooms populated with small, shadowy, and indistinguishable figures.)

PART ONE

Literary Eras

The Men's Magazines Era

Introduction

By 1960 Nelson Algren had written four novels: *Somebody in Boots* (1935), *Never Come Morning* (1942), *The Man with the Golden Arm* (1949), and *A Walk on the Wild Side* (1956). But by 1960, and for a variety of reasons, he decided to walk away from the Great American Novel. He could not, however, quit writing completely. He had to make a living, and as he told a *Chicago Daily News* reporter years later, "I write ... because there's really nothing else I can do."[1]

So Algren continued to write, but now with a different focus. From 1960 until his death in 1981, Algren wrote dozens of short stories and articles, poems and book reviews. To maximize his cash flow, Algren often submitted his work to magazines, because their editors made immediate payment. When he signed a book contract with a conventional publisher, he would negotiate an advance of money, which he used for living expenses while he worked on the book. When he wrote for magazines, he did not have to be concerned about working out the payment of advance money.[2]

Algren published much of his material in magazines like *Saturday Review*, *Atlantic Monthly*, and *The Nation*. But Algren also wrote for many of the so-called "men's magazines" that filled the newsstands at this time.[3]

The term, "men's magazines" conjures up images of sleazy "skin magazines" containing photographs of naked women in pornographic poses. Such a conclusion, however, is both overly broad and inaccurate. During the 1950s, Algren wrote for men's adventure magazines like *Stag*, *Man's Magazine*, and *Sensation*. Beginning in the late 1960s, men's adventure magazines fell out of favor; they were replaced by men's "girlie magazines"—magazines featuring attractive women in suggestive poses—magazines like *Escapade*, *Nugget*, and *Cavalier*. A study of Algren's magazine *oeuvre* reveals that Algren survived the transition; he wrote for both types of periodicals. In addition, he also wrote for crime fiction magazines like *Manhunt* and *Ellery Queen's Mystery Magazine*.

13

Each of these types of magazines, and Algren's contributions to these different men's magazines, are discussed in this essay.

Adventure Magazines

The Origin of Adventure Magazines

There were men's adventure magazines in the 1930s and 1940s with titles like *True*, *True Adventure Tales*, and *Argosy*. However, the adventure magazine did not fully develop into its own separate genre until the early 1950s, after World War II. Indeed, publishers of these magazines catered to World War II veterans.[4]

From the early 1950s to the mid–1970s, more than 150 different men's adventure magazines were published in the United States. In the early years these magazines were first and foremost *adventure* magazines. Granted, the covers would usually highlight a cheesecake pictorial or an article of a sexual nature, but such covers were just as often balanced by at least one reference to articles about action outside the bedroom. The format was always adventure first, sex second.[5]

Consider, for example, the January 1961 issue of *See* magazine, which is shown in Figure 3. The painted cover depicts six German soldiers being mowed down by machine gun fire. The cover heralds a short story by Nelson Algren and three articles.[6]

- BEAT THE TAX RACKET!—A Congressman's New Scheme
- BUTCHERY! by Nelson Algren, author of "The Man with the Golden Arm"
- Brother 12's Prescription: BEDS, BARBED WIRE, and BABES
- THE SNOW SOLDIERS DIE LIKE THIS, a shocking book-lengther of World War II

The magazine also contains a pictorial section called "See's She." One black-and-white photograph shows a woman apparently named Joy wearing a bikini. Another photograph is of Joy, topless, sitting on the floor, her back to the camera, looking over her shoulder. A third photograph shows Joy standing and wearing a short nightgown.[7]

Nelson Algren's Contributions to Adventure Magazines

The following is a chronological list of all of the known adventure magazines that contain Algren's work. Each of the magazines contains an Algren short story.

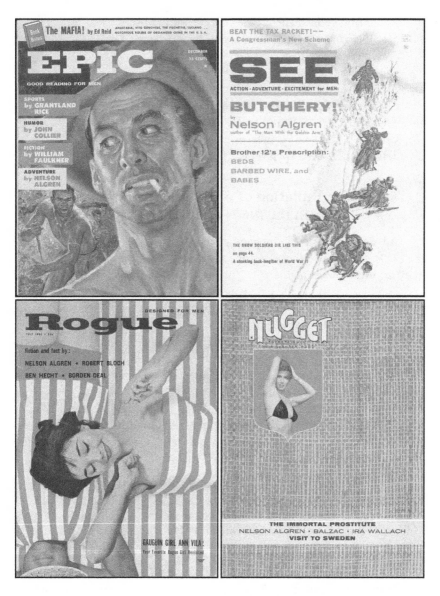

Figure 3: During his writing career, Nelson Algren wrote for a wide range of men's magazines. He started out with *Esquire* in the 1940s and later wrote for men's adventure magazines like *Epic* and *See*. The first issue of *Playboy* hit the newsstands in November of 1953, and soon Algren was writing for *Playboy* and also *Playboy* imitators like *Rogue* and *Nugget*. He even wrote for *Manhunt*, a men's crime magazine. (See Figure 4.) As shown in both this picture and in Figure 4, regardless of what type of men's magazine Algren wrote for, his name was often featured on the cover.

Man's Magazine, February 1958, "Depend on Aunt Elly!"
Stag, February 1958, "Venus Darling's Upstairs Lover"
Stag, May 1958, "Everyone Gets a Bum Rap"
Sensation, October 1958, "The Face on the Barroom Floor"
Epic, December 1958, "Kingdom City to Cairo"
Cavalcade, March 1959, "The Heroes"
See, January 1961, "Butchery!"
Climax, June 1962, "Cawfee Man"
True War Stories, April 1966, "The Heroes"

The Evolution of Adventure Magazines in the 1960s and the 1970s

Adventure magazines began to fall into disfavor in the late 1960s and the 1970s. There were three reasons for the changing content of magazines like *Stag* and *Man's Magazine*.[8]

The first reason is the passage of time. In the 1950s, men's magazines had made World War II a cottage industry. But as the years passed and as recollections of Pearl Harbor and Normandy faded into obscurity, the magazines were forced to publish new types of adventure stories. Unfortunately, the Korean War in the 1950s and the Vietnam War in the 1960s and 1970s did not engender tales of battlefield valor and derring-do like World War II did.[9]

Josh Alan Friedman, author of "When Men Were Men and Women Were Nymphos: Men's Adventure Magazines," identifies the second reason why adventure magazines abandoned their "cheesecake and testosterone" format in the late 1960s and the 1970s:

> Men's adventure magazines sold the common guy dreams of heroism. After he saved the world from the Nazis, or the Commies, or the Yellow Peril, or Half-Human Creatures from a Lost World, there'd be time to have his wounds dressed by an adoring Tina Louise or Jayne Mansfield. It was a fantasy of old fashioned paternalism, not to mention chauvinism of the purest kind, and by the 1970s that seemed pretty outdated.[10]

The third reason is sex. *Esquire* magazine premiered in the fall of 1933. It was designed to be a man's "contemporary guide to gracious living." It featured sections on such things as art, books, theater, sports, and men's clothing. It contained articles on men's fashion and serious fiction by writers like Ernest Hemingway and F. Scott Fitzgerald. But it also contained racy jokes and cartoons, and it featured airbrushed drawings of scantily clad beautiful women by George Petty and Alberto Vargas. These women came to be called the Petty Girl and the Varga (dropping the "s") Girl.[11]

Esquire was the first "men's magazine" that published one of Algren's works.

Seven years after *Esquire*'s 1933 debut, the March 1940 issue featured Algren's poem, "This Table on Time Only." His short story, "The Captain is a Card," was published two years later in the June 1942 issue. His work later appeared in *Esquire* in 1957, 1958, and 1960.[12]

During World War II *Esquire* added even more "cheesecake" illustrations to the magazine, thus increasing its appeal to American servicemen. At the same time, however, *Esquire* became entangled in a prolonged battle with the U.S. Post Office about these same illustrations. In order to qualify for second-class (and thus cheaper) mailing rates, a magazine had to be "originated and published for the dissemination of information of a public character, or devoted to literature, the sciences, arts or some special industry." Postmaster General Frank Walker maintained that this mailing rate was a "privilege" that was a "certificate of good moral character." He believed that he had the power to deny the permit, and in 1943 Postmaster Walker asked that *Esquire* show cause as to why its second-class mailing rate should not be withdrawn for failing to meet this requirement.[13]

The issue eventually reached the U.S. Supreme Court, and in a 1946 unanimous decision, Justice William O. Douglas ruled that the postal service did not have the authority to revoke a periodical's second-class mailing permit on the basis of material that it found objectionable but was not obscene.[14]

This U.S. Supreme Court decision was a hollow victory for *Esquire*. During the war, as long as there was a paper shortage or a court threat, *Esquire* faced little competition. But now, thanks to V-J Day and the U.S. Supreme Court, numerous "girlie" magazines with names like *Wink*, *Eyeful*, and *Flirt* appeared on the newsstands and in veterans' mailboxes. Before and during the war, *Esquire*'s formula was girls, cartoons, fiction, and lifestyle. Now that the war was over, *Esquire* still had its pinups, but they weren't being drawn by Petty or Vargas, and the sexy cartoons, serious fiction and men's lifestyle features had dissipated, replaced by articles on bowling and home remodeling. *Esquire* entered the post-war period lacking an editorial focus and beset by competitors. The time was ideal for the *Playboy* bunny to hop into the men's magazine marketplace.[15]

From the very beginning Hugh Hefner admitted that he wanted to develop a magazine like *Esquire*. In the early 1950s he wrote:

> I'd like to produce an entertainment magazine for the city-bred guy—breezy, sophisticated. The girlie features would guarantee the initial sale, but the magazine would have quality too. Later, with some money in the bank, we'll begin increasing the quality—reducing the girlie features, going after advertisers— and really making it an *Esquire*-type magazine.[16]

And Hefner succeeded. The first issue of *Playboy* was obviously influenced by *Esquire*. The magazine contained sexy cartoons, short stories by famous authors, party jokes, and a nude color photograph of Marilyn Monroe that was the photographic equivalent of *Esquire*'s Varga Girl.[17]

Hugh Hefner came out with *Playboy* in 1953. Nelson Algren first appeared in its pages only four years later. The year of 1957 was also the year the U.S. Supreme Court decided *Roth v. United States*, a case famous for establishing Justice William Brennan's obscenity doctrine, also called the Roth Test: "Whether, to the average person, applying contemporary community standards, the dominant theme of the material, taken as a whole, appeals to prurient interest." *Playboy*'s immediate success in 1953 and the *Roth v. United States* decision in 1957 were largely responsible for the marked increase in "girlie" magazines in the second half of the 1950s and into the 1960s.[18]

Magazines like *The Gent* and *The Dude* began to dominate the men's magazine market. Soon adventure magazines were changing their design, trying to duplicate Hefner's recipe for success by featuring more nude photographs, less artwork, and fewer action and adventure stories. The traditional "blood, guts, and cheesecake" adventure magazine now seemed an anachronism. By 1980 the genre had disappeared from the magazine racks. Some of the titles, though, remained. That is, some adventure magazines like *Climax*, *Stag*, and *Man's Magazine*, all of which had featured Algren's stories in the 1950s and early 1960s, kept their titles in the 1970s but changed their format by adding frontal nudity to their contents. Adventure magazines were out, and "girlie" magazines were in.[19]

The Playboy *Imitators*

During this time, many of these magazines adopted the template first used by *Esquire* and then by *Playboy*—that is, they combined Hefner's "girlie features" with literature. Often times this literature was in the form of articles. Some of them were erudite, such as "The Intellectual Maumaus," a look at white liberals and the New Hate, which appeared in the August 1965 issue of *Cavalier*. Others were entertainment, like the article about jazz pianist Dave Brubeck that was featured in the May 1959 issue of *Caper*. Still others sought to educate the modern male in various aspects of leisure activity. Consider, for example, "How to Beat the Horses" and "Low Hi-Fi" that appeared in the November 1957 issue of *Caper*.[20]

But the men who bought *Caper* and other post–*Playboy* periodicals didn't buy them just for the articles. These magazines also contained surprisingly serious fiction. Consider *Nugget*, one of the early Playboy wannabes. The first issue of *Nugget* (November 1955) named a stellar list of fiction contributors on its cover: James Joyce, Erskine Caldwell, and John Steinbeck. Nelson Algren followed less than a year later, appearing in *Nugget* (and on its cover) in the July 1956 and October 1956 issues. This trend of combining quality fiction with females continued into the 1960s, with, for example, the April 1963 issue of *Gent* featuring a short story by Evan Hunter, author of *The Blackboard Jungle*.[21]

The Disappearance of Nelson Algren and Serious Fiction from Men's "Girlie" Magazines

But the 1970s brought a men's magazine circulation battle that came to be known in the trade as the "Pubic Wars." When *Penthouse* made its debut in the United States in 1969, founder Bob Guccione announced the magazine's arrival with a full-page newspaper advertisement depicting the *Playboy* rabbit logo in the crosshairs of a rifle. The ad proclaimed, "We're going rabbit hunting." For all the notoriety of its centerfolds, *Playboy* had never crossed the line that seemed to separate erotic photography from pornography—the display of pubic hair. *Penthouse* drew first blood, crossing that line in its February 1970 and April 1970 issues. *Playboy* published its first full-frontal nude centerfold in January 1972. As *Playboy* and *Penthouse* fought the Pubic Wars, each publishing ever more sexually revealing photographs, *Swank*, *Nugget*, and the other *Playboy* imitators soon joined the battle. "Girlie" magazines quickly became "skin" magazines—that is, magazines containing full-frontal nude photographs of women in sexually explicit poses. Nelson Algren's last American men's magazine article or story was published in March of 1974. By this time quality fiction was vanishing from most of the men's magazines. Hard-core nudity eventually won out over fiction, and literature was the loser.[22]

Consider, e.g., *Nugget* magazine. *Nugget*—the same magazine that heralded James Joyce, Erskine Caldwell, and John Steinbeck on its cover in November 1955—featured the short story, "Flash: The World's Top Exhibitionist," on its cover in August 1974. Nelson Algren died on May 9, 1981. The June 1981 issue of *Nugget* contained fiction, but not by Joyce, Caldwell, or Steinbeck. The story was titled "Humbled," and it was described in the magazine's table of contents as "A forceful rape story where everyone gets what they want."[23]

The graphic nature of both the text and the pictures in men's magazines in the 1970s only partially explains the disappearance of Nelson Algren and other writers of serious fiction from the pages of *Swank* and *Stag*. Geoff Nicholson, author of "'For the Articles': Men's Magazines and Literature," offers another reason:

The slow death of quality fiction in men's magazines coincided with the rise of mainstream feminism, and this explains a great deal. In the 60s there was a symbiosis at work. Anything to do with sex was considered hip. The presence of good writers in men's magazines therefore increased the hip credentials of both sides. But with the broad acceptance of feminism, men's magazines became at best a guilty pleasure, at worst an instrument of oppression, and writers are reluctant to be seen as oppressors. The fact that magazines tended to become increasingly explicit only created more difficulties.[24]

Bettina Drew observes in her biography, *Nelson Algren: A Life on the Wild Side*, that "for a while, any low-class skin magazine could pick up an Algren story by paying a token sum to Doubleday [Algren's publisher]." In light of the quality fiction that once appeared in these magazines, one must ask: Is this somewhat disparaging comment a fair one?[25]

No, it is probably not a fair comment. When Algren was writing for *Caper* and *Cavalier,* these magazines were not low-class. Drew dates her observation circa 1959. The March 1959 issue of *Cavalcade* included Algren's "The Heroes." A month earlier *Escapade* (which published Algren in 1957 and 1958) featured a one-act drama by William Saroyan. A men's magazine that contains the fiction of William Saroyan, a novelist and playwright who won both the Pulitzer Prize and Academy Award, is *not* low class.[26]

Nor were these periodicals "skin magazines" in 1959. They are more appropriately described as men's "girlie" magazines. They included relatively modest pictures of women that today might be rated only a bit more severe than PG-13 but certainly not "R." *Cavalcade* in 1959 is not *Cavalcade* in 1979. For example, the featured fiction in the February 1979 issue of *Cavalcade* was "The Sex Pushers" and "Sexual Candy Store." Indeed, *Cavalcade* is a perfect example of the total transition of the formats of many of these men's magazines. The March 1959 issue of *Cavalcade* was an adventure magazine. Besides Algren's short story, "The Heroes," it contained a story about the legendary Western lawman Wyatt Earp and an article about the Civil War's Battle of Shiloh. By December 1961, less than three years later, *Cavalcade* was a traditional men's "girlie" magazine, an early 1960s *Playboy* clone with a slogan on the cover reading, "A New Entertainment Magazine for Men." It contained pictorials, fiction (five short stories), and articles like "The Pack"—that is, Frank Sinatra's "Rat Pack." The July 1964 issue of *Cavalcade*—still a "girlie" magazine—contained an Algren interview. But by March of 1977 *Cavalcade* had devolved into a raunchy skin magazine. The Table of Contents of this issue discloses only one short story. The title is, "His Last Piece of Ass," and it is labeled "Sex Fiction." Algren had appeared in *Cavalcade* when it was an adventure magazine and when it was a "girlie" magazine. He did not write for *Cavalcade* when it was a skin magazine.[27]

Again, if one were to define "skin magazines" as magazines containing full-frontal nude photographs of women in sexually explicit poses, there is no known skin magazine that includes a Nelson Algren short story or article. There is no full-frontal nudity in those issues of *Playboy* that contains Algren's work. The June 1973 issue of *Swank* and the March 1974 issue of *COQ* each featured pictorials of full-frontal (but not vulgar) nudity and Algren fiction. These two magazines are the last entries in the Algren chronological bibliography of American men's magazines. Why is this the case? Granted, it is likely that a raunchy skin magazine was not interested in printing what Algren was writing. But did Algren make a principled decision to stop writing for all men's magazines, even magazines like *Esquire* and *Playboy*? Was he taking a stand against Geoff Nicholson's aforementioned "instruments of oppression"? Or was there another reason why he quit writing for men's magazines in 1974? That question is answered later in this essay.

Nelson Algren's Contributions to "Girlie" Magazines

The following is a chronological list of all the known American "girlie" magazines that contain Nelson Algren's writing.

Esquire, March 1940, "This Table on Time Only"
Esquire, June 1942, "The Captain is a Card"
Nugget, July 1956, "Mr. Goodbuddy and the Mighty Dripolator"
Nugget, October 1956, "Lovers, Sec-fiends, Bugs in Flight"
The Gent, December 1956, "No Man's Laughter"
The Dude, January 1957, "Stickman's Laughter"
Playboy, April 1957, "All Through the Night"
Esquire, August 1957, "G-String Gomorrah"
Scamp, September 1957, "Depend on Aunt Elly!"
Escapade, December 1957, "A Bottle of Milk for Mother"
Escapade, June 1958, "The Heroes"
Esquire, August 1958, "Good-by to Old Rio"
Caper Annual, undated [1960], "A Bottle of Milk for Mother"
Esquire, June 1960, "How the Man with the Record One Eighth of an Inch Long was Saved by a Bessarabian Rye"
Swank, September 1960, "A Bottle of Milk for Mother"
The Gent, February 1961, "The Marquis of Kingsbury, You Could Have Him!"
Rogue, May 1961, "The South of England: Up from Piccadilly, or: What Makes the Low Life of Soho So High?"[28]

Rogue, July 1961, "The Bride Below the Black Coiffure"
Rogue, August 1961, "Moon of the Backstretch, Still and White"[29]
Scene, October 1961, "He Swung and He Missed"
Rogue, November 1961, "You Have Your People and I Have Mine"
Rogue, February 1962, "The Moon of King Minos Rose Seven-Eighths Full or There's Lots of Crazy Stuff in the Ocean"
The Dude, March 1962, "God Bless the Lonesome Gas Man"
Nugget, June 1962, "Fabulous Istanbul Isn't the Town for Me"
Cavalier, September 1962, "Afternoon in the Land of the Strange Light Sleep"
Playboy, December 1962, "The Father and Son Cigar"
The Men's Digest, Annual Edition, no. 49, undated [1963] (Book review of *F.S.C.*, by Con Sellers)
Cavalier, February 1963, "Shlepker, or White Goddess Say You Not Go That Part of Forest"
Harlequin, April 1963, "Whobody Knows My Name ... or, How to Be a Freedom-Rider Without Leaving Town"
Harlequin, August 1963, "The Unacknowledged Champion of Everything"
The Men's Digest, no. 51, January 1964 (Book review of *F.S.C.*, by Con Sellers)
Cavalier, February 1965, "Hemingway All the Way"
Playboy, June 1970, "Get All the Money"
Playboy, February 1972, "The Last Carrousel"
Playboy, December 1972, "The Way to Médenine"
Swank, June 1973, "The House of the Hundred Grassfires"
COQ, March 1974, "$22.50 by Wieboldt's"
Lui Deutschland, June 1980, "Ein Mann und Seine Welt: Detective Roy Finer von der New Yorker Mordkommission" ["A Man and His World: Detective Roy Finer of the New York Homicide Commission"]
Lui Deutschland, July 1980, "Nelson Algren und Simone de Beauvoir: Ein Mann und eine Frau" ["Nelson Algren and Simone de Beauvoir: A Man and a Woman"][30]

Obvious questions arise after reviewing these titles in chronological order. Algren wrote for *Escapade* in 1957 and 1958, but then he stopped. *Escapade* published fiction in 1959. Why didn't Algren appear in *Escapade* that year or in later years? *Escapade* featured a column by *On the Road* author Jack Kerouac in 1959 and 1960. Did Algren stop writing for *Escapade* because he was upset that Kerouac got the column and he did not? That is possible; writer Warren Leming knew Algren, and Lemming suggests that Algren resented the attention given to Kerouac and the other Beat Generation authors.[31]

Algren's work was featured in five different issues of *Rogue* in 1961 and 1962. Furthermore, not only was his name on the cover of all five issues, his name was at the top of all five covers. Algren had great name recognition—but he never again appeared in *Rogue* after 1962. *Rogue* still published fiction in 1963. Indeed, the early 1960s seem to be *Rogue*'s glory days for fiction. Science fiction writer Harlan Ellison was editor of *Rogue* in 1959 and 1960, and Ellen Weil and Gary K. Wolfe write in their biography of Ellison that "Ellison is credited by [Frank Robinson, editor of *Rogue* in the early 1960s] as having been the creative spark that, for a time, turned *Rogue* into a legitimate competitor with *Playboy*, at least in terms of the quality of its writing." This spark was obviously still lit in 1963 and 1964 when Robinson was editor of *Rogue*. For example, the June 1963 issue featured a short story by William Saroyan. The December 1964 issue included fiction by Graham Greene. This issue also included an article by Willard Motley. Motley worked with Algren on the Illinois Writers' Project, one of President Franklin Roosevelt's Depression-era "New Deal" programs. Algren and Motley appear together in a photograph in Jerre Mangione's book, *The Dream and the Deal: The Federal Writers' Project, 1935–1943*. Algren was with Motley in this picture. Why wasn't Algren with Motley in the December 1964 issue of *Rogue*? Why is there nothing by Algren in *Rogue* after 1962?[32]

Why did Algren write for *The Gent* in 1956 and then not again until 1961? Why did his work appear in *The Dude* in 1957 but then not resurface in that magazine until 1962? Why was Algren in *Playboy* in 1957 but then not again until 1962? Does the answer to all these questions concern money? Was Algren constantly "following the money"? Was he always seeking out the men's magazine editor who paid the most? This was possibly the case. In a 1973 interview he said, "I live on book reviews and by giving talks…. I write for financial reasons."[33]

On the other hand, was Algren more concerned with artistic freedom than financial freedom? Consider, for example, the literary motives of Harlan Ellison, who wrote dozens of short stories for men's magazines in the 1950s and 1960s. Ellison wrote for *Rogue* in the 1950s and later wrote for *Knight*, another "girlie" magazine. From 1963 through 1972 *Knight* published fifteen of Ellison's stories.[34]

In 1967 Ellison explained why he had chosen to write for *Knight* and not (in his words) *Saturday Review* or *Harper's*:

> *Knight* does not edit my stories but prints them untouched as I submit them … [they] pay me much less than many other markets, but very much a top dollar as far as their own rates are concerned; they let me experiment.[35]

Ellen Weil and Gary K. Wolfe note in their biography of Ellison that the entire men's magazine industry (and not just *Knight*) fostered the creative freedom that might have lured Algren to *Rogue, Nugget,* and *Cavalier*:

> The men's magazine market was not defined by the fiction alone, but by a mix of articles, cartoons, jokes, reviews, and—probably most important—photo layouts. Since no particular fiction genre had defined this market, the market placed considerably fewer generic restrictions on its contributors, and for writers like Ellison this meant a new dimension of creative freedom. More immediate social issues such as civil rights or "sick" humor could be addressed, and stories didn't have to be targeted to a particular science fiction or crime or western market.[36]

Was it jealousy? Was it money? Was it artistic freedom? The questions remain unanswered.[37]

Crime and Mystery Fiction

The term, "men's magazines" encompasses both adventure magazines and "girlie" magazines. The term, however, is a broad one. There is one more men's magazine genre that Nelson Algren wrote for—crime and mystery fiction. Algren's work appears in one mystery magazine and one "hard boiled" crime fiction magazine.

Ellery Queen's Mystery Magazine

In 1934 Lawrence Spivak became the business manager of *The American Mercury,* a literary magazine founded by H.L. Mencken ten years earlier. (This magazine published Algren's work in 1934, 1942, 1943, and 1947.) In 1939 Spivak purchased *The American Mercury*. Like many of Mencken's projects, the magazine bled money, and other means were required to support this literary venture. After reading a pulp magazine, Spivak became intrigued with the idea of publishing a "respectable" mystery magazine. He approached Frederic Dannay and Manfred B. Lee, two cousins who wrote detective novels using the joint pseudonym, "Ellery Queen," about the idea. They were skeptical at first, as they had unsuccessfully tried magazine publishing before, but Spivak assured them that this magazine would be different from their earlier attempt.[38]

The first issue of *Ellery Queen's Mystery Magazine,* or *EQMM,* was published in the fall of 1941. Page one indicates that it was "published by Lawrence E. Spivak" and "edited by Ellery Queen."[39]

Nelson Algren's work appears only once in *EQMM*. His contribution, the short story, "He Swung and He Missed," was published in the October

1957 issue. This story is a slight revision of "He Swung and He Missed" that originally appeared in the July 1942 issue of *The American Mercury*. The EQMM version was later reprinted in *The Neon Wilderness* (1947).[40]

Manhunt

Gritty and grim crime fiction—the so-called "hard-boiled" crime fiction—grew out of the pages of *Black Mask* magazine. First published in 1920, *Black Mask* eventually attracted a nucleus of writers that included Raymond Chandler and Dashiell Hammett. Circulation peaked in 1930 at 103,000 copies a month, but in later years sales declined, and *Black Mask* ended its run in 1951.[41]

By this time *EQMM* was well established; however, *EQMM* rarely published a hard-boiled story. The reason was simple—except for Hammett's work, Dannay was not a proponent of this type of crime fiction. Consequently, with the demise of *Black Mask*, the time was ripe for a new magazine devoted to "tough, downbeat, violent stories of 'the seamier side' of contemporary life." That magazine was *Manhunt*.[42]

The premier issue was dated January 1953, and it featured the first installment of "a new mystery thriller" by Mickey Spillane and stories by Kenneth Millar and Evan Hunter. Writing as Ross Macdonald, Millar would go on to earn considerable fame as the author of the Lew Archer detective novels. Evan Hunter would later write the 87th Precinct crime novels under the name Ed McBain.[43]

Manhunt was an immediate hit—that first issue sold almost 500,000 copies. The magazine was so successful in its early years that it was able to solicit hard-edged original stories from such respected mystery writers as Erle Stanley Gardner, Rex Stout, and Fredric Brown. It also solicited a story from Nelson Algren. Algren's one contribution to *Manhunt* (June 1958), entitled "Say a Prayer for the Guy," was a dark account about a man dropping dead while playing poker.[44] (Figure 4)

Nelson Algren's Contributions to Crime and Mystery Fiction Magazines:

Ellery Queen's Mystery Magazine, "He Swung and He Missed,"
    October 1957
Manhunt, "Say a Prayer for the Guy," June 1958

Nelson Algren in the 1970s

The traditional girlie magazine was all but killed off in the Pubic Wars. There were, though, at least two survivors: *Esquire*, which started

K

MANHUNT

WORLD'S BEST SELLING CRIME-FICTION MAGAZINE

JUNE, 1958   35 CENTS

A Tough, New Story by

NELSON

("The Man With The Golden Arm")

ALGREN

EVERY STORY
NEW!

Plus—C. B. GILFORD • MAX FRANKLIN • ARNOLD ENGLISH
D. E. FORBES • WILLIAM O'FARRELL • NORMAN STRUBER

the genre, and *Playboy*, which copied it. *Esquire* chose to sit out the wars completely, and Hefner surrendered the battle. *Esquire* reinvented itself as a literary magazine, popularizing a new form of writing called "New Journalism"—factual writing that read like fiction. By the mid–1970s, Hefner conceded his rivals' domination of the coarser segment of the men's magazine market and began to temper *Playboy*'s explicit pictures. However, the relative modesty of the 1950s and early 1960s did not return to the pages of *Playboy* in the late 1970s and thereafter.[45]

The March 1974 issue of *COQ* featured Algren's short story, "$22.50 by Wieboldt's." It marked the end of the men's magazine era for Nelson Algren. He could have submitted some fiction to *Esquire* for publication in 1974, but nothing by Algren appeared in *Esquire* that year. Instead, the December 1974 issue featured a story by fellow Chicago writer Saul Bellow. Algren could have submitted a short story to *Playboy* in 1975. At first one might think that *Playboy* would be unwilling to publish Algren's work because of his vicious attack on Hugh Hefner and *Playboy* that he wrote for his 1963 book, *Who Lost an American?* Although the article contained such statements as, "Hefner has perceived that the American businessman's most erotic zone is the skin of his wallet," Algren still appeared in the pages of *Playboy* in 1970 and 1972. Nothing, however, by Algren appeared in *Playboy* after 1972. *Playboy* continued to feature serious fiction after March of 1974—for example, it published John Updike twice in 1975—but nothing by Nelson Algren.[46]

In 1975 and later years, Algren could have written for *Esquire*, *Playboy*, or even *Ellery Queen's Mystery Magazine*, but he did not. *Why* did Algren stop writing for men's magazines after 1974?[47]

It appears that Algren stopped because of a fateful decision he made at about the same time that *COQ* published "$22.50 by Wieboldt's." In

Opposite: Figure 4: *Manhunt* was a 1950s and 1960s hard-boiled crime fiction magazine. While *Ellery Queen's Mystery Magazine* was at one end of the crime fiction spectrum, specializing in traditional mysteries, *Manhunt* was at the opposite end. *Manhunt* focused on a market that wanted gritty realism and hard-hitting crime, with an emphasis on sex and violence. This philosophy was made clear by the magazine's lurid painted covers. (The cover of this June 1958 issue is rather tame. The July 1954 magazine, featuring James T. Farrell's short story, "I Want a French Girl," depicts on its cover a woman in a low-cut dress pointing a gun at a nude standing woman.)

The cover shown here announced "A Tough, New Story" by Nelson Algren. The story was "Say a Prayer for the Guy." Even though the story was not hard-boiled crime fiction, it appears that *Manhunt* published it because Algren was an established writer and the story fit loosely into the crime fiction genre.

early 1974 *Esquire* offered Algren $1,250 for an article about boxer Rubin "Hurricane" Carter. Carter and his friend John Artis had been convicted of triple murder in 1967. The convictions, though, seemed shaky. One of the prosecution's main witnesses could not identify Carter on the night of the murders, and firearm ballistic experts found no similarities between the bullets used in the shootings and two bullets allegedly found in Carter's car.[48]

Algren was an ardent boxing fan. He had written about boxing in his books and short stories, and he had seen Carter at St. Nick's Arena in New York. But Carter was more than just a boxer to Algren. Algren believed that a writer should function as a conscience of society. In 1961 he wrote, "I submit that literature is made upon any occasion that a challenge is put to the legal apparatus by a conscience in touch with humanity." The Carter case represented just such a challenge. Boxing and a miscarriage of justice—the story of "Hurricane" Carter was perfect for Algren, and he accepted *Esquire*'s offer.[49]

Algren met with Carter and wrote the article, but in the summer of 1974, *Esquire* rejected it. *Playboy* also turned it down, but by this time Algren felt that that he was onto something and that he had found a cause worth pursuing. Algren's friend Sue McNear later recalled that Algren "needed a project, and there it was."[50]

The murders took place in Paterson, New Jersey, and Algren moved from Chicago to Paterson in March of 1975. He visited Carter and pored over old newspaper accounts of the case in the New York Public Library. Towards the end of 1975, after Algren's landlady served him with an eviction notice because of a rent dispute, Algren moved to Hackensack, New Jersey.[51]

In early 1976 the New Jersey Supreme Court struck down the Carter and Artis convictions and granted the men a new trial. Algren was now trying to market a book based on his research. The timing was perfect. Public opinion seemed increasingly favorable towards Carter and his friend; it appeared that they were bound to be exonerated in the second trial.[52]

But public opinion does not sway book publishers. Putnam's, Random House, and other publishers rejected Algren's book, which was titled *Carter*. The general consensus was that the manuscript contained too much trial testimony and not enough Algren.[53]

In December of 1976 Carter and Artis were retried and again found guilty. Carter was now yesterday's news. In 1960 a dejected Nelson Algren, disheartened in part by the negative reviews of his 1956 novel, *A Walk on the Wild Side*, had written a friend that he would never write another one. But after the jury rendered its guilty verdict, Algren realized that his only hope to salvage something out of his years of work was to do what he had earlier said he would not do—write another novel. He started revising his book in the fall of 1977.[54]

In April 1979 Algren gave his agent the manuscript he called *China-town*. Algren continued to work on the book, and in February 1980 he gave his agent the final version of a novel renamed *The Devil's Stocking*. Algren, now free of endless revisions, moved from New Jersey to Sag Harbor, Long Island, New York, in the summer of 1980. The book, titled *Calhoun*, was published in Germany in October 1981. Unfortunately, Algren did not live to see it published—he died of a heart attack on May 9, 1981. *The Devil's Stocking* eventually appeared in America in 1983, two years after Algren's death.[55]

Equally unfortunately, the book was released to decidedly mixed reviews. Algren's friend, Budd Schulberg, admitted in the *Chicago Tribune* that "there are times when the lengthy Q's and A's of the trials seem a little too close to undigested transcripts, times when one too many brothel scene becomes a distracting echo of other books in which he did his janes, johns, pimps and madams to perfection." Phoebe-Lou Adams writes in *The Atlantic*, "But if the whole is a bit shaky, many of the parts are splendid, and worth reading for their own brilliant sake." But on the other hand, an unnamed reviewer in the *Virginia Quarterly Review* writes that "the rhythms are too often choppy; the narrative too clearly episodic." A.J. Anderson minces no words in his *Library Journal* review, maintaining that "one's concluding impression is of magnificent writing gifts neutralized by structural carelessness or ineptitude."[56]

A.J. Anderson was right. Algren should never have agreed to Esquire's 1974 offer, as it led to six years of work with little to show for it but a lackluster novel. Instead of taking on "Hurricane" Carter, Algren should have continued to write short stories. He had already established a working relationship with *Esquire*, *Playboy*, and *Ellery Queen's Mystery Magazine*. Algren could have continued the trend started by writers like Raymond Chandler and Dashiell Hammett. These authors are obviously known for their novels, but they were also the premier short story contributors to *Black Mask* magazine. Admittedly, many of Algren's men's magazine articles are excerpts or adaptations from Algren's earlier books, but some are not. Going forward from 1974, Algren could have improved on that record by writing and publishing more original work. Instead, he wasted almost all of the last years of his life researching and writing *The Devil's Stocking*. Consider the timeline: *Esquire* made Algren the offer in early 1974; he finished the book in February 1980; he died on May 9, 1981.[57]

Chicago writer Rick Kogan is the son of Herman and Marilew Kogan, who were friends of Algren. Mary Wisniewski interviewed Rick for her

Algren biography, and Rick suggested that Algren's use of language is more apparent in some of his short stories than it is in his novels. He then added this observation: "I think that's where his literary genius lies."[58]

Rick Kogan was right.

Pieces Published Only Once

Although Nelson Algren's men's magazine career was cut short by his ill-fated venture into the Rubin "Hurricane" Carter case, he left behind dozens of short stories, articles, and poems. Some of them were excerpts from his earlier novel, *A Walk on the Wild Side* (1956), and some were reprints or variations of stories that originally appeared in his 1947 book, *The Neon Wilderness*. Many of them were recycled into his post—*A Walk on the Wild Side* (1956) "collection" books: *Who Lost an American?* (1963), *Notes from a Sea Diary: Hemingway All the Way* (1965), and *The Last Carousel* (1973). But a few items were both original and published just once and then never again in Algren's lifetime. (Some of them, however, were reprinted many years after his death in the 2009 book, *Entrapment and Other Writings*.) Remarkably, these writings, published only one time when Algren was alive, represent some of his finest work, and they are discussed in this section.[59]

"This Table on Time Only," *Esquire*, March 1940, 78–79.

Nelson Algren's first published work of the 1940s was the poem, "This Table on Time Only," which appeared in the March 1940 issue of *Esquire* magazine. The poem tells the story of the murder of a man by at least three other men. The motive is unclear; he was "born above a rear-lot garage facing an alley" and raised "between the clack of an ivory-tipped cue in a North Avenue poolroom and the fall of the fifteen ball into a corner pocket." Had he not paid a pool hall gambling debt? Did he owe money to a loan shark? Regardless, the men "found him necking his waltz-night girl at the Cherry Gardens." They force him into a car and drive him to an alley beneath the Congress Street elevated train station "until the groan of the El overhead could muffle the shot." They then drape him over the side of the car "to let him drip." The men continue to drive "and got rid of him at last, without slowing down, passing the darkened park".[60]

> He lay among other undersized weeds
> In the prairie behind the grandstand.
> The grey-gloved fingers twitched once
> And the trouser legs stirred in the wind.[61]

"G-String Gomorrah," *Esquire,* August 1957, 47–48.

"G-String Gomorrah" is a marvelously descriptive account of the strip clubs in Calumet City, Illinois:

> One hour south of Chicago, just this side of the Indiana line, there's a patch-work burg that looks by day like any midland patch you see from any railroad right-of-way: the same small frame houses, quietly curtained, where 20,000 squares bless their state of grace and gratefully tuck themselves in by ten....
>
> Under the patchwork a baby Babylon lies sleeping....
>
> Rest till that hour that twilight falls in, and squares begin to feel tuckered; then the baby Babylon will stretch and yawn. The night's first juke will waken, neighing, *Your cheating heart will tell on you.*[62]

"Say a Prayer for the Guy," *Manhunt,* June 1958, 31–35.

Although this short story was never recycled into one of Algren's subsequent books, it is slightly similar to "A Ticket on Skoronski," which was first published in the November 5, 1966, issue of the *Saturday Evening Post* and later collected in *The Last Carousel* (1973).

"Say a Prayer for the Guy" concerns a poker player who dies at the table. The writing is Algren at his best:

> The juke coughed on a note, and went on coughing, how it does when some-one leans against it. I saw Joe's hands shuffling, but he shuffled too slow. A red deuce twisted out of the deck and dropped to the floor like a splash of blood. Joe fell forward onto the table, without a gasp, without a sound.[63]

"How the Man with the Record One Eighth of an Inch Long was Saved by a Bessarabian Rye," *Esquire,* June 1960, 105.

In 1962 and 1963 writer H.E.F. Donohue conducted a series of interviews with Algren. Their conversations became the book appropriately titled, *Conversations with Nelson Algren.* During one interview Algren indicated that he "thought a lot of" Mark Twain. Therefore, it is probably not a coincidence that "Bessarabian Rye" is similar to Twain's famous short story, "The Notorious Jumping Frog of Calaveras County" in that both Algren and Twain use humor, irony, dialect, and satire in their respective stories.[64]

For example, three of these four elements—humor, dialect, and satire—are present in the following two paragraphs from "Bessarabian Rye."

(The title of the story refers to the protagonist's police record, which was "nearly an eighth of an inch long.")

One night in January, eleven years ago, Willie was standing in front of a bakery pressing his nose against the pane to see what the woman inside was doing. It looked to Willie like what she was doing was slicing pumpernickel, but he couldn't be sure because of the way his cap shaded his eyes. It might really be Swedish rye for all he could tell. The woman inside noticed this cap looking in at her and after a while one of the darker, seedier loaves, a kind of Bessarabian dock-type rye, began eying her too. It became plain enough that what this swarthy old-country loaf had in mind was to assault her under the cake-flour bin, so she phoned Po-*lees* Thirteen Thirteen Thirteen Thirteen.

The operator immediately sensed that a man with a record nearly an eighth of an inch long was on the loose in the city and called Central Po-*lees*, who radioed four officers who were drinking Mogen David out of a gallon jug and smoking tea with a sixteen-fingered pickpocket from Milford Junction, Ohio, in the back room of Mieczyslaw Wysocki's Family-Corner Bar, a place that has since been transformed to a pizza parlor under the management of Al Naoyuki Muramoto.[65]

"Moon of the Backstretch, Still and White," *Rogue*, August 1961, 12–16, 24.

The August 1961 issue of *Rogue* featured Algren's article, "Moon of the Backstretch, Still and White." The article includes Algren's recollections of the 1958 Kentucky Derby. Here is an excerpt:[66]

Night, falling in those wooden hills, carried remembrance back to the night that had fallen onto the infield at Louisville after the infield bettors had left on Derby Day of 1958.

They had brought their box lunches of fried chicken like baskets of good wishes for Silky Sullivan in the blue forenoon. Their picnic-time morning had worn on toward post, with their good wishes spread on the good green grass. And the holiday air so white, so blue: and the sky wide as all Kentucky. They had bet Sullivan down to two to one, a horse no better than a plater.

Up in the pressbox we knew better. The word up there was Tim-Tam all the way.

But John L. Sullivan had once been something more than a man. So Silky Sullivan, that big green forenoon, became something more than a horse. He was going to run for everyone now trailing the field. For everyone whose old man had been no more than a plater too.

I remembered the big shout that had gone up when Sullivan started his run from so far back it was almost no hope—then came on, closing ground in an off-the-ground charge that looked as if here *lifted*—then lost stride as the big shout died and Derby Day was done for a horse that was, after all, nothing more than another horse.

And a low small wind passed over the infield and stayed on after the infield bettors had gone, moving like a ragpicking wind in the litter of emptied box-lunches; among the lily cups and drumsticks that had once been good wishes.[67]

John L. Sullivan was, of course, a heavyweight champion boxer. Algren loved gambling, horse racing, and prize-fighting, and he managed to combine references to all three in this article.[68]

"Afternoon in the Land of the Strange Light Sleep," *Cavalier*, September 1962, 24–25, 27.

In "Afternoon in the Land of the Strange Light Sleep" Algren writes of the lives of young people caught up in the throes of drug addiction. He asks a girl, "How did you get on stuff in the first place?" and she replies, "There were so many little troubles floatin' around, I figured why not roll 'em all up into one big trouble?" Algren responds, "Why should a young girl like yourself want to live like this?" She answers, "Don't bother me with *why*. For God's sake, only tell me *how*."[69]

The penultimate paragraph is suggestive of Ecclesiastes 3:1–8. "M" and "H" are morphine and heroin. "Jack-The-Rabbit" is, in Algren's words, the drug "peddler":[70]

> Where the time is always a time for M or a time for H, a time to goof or a time to taper. Where the rhythms of the night or day forever follow the rhythms of the blood. For the blood that moves as the Jack-The-Rabbit moves. As time is told only by the chill that comes up from deep inside and the user needs no watch to know he is starting to freeze. And there is no other time.[71]

The editors of *Cavalier* called this article "a prose poem in a new dimension."[72]

Conclusion

Nelson Algren's work appeared fifty times in a wide variety of men's magazines. Algren scholar James R. Giles comments in his book, *The Naturalistic Inner-City Novel in America*, that "Algren has yet to be welcomed without reservation into the canon of twentieth-century American literature." When one reads these works—especially these six pieces he published only one time and then never again—one has to ask: Why isn't he in the canon?[73]

NOTES

1. Matthew J. Bruccoli, *Nelson Algren: A Descriptive Bibliography* (Pittsburgh: University of Pittsburgh Press, 1985), 2, 9, 25, 40; John Clellon Holmes, "Arm: A Memoir," in

Representative Men: The Biographical Essays, Selected Essays by John Clellon Holmes, vol. 2 (Fayetteville: University of Arkansas Press, 1988), 251; Bettina Drew, *Nelson Algren: A Life on the Wild Side* (Austin: University of Texas Press, 1991), 297–98, 303; Henry Kisor, "Nelson Algren, Hale and Salty at 64," *Chicago Daily News Panorama*, 27–28 October 1973, 2.

2. Drew, *Nelson Algren*, 252–53, 255, 274–75, 291, 301; Bruccoli, *Nelson Algren*, 113–31; Matthew J. Bruccoli, "Addenda to Bruccoli, *Nelson Algren*," *The Papers of the Bibliographical Society of America* 82 (September 1988), 368–69; Robert A. Tibbetts, "Further Addenda to Bruccoli, *Nelson Algren*," *The Papers of the Bibliographical Society of America* 83 (June 1989), 214–15; Henry Kisor, "Nelson Algren, That Hackensack Homebody," *Chicago Daily News Panorama*, 12–13 June 1976, 7.

3. Drew, *Nelson Algren*, 273–303 passim; Bruccoli, *Nelson Algren*, 113–28; 147–56.

4. [Steven Heller], "Blood, Sweat, and Tits: A History of Men's Adventure Magazines," in *Men's Adventure Magazines in Postwar America*, by Max Allan Collins and George Hagenauer (Cologne, Germany: Taschen, 2008), 9, 11–14, 16–17; Adam Parfrey, "From Pulp to Posterity: The Origins of Men's Adventure Magazines," in *It's a Man's World: Men's Adventure Magazines, The Postwar Pulps*, ed. Adam Parfrey, expanded edition (Port Townsend, Wash.: Feral House, 2015), 31; Adam Parfrey, "The Illustrators," in Parfrey, *It's a Man's World*, 63; Josh Alan Friedman, "Throw 'Em a Few Hot Words," in Parfrey, *It's a Man's World*, 45; David M. Earle, *All Man! Hemingway, 1950s Men's Magazines, and the Masculine Persona* (Kent, Ohio: Kent State University Press, 2009), 20–21, 79, 82, 84; Wyatt Doyle, foreword to *Weasels Ripped My Flesh!*, ed. Robert Deis (n.p.: New Texture, 2012), 17–20; Robert Deis, introduction to Deis, *Weasels Ripped My Flesh!*, 24; Mike Kamens, "Weasels Ripped My Flesh" in Deis, *Weasels Ripped My Flesh!*, 33; Josh Alan Friedman, "When Men Were Men and Women Were Nymphos: Men's Adventure Magazines," in *The History of Men's Magazines, Volume 3: 1960s at the Newsstand*, ed. Dian Hanson (Cologne, Germany: Taschen, 2005), 367, 375; Bruce Jay Friedman, *Even the Rhinos Were Nymphos* (Chicago: University of Chicago Press, 2000), 20–22; Robert F. Dorr, "My Plan Was to Be a Writer and an Adventurer," in *A Handful of Hell: Classic War and Adventure Stories*, ed. Robert Deis and Wyatt Doyle (n.p.: New Texture, 2016), 16–17.

5. Parfrey, "From Pulp to Posterity: The Origins of Men's Adventure Magazines," in Parfrey, *It's a Man's World*, 29, 31; Bruce Jay Friedman, *Even the Rhinos Were Nymphos*, 20–23; Doyle, foreword to Deis, *Weasels Ripped My Flesh!*, 15; Deis, introduction to Deis, *Weasels Ripped My Flesh!*, 24; Josh Alan Friedman, "When Men Were Men and Women Were Nymphos: Men's Adventure Magazines," in Hanson, *The History of Men's Magazines, Volume 3, 1960s at the Newsstand*, 375–81.

6. This short story is the fight between Achilles Schmidt and Dove Linkhorn that appears at the end of *A Walk on the Wild Side*. See Nelson Algren, *A Walk on the Wild Side* (N.p.: Thunder's Mouth Press, 1990), 266–69, 338–46.

7. "Joy!," *See*, January 1961, 29–31.

8. "The War Comes Home," in Parfrey, *It's a Man's World*, 269; Dorr, "My Plan Was to Be a Writer and an Adventurer," in Deis and Doyle, *A Handful of Hell*, 37.

9. Parfrey, "From Pulp to Posterity: The Origins of Men's Adventure Magazines," in Parfrey, *It's a Man's World*, 29, 31, 34; "The War Comes Home," in Parfrey, *It's a Man's World*, 269; Bruce Jay Friedman, "Even the Rhinos Were Nymphos," in Parfrey, *It's a Man's World*, 37–41, 43; Josh Alan Friedman, "Throw 'Em a Few Hot Words," in Parfrey, *It's a Man's World*, 45–46, 55; Josh Alan Friedman, "When Men Were Men and Women Were Nymphos: Men's Adventure Magazines," in Hanson, *The History of Men's Magazines, Volume 3, 1960s at the Newsstand*, 371, 375, 379, 381.

10. Josh Alan Friedman, "When Men Were Men and Women Were Nymphos: Men's Adventure Magazines," in Hanson, *The History of Men's Magazines, Volume 3, 1960s at the Newsstand*, 379, 381; Deis, introduction to Deis, *Weasels Ripped My Flesh!*, 25.

11. Elizabeth Fraterrigo, *"Playboy" and the Making of the Good Life in Modern America* (New York: Oxford University Press, 2009), 22–24; James R. Petersen, *The Century of Sex: Playboy's History of The Sexual Revolution: 1900–1999* (New York: Grove Press, 1999), 126; Hugh Merrill, *Esky: The Early Years at "Esquire"* (New Brunswick, N.J.: Rutgers University Press, 1995), 4, 39, 85.

12. Bruccoli, *Nelson Algren*, 109, 110, 114, 116.

13. Fraterrigo, *"Playboy" and the Making of the Good Life in Modern America*, 25; Petersen, *The Century of Sex*, 173; Merrill, *Esky*, 104–105, 109.

14. Merrill, *Esky*, 115–18; Petersen, *The Century of Sex*, 173–74. The U.S. Supreme Court decision was *Hannegan v. Esquire, Inc.*, 327 U.S. 146 (1946). The plaintiff in the case was Robert E. Hannegan. Frank Walker resigned as postmaster general in 1945, and Hannegan was the successor postmaster general. See Merrill, *Esky*, 117.

15. Merrill, *Esky*, 119, 127–30; Fraterrigo, *"Playboy" and the Making of the Good Life in Modern America*, 23–25; Petersen, *The Century of Sex*, 228; Frank Brady, *Hefner* (New York: Macmillan Publishing, 1974), 56–57.

16. Brady, *Hefner*, 56; Fraterrigo, *"Playboy" and the Making of the Good Life in Modern America*, 20; Russell Miller, *Bunny: The Real Story of "Playboy"* (New York: Holt, Rinehart and Winston, 1984), 30–31; Merrill, *Esky*, 138.

17. Jaccoma and Hanson, "Hugh Hefner: Playboy of the Western World," in *The History of Men's Magazines, Volume 2: Postwar to 1959*, ed. Dian Hanson (Cologne, Germany: Taschen, 2004), 206, 208; Merrill, *Esky*, 139; Miller, *Bunny*, 32–33.

18. Nelson Algren, "All Through the Night," *Playboy*, April 1957, 29, 69–72; Fraterrigo, *"Playboy" and the Making of the Good Life in Modern America*, 20; Merrill, *Esky*, 139; "Rabbit and Strippers Neck and Neck: The Race to the 60s," in Hanson, *The History of Men's Magazines, Volume 2, Postwar to 1959*, 295–96, 298; Dian Hanson, "Ten Years that Shook the (Men's Magazine) World," in Hanson, *The History of Men's Magazines, Volume 3, 1960s at the Newsstand*, 10, 12; [Heller], "Blood, Sweat, and Tits," in Collins and Hagenauer, *Men's Adventure Magazines in Postwar America*, 20–21; Petersen, *The Century of Sex*, 231, 250–53; Whitney Strub, *Obscenity Rules: "Roth v. United States" and the Long Struggle over Sexual Expression* (Lawrence: University Press of Kansas, 2013), 167, 235; *"Samuel Roth v. United States of America*: How *Good Times* Defined Obscenity," in Hanson, *The History of Men's Magazines, Volume 2, Postwar to 1959*, 395–400; "A Timeline of History with Men's Magazines," in Hanson, *The History of Men's Magazines, Volume 2, Postwar to 1959*, 17; Brady, *Hefner*, 82–88; Milton Moskowitz, "Newsstand Strip-Tease," *The Nation*, 20 July 1957, 24; *Roth v. United States*, 354 U.S. 476 (1957).

19. Bruce Jay Friedman, *Even the Rhinos Were Nymphos*, 25; Dorr, "My Plan Was to Be a Writer and an Adventurer," in Deis and Doyle, *A Handful of Hell*, 37; Deis, introduction to Deis, *Weasels Ripped My Flesh!*, 25; Josh Alan Friedman, "Throw 'Em a Few Hot Words," in Parfrey, *It's a Man's World*, 55; Parfrey, "From Pulp to Posterity: The Origins of Men's Adventure Magazines," in Parfrey, *It's a Man's World*, 34; "The War Comes Home," in Parfrey, *It's a Man's World*, 269; Earle, *All Man!*, 101; Josh Alan Friedman, "When Men Were Men and Women Were Nymphos: Men's Adventure Magazines," in Hanson, *The History of Men's Magazines, Volume 3:1960s at the Newsstand*, 379, 381; "Rabbit and Strippers Neck and Neck: The Race to the 60s," in Hanson, *The History of Men's Magazines, Volume 2, Postwar to 1959*, 296; Richard Jaccoma, "Full Frontal Assault: Bob Guccione and 'Penthouse,'" in Hanson, *The History of Men's Magazines, Volume 3, 1960s at the Newstand*, 277, 279; [Heller], "Blood, Sweat, and Tits: A History of Men's Adventure Magazines," in Collins and Hagenauer, *Men's Adventure Magazines in Postwar America*, 21; Fraterrigo, *"Playboy" and the Making of the Good Life in Modern America*, 20, 169–70; Petersen, *The Century of Sex*, 231, 353; Miller, *Bunny*, 170, 182–89; Bill Devine, "Devine's Guide to Men's Adventure Magazines," in Parfrey, *It's a Man's World*, 305–11.

20. Jaccoma and Hanson, "Hugh Hefner: Playboy of the Western World," in Hanson, *The History of Men's Magazines, Volume 2, Postwar to 1959*, 206, 208; Geoff Nicholson, "'For the Articles': Men's Magazines and Literature," in Hanson, *The History of Men's Magazines, Volume 2, Postwar to 1959*, 243, 246; Jack Newfield, "The Intellectual Maumaus," *Cavalier*, August 1965, 36–37, 80–82; Arthur J. Sasso, "The Sounds of Brubeck," *Caper*, May 1959, 18–21; Sol Coppola, "How to Beat the Horses," *Caper*, November 1957, 10–12; Ray Rich, "Low Hi-Fi," *Caper*, November 1957, 28–29, 45.

21. Evan Hunter, "S.P.Q.R.," *Gent*, April 1963, 8–10, 69–71; Geoff Nicholson, "'For the Articles': Men's Magazines and Literature," in Hanson, *The History of Men's Magazines, Volume 2, Postwar to 1959*, 250.

22. Fraterrigo, *"Playboy" and the Making of the Good Life in Modern America*, 169–171; Geoff Nicholson, "'For the Articles': Men's Magazines and Literature," in Hanson, *The History of Men's Magazines, Volume 2, Postwar to 1959*, 254, 257; "All Hail the Age of Aquarius: The American Newsstand 1959–1969" in Hanson, *The History of Men's Magazines, Volume 3, 1960s at the Newsstand*, 41; "Full Frontal Assault: Bob Guccione and '*Penthouse*,'" in Hanson, *The History of Men's Magazines*, Volume 3, *1960s at the Newsstand*, 277, 279; [Heller], "Blood, Sweat, and Tits," in Collins and Hagenauer, *Men's Adventure Magazines in Postwar America*, 21; Miller, *Bunny*, 170–71, 176–89; Petersen, *The Century of Sex*, 231, 353.

23. Geoff Nicholson, "'For the Articles': Men's Magazines and Literature," in Hanson, *The History of Men's Magazines, Volume 2, Postwar to 1959*, 254, 257; Tom Stratton, "Flash," *Nugget*, December 1974, 26–28, 33, 51; Nicholas Loungo, "Humbled," *Nugget*, June 1981, 36–38, 76–77, 84–86.

24. Geoff Nicholson, "'For the Articles': Men's Magazines and Literature," in Hanson, *The History of Men's Magazines, Volume 2, Postwar to 1959*, 257.

25. Drew, *Nelson Algren*, 301–02.

26. Drew, *Nelson Algren*, 301–02; Nelson Algren, "The Heroes," *Cavalcade*, March 1959, 20–21, 75–78; William Saroyan, "Hello Out There," *Escapade*, February 1959, 50–52, 60–62. In a 1962 *Washington Post Times Herald* article, Al Horne writes: "There's something to be said for the writing that turns up occasionally in the girlie books. Some, like a Nelson Algren story in *Cavalier*, is window-dressing, … but often you'll find brains among the bosoms." Al Horne, "The Magazine Rack," *Washington Post Times Herald*, 12 August 1962, E7.

27. "The Sex Pushers," *Cavalcade*, February 1979, 10–12, 75–76; "Sexual Candy Store," *Cavalcade*, February 1979, 20–22, 67–68; Stuart James, "Wyatt Earp and the Rustled Redhead!," *Cavalcade*, March 1959, 32–33, 81–84; Charles Richards, "The Battle That Won the Civil War," *Cavalcade*, March 1959, 44–47, 94, 96–97; William Bradley Bennet, "The Pack," *Cavalcade*, December 1961, 44–46, 69; Wayne C. Ulsch, "His Last Piece of Ass," *Cavalcade*, March 1977, 25–26, 74.

28. In a letter to *Rogue* published in the July 1961 issue, Algren commented about this article.

29. In a letter to *Rogue* published in the October 1961 issue, Algren commented about this article.

30. The March 1974 issue of *COQ* featured Algren's last American men's magazine contribution. Bettina Drew notes, however, that "German literary people had unfailingly treated Algren with the respect due an important novelist." In the late 1970s there was an increased German interest in his work. After the German *Playboy* paid hefty prices for two Algren pieces, Algren sought out other possible German sales. He sold two articles to *Lui Deutschland*, a German men's magazine, and they were published in the June 1980 and the July 1980 issues. See Drew, *Nelson Algren*, 365, 367–68.

31. "Rabbit and Strippers Neck and Neck: The Race to the 60s," in Hanson, *The History of Men's Magazines, Volume 2, Postwar to 1959*, 296; Tom Clark, *Kerouac's Last Word: Jack Kerouac in "Escapade"* (Sudbury, Mass.: Water Row Press, 1986), 5; Jack Kerouac, *Good Blonde & Others*, rev. and enl. ed. (San Francisco: Grey Fox Press, 1998), 217; Warren Leming, "Hanging with Nelson Algren: A Brief Look at the Author and His Milieu," in *Nelson Algren: A Collection of Critical Essays*, ed. Robert Ward (Madison, N.J.: Fairleigh Dickinson University Press, 2007), 169.

32. Ellen Weil and Gary K. Wolfe, *Harlan Ellison: The Edge of Forever* (Columbus: Ohio State University Press, 2002), 14, 40, 89–90; William Saroyan, "My Back to the World," *Rogue*, June 1963, 54–56, 60; Graham Greene, "Cheap in August," *Rogue*, December 1964, 10–12+; Jerre Mangione, *The Dream and the Deal: The Federal Writers' Project, 1935–1943* (Boston: Little, Brown and Co., 1972), 119, 121, 126; Earl Kemp and Luis Ortiz, eds., *Cult Magazines A to Z* (New York: Nonstop Press, 2009), s.v. "Rogue."

33. Kisor, "Nelson Algren, Hale and Salty at 64," 2; Drew, *Nelson Algren*, 342.

34. Weil and Wolfe, *Harlan Ellison*, 90–91.

35. Weil and Wolfe, *Harlan Ellison*, 90; Harlan Ellison, *I Have No Mouth and I Must Scream* (New York: Open Road Integrated Media, 2014), 73.

36. Weil and Wolfe, *Harlan Ellison*, 14.

37. Men's magazines published articles by Nelson Algren, and they also featured articles about Algren. These articles about Algren include the following: Bob Ellison, "A Walk on the Wild Side with Nelson Algren," *Fling*, January 1963; Paul Romney, "Nelson Algren: Writer on the Wild Side," *Caper*, July 1963; Hendrik L. Leffelaar, "Nelson Algren Off the Cuff," *Cavalier*, November 1963; Bob Ellison, "Three Best-Selling Authors: Conversations," *Rogue*, December 1963; David Ray, "A Talk on the Wild Side: A *Cavalcade* Interview with Nelson Algren," *Cavalcade*, July 1964; Sam Baker, "Author of the Issue—A Walk on the Wild Side with Nelson Algren," *Jaguar*, March 1967; William Penrod, "My First Literary Cocktail Party," *Gallery*, February 1973.

38. Jeffrey Marks, "In the Beginning," *Ellery Queen's Mystery Magazine*, September/October 2016, 65–66; Francis M. Nevins, Jr., *Royal Bloodline: Ellery Queen, Author and Detective* (Bowling Green, Ohio: Bowling Green University Popular Press, 1974), 1–6, 227.

39. Marks, "In the Beginning," *Ellery Queen's Mystery Magazine*, 67; Ellery Queen, ed., *Ellery Queen's Mystery Magazine*, Fall 1941, 1.

40. Nelson Algren, "He Swung and He Missed," *Ellery Queen's Mystery Magazine*, October 1957, 29–35; Nelson Algren, "He Swung and He Missed," *The American Mercury*, July 1942, 57–63. There are three versions of the October 1957 issue of *EQMM*: plain cover, pictorial cover, and British edition. Each version contains "He Swung and He Missed."

41. Bill Pronzini and Jack Adrian, eds., *Hard-Boiled: An Anthology of American Crime Stories* (Oxford: Oxford University Press, 1995), 3–4, 8–11; Keith Alan Deutsch, introduction to *The Black Lizard Big Book of "Black Mask" Stories*, ed. Otto Penzler (New York: Vintage Books, 2010), xi.

42. Pronzini and Adrian, *Hard-Boiled*, 15.

43. Mickey Spillane, "Everybody's Watching Me," *Manhunt*, January 1953, 1–15; Evan Hunter, "Die Hard," *Manhunt*, January 1953, 16–29; Kenneth Millar, "Shock Treatment," *Manhunt*, January 1953, 71–80; Pronzini and Adrian, *Hard-Boiled*, 15, 301–02, 388–89.

44. Nelson Algren, "Say a Prayer for the Guy," *Manhunt*, June 1958, 31–35; Pronzini and Adrian, *Hard-Boiled*, 15; Brooke Horvath, *Understanding Nelson Algren* (Columbia: University of South Carolina Press, 2005), 115–16.

45. Fraterrigo, *"Playboy" and the Making of the Good Life in Modern America*, 170–71; Merrill, *Esky*, 146–149; Tom Wolfe, *The New Journalism*, with an anthology edited by Tom Wolfe and E.W. Johnson (New York: Harper & Row, 1973), 9–22 passim.

46. Nelson Algren, "$22.50 by Wieboldt's," *COQ*, March 1974, 32–34, 36, 88; Saul Bellow, "Burdens of a Lone Survivor," *Esquire*, December 1974, 176–85+; Nelson Algren, "Chicago IV: The Irishman in the Grotto, the Man in the Iron Suit, and the Girl in Gravity-Z: The *Playboy* Magazine Story *or* Mr. Peepers as Don Juan" in *Algren at Sea: Who Lost an American? & Notes from a Sea Diary–Travel Writings* (New York: Seven Stories Press, 2008), 252; James R. Giles, *Confronting the Horror: The Novels of Nelson Algren* (Kent, Ohio: Kent State University Press, 1989), 85, 92–93; John Updike, "A Month of Sundays," *Playboy*, January 1975, 82–84+; John Updike, "Bech Third-Worlds It," *Playboy*, August 1975, 104–106, 144–147. Drew writes that "Candida [Donadio, Algren's agent] pulled him out of the hole by selling a section of the abandoned racetrack novel to *Playboy* for $3,000; this seemed to patch up all bad feelings between Algren and the enterprise." It appears that *Playboy* published this section as "Get All the Money," which appeared in the June 1970 issue. See Drew, *Nelson Algren*, 339. But not only did *Playboy* not publish Algren's work after 1972, *Playboy* did not invite Algren to its 1974 twentieth anniversary party. Did *Playboy* snub Algren because it felt he was a has-been or because of his behavior? In his prose poem "The Old Life" (1996) Donald Hall writes: "At the opening cocktail party of *Playboy's* conference, 'Great Young American Novelists,' Styron and Bourjaily speculated about procedures or engines by which they might rectify certain reviewers. Their words exemplified the spirit of this writers' weekend, which ended when Nelson Algren stubbed his cigar on a teacher of English's grand piano." See Mary Wisniewski, *Algren: A Life* (Chicago: Chicago Review Press, 2017), 289–90; Donald Hall, *The Old Life* (Boston: Houghton Mifflin, 1996), 70; "Wednesday's TV Highlights," *Chicago Tribune*, 23 October 1974, sec. 3, 15. Although *Playboy* magazine did not publish any of Algren's work after 1972, he continued to appear

in *Playboy*'s books. See Nelson Algren, "The Last Carrousel," in "*Playboy*" *Stories: The Best of Forty Years of Short Fiction*, ed. Alice K. Turner (New York: Dutton, 1994), 277–302; Nelson Algren, "All Through the Night," in *All Through the Night: Stories of the World's Oldest Profession* (Chicago: Playboy Press, 1975), 177–90.

47. As described in note 30, Algren published articles in the June 1980 and the July 1980 issues of *Lui Deutschland*, a German men's magazine. This magazine featured full-frontal (but not vulgar) nudity, similar to the nudity in *COQ*. It appears that Algren's brief appearance in this German men's magazine was merely an acceptance of an offer to make some quick and easy money and not an intention to continue publishing in men's magazines. See Drew, *Nelson Algren*, 365, 367–68.

48. Drew, *Nelson Algren*, 350–52.

49. Drew, *Nelson Algren*, 355; Jan Herman, "Nelson Algren: The Angry Author," *Chicago Sun-Times Chicagostyle*, 21 January 1979, 11; Giles, *Confronting the Horror*, 113; Nelson Algren, *Chicago: City on the Make* (Sausalito, Calif.: Contact Editions, 1961), 9; Arthur Shay, "Author on the Make: Nelson Algren's Bittersweet Affair with Chicago," *Chicago Tribune Magazine*, 14 September 1986, 14; Art Shay, *Chicago's Nelson Algren* (New York: Seven Stories Press, 2007), 136–39; Art Shay, *Nelson Algren's Chicago* (Urbana: University of Illinois Press, 1988), xiv; Martha Heasley Cox and Wayne Chatterton, *Nelson Algren* (Boston: Twayne Publishers, 1975), 52–54, 146n22; Nelson Algren, *The Devil's Stocking* (New York: Arbor House, 1983), 4. Carter wrote an autobiography; see Rubin "Hurricane" Carter, *The Sixteenth Round: From Number 1 Contender to # 45472* (New York: Viking Press, 1974). For more information about Algren's work on the Hurricane Carter case, see Linda Kay, *The Reading List* (Lanham, Md.: Hamilton Books, 2005).

50. Drew, *Nelson Algren*, 340, 350–52, 402; Jan Herman, *Ticket to New Jersey: A Portrait of Nelson Algren* (Lexington, Ky.: Impromptu Editions, 2014), 8–9; Kay, *The Reading List*, 71.

51. Kay, *The Reading List*, ix, xii; Drew, *Nelson Algren*, 352–56.

52. Drew, *Nelson Algren*, 357; Kay, *The Reading List*, 54–55.

53. Drew, *Nelson Algren*, 357–60; John Blades, "The Novel Nelson Algren Didn't Want to Write," *Chicago Tribune Book World*, 21 August 1983, sec. 13, 39; Budd Schulberg, "*The Devil's Stocking*: Algren's Last Look at the Inner Circle of Outcasts," review of *The Devil's Stocking*, by Nelson Algren, *Chicago Tribune Book World*, 21 August 1983, sec. 13, 38.

54. Drew, *Nelson Algren*, 273–99 passim, 360–62, 399; Wisniewski, *Algren*, 293–94; Holmes, "Arm: A Memoir," 251; Kay, *The Reading List*, 58–59.

55. Drew, *Nelson Algren*, 364–77; Horvath, *Understanding Nelson Algren*, 150; Bruccoli, *Nelson Algren*, 86, 91; Nelson Algren, *Calhoun* (Frankfurt, Germany: Zweitausendeins, 1981). Herbert Mitgang of *The New York Times* wrote the foreword to *The Devil's Stocking*, and in the foreword Mitgang claims that the book's title refers to Algren's statement: "A woman once told me that I was a devil's stocking—knitted backwards." But journalist Jan Herman, who knew Algren, maintains that a prostitute Algren interviewed while researching the book gave her boyfriend this description. Herman writes: "The novel took its final title from her phrase for her boyfriend. 'You're like the devil's stocking, Tiger,' she tells him. 'You're knitted backwards.'" See Drew, *Nelson Algren*, 370; Herbert Mitgang, foreword to Algren, *The Devil's Stocking*, 4; Jan Herman, "'In' at Last: Nelson Algren's Final Happy Days," *Chicago Sun-Times Book Week*, 17 May 1981, 31.

56. Schulberg, "*The Devil's Stocking*: Algren's Last Look at the Inner Circle of Outcasts," sec. 13, 37, 38; Phoebe-Lou Adams, review of *The Devil's Stocking*, by Nelson Algren, *The Atlantic*, October 1983, 122; "Notes on Current Books," review of *The Devil's Stocking*, by Nelson Algren, *The Virginia Quarterly Review* 60, no. 1 (Winter 1984): 27; A.J. Anderson, review of *The Devil's Stocking*, by Nelson Algren, *Library Journal* 108, no. 14 (1 August 1983): 1500. Buried deep in *The Devil's Stocking* is Algren's quintessential inside joke. On Saturday, November 26, 1977, someone (possibly a student group) managed to hack a television transmitter in southern England. At 5:06 PM, during a television news program, "a deep voice, accompanied by an eerie booming sound," drowned out the newscaster and delivered the following message: "This is the voice of Asteron. I am an authorized representative of the Intergalactic Mission, and I have a message for the planet Earth. We are

beginning to enter the period of Aquarius and there are many corrections which have to be made by Earth people. All your weapons of evil must be destroyed. You only have a short time to learn to live together in peace. You must live in peace ... or leave the galaxy." In *The Devil's Stocking*, a "raving" person named Kenyatta Islam makes an announcement that is almost identical to Asteron's message: "'I am an authorized representative of the Intergalactic Mission,' Kenyatta finally disclosed his credentials. 'I have a message for the Planet Earth. We are beginning to enter the period of Aquarius. Many corrections have to be made by Earth people. All your weapons of evil must be destroyed. You have only a short time to learn to live together in peace. You must live in peace'—here he paused to gain everybody's attention—'you must live in peace or leave the galaxy!'" See Robert JM Rickard, ed., "News," *Fortean Times: A Contemporary Record of Strange Phenomena*, no. 24 (Winter 1977): 50–51; reprint, Paul Sieveking, ed., *Fortean Times 16–25: Diary of a Mad Planet* (London: John Brown Publishing, 1995); Burton Paulu, *Television and Radio in the United Kingdom* (Minneapolis: University of Minnesota Press, 1981), 179–80; "Mysterious Voice Shakes Up Britons," *Chicago Tribune*, 27 November 1977, 2; Algren, *The Devil's Stocking*, 202, 204–05.

57. William F. Nolan, *The "Black Mask" Boys: Masters in the Hard-Boiled School of Detective Fiction* (New York: William Morrow, 1985), 27–28; Horvath, *Understanding Nelson Algren*, 150.

58. Rick Kogan, "2 Movies Try to Unravel the Mystery that is Algren," *Chicago Tribune*, 19 October 2014, sec. 4, 9; Wisniewski, *Algren*, 196. Martha Heasley Cox and Wayne Chatterton echo Kogan's belief, commenting that in short stories Algren "has demonstrated the complete range of his literary attainments." See Cox and Chatterton, *Nelson Algren*, 57. Maxwell Geismar also agrees with Rick Kogan. Geismar writes that "[Algren] was basically a short story writer, like Ernest Hemingway, whom he so admired." See Maxwell Geismar, "Nelson Algren: Unsung Proletarian of Letters," *Los Angeles Times Calendar*, 24 May 1981, 5.

59. Bruccoli, *Nelson Algren*, 113–31; Bruccoli, "Addenda to Bruccoli, *Nelson Algren*," 368–69; Tibbetts, "Further Addenda to Bruccoli, *Nelson Algren*," 214–15; Nelson Algren, *Entrapment and Other Writings*, eds. Brooke Horvath and Dan Simon (New York: Seven Stories Press, 2009).

60. Nelson Algren, "This Table on Time Only," *Esquire*, March 1940, 78–79; Horvath, *Understanding Nelson Algren*, 35.

61. Algren, "This Table on Time Only," 79. "This Table on Time Only" has been reprinted; see Algren, "This Table on Time Only," in *Entrapment and other Writings*, 58–60.

62. Nelson Algren, "G-String Gomorrah," *Esquire*, August 1957, 47. The italics in the text are in the original.

63. Algren, "Say a Prayer for the Guy," 32.

64. H.E.F. Donohue, *Conversations with Nelson Algren* (New York: Hill and Wang, 1964), 156, 331–32; S.J. Krause, "The Art and Satire of Twain's 'Jumping Frog' Story," *American Quarterly* 16, no. 4 (Winter 1964): 562–76; Mark Twain, "The Notorious Jumping Frog of Calaveras County," in *Sketches, New and Old* (New York: Oxford University Press, 1996), 29–35. For further discussion of Twain's "Jumping Frog" story, see Edgar Marquess Branch, *The Literary Apprenticeship of Mark Twain* (Urbana: University of Illinois Press, 1950), 120–29.

65. Nelson Algren, "How the Man with the Record One Eighth of an Inch Long was Saved by a Bessarabian Rye," *Esquire*, June 1960, 105. The use of the word "poleese" as "police" is not solely urban slang. Instead, its provenance as a type of dialect dates back to at least 1864. For example: "Persimmon Jake and ten others planned the robbery of your house this very night. I'm a poleese officer, Mr. Goodleigh, I am." See George Lippard, *The Memoirs of a Preacher; or, The Mysteries of the Pulpit* (Philadelphia: T.B. Peterson & Bros., 1864), 104. See also this 1876 example: "Then they held a long confab as to what they'd better do, an' th' wimmen sed they thowt it wor th' duty o' th' poleese to goa in an' tak him up whativver he wor; but th' poleese didn't see it, for, sed one on 'em, 'If he's th' chap aw think he is he might tak us daan wol we wor tryin to tak him up." See John Hartley, *Yorksher*

Puddin': A Collection of the Most Popular Dialect Stories (London: W. Nicholson & Sons, 1876), 356.

66. *Sports Illustrated* had asked Algren to attend the 1958 Kentucky Derby and to write an article about it for the magazine. Algren did both, but the magazine never printed his article. See Whitney Tower, "Prose for the Roses," *Sports Illustrated*, 28 April 1986, 38–40, 42, 45; Drew, *Nelson Algren*, 292–93; Colin Asher, *Never a Lovely So Real: The Life and Work of Nelson Algren* (New York: W.W. Norton, 2019), 372–74.

67. Nelson Algren, "Moon of the Backstretch, Still and White," *Rogue*, August 1961, 16, 24.

68. Shay, *Nelson Algren's Chicago*, xii, xiv, xxi; Cox and Chatterton, *Nelson Algren*, 49, 52–54, 138, 146n22.

69. Nelson Algren, "Afternoon in the Land of the Strange Light Sleep," *Cavalier*, September 1962, 25.

70. Algren identifies the drug peddler in the article: "In the night-blue bars of the wilderness where the peddler's name is always Jack-The-Rabbit." See Algren, "Afternoon in the Land of the Strange Light Sleep," 27.

71. Algren, "Afternoon in the Land of the Strange Light Sleep," 27.

72. Algren, "Afternoon in the Land of the Strange Light Sleep," 25.

73. James R. Giles, *The Naturalistic Inner-City Novel in America: Encounters with the Fat Man* (Columbia: University of South Carolina Press, 1995), 96.

Selected Bibliography

Adams, Phoebe-Lou. Review of *The Devil's Stocking*, by Nelson Algren. *The Atlantic*, October 1983, 122.

Algren, Nelson. "Afternoon in the Land of the Strange Light Sleep." *Cavalier*, September 1962, 24–25, 27.

Algren, Nelson. *Algren at Sea: Who Lost an American? & Notes from a Sea Diary—Travel Writings*. New York: Seven Stories Press, 2008.

Algren, Nelson. "All Through the Night." In *All Through the Night: Stories of the World's Oldest Profession*, 177–90. Chicago: Playboy Press, 1975.

Algren, Nelson. *Calhoun*. Frankfurt, Germany: Zweitausendeins, 1981.

Algren, Nelson. *Chicago: City on the Make*. Sausalito, Calif.: Contact Editions, 1961.

Algren, Nelson. *The Devil's Stocking*. New York: Arbor House, 1983.

Algren, Nelson. *Entrapment and Other Writings*, edited by Brooke Horvath and Dan Simon. New York: Seven Stories Press, 2009.

Algren, Nelson. "G-String Gomorrah." *Esquire*. August 1957, 47–48.

Algren, Nelson. "How the Man with the Record One Eighth of an Inch Long Was Saved by a Bessarabian Rye." *Esquire*, June 1960, 105.

Algren, Nelson. "The Last Carrousel." In *Playboy Stories: The Best of Forty Years of Short Fiction*, edited by Alice K. Turner, 277–302. New York: Dutton, 1994.

Algren, Nelson. "Moon of the Backstretch, Still and White." *Rogue*, August 1961, 12–16, 24.

Algren, Nelson. "Say a Prayer for the Guy." *Manhunt*, June 1958, 31–35.

Algren, Nelson. "This Table on Time Only." *Esquire*, March 1940, 78–79.

Algren, Nelson. *A Walk on the Wild Side*. N.p.: Thunder's Mouth Press, 1990.

Anderson, A.J. Review of *The Devil's Stocking*, by Nelson Algren. *Library Journal* 108, no. 14 (1 August 1983): 1500.

Asher, Colin. *Never a Lovely So Real: The Life and Work of Nelson Algren*. New York: W.W. Norton, 2019.

Blades, John. "The Novel Nelson Algren Didn't Want to Write." *Chicago Tribune Book World*, 21 August 1983, sec. 13, 37, 39.

Brady, Frank. *Hefner*. New York: Macmillan Publishing, 1974.

Branch, Edgar Marquess. *The Literary Apprenticeship of Mark Twain*. Urbana: University of Illinois Press, 1950.

Bruccoli, Matthew J. "Addenda to Bruccoli, *Nelson Algren*." *The Papers of the Bibliographical Society of America*, September 1988, 367–69.

Bruccoli, Matthew J. *Nelson Algren: A Descriptive Bibliography*. Pittsburgh: University of Pittsburgh Press, 1985.

Carter, Rubin "Hurricane." *The Sixteenth Round: From Number 1 Contender to # 45472*. Toronto: Penguin Canada, 1974.

Clark, Tom. *Kerouac's Last Word: Jack Kerouac in "Escapade."* Sudbury, Mass.: Water Row Press, 1986.

Collins, Max Allan, and George Hagenauer. *Men's Adventure Magazines in Postwar America*. Cologne, Germany: Taschen, 2008.

Cox, Martha Heasley, and Wayne Chatterton. *Nelson Algren*. Boston: Twayne, 1975.

Deis, Robert, ed. *Weasels Ripped My Flesh!* N.p.: New Texture, 2012.

Deutsch, Keith Alan. Introduction to *The Black Lizard Big Book of "Black Mask" Stories*, xi–xix. Edited by Otto Penzler. New York: Vintage Books, 2010.

Donohue, H.E.F. *Conversations with Nelson Algren*. New York: Hill and Wang, 1964.

Dorr, Robert F. *A Handful of Hell: Classic War and Adventure Stories*. Edited by Robert Deis and Wyatt Doyle. N.p.: New Texture, 2016.

Drew, Bettina. *Nelson Algren: A Life on the Wild Side*. Austin: University of Texas Press, 1991.

Earle, David M. *All Man! Hemingway, 1950s Men's Magazines, and the Masculine Persona*. Kent, Ohio: Kent State University Press, 2009.

Ellison, Harlan. *I Have No Mouth and I Must Scream*. New York: Open Road Integrated Media, 2014.

Fraterrigo, Elizabeth. *"Playboy" and the Making of the Good Life in Modern America*. New York: Oxford University Press, 2009.

Friedman, Bruce Jay. *Even the Rhinos Were Nymphos*. Chicago: University of Chicago Press, 2000.

Geismar, Maxwell. "Nelson Algren: Unsung Proletarian of Letters." *Los Angeles Times Calendar*, 24 May 1981, 5.

Giles, James R. *Confronting the Horror: The Novels of Nelson Algren*. Ohio: Kent State University Press, 1989.

Giles, James R. *The Naturalistic Inner-City Novel in America: Encounters with the Fat Man*. Columbia: University of South Carolina Press, 1995.

Hall, Donald. *The Old Life*. Boston: Houghton Mifflin, 1996.

Hanson, Dian, ed. *The History of Men's Magazines, Volume 2: Postwar to 1959*. Cologne, Germany: Taschen, 2004.

Hanson, Dian, ed. *The History of Men's Magazines, Volume 3: 1960s at the Newsstand*. Cologne, Germany: Taschen, 2005.

Hartley, John. *Yorksher Puddin': A Collection of the Most Popular Dialect Stories*. London: W. Nicholson & Sons, 1876.

Herman, Jan. "Nelson Algren: The Angry Author." *Chicago Sun-Times Chicagostyle*. 21 January 1979, 8–11.

Herman, Jan. "'In' at Last: Nelson Algren's Final Happy Days." *Chicago Sun-Times Book Week*, 17 May 1981, 24, 31.

Herman, Jan. *Ticket to New Jersey: A Portrait of Nelson Algren*. Lexington, Ky.: Impromptu Editions, 2014.

Holmes, John Clellon. "Arm: A Memoir." In *Representative Men: The Biographical Essays, Selected Essays by John Clellon Holmes*. Vol. 2. Fayetteville: University of Arkansas Press, 1988.

Horne, Al. "The Magazine Rack." *Washington Post Times Herald*, 12 August 1962, E7.

Horvath, Brooke. *Understanding Nelson Algren*. Columbia: University of South Carolina Press, 2005.

Kay, Linda. *The Reading List*. Lanham, Md.: Hamilton Books, 2005.

Kemp, Earl, and Luis Ortiz, eds. *Cult Magazines A to Z*. New York: Nonstop Press, 2009.

Kerouac, Jack. *Good Blonde & Others*. Rev. and enl. ed. San Francisco: Grey Fox Press, 1998.

Kisor, Henry. "Nelson Algren, Hale and Salty at 64." *Chicago Daily News Panorama*, 27–28 October 1973, 2–3.

Kisor, Henry. "Nelson Algren, That Hackensack Homebody." *Chicago Daily News Panorama*, 12–13 June 1976, 7.

Kogan, Rick. "2 Movies Try to Unravel the Mystery that is Algren." *Chicago Tribune*, 19 October 2014, sec. 4, 9.

Krause, S.J. "The Art and Satire of Twain's 'Jumping Frog' Story." *American Quarterly* 16, no. 4 (Winter 1964): 562–76.

Leming, Warren. "Hanging with Nelson Algren: A Brief Look at the Author and His Milieu." In *Nelson Algren: A Collection of Critical Essays*, edited by Robert Ward, 162–72. Madison, N.J.: Fairleigh Dickinson University Press, 2007.

Lippard, George. *The Memoirs of a Preacher; or, The Mysteries of the Pulpit*. Philadelphia: T.B. Peterson & Bros., 1864.

Mangione, Jerre. *The Dream and the Deal: The Federal Writers' Project 1935–1943*. Boston: Little Brown, 1972.

Marks, Jeffrey. "In the Beginning." *Ellery Queen's Mystery Magazine*, September/October 2016, 65–68.

Merrill, Hugh. *Esky: The Early Years at "Esquire."* New Brunswick, N.J.: Rutgers University Press, 1995.

Miller, Russell Miller. *Bunny: The Real Story of "Playboy."* New York: Holt, Rinehart and Winston, 1984.

Moskowitz, Milton. "Newsstand Strip-Tease." *The Nation*, 20 July 1957, 24.

"Mysterious Voice Shakes Up Britons." *Chicago Tribune*, 27 November 1977, 2.

Nevins, Francis M., Jr. *Royal Bloodline: Ellery Queen, Author and Detective*. Bowling Green, Ohio: Bowling Green University Popular Press, 1974.

Nolan, William F. *The "Black Mask" Boys: Masters in the Hard-Boiled School of Detective Fiction*. New York: William Morrow, 1985.

"Notes on Current Books." Review of *The Devil's Stocking*, by Nelson Algren. *The Virginia Quarterly Review* 60, no. 1 (Winter 1984): 27.

Parfrey, Adam, ed. *It's a Man's World: Men's Adventure Magazines, The Postwar Pulps*, expanded edition. Port Townsend, Wash.: Feral House, 2015.

Paulu, Burton. *Television and Radio in the United Kingdom*. Minneapolis: University of Minnesota Press, 1981.

Petersen, James R. *The Century of Sex: Playboy's History of The Sexual Revolution: 1900–1999*. New York: Grove Press, 1999.

Pronzini, Bill, and Jack Adrian, eds. *Hard-Boiled: An Anthology of American Crime Stories*. Oxford: Oxford University Press, 1995.

Rickard, Robert JM, ed. "News." *Fortean Times: A Contemporary Record of Strange Phenomena*, no. 24 (Winter 1977): 50–51; reprint, Paul Sieveking, ed. *Fortean Times 16–25: Diary of a Mad Planet*. London: John Brown Publishing, 1995.

Schulberg, Budd. "'The Devil's Stocking': Algren's Last Look at the Inner Circle of Outcasts." Review of *The Devil's Stocking*, by Nelson Algren. *Chicago Tribune Book World*, 21 August 1983, sec. 13, 37–38.

Shay, Arthur. "Author on the Make: Nelson Algren's Bittersweet Affair with Chicago." *Chicago Tribune Magazine*, 14 September 1986, 10–12, 14–17, 32, 39.

Shay, Art. *Chicago's Nelson Algren*. Seven Stories Press: New York, 2007.

Shay, Art. *Nelson Algren's Chicago*. Urbana: University of Illinois Press, 1988.

Strub, Whitney. *Obscenity Rules: "Roth v. United States" and the Long Struggle over Sexual Expression*. Lawrence: University Press of Kansas, 2013.

Tibbetts, Robert A. "Further Addenda to Bruccoli, *Nelson Algren*." *The Papers of the Bibliographical Society of America*, June 1989, 214–17.

Tower, Whitney. "Prose for the Roses." *Sports Illustrated*, 28 April 1986, 38–40, 42, 45.

Twain, Mark. "The Notorious Jumping Frog of Calaveras County." In *Sketches, New and Old*, 29–35. New York: Oxford University Press, 1996.

Weil, Ellen, and Gary K. Wolfe. *Harlan Ellison: The Edge of Forever*. Columbus: Ohio State University Press, 2002.

Wisniewski, Mary. *Algren: A Life*. Chicago: Chicago Review Press, 2017.

Wolfe, Tom. *The New Journalism*. With an anthology edited by Tom Wolfe and E.W. Johnson. New York: Harper & Row, 1973.

The *Chicago Free Press* Era

Nelson Algren graduated from the University of Illinois in 1931 with a degree in journalism. Thirty-nine years later, he landed what many journalists might think was a dream job—a contributing writer for the *Chicago Free Press*. Brian D. Boyer and Christopher Chandler, the publisher and editor, respectively, of the *Chicago Free Press*, describe this publication in the January 18, 1970, prototype edition (Volume 1, No. 0) as "a new, old-fashioned muckraking newsmagazine for metropolitan Chicago." Brian Boyer recalls talking with Chandler as to who they could get to write for their magazine. Chandler, who knew Algren, suggested contacting the author. It was a dream job for Algren because of his dream job description—In the first "regular" issue (Volume 1, No. 1) dated September 28, 1970, Algren is identified in the masthead and in an editorial as a "contributing writer" who "will write about whatever he wants to." Algren was given free rein; he only had to meet the magazine's weekly deadlines for submitting his work.[1]

NELSON ALGREN ABRAHAM . . . . . *Chicago*

Journalism

Daily Illini (4)

Figure 5: Nelson Algren graduated from the University of Illinois in 1931 with a degree in journalism. This is his graduation picture from the 1931 university yearbook, *The Illio*. Nelson Algren was born Nelson Algren Abraham, his first and middle names being a variation of his grandfather's name, Nels Ahlgren. When he started to write, a magazine editor suggested that he shorten his name to Nelson Algren. When he went into the army, he legally changed his name to Nelson Algren.

43

Unfortunately, the *Chicago Free Press* was short-lived. Disregarding the January prototype issue, the magazine ran from September 28, 1970, through November 23, 1970. Chicago real estate developer Bernard "Barney" Weissbourd had initially contributed $50,000 towards start-up costs. But the staff was writers, not ad salesmen. The magazine contained advertising, but it did not generate sufficient revenue to keep the magazine afloat. Barney's money ran dry after nine issues. Algren's contributions to the magazine, consisting of seven articles, one story, and one book review, are discussed in the following pages.[2]

Chicago Free Press *(Prototype edition) 1, No. 0 (18 January 1970): Nothing*

"Upside-Down Emil," Chicago Free Press *1, No. 1 (28 September 1970): 12–13*

"Upside-Down Emil" is a rather sad story about a young man who, wearing an ironworker's helmet with an attached pulley, would ride a tightrope upside down. After trying to convert his Model-T car into an oil burning vehicle, he is sent to a "psyche ward" for thirty days. When he comes back, Emil goes to work "for a factory that made endless belting, and some magic that had been in the world was gone." After a machine was invented that could do his job, "Emil went to the bars. He never tried anything again except whiskey." An earlier version of this story first appeared in the *New York Herald Tribune Book Week* in 1963. "Upside-Down Emil" is reprinted in *The Last Carousel*.[3]

"The Rest of the Way is by the Stars," Chicago Free Press *1, No. 2 (5 October 1970): 22–27*

In the spring of 1968, Nelson Algren decided to go to Vietnam, hoping to find material for a possible book, a book similar to Truman Capote's 1966 non-fiction novel, *In Cold Blood*. Algren arranged passage on a freighter that left San Francisco on November 14, 1968. He first sailed to Japan; Algren stayed a week in Yokohama and Tokyo, and then he continued on to Vietnam, arriving in Saigon on December 15. His trip was financed by a variety of sources: a grant from the Illinois Arts Council; a writers' conference fee; horse track gambling winnings; and an advance from the *Atlantic Monthly*—the magazine had agreed to provide press credentials and money in exchange for four articles about Saigon.[4]

Algren wrote three articles for the *Atlantic Monthly*, but the magazine rejected them. (Algren's friend Studs Terkel claimed that the magazine "didn't print a thing because the essays were so outrageous.") Perhaps "The Rest of the Way is by the Stars" was a revision of one of the rejected articles, or perhaps Algren wrote it especially for the *Chicago Free Press*. Regardless of its provenance, this long article (six pages) is about Saigon's *Chieu Hoi* or Open Arms amnesty program, where the U.S. government provides housing and aid to North Vietnamese defectors. Algren describes *Chieu Hoi* in the article: "Its purpose is to turn the insurgent into a friend by rewarding him with a respected place in the Establishment. Something like offering a member of the Black Panthers a job as an executive in Head Start."[5]

"A Ticket to Biro-Bidjan," Chicago Free Press 1, No. 2 (5 October 1970): 37–38

"A Ticket to Biro-Bidjan" is an article about King Levinsky, a washed-up Chicago boxer, grilling hot dogs for a living, who welches on a horse racing gambling bet:[6] (Figure 6)

> It was plain enough that he'd pocketed the fifty and didn't have a dime of his own. Now I could either come in on him to the people he'd held out on, and get his head split with a baseball bat if not something heavier. Such as a crowbar. But how would *that* get me five hundred and ninety-five dollars?[7]

The article is about 1300 words in length, and it is amusing. But Algren had been a boxing fan all his life, and so this article did not have to be just a 1300-word anecdote. Instead, he could have taken his cue from Gay Talese, who was a new journalist—he wrote nonfiction journalistic prose that read like fiction. In 1964 Talese wrote an article for *Esquire* called, "The Loser." It was about boxer Floyd Patterson and his life after his second loss to Sonny Liston. Moving from scene-by-scene—first a dirt road, then Patterson's apartment, then his daughter's school—Talese poignantly and sympathetically reveals Patterson as a fallen sports hero.[8]

New Journalism eventually became its own literary genre, and Tom Wolfe became its literary guru, with books such as *The Kandy-Kolored Tangerine-Flake Streamline Baby* (1965) and *The Electric Kool-Aid Acid Test* (1968).[9]

Tom Wolfe writes of four "devices"—four "techniques of realism" that give New Journalism what has variously been called its "immediacy,"

Figure 6: This cover of the May 1934 issue of *The Ring* magazine features King Levinsky; it describes him as "Chicago's Heavyweight Challenger." Nelson Algren wrote about Levinsky in the October 5, 1970, issue of the *Chicago Free Press* magazine. Levinsky gained national prominence by going four rounds with onetime heavyweight champion Jack Dempsey in a 1932 exhibition match. There was no official decision, but eighteen of twenty-four sportscasters (*continued*)

its "concrete reality," its "emotional involvement," and its "gripping or absorbing quality." These four devices are:[10]

One: Scene-by-Scene Construction. The writer tells the story by moving from scene to scene, resorting as little as possible to narrating the story.[11]

Two: Recording the Dialogue in Full. Realistic dialogue gets the reader involved in the story. It establishes and defines the characters in the story.[12]

Three: Third-Person Point of View. The writer presents every scene to the reader through the eyes of a particular character. This gives the reader the feeling of being inside the character's mind, with the reader experiencing the emotional reality of the scene in the same way as the character experiences it.[13]

Four: Recording Status-Life Details. This is the recording of everyday gestures, habits, manners, customs, styles of furniture, clothing, decorations, styles of traveling, eating, styles of walking, and other symbolic details that might exist within a scene. These details are symbols of what Wolfe calls a person's *status life*. These details make the story more realistic because they are indications as to how people live. These details are basically background colors, noises, and tastes. The inclusion of details like hair styles, brand names, gestures, habits, and mannerisms give stories added realism.[14]

New Journalism was still popular in 1970—Tom Wolfe had published *Radical Chic & Mau-Mauing the Flak Catchers* that year. Using the four techniques of New Journalism, Algren could have compassionately traced Levinsky's career from the time Levinsky brought Jack Dempsey's "comeback" tour to an abrupt end when Levinsky pounded the former champion in a 1932 four-round exhibition match that broke the Chicago Stadium attendance records, to Levinsky's 1935 loss in the first round against Joe Louis, when Levinsky begged the referee, "Please don't let him hit me no more!" Algren could have asked Levinsky, who had earned $250,000 in the ring, why he was now grilling hot dogs in a Chicago snack shop. Algren could have used status-life details to describe the snack shop. He could have coupled these details with extended dialogue to illustrate Levinsky's

agreed that Levinsky won. The event broke the Chicago Stadium attendance record, drawing a crowd of 23,332 spectators. Levinsky was big and strong, and he had stamina and a powerful right hand. Unfortunately, he had virtually no defense, and so he lost as many fights as he won. After his boxing career ended, he turned to selling neckties. When Algren met Levinsky, he was grilling hot dogs in a Chicago snack shop (Getty Images).

demeanor and frame of mind as he stood in front of the hot dog grill. Algren could have persuaded Levinsky to talk about Joe Louis (and himself) the way Gay Talese convinced Floyd Patterson to talk about Sonny Liston (and himself) in his famous 1964 *Esquire* article.[15]

But Algren did not do any of these things. For example, he devotes just one sentence to Levinsky's post-boxing employment: "The King was grilling hot dogs in a North Clark Street snackery the next time I saw him." Compare this description of where Levinsky worked to Talese's "The Loser" description of where Floyd Patterson lived—a two-room apartment in upstate New York:[16]

> In the smaller room is a large bed he makes up himself, several record albums he rarely plays, a telephone that seldom rings. The larger room has a kitchen on one side and, on the other, adjacent to a sofa, is a fireplace from which are hung boxing trunks and T-shirts to dry, and a photograph of him when he was the champion, and also a television set. The set is usually on except when Patterson is sleeping, or when he is sparring across the road inside the clubhouse (the ring is rigged over what was once the dance floor), or when, in a rare moment of painful honesty, he reveals to a visitor what it is like to be the loser.[17]

Status-life details like gestures, clothing, and mannerisms make a story more realistic, as they are indications of what people do and how they live. In the above passage from Talese's "The Loser," the status-life details of Patterson's apartment add a sense of resignation, perhaps even melancholy, to Patterson's life. On the other hand, there is little sense of *anything* in "A Ticket to Biro-Bidjan." There are, for example, a few cursory status-life details in Algren's description of Levinsky, but they tell the reader almost nothing about his life:[18]

> The next time I saw him he was leaning on the grandstand rail at Sportsman's Park. He was wearing a heavy white turtleneck sweater, a small cap perched on the very back of his skull, and was smoking an expensive-looking cigar.[19]

Wolfe writes that with New Journalism, "the writer is one step closer to the absolute involvement of the reader." In "The Loser," the reader is inside Floyd Patterson's apartment and sitting on the furniture while Patterson is "pacing slowly around the room near the sofa." In "A Ticket to Biro-Bidjan," the reader is barely in Chicago. Algren writes about King Levinsky as if he were writing a feature article for a news magazine. Which, of course, he was. In 1970 Nelson Algren was a self-proclaimed journalist, and so Algren's story was journalism. But it wasn't New Journalism. It was good, but it was not memorable.[20]

But is that so bad, not being memorable? Not really. But what might it have been? In 1949 Art Shay, a free-lance photographer for *Life* magazine and a former staff reporter for *Life*, decided to do a photo essay about

"Algren in His World." The two men prowled the streets of Chicago, with Shay taking pictures of all-night restaurants, bars, and tattoo parlors. Shay photographed a heroin buy being made in a Chicago doorway.[21]

Life laid out the story for eight pages, but at the last minute, *Life* changed its mind. When the presses rolled in the spring of 1950, the April 3 issue did not include "Algren in His World." Instead, the issue featured "The Black Palace," a ten-page pictorial about life in a Mexican prison that granted conjugal rights to prisoners. Art Shay later commented about his Algren photo essay to Algren biographer Bettina Drew: "It would have *made* Nelson."[22]

Twenty years later, what if Algren had adopted the "New Journalism" style of writing nonfiction for his article about King Levinsky? "A Ticket to Biro-Bidjan," based on one or more interviews with the former boxer, but written in the style of Gay Talese's "The Loser," first published in the *Chicago Free Press*, then expanded for *Esquire* or *Playboy*, would have *made* Algren.[23]

"Early Chicago Journalism," Chicago Free Press 1, No. 3 (12 October 1970): 28–30

"Early Chicago Journalism" is a brilliantly comedic account of Algren's four so-called "starts in Chicago journalism." His second start is the most humorous—when Emmett Dedmon of the *Chicago Sun-Times* hired him to write about the Chicago White Sox and the 1959 World Series:

> The moment each game was finished, I cabbed north to Dedmon's office, composing my story on the way. Dedmon, wearing a green eye-shade, would be striding up and down shouting things like, "Hit that story! The presses are rolling! Get on the streets before the *Trib*! *Scoop* 'em!" To which nobody paid the least attention. It wasn't until some years later, when I chanced to see a revival of "The Front Page," that I realized he was doing Hildy Johnson.[24]

"Previous Days," Chicago Free Press 1, No. 4 (19 October 1970): 30–31

This article consists of various remembrances of Algren's childhood days. One of them is about a girl named Ethel: "When I was five I fell in love with a girl of six. Her name was Ethel, she was Catholic, she lived upstairs, she could read and write and she liked me too. We were to be married as soon as I learned to read and write."[25]

In this article Algren shows his mastery of dialogue. Ethel goes to school at St. Columbanus, the church across the street from where he lived. When Algren learns that he cannot go to school with Ethel because he is not Catholic, but instead has to go to Park Manor Public School, Ethel sprinkles holy water on his head and proclaims that he is a Catholic:[26]

> I ran downstairs to give the good news to my parents.
> "Be whatever you want," my mother compromised with The Pope, "but you're going to Park Manor all the same."
> "That girl is sure one holy wonder," was all my father had to say.
> "I'm an atheist," my sister piped in.
> "Just finish your carrots before you eat the tapioca," my mother had the last word.[27]

"Pottawattomie Ghosts," Chicago Free Press 1, no. 5 (26 October 1970): 30–31

In the article, "Pottawattomie Ghosts," Algren offers up his own interpretation of Chicago history. In the following excerpt he comments on the Chicago Race Riots of 1919:[28]

> The press attributed the murders to racial hate. Yet poverty, not color, was the spur. For poverty was what the Irish were just rising from, and what the blacks threatened to push them back into. The Irish would have taken off after any anyone, black or white, who'd stick pigs for [meat packers] Armour, Cudahy and Swift for half of what they themselves were earning.
> By raising the blacks' standard of living to that of the whites, Carl Sandburg suggested, the conflict in the slums could be resolved.
> "The slums take their revenge," he warned Armour, Cudahy and Swift....
> Yet neither Armour, Cudahy nor Swift got mad at Sandburg. They *tried* to see things his way. The only thing that stopped them from coming right out for low-income housing was their investment in bacon. Naturally, the *Chicago Tribune* gave them a big "E" for Effort. Thus keeping the stockyards advertising.[29]

Algren sometimes used satire in his *Chicago Free Press* columns. Chicago newspaper columnist Mike Royko was Algren's friend, and he also used satire in his columns, and so their writing styles at times seems similar. Here both Algren and Royko are writing about Mayor Richard J. Daley of Chicago and the rioting during the 1968 Democratic National Convention:

Nelson Algren, "Pottawattomie Ghosts":

> Putting up barbed wire to protect his politics, organizing a massive defense against children and issuing a shoot-to-kill order against looters were not tactics Richard Daley picked up at the Nativity of Our Lord Church.[30]

Mike Royko, "Cops Threaten Law and Order":

> But our mayor, the architect of the grand plan for head-bashing, is wandering around loose and making predictable statements.
>
> The great dumpling says newspapermen ought to move faster when cops come at them. That way they won't be banged about.
>
> How in the hell, the mayor might demonstrate, can you move fast when there are six people slugging you from one direction and a parked car is blocking your retreat from another?
>
> If the mayor will put that trick on film, I'll sell tickets and guarantee a full house.[31]

"Let's See Your Hands," Chicago Free Press *1, No. 6 (2 November 1970): 25–27*

Nelson Algren met Richard Wright in 1933. They worked together for the Illinois Writers' Project during the Great Depression, and Wright would eventually write the introduction to Algren's second novel, *Never Come Morning* (1942). (President Roosevelt's New Deal had the task of putting writers and other people in the creative professions back to work. The Illinois Writers' Project was the Illinois office of the Federal Writer's Project, which was one of President Roosevelt's New Deal programs.)[32]

Richard Wright died on November 28, 1960. Algren had not seen Wright since 1949, but he had such tremendous respect for Wright, he felt compelled to write an essay in honor of his friend. "Remembering Richard Wright" appeared in the January 28, 1961, issue of *The Nation*.

Almost ten years later, Algren revised "Remembering Richard Wright" for the *Chicago Free Press*, calling it, "Let's See Your Hands."[33]

In just one paragraph of "Let's See Your Hands," Algren manages to capture the essence of Richard Wright:

> Beginning himself as a face without a name among a multitude of nameless faces, an inarticulate man of no permanent address, a being entitled to survive only so long as he put in no claim to his own individuality, he became the voice of multitudes now claiming not only an address, but their individuality as men, from Johannesburg to DaNang. His voice forced a wedge for the inarticulate of the world to force their way into the company of men.[34]

Algren concluded his article with this observation:

> Ten years after his death in Paris, November 28, 1960, Wright's impact upon Chicago, it is my own surmise, will be more enduring than that of any merchant prince, mayor or newspaper owner. For his impact was not upon City Hall but upon the city's conscience. Therefore upon the conscience of humanity everywhere.[35]

"The Cop Mentality," Chicago Free Press 1, No. 7 (9 November 1970): 27–28

During the 1960s Nelson Algren wrote two short stories and one article for the *Saturday Evening Post*. They were "The Moon of the Arfy Darfy," "A Ticket on Skoronski," and "Down with Cops." They are significant because they encapsulate in the microcosm of a national magazine the wide range of Algren's writing. "The Moon of the Arfy Darfy" is a gritty story of horse racing deceit. "A Ticket on Skoronski" is a dark story about a man dying of a heart attack at a poker table.[36]

But "Down with Cops" is completely different. In this essay Algren writes of the rogue Chicago policeman with the so-called "cop mentality," the policeman with the inferiority complex who believes that once he gets his badge, "now at last those who have made him toe the mark are going to have to take their turn at toeing."[37]

Algren condensed "Down with Cops" for the *Chicago Free Press*. In "The Cop Mentality" he argues that policemen are people who hide their own feelings of inferiority behind a badge as they administer society's "vindictiveness":[38]

> The devil being at the bottom of it all, it's the cop's duty, he feels, to keep people from acting funny be*fore* they do something funny.
>
> Ultimately, the cop is no more than the instrument which fulfills us; no more than the extension of our own vindictiveness. And his secret enjoyment of flashing the parked couple or of crying "Open the door!" on the midnight stair, no more than our own secret enjoyment....
>
> "I call upon you to remember," Sir Samuel Romilly warned a century and a half ago, "that cruel punishments have an inevitable tendency to produce cruelty in the people."[39]

"A Guy Who Got Wiped," review of Blue Movie, by Terry Southern, Chicago Free Press 1, No. 8 (16 November 1970): 32–3

Algren broke format in writing his last contribution to the *Chicago Free Press*—he wrote a book review of Terry Southern's book, *Blue Movie* (1970).

Algren reviewed Southern's 1959 novel, *The Magic Christian*, for the *Chicago Sun-Times* newspaper. He was effusive in his praise, writing that the book was "the most profoundly satiric and wildly comic account of our life and times in years." But praise for one book does not merit a free pass for a later book. Eleven years later, Algren ripped into *Blue Movie*:[40]

What ultimate personal realization the author had in mind in turning out *Blue Movie* could scarcely have been anything else than truckloads of bread gained by a great pornographic breakthrough. Unhappily, *Blue Movie* is no greater a breakthrough than were the sex-orientation films, presented by the chaplain of the 124th Field Evacuation Hospital, which we had to sit through to qualify for a pass to Marseilles.[41]

Chicago Free Press *1, no. 9 (23 November 1970): Nothing*

This was the last issue of the *Chicago Free Press*. Although Algren is still listed in this issue as a contributing writer, it contains nothing by Algren. Barney Weissbourd's seed money was gone. Boyer and Chandler had barely enough left to publish the ninth issue; they did not have enough money to pay Algren for his weekly column. When they explained this to Algren, he told them that he was not going to write if he was not going to be paid.[42]

Conclusion

Algren's first *Chicago Free Press* contribution was a story. His last was a book review. In between he wrote seven articles. Of these nine pieces, only three of them—"Upside-Down Emil," "Let's See Your Hands," and "The Cop Mentality"—were recycled from earlier writings. The rest of them were all original works. Viewed as a group through a

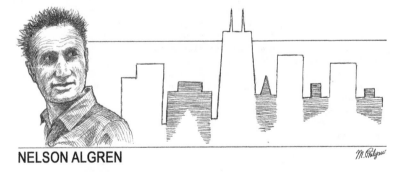

NELSON ALGREN

Figure 7: In 1970 Nelson Algren wrote seven articles, one story, and one book review for the *Chicago Free Press*, a weekly newsmagazine. Algren's contributions to this magazine were highlighted by a byline illustration that depicted his name and face set against a backdrop of Chicago's skyline. Artist Marshall Philyaw has stylistically recreated this *Chicago Free Press* artwork with the permission of Brian D. Boyer, former publisher of the magazine.

twenty-first-century lens, Algren's *Chicago Free Press* work is fresh, innovative, and entertaining, even more than fifty years after it was written.

NOTES

1. Bettina Drew, *Nelson Algren: A Life on the Wild Side* (Austin: University of Texas Press, 1991), 25, 31; Brian D. Boyer and Christopher Chandler, [editorial], *Chicago Free Press* 1, no. 0 (18 January 1970): 3; [masthead], *Chicago Free Press* 1, no. 1 (28 September 1970): 3; "Editorial," *Chicago Free Press* 1, no. 1 (28 September 1970): 5; Brian D. Boyer, interview by Richard F. Bales, July 1, 2021.

2. Brian D. Boyer, interview by Richard F. Bales, July 1, 2021; Matthew J. Bruccoli, *Nelson Algren: A Descriptive Bibliography* (Pittsburgh: University of Pittsburgh Press, 1985), 124, 154.

3. Nelson Algren, "Upside-Down Emil," *Chicago Free Press* 1, no. 1 (28 September 1970):13; Nelson Algren, "Stanley Upside Down Or: Why Trail Bullfighters When You Can Teach Iambic Pentameter?," *New York Herald Tribune Book Week*, 8 December 1963, 1, 12, 14; Nelson Algren, "The Passion of Upside-Down-Emil: A Story from Life's Other Side," in *The Last Carousel* (New York: Seven Stories Press, 1997), 226–28; Brooke Horvath, *Understanding Nelson Algren* (Columbia: University of South Carolina Press, 2005), 139; Bruccoli, *Nelson Algren*, 120. "Upside-Down Emil" was later revised; see "July 14th: Rafts of a Summer Night," in *Algren at Sea: Who Lost an American? & Notes from a Sea Diary–Travel Writings* (New York: Seven Stories Press, 2008), 341–347.

4. Drew, *Nelson Algren*, 334–37; Colin Asher, *Never a Lovely So Real: The Life and Work of Nelson Algren* (New York: W.W. Norton, 2019), 433.

5. Drew, *Nelson Algren*, 339–40; Nelson Algren, "The Rest of the Way is by the Stars," *Chicago Free Press* 1, no. 2 (5 October 1970): 22–23; Studs Terkel, *Touch and Go: A Memoir* (New York: The New Press, 2007), 198. The Black Panther Party was a Black Power political organization founded by college students Bobby Seale and Huey P. Newton in 1966 in Oakland, California. Head Start is a U.S. government program that provides aid to low-income children and families.

6. Nelson Algren, "A Ticket to Biro-Bidjan," *Chicago Free Press* 1, no. 2 (5 October 1970): 37–38. In a 1974 newspaper article, Algren described Levinsky as a "kind of an underworld figure." See Michaela Tuohy, "A Day at the Races with Nelson Algren," *Chicago Tribune Magazine*, 30 June 1974, 19. Algren later recycled, at times almost word-for-word, this *Chicago Free Press* story of Levinsky refusing to pay a gambling bet. The name is changed from King Levinsky to "Max" in the new story. See Nelson Algren, "Otto Preminger's Strange Suspenjers," in *The Last Carousel* (New York: Seven Stories Press, 1997), 27–28.

7. Algren, "A Ticket to Biro-Bidjan," 38.

8. Gay Talese, "The Loser," *Esquire*, March 1964, 65–68, 70, 139–143; Tom Wolfe, *The New Journalism*, with an anthology edited by Tom Wolfe and E.W. Johnson (New York: Harper & Row, 1973), 9–11; Drew, *Nelson Algren*, 355.

9. Wolfe, *The New Journalism*, 14–24 passim, 204; Ronald Weber, "Some Sort of Artistic Excitement," in *The Reporter as Artist: A Look at The New Journalism Controversy*, ed. Ronald Weber (New York: Hastings House, 1974), 13–14.

10. Wolfe, *The New Journalism*, 31.

11. Wolfe, *The New Journalism*, 31.

12. Wolfe, *The New Journalism*, 31–32.

13. Wolfe, *The New Journalism*, 32.

14. Wolfe, *The New Journalism*, 32–33; William McKeen, *Tom Wolfe* (New York: Twayne, 1995), 37; John Hollowell, *Fact & Fiction: The New Journalism and the Nonfiction Novel* (Chapel Hill: University of North Carolina Press, 1977), 28; Richard A. Kallan, "Style and the New Journalism: A Rhetorical Analysis of Tom Wolfe," in *Tom Wolfe*, ed. Harold Bloom (Philadelphia: Chelsea House, 2001), 74–75; Joel Best, "'Status! Yes!': Tom Wolfe as a Sociological Thinker," *The American Sociologist* 32, no. 4 (Winter 2001): 6–7;

Brant Mewborn, "Tom Wolfe," interview with Tom Wolfe, *Rolling Stone*, no. 512 (November 5th–December 10th, 1987): 216.

15. J.J. Johnston and Sean Curtin, *Chicago Boxing* (Charleston, S.C.: Arcadia, 2005), 62; Paul Martin, "Fight Nights (and Days)," *Chicago Tribune Magazine*, 19 August 1990, 22; Richard Bak, *Joe Louis: The Great Black Hope* (Dallas: Taylor Publishing, 1996), 92; George Kirksey, "Levinksy [sic] Foe of Dempsey Tonight," *Washington Post*, 18 February 1932, 11; "Dempsey v. Fish," *Time*, 29 February 1932, 39; Chris Mead, *Champion: Joe Louis: Black Hero in White America* (New York: Charles Scribner's Sons, 1985), 66; Leo Fischer, "The Royal Road to Wrestling," *Esquire*, February 1939, 43; Gilbert Odd, "He Was 'Managed' by His Sister," in *The Woman in the Corner* (London: Pelham Books, 1978), 35–36; Gay Talese, "The Loser," 68, 70, 141.

16. Algren, "A Ticket to Biro-Bidjan," 37.

17. Talese, "The Loser," 65.

18. Tom Wolfe, "Why They Aren't Writing the Great American Novel Anymore," *Esquire*, December 1972, 272.

19. Algren, "A Ticket to Biro-Bidjan," 37.

20. Wolfe, "Why They Aren't Writing the Great American Novel Anymore," 272; Talese, "The Loser," 65; Drew, *Nelson Algren*, 303; Martha Heasley Cox and Wayne Chatterton, *Nelson Algren* (Boston: Twayne, 1975), 134.

21. Arthur Shay, "Author on the Make: Nelson Algren's Bittersweet Affair with Chicago," *Chicago Tribune Magazine*, 14 September 1986, 10, 14, 32; Art Shay, *Nelson Algren's Chicago* (Urbana: University of Illinois Press, 1988), ix, xiii; Drew, *Nelson Algren*, 211–12.

22. Shay, "Author on the Make," 32; Drew, *Nelson Algren*, 218–19, 394; "The Black Palace," *Life*, 3 April 1950, 106–115; Asher, *Never a Lovely So Real*, 297–98.

23. Book reviewer Bruce Cook suggests in his review of *The Last Carousel* (1973) that Algren was a new journalist. Using Tom's Wolfe's devices as a four-sided touchstone, however, it seems clear that Algren was *not* a new journalist. See Bruce Cook, review of *The Last Carousel*, by Nelson Algren, *Commonweal*, 8 February 1974, 467–69.

24. Nelson Algren, "Early Chicago Journalism," *Chicago Free Press* 1, no. 3 (12 October 1970): 29. *The Front Page* is a Broadway comedy about newspaper reporters who work the police beat. The play was first produced in 1928. In the play, Hildy Johnson is a reporter for the *Examiner* newspaper. See Ben Hecht and Charles MacArthur, *The Front Page* (New York: Covici, Friede (1928). Algren should have stopped after his second start in New Journalism. The third and fourth starts deteriorated into personal feuds with newspaper columnists Maggie Daly and Jack Mabley. Algren revised this article and published it in *The Last Carousel*. See Nelson Algren, "Different Clowns for Different Towns," *The Last Carousel*, 257–61.

25. Nelson Algren, "Previous Days," *Chicago Free Press* 1, no. 4 (19 October 1970): 31.

26. Algren, "Previous Days," 31.

27. Algren, "Previous Days," 31. Algren later expanded and republished this article. See Nelson Algren, "Previous Days," *The Last Carousel*, 209–24; Nelson Algren, "Blanche Sweet under the Tapioca," *Chicago Tribune Magazine*, 30 April 1972, 42–45.

28. In "Pottawattomie Ghosts" Algren mistakenly writes that the riots occurred in 1917. The correct year is 1919. See Nelson Algren, "Pottawattomie Ghosts," *Chicago Free Press* 1, no. 5 (26 October 1970): 27–28; Carl Sandburg, *The Chicago Race Riots July, 1919* (New York: Harcourt, Brace and World, 1969).

29. Algren, "Pottawattomie Ghosts," 27.

30. Algren, "Pottawattomie Ghosts," 28.

31. Mike Royko, "Cops Threaten Law and Order," *One More Time: The Best of Mike Royko* (Chicago: University of Chicago Press, 1999), 38.

32. Addison Gayle, *Richard Wright: Ordeal of a Native Son* (Garden City, N.Y.: Anchor Press/Doubleday, 1980), 67; Hazel Rowley, *Richard Wright: The Life and Times* (New York: Henry Holt, 2001), 74–76, 78; Jerre Mangione, *The Dream and the Deal: The Federal Writers' Project 1935–1943* (Boston: Little Brown, 1972), 121; Nelson Algren, *Never Come Morning* (New York: Harper & Brothers, 1942), ix–x; *The WPA Guide to Illinois: The Federal Writers' Project Guide to 1930s Illinois* (New York: Pantheon Books, 1983), xvii–xviii;

David A. Taylor, *Soul of a People: The WPA Writers' Project Uncovers Depression America* (Hoboken, N.J.: John Wiley & Sons, 2009), 14; Douglas Wixson, *Worker-Writer in America: Jack Conroy and the Tradition of Midwestern Literary Radicalism, 1898–1990* (Urbana: University of Illinois Press, 1994), 407, 438; Drew, *Nelson Algren*, 100–101.

    33. Rowley, *Richard Wright*, 380–81, 523–24, 528; Drew, *Nelson Algren*, 204–06; Nelson Algren, "Remembering Richard Wright," *The Nation*, 28 January 1961, 85. "Remembering Richard Wright" was later reprinted; see Nelson Algren, "Remembering Richard Wright," in *Twentieth Century Interpretations of "Native Son,"* ed. Houston A. Baker, Jr. (Englewood Cliffs, N.J.: Prentice-Hall, 1972), 115–16.

    34. Nelson Algren, "Let's See Your Hands," *Chicago Free Press* 1, no. 6 (2 November 1970): 27. In a letter to Algren dated March 5, 1961, Simone de Beauvoir suggested that Algren wrote "Remembering Richard Wright" only because he had to and not because he wanted to: "I got the *Nation* with the paper about Wright; I felt you wrote it because you had to, not from the deepest depth of your heart, but I guess nobody will feel it." See Simone de Beauvoir, *A Transatlantic Love Affair: Letters to Nelson Algren*, comp. and annot. by Sylvie Le Bon de Beauvoir (New York: New Press, 1998), 543.

    35. Algren, "Let's See Your Hands," 27.

    36. Nelson Algren, "The Moon of the Arfy-Darfy," *The Saturday Evening Post*, 26 September 1964, 44–45, 48–49; Nelson Algren, "A Ticket on Skoronski," *The Saturday Evening Post*, 5 November 1966, 48, 52, 54–56; Nelson Algren, "Down with Cops," *The Saturday Evening Post*, 23 October 1965, 10, 14.

    37. Algren, "Down with Cops," 10, 14.

    38. Horvath, *Understanding Nelson Algren*, 116.

    39. Nelson Algren, "The Cop Mentality," *Chicago Free Press* 1, no. 7 (9 November 1970): 28.

    40. Nelson Algren, "Wild Times of Big Spender—This Baby Packs a Satire," review of *The Magic Christian*, by Terry Southern, *Chicago Sun-Times Book Week*, 21 February 1960, 4.

    41. Nelson Algren, "A Guy Who Got Wiped," review of *Blue Movie*, by Terry Southern, *Chicago Free Press* 1, no. 8 (16 November 1970): 33.

    42. Brian D. Boyer, interview by Richard F. Bales, July 1, 2021.

Selected Bibliography

Algren, Nelson. "Blanche Sweet under the Tapioca." *Chicago Tribune Magazine*, 30 April 1972, 42–45.

Algren, Nelson. "The Cop Mentality." *Chicago Free Press* 1, no. 7 (9 November 1970): 27–28.

Algren, Nelson. "Different Clowns for Different Towns." In *The Last Carousel*. New York: Seven Stories Press, 1997, 257–61.

Algren, Nelson. "Down with Cops." *The Saturday Evening Post*, 23 October 1965, 10, 14.

Algren, Nelson. "Early Chicago Journalism." *Chicago Free Press* 1, no. 3 (12 October 1970): 28–30.

Algren, Nelson. "A Guy Who Got Wiped." Review of *Blue Movie*, by Terry Southern. *Chicago Free Press* 1, no. 8 (16 November 1970): 32–33.

Algren, Nelson. "Let's See Your Hands." *Chicago Free Press* 1, no. 6 (2 November 1970): 25–27.

Algren, Nelson. "The Moon of the Arfy-Darfy." *The Saturday Evening Post*, 26 September 1964, 44–45, 48–49.

Algren, Nelson. *Never Come Morning*. New York: Harper & Brothers, 1942.

Algren, Nelson. "Otto Preminger's Strange Suspenjers." In *The Last Carousel*. New York: Seven Stories Press, 1997, 21–36.

Algren, Nelson. "The Passion of Upside-Down-Emil: A Story from Life's Other Side." In *The Last Carousel*. New York: Seven Stories Press, 1997, 226–28.

Algren, Nelson. "Pottawattomie Ghosts." *Chicago Free Press* 1, no. 5 (26 October 1970): 30–31.

Algren, Nelson. "Previous Days." *Chicago Free Press* 1, no. 4 (19 October 1970): 30–31.

Algren, Nelson. "Previous Days." In *The Last Carousel*. New York: Seven Stories Press, 1997, 209–24.

Algren, Nelson. "Remembering Richard Wright." *The Nation*, 28 January 1961, 85.

Algren, Nelson. "Remembering Richard Wright." In *Twentieth Century Interpretations of "Native Son,"* edited by Houston A. Baker, Jr., 115–16. Englewood Cliffs, N.J.: Prentice-Hall, 1972.

Algren, Nelson. "The Rest of the Way is by the Stars." *Chicago Free Press* 1, no. 2 (5 October 1970): 22–27.

Algren, Nelson. "A Ticket on Skoronski." *The Saturday Evening Post*, 5 November 1966, 48, 52, 54–56.

Algren, Nelson. "A Ticket to Biro-Bidjan." *Chicago Free Press* 1, no. 2 (5 October 1970): 37–38.

Algren, Nelson. "Upside-Down Emil." *Chicago Free Press* 1, no. 1 (28 September 1970): 12–13.

Algren, Nelson. "Wild Times of Big Spender—This Baby Packs a Satire." Review of *The Magic Christian*, by Terry Southern. *Chicago Sun-Times Book Week*, 21 February 1960, 4.

Asher, Colin. *Never a Lovely So Real: The Life and Work of Nelson Algren*. New York: W.W. Norton, 2019.

Bak, Richard. *Joe Louis: The Great Black Hope*. Dallas: Taylor Publishing, 1996.

Beauvoir, Simone de. *A Transatlantic Love Affair: Letters to Nelson Algren*. Comp. and annot. by Sylvie Le Bon de Beauvoir. New York: New Press, 1998.

Best, Joel. "'Status! Yes!': Tom Wolfe as a Sociological Thinker." *The American Sociologist* 32, no. 4 (Winter 2001): 5–22.

"The Black Palace." *Life*, 3 April 1950, 106–115.

Boyer, Brian D. and Christopher Chandler. [editorial]. *Chicago Free Press* 1, no. 0 (18 January 1970): 3.

Boyer, Brian D. Interview by Richard F. Bales, July 1, 2021.

Bruccoli, Matthew J. *Nelson Algren: A Descriptive Bibliography*. Pittsburgh: University of Pittsburgh Press, 1985.

Cook, Bruce. Review of *The Last Carousel*, by Nelson Algren. *Commonweal*, 8 February 1974, 467–69.

Cox, Martha Heasley, and Wayne Chatterton. *Nelson Algren*. Boston: Twayne, 1975.

"Dempsey v. Fish." *Time*, 29 February 1932, 39.

Drew, Bettina. *Nelson Algren: A Life on the Wild Side*. Austin: University of Texas Press, 1991.

Fischer, Leo. "The Royal Road to Wrestling." *Esquire*, February 1939, 43, 106–07.

"Editorial." *Chicago Free Press* 1, no. 1 (28 September 1970): 5.

Gayle, Addison. *Richard Wright: Ordeal of a Native Son*. Garden City, N.Y.: Anchor Press/Doubleday, 1980.

Hecht, Ben, and Charles MacArthur. *The Front Page*. New York: Covici, Friede, 1928.

Hollowell, John. *Fact & Fiction: The New Journalism and the Nonfiction Novel*. Chapel Hill: University of North Carolina Press, 1977.

Horvath, Brooke. *Understanding Nelson Algren*. Columbia: University of South Carolina Press, 2005.

Johnston, J. J., and Sean Curtin. *Chicago Boxing*. Charleston, S.C.: Arcadia, 2005.

Kallan, Richard A. "Style and the New Journalism: A Rhetorical Analysis of Tom Wolfe." In *Tom Wolfe*, edited by Harold Bloom, 71–83. Philadelphia: Chelsea House, 2001.

Kirksey, George. "Levinksy [sic] Foe of Dempsey Tonight." *Washington Post*, 18 February 1932, 11.

Mangione, Jerre. *The Dream and the Deal: The Federal Writers' Project 1935–1943*. Boston: Little Brown, 1972.

Martin, Paul. "Fight Nights (and Days)." *Chicago Tribune Magazine*, 19 August 1990, 20, 22–26, 34.

McKeen, William. *Tom Wolfe*. New York: Twayne, 1995.

Mead, Chris. *Champion: Joe Louis: Black Hero in White America*. New York: Charles Scribner's Sons, 1985.

Mewborn, Brant. "Tom Wolfe." Interview with Tom Wolfe. *Rolling Stone*, no. 512 (November 5–December 10, 1987): [214]-19.

Odd, Gilbert. "He Was 'Managed' by His Sister." In *The Woman in the Corner*, [32]-36. London: Pelham Books, 1978.

Rowley, Hazel. *Richard Wright: The Life and Times*. New York: Henry Holt, 2001.

Royko Mike. "Cops Threaten Law and Order." *One More Time: The Best of Mike Royko*. Chicago: University of Chicago Press, 1999, 37–39.

Sandburg, Carl. *The Chicago Race Riots July, 1919*. New York: Harcourt, Brace and World, 1969.

Shay, Arthur. "Author on the Make: Nelson Algren's Bittersweet Affair with Chicago." *Chicago Tribune Magazine*, 14 September 1986, 10–12, 14–17, 32, 39.

Shay, Art. *Nelson Algren's Chicago*. Urbana: University of Illinois Press, 1988.

Talese, Gay. "The Loser." *Esquire*, March 1964, 65–68, 70, 139–143.

Taylor, David A. *Soul of a People: The WPA Writers' Project Uncovers Depression America*. Hoboken, N.J.: John Wiley & Sons, 2009.

Terkel, Studs. *Touch and Go: A Memoir*. New York: The New Press, 2007.

Tuohy, Michaela. "A Day at the Races with Nelson Algren." *Chicago Tribune Magazine*, 30 June 1974, 18–19, 22.

The WPA Guide to Illinois: The Federal Writers' Project Guide to 1930s Illinois. New York: Pantheon Books, 1983.

Weber, Ronald. "Some Sort of Artistic Excitement." In *The Reporter as Artist: A Look at The New Journalism Controversy*, edited by Ronald Weber, 13–26. New York: Hastings House, 1974.

Wixson, Douglas. *Worker-Writer in America: Jack Conroy and the Tradition of Midwestern Literary Radicalism, 1898–1990*. Urbana: University of Illinois Press, 1994.

Wolfe, Tom. *The New Journalism*. With an anthology edited by Tom Wolfe and E.W. Johnson. New York: Harper & Row, 1973.

Wolfe, Tom. "Why They Aren't Writing the Great American Novel Anymore." *Esquire*, December 1972, 152–59+.

The *Chicago* Magazine Era

The Chicago magazine era is a significant one. After Algren walked away from the novel in the late 1950s, he began writing short stories and articles for magazines, especially men's magazines. But after *Esquire* asked him to write an article about boxer Rubin "Hurricane" Carter in 1974, he all but abandoned short stories and articles in favor of book reviews. A notable exception is his writing for *Chicago* magazine. Over a course of six years—from 1975 to 1981—Nelson Algren wrote three articles and two short stories for *Chicago*. (The magazine had also reprinted his 1942 prose poem, "The Swede Was a Hard Guy," in 1956.) In comparison, from 1975 until 1981 he wrote eight additional articles, but for a variety of other periodicals.[1]

Algren's varied contributions to the "*Chicago* Magazine Era" are the topic of this essay.

"*The Swede Was a Hard Guy*," Chicago, *June 1956, 30–34*

This is a reprint of the prose poem that was originally published in the *Southern Review* in 1942. The poem is about the infamous Black Sox Scandal—when the Chicago White Sox lost the 1919 World Series to the Cincinnati Reds. Eight Chicago players, including "Swede" Risberg, Algren's childhood favorite player, and the legendary "Shoeless" Joe Jackson, were later accused of intentionally losing games. This poem is discussed in this book's essay, "Chicago White Sox Literature."[2]

The editors of *Chicago* magazine write about Algren in their introduction to the poem:

Algren has missed few opening days at Comiskey Park since 1920, and after he had become an adult fan, he decided to find out more about the Black Sox scandal. He read the contemporary newspaper accounts at the library and did some other research. He formed the opinion that the dividing line between the seven players who were expelled from baseball and some of their teammates was thin, and that the biggest villain was Charles Comiskey, their frugal owner. In 1941 he wrote this poem, which was published the following year in the *Southern Review*.[3]

"Requiem," Chicago, *September 1975, 120–24*

In March of 1975 Algren moved from Chicago to Paterson, New Jersey, to work on the murder conviction case of boxer Rubin "Hurricane" Carter. A few months later, *Chicago* magazine published "Requiem," his farewell to not only the city that had been his home since he was four years old, but also, to a lost way of life:[4]

Hugh Hefner made it possible for men who never found a personality uniquely their own to buy one. A ring bearing two bunny ears made him somebody at last: a *Playboy*.

Although closer, chronologically, to Hugh Hefner's Chicago, my own Chicago is actually nearer to that of Sandburg. Sandburg's farm boys eyeing women under gas lamps are as remote today as Wordsworth; and my own town, too....

And now that we have sensed that consumption for its own sake can no longer be sustained, a faint tremor shakes the *Playboy* offices. Adumbrating the day five years hence, or ten, when the whole enterprise, built upon a fantasy, will come down crashing.

So say *sayonara* and then goodbye, old broken-nose whore of a city in whose arms I've slept ten thousand nights.

I'll not be sleeping in them again.[5]

"There Will Be No More Christmases," Chicago, *July 1980, 132–34*

"There Will Be No More Christmases" (*Chicago*, July 1980) is the comic story of a Chicago policeman named Oliver who bungles a purse snatching incident. When the *Daily News* newspaper prints an article about what happened (together with his photograph), Oliver realizes that he has become "the butt of a story on police ineptitude," and he loses his mind.[6]

Oliver's friends are "Little Stash" and "Big Stash." They run an illegal off-track betting facility—"the biggest bookie on Milwaukee Avenue between Grand Avenue and West Division." In just a few words, Algren vividly describes both this horse racing "bookie" and Oliver's descent into madness:[7]

"Are they laughing *now*?" Oliver asked quietly. He sounded like someone in another room asking if it looked like rain.

Figure 8: On Saturday and Sunday, March 8 and 9, 1975, Nelson Algren held a moving sale at his West Evergreen Avenue apartment in Chicago. He had decided to move to New Jersey to work on the Rubin "Hurricane" Carter case. This picture was taken on the first day of the sale. Algren is standing next to a table; it bears a $150.00 price tag and a note that reads: "This table is the one on which I played while gathering material for *The Man with the Golden Arm*. Several of the players later materialized as fictional characters of that novel. One of them I named 'Sparrow Saltskin' and another 'Frankie Machine.' [Signed] Nelson Algren, 8 March 1975, Chicago Ill." Eleanor Randolph of the *Chicago Tribune* reported only that "a writer" purchased the table. That writer was journalist Michael Miner, and in a 2009 online comment, he indicates that buying "a poker table from Nelson Algren was a way to feel really happy" (Gene Pesek, photographer, courtesy *Chicago Sun-Times*).

"*Laughing*? Are they *laughing*?" Little Stash asked. "They been laughing all day. The whole West Side is laughing...."

Oliver squeezed himself from between them and smoothed down his uniform. He saw the crowd of bettors consulting *Forms* and reading the results from Hawthorne, Belmont, Golden Gate, and Hialeah. He saw the morning line and he saw the mutuel window. He saw the man posting results. He pulled out his .38 and shot a clean hole into the results from Belmont. The crowd turned, gaping. When Oliver raised the gun at the results from Hawthorne, the whole mob bolted for the door....

"They're off and running at Hialeah!" Oliver announced, and fired his last shot into the air. "They're off and running at Golden Gate!" He pressed the trigger but the gun was empty. Yet he kept pressing it—"They're off and running at Belmont! They're off and running at Hawthorne! Let them all keep running! Let them horses run! Let them dogs howl! Let them cats meow! Let them lions roar! Let them kangaroos hop! Let them railroad trains whistle! Let them go! Let them all go!"[8]

Both the prose and the dialogue of "There Will Be No More Christmases" sparkles with wit and authenticity. It is a superb short story, one of Algren's best.[9]

"Last Rounds in Small Cafés: Remembrances of Jean-Paul Sartre and Simone de Beauvoir," Chicago, *December 1980, 210–13, 237–38, 240*

In 1980 Nelson Algren went back to the well of reminiscences that he had dug ten years earlier for the *Chicago Free Press*. But this time his recollections were not about his childhood. Instead, they were of Jean-Paul Sartre and Simone de Beauvoir.[10]

Algren met French philosopher and author Simone de Beauvoir in 1947, and they immediately began a long-distance love affair. After Algren read excerpts of Beauvoir's book, *Force of Circumstance*, in *Harper's Magazine* in 1964 in which she wrote of their relationship, he never spoke to her again. He was angry that she wrote about the intimate details of their affair. Furthermore, these excerpts revealed that that from the very beginning of his relationship with Beauvoir, Jean-Paul Sartre had always been number one with her, and he had always been number two. Deirdre Bair, Beauvoir's biographer, was not exaggerating when she wrote that he spent the rest of his life "denouncing her to anyone who would listen." On May 8, 1981, W.J. Weatherby interviewed Algren for *The Times* of London. During the interview Algren railed against Beauvoir. Algren died only hours later, in the early morning of May 9.[11]

Weatherby's article, "The Last Interview," which details his meeting with Algren, appears in Algren's posthumously published novel, *The Devil's Stocking*, sandwiched between the foreword and the first chapter. Weatherby writes that "the topic that seemed to excite [Algren] more than anything was a love affair of twenty-five years ago…. Algren still hadn't forgiven [Beauvoir]." But Algren's article, "Last Rounds in Small Cafés," that was published in the December 1980 issue of *Chicago* magazine, only a few months prior to the May 8, 1981, interview, contains none of the anger that Weatherby describes in "The Last Interview":[12]

> Algren had become very excited, and mindful of that "heaviness" in his chest, I tried to get him back to the safer topic of the new novel. So some prostitutes are becoming millionaires, I said. The diversion was a failure. He was too steamed up about de Beauvoir.[13]

Instead, there is only a hint of forced formality in "Last Rounds in Small Cafés." Algren mentions Beauvoir's name only three times in the article; otherwise, she is always simply "Madame." He mentions Beauvoir's and Sartre's pact that allowed for "contingent affairs," but he does so without comment and in fact, with a little humor:[14]

> In the spring of 1949 I went to Paris to live with Simone de Beauvoir. Madame lived in a large room four flights up an ancestral stair on the Rue de la Bûcherie….
> After Sartre and Madame had agreed to lead separate love lives, based on what they termed contingency (and which American hookers name, more simply, chippying), Sartre embarked on a series of such affairs. Despite the fact that he was undersized, wall-eyed, and shabbily dressed, he had no more difficulty finding women to sleep with than Cary Grant.[15]

One has to wonder: If, as Bair says, Algren spent the rest of his life "denouncing" Beauvoir, why did Algren write these remembrances *sans* invective? Bettina Drew indicates in her Algren biography that the author may have written these reminiscences of Sartre and Beauvoir years before he sold the article to *Chicago*. Did *Chicago* read it and agree to print it, but only if Algren toned down its original rancor? Or did Algren submit the article to *Chicago* as published, knowing that it would sell magazines, but also knowing that it would sell magazines only if the article were diatribe-free? The December 1980 issue of *Chicago* gives no clue.[16]

"Walk Pretty All the Way," Chicago, June 1981, 160–64

Algren was in *Chicago* magazine again only six months later. Algren scholar Brooke Horvath describes "Walk Pretty All the Way" (*Chicago*,

Figure 9: Nelson Algren met Simone de Beauvoir in 1947, the same year that his collection of short stories entitled *The Neon Wilderness* was published. They exchanged hundreds of letters and packages until their "transatlantic love affair" ended in 1964. On November 13, 1949, Beauvoir wrote Algren: "In big yellow envelope, you came in, not a ghost, really you, sitting in the Chicago street among the Chicago dirt.... I know the place, so often we went beneath this iron bridge, coming back to Wabansia nest. I want to be there again, among the old newspapers flying in the wind, near you." The picture that Beauvoir is writing about is undoubtedly this photograph. She continued to refer to it in subsequent letters to Algren. On May 8, 1950, she wrote, "I want to meet the man who sat in the little cave with such a faraway, sullen, misty sweet face, just sitting in Chicago fall streets as he sits in my heart." In October of 1954 she wrote, "But here is a nice picture of you, the one I have in my room, when you are sitting beneath the iron bridge in Chicago."

Beauvoir refers to a "Wabansia nest" in her 1949 letter; that is Algren's Chicago apartment at 1523 West Wabansia Avenue. The building was eventually demolished to make way for the Kennedy Expressway (photograph by Robert McCullough, Universal History Archive, Getty Images).

June 1981) as "the story of two runaway fourteen-year-old girls headed for lives on the wild side."[17]

Unfortunately, the prose in "Walk Pretty All the Way" is not anywhere near the wild side; it is flat and lifeless. The following example is typical:

> It was exactly at that moment—I was closing the handbag—that I got a full whiff of something awful yet familiar—and sure enough here he comes, right off the gump truck, right down the middle of the aisle, the world's most ignorant man: Old Tom.
>
> Old gump-snatching Tom the dead-chicken man, he can't read, he can't write, but he sure can count good.[18]

Chicago editor John Fink writes about "Walk Pretty All the Way" in the June 1981 issue of *Chicago*: "Nelson Algren, one of our best writers, died last month in New York. As his friend Studs Terkel said, 'He never put a sentence on paper unless it rang.' See for yourself; there is an Algren short story on page 160." In this case, Studs Terkel was wrong; there is little ringing in "Walk Pretty All the Way."[19]

But the sentences could have rung. After the twin sisters help steal furniture from an apartment, they are caught by the police, who trick them into thinking they are going to go on a picnic the next morning. Instead, they go to court. The idea has much comic potential, and Algren could have embellished it with some wonderful humor and dialogue, just as he used humor and dialogue a year earlier in "There Will Be No More Christmases." Instead, he falls short. "There Will Be No More Christmases" sparkles, but "Walk Pretty All the Way" is as colorless as a piece of Lake Michigan driftwood.

"So Long, Swede Risberg," Chicago, July 1981, 138–41, 158

Chicago published "Walk Pretty All the Way," Algren's last short story, in the June 1981 issue, and the magazine featured "So Long, Swede Risberg," Algren's last article, the following month. This article consists of perhaps one-fourth baseball reminiscences and three-fourths baseball history—the story of the 1919 World Series and the Black Sox Scandal.[20]

Did Studs Terkel hear ringing in "So Long, Swede Risberg?" Admittedly, there are some memorable sentences in this article. For example: "The Swede was a hard guy. He took to fighting as easily as he did to baseball and occasionally confused these crafts." However, there are only a few.[21]

Algren, as always, does a great job with his recollections; unfortunately, his Chicago baseball history has all the verve of a college term paper.

But again, it did not have to be this way. Algren's 1970 article, "Pottawattomie Ghosts," is also a history of Chicago, but of a much earlier time. The following account of the aftermath of the Fort Dearborn Massacre of 1812 is one of the opening paragraphs, and surely Studs Terkel would agree that every sentence rings in this *Chicago Free Press* article:[22]

> The skeletons on the shore were given coffined burial the following spring. But the waters washed the sands until the coffins rose from their graves. Then the boxes fell in and lake winds thinned those dry grey bones. Till they strangely

turned into Pottawattomie ghosts spreading false rumors through dunes and town: *The last ambush is not yet.*[23]

But to give Algren his due: he was a lifelong fan of the Chicago White Sox. He had already mined White Sox gold with the 1942 publication of his prose poem, "The Swede is a Hard Guy." Almost forty years later, perhaps Algren wanted to revisit the Black Sox Scandal, but this time by writing a more traditional account of the 1919 World Series. After all, just as if he were writing that college term paper, he quotes two sources in "So Long, Swede Risberg": *My Baseball Diary*, by James T. Farrell, and *Eight Men Out*, by Eliot Asinof.[24]

Algren died on May 9, 1981, and so he probably never saw "So Long, Swede Risberg" in print. The article appeared in the July 1981 issue of *Chicago* magazine, and so it is likely that he died before this issue was published.[25]

Final Observations

Working with Brian D. Boyer and Christopher Chandler, Nelson Algren produced some stellar work in 1970 during the *Chicago Free Press* era. Unfortunately, Algren's writing during the final era of his career, the *Chicago* magazine era, was not an encore performance. He started out strong, but he phoned in his last two contributions—the uninspired last short story of his career ("Walk Pretty All the Way") and the equally uninspired last article of his career ("So Long, Swede Risberg.")

It is possible that Algren hurriedly threw together this short story and article only to make a few quick dollars. If that is the case, that would be unfortunate. Algren and Kurt Vonnegut, Jr., had both been teachers at the Iowa Writers' Workshop at the University of Iowa in 1965. Vonnegut wrote the introduction to the 1987 edition of *Never Come Morning*, and in the introduction, Vonnegut recalled that "another thing I heard from others, but never from Algren himself, was how much he hoped to be remembered after he was gone." Colin Asher writes in his biography of Algren that during the last year of Algren's life, "he dwelled on the past and wondered how he would be remembered when he was gone." Nelson Algren should not be remembered for writing these two works.[26]

Nonetheless, Algren's *Chicago* magazine era still gets an overall grade of B minus. His Black Sox term paper and the prosaic "Walk Pretty All the Way" are more than offset by the frank honesty of "Requiem" and the comic brilliance and perfection of "There Will Be No More Christmases."[27]

Conclusion

Chicago magazine continued to publish Nelson Algren even after his death, appearing twice in *Chicago* in 1983. In 1957, a year after the release of *A Walk on the Wild Side*, Algren took part in a discussion about Chicago's contributions to the American arts. The event was held in the Grand Ballroom of Chicago's Hotel Sherman, and it was tape-recorded by Chicago radio station WFMT. The tape was presumed lost, but it was later discovered in 1982.[28]

Chicago magazine published an edited transcript of the tape in the January 1983 issue. The magazine identified the panelists as "Frank Lloyd Wright the architect, Nelson Algren the novelist, Archibald MacLeish the poet and playwright, and Rudolph Ganz the musician." The moderator was Leo A. Lerner, who was then Chairman of the Board of Roosevelt University. *Chicago* magazine was clearly impressed by the group, writing that "the panelists, who are all now dead, may well have made up one of the most formidable groups of Chicago talent ever to have been gathered together."[29]

Chicago: City on the Make was reissued in 1983 with a new introduction by Studs Terkel. Terkel's new introduction and portions of the book were reprinted in the May 1983 issue of *Chicago*.[30]

Chicago magazine also published articles about Algren in the years after his death. Algren moved from Hackensack, New Jersey, to Sag Harbor, Long Island, New York, in June of 1980. He would spend the last year of his life in Sag Harbor. "Algren in Exile," by Joe Pintauro, the cover story of the February 1988 issue of *Chicago*, tells the story of that year—what the magazine describes on the cover as, "The Remarkable Last Year of Chicago's Angriest Man."[31]

Algren's *Chicago: City on the Make* was published in 1951. A.J. Liebling's *Chicago: The Second City* came out a year later. Both books lampooned the city. In "Chicago in Their Sights," published in the March 2001 issue of the magazine, Bill Beuttler reexamines both books in a twenty-first-century light.[32]

Notes

1. Matthew J. Bruccoli, *Nelson Algren: A Descriptive Bibliography* (Pittsburgh: University of Pittsburgh Press, 1985), 128–31; Matthew J. Bruccoli, "Addenda to Bruccoli, *Nelson Algren*," *The Papers of the Bibliographical Society of America*, September 1988, 369; Robert A. Tibbetts, "Further Addenda to Bruccoli, *Nelson Algren*," *The Papers of the Bibliographical Society of America*, June 1989, 215; Bettina Drew, *Nelson Algren: A Life on the Wild Side* (Austin: University of Texas Press, 1991), 350–52; Nelson Algren, "The Swede Was a Hard Guy," *Southern Review*, Spring 1942, 873–79.

2. Algren, "The Swede Was a Hard Guy," 873–79; Eliot Asinof, *Eight Men Out: The Black Sox and the 1919 World Series* (New York: Holt, Rinehart and Winston, 1963), [iv], 5, 17, 18.

3. [Untitled], *Chicago*, June 1956, 30.

4. Drew, *Nelson Algren*, 13–14, 350–55; Rick Soll, "Nelson Algren Bids Final Farewell," *Chicago Tribune*, 10 March 1975, sec. 1, 2; Brooke Horvath, *Understanding Nelson Algren* (Columbia: University of South Carolina Press, 2005), 133.

5. Nelson Algren, "Requiem," *Chicago*, September 1975, 124. Years after Algren left Chicago, Algren's friend, newspaper columnist Mike Royko, recalled that Algren "moved from Chicago a few years ago, and had a great time announcing that he no longer liked this city, and that it had never appreciated him. Neither statement was true, and he knew it. But he liked saying such things to create a controversy. We had dinner the night before he left and the fact was, he was moving because he felt like moving." But Royko may have been wrong. Algren may have believed that the City of Chicago did *not* appreciate him. Suzanne McNear was Algren's friend, and in her memoir (written in the third person), she writes of Algren: "On her desk she kept a framed formal photograph he'd sent, a letter, so bitter, about the years in Chicago, when he felt he'd been ignored." See Mike Royko, "Algren's Golden Pen," *Chicago Sun-Times*, 13 May 1981, 2; Mary Wisniewski, *Algren: A Life* (Chicago: Chicago Review Press, 2017), 289–92; Drew, *Nelson Algren*, 340; Suzanne McNear, *Knock Knock: A Life* (Sag Harbor, N.Y.: The Permanent Press, 2012), 197. Algren's reference to Chicago as a "broken-nose whore of a city" comes from his 1951 book, *Chicago: City on the Make*: "Yet once you've come to be part of this particular patch, you'll never love another. Like loving a woman with a broken nose, you may well find lovelier lovelies. But never a lovely so real." See Nelson Algren, *Chicago: City on the Make*, 60th Anniversary Edition (Chicago: University of Chicago Press, 2011), 23.

6. Nelson Algren, "There Will Be No More Christmases," *Chicago*, July 1980, 132–34; Horvath, *Understanding Nelson Algren*, 184–85n2.

7. Algren, "There Will Be No More Christmases," 133.

8. Algren, "There Will Be No More Christmases," 134.

9. "There Will Be No More Christmases" has been reprinted; see Nelson Algren, "There Will Be No More Christmases," in Nelson Algren, *Entrapment and other Writings*, eds. Brooke Horvath and Dan Simon (New York: Seven Stories Press, 2009), 261–69.

10. Nelson Algren, "Last Rounds in Small Cafés: Remembrances of Jean-Paul Sartre and Simone de Beauvoir," *Chicago*, December 1980, 210–13, 237–38, 240.

11. W.J. Weatherby, "The Last Interview," in Nelson Algren, *The Devil's Stocking* (New York: Arbor House Publishing, 1983), 10–11; Horvath, *Understanding Nelson Algren*, 150; Deirdre Bair, *Simone de Beauvoir: A Biography* (New York: Summit Books, 1990), 500–502; Drew, *Nelson Algren*, 322–23, 375–76; Joe Pintauro, "Algren in Exile," *Chicago*, February 1988, 158; Simone de Beauvoir, *A Transatlantic Love Affair: Letters to Nelson Algren*, comp. and annot. by Sylvie Le Bon de Beauvoir (New York: New Press, 1998), 9–10.

12. Weatherby, "The Last Interview," 10.

13. Weatherby, "The Last Interview," 11.

14. Algren, "Last Rounds in Small Cafés," 210, 213, 237.

15. Algren, "Last Rounds in Small Cafés," 210, 237.

16. Drew, *Nelson Algren*, 341, 344, 365, 367.

17. Nelson Algren, "Walk Pretty All the Way," *Chicago*, June 1981, 160–64; Horvath, *Understanding Nelson Algren*, 150; Bruccoli, *Nelson Algren*, 131.

18. Algren, "Walk Pretty All the Way," 163. "Walk Pretty All the Way" has been reprinted; see Algren, "Walk Pretty All the Way," in *Entrapment*, 271–80.

19. John Fink, [untitled], *Chicago*, June 1981, 2; [Masthead], *Chicago*, June 1981, 4.

20. Nelson Algren, "So Long, Swede Risberg," *Chicago*, July 1981, 138–41, 158; Bruccoli, *Nelson Algren*, 131.

21. Algren, "So Long, Swede Risberg," 138.

22. Mrs. John H. Kinzie, *Wau-Bun: The "Early Day" in the North-West* (Chicago: Lakeside Press, 1932), 233–87.

23. Nelson Algren, "Pottawattomie Ghosts," *Chicago Free Press* 1, no. 5 (26 October 1970): 26.

24. Nelson Algren, "The Swede Was a Hard Guy," 873–79. Algren does more than just quote from *My Baseball Diary* and *Eight Men Out*; he rewrites, albeit very slightly, what Farrell and Asinof state in their respective books. For example, Algren writes in "So Long, Swede Risberg" that "James T. Farrell remembers [Swede Risberg] as 'snaring a grounder deep over second base and getting the ball to first base like a bullet.'" But Farrell wrote, "Now, in memory, scenes re-occur in my mind…. Risberg snaring a grounder deep over second base and getting the ball to Gandil or Shano Collins at first in time as though the ball were a bullet." Other examples are: Algren: "Landis wanted me to tell him something I didn't know." Farrell: "Landis wanted me to tell him something that I didn't know." Algren: "A murderer serves his sentence and is let out. I got life." Farrell: "A murderer even serves his sentence and is let out. I got life." Algren: "His curve ball dropped, that day, with startling suddenness." Asinof: "His curve ball dropped with startling suddenness." See James T. Farrell, *My Baseball Diary* (New York: A.S. Barnes, 1957), 101, 177, 179; Asinof, *Eight Men Out*, 97; Algren, "So Long, Swede Risberg," 138, 140, 141. "So Long, Swede Risberg" has been reprinted; see Algren, "So Long, Swede Risberg," in *Entrapment*, 281–92.

25. Horvath, *Understanding Nelson Algren*, 150.

26. Colin Asher, *Never a Lovely So Real: The Life and Work of Nelson Algren* (New York: W.W. Norton, 2019), 478–79; Kurt Vonnegut, Jr., introduction to *Never Come Morning*, by Nelson Algren (New York: Four Walls Eight Windows, 1987), xvii, xix. Kurt Vonnegut's introduction has been reprinted. See Kurt Vonnegut, "Algren As I Knew Him," in Nelson Algren, *The Man with the Golden Arm*, eds. William J. Savage Jr., and Daniel Simon, 50th Anniversary Critical Edition (New York: Seven Stories Press, [1999]), 367–70.

27. Literary critic Maxwell Geismar wrote the following of Algren: "He once confided that he was a 'writer on the run,' and in fact his later work was often careless and repetitious. Somehow he lost the ability for patient and sustained work that is the mark of a serious writer." See Maxwell Geismar, "Nelson Algren: Unsung Proletarian of Letters," *Los Angeles Times Calendar*, 24 May 1981, 5.

28. "Searching for the Real Chicago," *Chicago*, January 1983, 125; "4 Intellects Discourse on State of Culture Here," *Chicago Sun-Times*, final edition, 22 November 1957, 18.

29. "Searching for the Real Chicago," 125.

30. Nelson Algren, "Chicago: City on the Make," *Chicago*, May 1983, 2, 146–153.

31. Pintauro, "Algren in Exile," cover, 96; Drew, *Nelson Algren*, 356, 367–76.

32. Bill Beuttler, "Chicago in Their Sights," *Chicago*, March 2001, 105–07, 154.

SELECTED BIBLIOGRAPHY

Algren, Nelson. *Chicago: City on the Make.* 60th anniversary edition. Chicago: University of Chicago Press, 2011.

Algren, Nelson. "Chicago: City on the Make," *Chicago*, May 1983, 2, 146–153.

Algren, Nelson. *Entrapment and other Writings.* Edited by Brooke Horvath and Dan Simon. New York: Seven Stories Press, 2009.

Algren, Nelson. "Last Rounds in Small Cafés: Remembrances of Jean-Paul Sartre and Simone de Beauvoir." *Chicago*, December 1980, 210–13, 237–38, 240.

Algren, Nelson. "Pottawattomie Ghosts." *Chicago Free Press* 1, no. 5 (26 October 1970): 26–29.

Algren, Nelson. "Requiem." *Chicago*, September 1975, 120–24.

Algren, Nelson. "So Long, Swede Risberg." *Chicago*, July 1981, 138–41, 158.

Algren, Nelson. "The Swede Was a Hard Guy." *Southern Review*, Spring 1942, 873–79.

Algren, Nelson. "There Will Be No More Christmases." *Chicago*, July 1980, 132–34.

Algren, Nelson. "Walk Pretty All the Way." *Chicago*, June 1981, 160–64.

Asher, Colin. *Never a Lovely So Real: The Life and Work of Nelson Algren.* New York: W.W. Norton, 2019.

Asinof, Eliot. *Eight Men Out: The Black Sox and the 1919 World Series.* New York: Holt, Rinehart and Winston, 1963.

Bair, Deirdre. *Simone de Beauvoir: A Biography*. New York: Summit Books, 1990.

Beauvoir, Simone de. *A Transatlantic Love Affair: Letters to Nelson Algren*. Comp. and annot. by Sylvie Le Bon de Beauvoir. New York: New Press, 1998.

Beuttler, Bill. "Chicago in Their Sights." *Chicago*, March 2001, 105–07, 154.

Bruccoli, Matthew J. "Addenda to Bruccoli, *Nelson Algren*." *The Papers of the Bibliographical Society of America*, September 1988, 367–69.

Bruccoli, Matthew J. *Nelson Algren: A Descriptive Bibliography*. Pittsburgh: University of Pittsburgh Press, 1985.

Drew, Bettina. *Nelson Algren: A Life on the Wild Side*. Austin: University of Texas Press, 1991.

Farrell, James. T. *My Baseball Diary*. New York: A.S. Barnes, 1957.

"4 Intellects Discourse on State of Culture Here." *Chicago Sun-Times*, final edition, 22 November 1957, 18.

Geismar, Maxwell. "Nelson Algren: Unsung Proletarian of Letters." *Los Angeles Times Calendar*, 24 May 1981, 5.

Horvath, Brooke. *Understanding Nelson Algren*. Columbia: University of South Carolina Press, 2005.

Kinzie, Mrs. John H. *Wau-Bun: The "Early Day" in the North-West*. Chicago: Lakeside Press, 1932.

McNear, Suzanne. *Knock Knock: A Life*. Sag Harbor, N.Y.: The Permanent Press, 2012.

Pintauro, Joe. "Algren in Exile." *Chicago*, February 1988, 92–101, 156–63.

Royko, Mike. "Algren's Golden Pen." *Chicago Sun-Times*, 13 May 1981, 2.

"Searching for the Real Chicago." *Chicago*, January 1983, 125–27, 153–55.

Soll, Rick. "Nelson Algren Bids Final Farewell." *Chicago Tribune*, 10 March 1975, sec. 1, 2.

Tibbetts, Robert A. "Further Addenda to Bruccoli, *Nelson Algren*." *The Papers of the Bibliographical Society of America*, June 1989, 214–17.

Vonnegut, Kurt. "Algren as I Knew Him." In *The Man with the Golden Arm*, by Nelson Algren. Edited by William J. Savage, Jr., and Daniel Simon, 367–70. 50th Anniversary Critical Edition New York: Seven Stories Press, 1999.

Vonnegut, Kurt, Jr. Introduction to *Never Come Morning*, by Nelson Algren, xvii–xx. New York: Four Walls Eight Windows, 1987.

Weatherby, W.J. "The Last Interview." In *The Devil's Stocking*, by Nelson Algren, [7]-12. New York: Arbor House Publishing, 1983.

Wisniewski, Mary. *Algren: A Life*. Chicago: Chicago Review Press, 2017.

PART TWO

Specific Genres

Poetry

Introduction

Many people know that Nelson Algren was a novelist. They may not know, however, that he was also a gifted poet. In 1973 Richard Studing gathered bibliographic information concerning Nelson Algren's poems for his compilation, "A Nelson Algren Checklist." Kenneth G. McCollum also collected Algren's poems for his 1973 book, *Nelson Algren: A Checklist*. Martha Heasley Cox and Wayne Chatterton did the same thing two years later for their book, *Nelson Algren*. Matthew J. Bruccoli did it in 1985 for his work, *Nelson Algren: A Descriptive Bibliography*, and Brooke Horvath did it again in 2005 for *Understanding Nelson Algren*. This is now the sixth attempt to bring together all of Algren's poetry.[1]

This compilation of poetry is limited to published poems—more specifically, the poems that Nelson Algren wrote that were published originally and separately as poems. Thus, Algren's poem to Simone de Beauvoir that he inscribed in a copy of *Never Come Morning* is not noted in this essay. Although this poem has been reprinted in other books, it was never formally published as a poem. Bettina Drew writes in her Algren biography of a twenty-five-page poem that Algren wrote to his friend Margo. This poem is also not listed, as it too was never published. The poem, "Quais of Calcutta" that appears as the "Epilogue" in *Notes from a Sea Diary: Hemingway All the Way* is not in the list, because this poem was originally published as the epilogue to *Notes from a Sea Diary*. Although Studs Terkel called *Chicago: City on the Make*, a "prose poem," it is not listed here, as it was published separately as a book. On the other hand, "Afternoon in the Land of the Strange Light Sleep" is listed, but only because the editors of *Cavalier* called it a "prose poem in a new dimension."[2]

All the poems shown in this essay are listed chronologically in the order of their date of publication. Listed in this manner, several questions immediately become apparent:

- Algren died in 1981. Why did he stop writing poetry in 1972? Was he too busy researching and writing (and later rewriting), his last novel, *The Devil's Stocking*, to write poetry?
- Why did Algren stop writing poetry for *Poetry* magazine in 1947? He continued to write and publish poetry for other magazines, but he stopped writing for *Poetry* fairly early in his career.[3]
- Algren recycled much of his work throughout his career. Why didn't he reprint more of his poetry in *The Last Carousel* (1973) or in one of the other collections of his writings?

"Goodbye Lilies Hello Spring," Algren's poetic rant against Simone de Beauvoir, is in the Summer 1966 issue of *Zeitgeist*, a long-defunct East Lansing, Michigan, literary journal. Matthew J. Bruccoli does not mention it in his 1985 book, *Nelson Algren: A Descriptive Bibliography*. The first issue (Winter 1967) of *Lillabulero*, a relatively short-lived (fourteen issues) literary magazine edited by Algren aficionado Russell Banks, features the poems, "The Cockeyed Hooker of Bugis Street" and "The Country of Kai-Li." These poems, as originally published in 1967 in *Lillabulero*, are also not in Bruccoli's book. (Algren later revised these two poems, and he published them in the October 8, 1972, *Chicago Tribune*. Bruccoli lists only the *Tribune* publication information for these poems in his bibliography.) One has to wonder: did Algren publish other poems in nonextant literary magazines that are not in Bruccoli's bibliography and have yet to be discovered by Algren scholars?[4]

Algren was the literary equivalent of a "hired gun." That is, in addition to writing, he earned money by giving lectures, teaching classes, and leading seminars. Algren gave *Zeitgeist* his poem about Simone de Beauvoir when he was in East Lansing taking part in a "reading and discussion of his works." In an accompanying letter that was also published in *Zeitgeist*, he states that he "made fourteen campus stops." While speaking about "his works" like *The Man with the Golden Arm* in college towns across the Midwest, is it possible that Algren gave away other unknown poems to obscure and now extinct college magazines and journals? Colin Asher, author of *Never a Lovely So Real: The Life and Work of Nelson Algren*, writes of Algren being interviewed by "two student journalists writing for a college magazine that doesn't have an archive and hasn't been digitized." Student journalists could have interviewed Algren at all fourteen of these campus stops. In addition to an interview, Algren could have given at least one or two of these students an original poem for publication in their college magazine. If a college magazine "doesn't have an archive and hasn't been digitized," will this poem ever be discovered?[5]

The Poetry of Nelson Algren

Algren published his first work—a story called "So Help Me"—in 1933. He did not publish his first poem until six years later, but when he did, he published five during that one year.[6]

"Makers of Music," *The New Anvil*, March 1939, 23

In 1939 writer Jack Conroy and Nelson Algren joined forces to publish the *New Anvil*, a proletarian literary magazine. Page one of the first issue (March 1939) indicates that Conroy was the editor, and Algren was the managing editor.[7]

But Algren was also a contributor to the *New Anvil*. This inaugural issue contains Algren's poem, "Makers of Music." The first stanza sets the tone of what Algren scholar Brooke Horvath calls a "glum portrait of Chicago":[8]

> The city is a sleeper, without a friend:
> Walk slow past a million friendless faces,
> Avoiding a million friendless hands.
> Who will play Lenin to Chicago,
> Touching faces, touching hands?[9]

"Utility Magnate," *The New Anvil*, April–May 1939, 16–17

Algren wrote the poem, "Utility Magnate" for the second (April–May 1939) issue of the *New Anvil*. As a joke, he wrote it under the pseudonym, "Lawrence O'Fallon." (Lawrence "Bud" Fallon was an acquaintance of Algren's.) Algren even fabricated a "Notes on Contributors" paragraph, describing the fictional O'Fallon:[10]

LAWRENCE O'FALLON, ex-seaman and aluminum worker, is surveying the annals of Labor and Industry of East St. Louis for the Illinois Federal Writers' Project.[11]

Perhaps Algren should have signed his own name to "Utility Magnate." Throughout this prose poem Algren deftly contrasts the life of an unnamed deceased business tycoon with the cynicism of the newspaper writer assigned to write a feature story about the man:[12]

"I was just another helpless victim of the depression,"
    Explained the man who had used hard times like a knife, to cut wages to the bone.

"I went down with my ship because I had too much faith in my country,"
Said the man who had scuttled the ship, then deserted it before the others
aboard even knew,
And had never had faith in anything save a personal savings account.[13]

Who was Algren's so-called "Utility Magnate"? The poem is clearly about electric company giant Samuel Insull. There are references in the poem to the Chicago Civic Opera Company, the Midland Utilities Company, and "Slinky Sam." In 1929 Samuel Insull built the Civic Opera House for the Chicago Civic Opera. Insull was president of the Midland Utilities Company, a utility holding company. Algren confirmed that "Slinky Sam" was Samuel Insull in a 1972 letter to Algren bibliographer Ken McCollum.[14]

Figure 10: In the prose poem, "Utility Magnate," Nelson Algren, using the pseudonym, "Lawrence O'Fallon," writes sarcastically of "Slinky Sam" and the Midland Utilities Company.
Algren's poem was obviously about electric company giant Samuel Insull. Shown here is a Midland Utilities Company stock certificate that is signed by Samuel Insull, President.

"Program for Appeasement," *The New Anvil*, June–July 1939, 12.

In 1939 Neville Chamberlain was the prime minister of Britain. Chamberlain has been historically associated with the term, "Appeasement." Appeasement is the diplomatic policy of negotiating with and making political or material concessions to an aggressive power in order to prevent war. It is the term given to Britain's policy in the 1930s of allowing Hitler to expand German territory unchecked.[15]

In September 1938 Germany, Britain, France, and Italy entered into the Munich Agreement, allowing Germany to annex the Sudetenland, a region in Czechoslovakia. Chamberlin viewed this agreement as a victory for appeasement, claiming that it represented "peace for our time." He was wrong; German troops occupied Prague by March 1939. Perhaps this convinced Algren that appeasement was not working. The June–July 1939 issue of the *New Anvil* featured Algren's "Program for Appeasement," a prose poem in which Algren sarcastically disparages appeasement. He compares a world on the brink of war to a theater on fire, suggesting that even if only half of the people in the theater get out unhurt, "that's better than they've done at some other fires":[16]

> In the event of fire, consult your program
> Then walk, do not run, to the nearest exit.
> We can all get out. If nobody runs.
> And even if somebody should get excited,
> Most of us will get out into the air again just the same.
> Even if only half get out,
> That's better than they've done at some other fires.
> Or the time the *Eastland* turned on her side in the river.
> Or the time somebody decided to picket a block from Republic Steel.[17]

Algren mentions both the *Eastland* and Republic Steel in this 1939 poem. On July 24, 1915, the steamer *Eastland* capsized into the Chicago River, killing a reported 844 people. On May 30, 1937, striking Republic Steel workers attempted to establish a picket line at the front of a steel mill. Protesting marchers were met by Chicago police in a field north of the mill gate, and in the ensuing violence, ten protestors were killed and approximately ninety were injured.[18]

Twelve years after Algren published "Program for Appeasement," he made dozens of similar historical references to people, places, and events in his 1951 prose poem, *Chicago: City on the Make*. For example:

> The cemetery that yet keeps the Confederate dead is bounded by the same tracks that run past Stephen A. Douglas' remains. The jail where Parsons hung is gone, and the building from which Bonfield marched is no more. Nobody remembers the Globe on Desplaines, and only a lonely shaft remembers the four who died, no one ever understood fully why. And those who went down with the proud steamer *Chicora* are one with those who went down on the *Eastland*.[19]

"Program for Appeasement" was Algren's last contribution to the *New Anvil*.

"Home and Goodnight," *Poetry,* November 1939, 74–76

Algren published his first poetry during the Great Depression. President Roosevelt's New Deal had the task of putting writers and other people in the creative professions back to work. The Federal Writers' Project, or FWP, was part of the Works Progress Administration, or WPA. The FWP established offices in every state. The Illinois office of the FWP was called the Illinois Writers' Project, or ILWP. The ILWP hired Algren in or about September 1936.[20]

While working for the Illinois Writers' Project, Algren attended the third American Writers' Congress, which was held in New York City in the first week of June 1939. Benjamin A. Botkin and Hyde Partnow of the Federal Writers' Project spoke at the Congress, and it appears that what these men told those in attendance would indelibly change Algren as a writer.[21]

One of the sessions at the Congress was on folklore. Botkin was the chairman of the session, and in a speech entitled "The Folk and the Writer," Botkin described the importance of listening:[22]

> For the writer who would successfully utilize folk sources there are certain requisites. First, he must be a good listener with a good ear for recording or remembering both what is said and how it is said. For folklore, like preaching, in Steinbeck's phrase, is "a kinda tone of voice, an' a way a lookin' at things." Like Casey, the ex-preacher in *The Grapes of Wrath*, the writer must make up his mind to "cuss and swear an' hear the poetry of folks talkin'."[23]

During his lecture, entitled "Creative Listening," Partnow talked about how he writes down what he hears:[24]

> I record what I've heard on my typewriter. What I attempt to do is: one, build up a unique person; two, relate that person to the group in which I found him, or in which he found himself; three, use his own idiom and lyric.[25]

The third American Writers' Congress was held on June 2–4, 1939. A few weeks later, on July 13, Nelson Algren, now a supervisor at the Illinois Writers' Project, led a so-called "staff conference in industrial folklore." Bessie Jaffey, a shorthand reporter, took notes during this meeting, and a complete transcript of this conference is on file in the Manuscript Division of the Library of Congress. Writer Jack Conroy and other Illinois Project members were in attendance.[26]

William F. McDonald, author of *Federal Relief Administration and the Arts*, writes that Algren spoke at this staff conference "after a visit to the New York City Project." Algren probably visited this writers' project while he was in New York at the third American Writers' Congress. Jaffey's

Figure 11: In the late 1930s Nelson Algren and his wife lived at 3569 Cottage Grove Avenue, on Chicago's South Side. They lived in what was then called the Arcade, a passageway flanked by storefront studios that were built, according to legend, to house shops catering to visitors of the World's Columbian Exposition of 1893. Marshall Philyaw's drawing of the Arcade is based on a 1940 photograph by John G. Rogers.

The Arcade was also known as Rat Alley, named after the four-legged tenants who also lived in the area. How big were the rats? In 1973 Algren wrote Kenneth G. McCollum, author of *Nelson Algren: A Checklist* (1973): "The rats were so large, and ran in such hordes, that, when they raced, late at night, across our roof, it sounded like cavalry charge. Hoofbeats! Getting one cornered didn't solve the problem. With all the furniture piled in a corner, and the door locked behind you, and a baseball bat in your hand, the problem became more acute: then you had to fight him."

transcript of the meeting indicates that Algren was impressed, perhaps even excited, by what he had heard in New York at the third Congress and at what the New York City Project was doing.[27]

Algren began the meeting with some introductory remarks:[28]

The purpose of this meeting is to inaugurate a new line in the accumulation of industrial folklore. We're going to … collect material appropriate to a national volume.[29]

The people on the New York Project are doing almost straight dialogue for this volume. We have an example here from the recent American Writers'

Congress in New York. It's the feeling of the New York writers that realism in American letters will become increasingly documentary.[30]

Algren later expressed his interest in and approval of what the New York City Project is doing:

The point of these documents is that they reveal what is really a new way of writing—which we'll attempt here.[31]

Jaffey's transcript indicates that Jack Conroy read Botkin's Congress presentation, "The Folk and the Writer," to Algren and the others at the July 13, 1939, staff conference.[32]

Botkin spoke about how a writer "must be a good listener with a good ear for recording or remembering both what is said and how it is said." Algren describes "how it is said" in his poem, "Home and Goodnight," which appeared in the November 1939 issue of *Poetry* magazine. The poem is about late-night workers at the end of their day. One of the lines of the poem is the New York Project's "straight dialogue"—a "come-on girl" speaking in her own (as Hyde Partnow described) "idiom and lyric":[33]

> The boys in the three-piece orchestra can go home now,
> And the come-on girl fingering a pink paper gardenia and saying,
> "My feet is killen me but I'm still dancen"—
> Can walk two blocks east and have breakfast No. 9 at the Greek's
> with her best boyfriend
> And be back dancing in bed; all in twenty-five minutes flat.[34]

"My feet is killen me but I'm still dancen"—Algren's use of colloquial language in "Home and Goodnight" is subtle and subdued. It is not cartoonish or extreme, like it was in his first novel, *Somebody in Boots* (1935). Bettina Drew describes the latter in her biography, *Nelson Algren: A Life on the Wild Side*:

The West Texas accents, rendered through Algren's urban, sophisticated ear, seem hokey and heavy-handed, almost caricature. "What good's it do fo' us to know folks or fo' folks to know we?" Cass's sister asks clumsily. "All folks us know is plum harder up 'an we." The insistence on dialect, despite his lack of intimacy with the nuances of southern speech, hindered the very realism he sought to create.[35]

On July 17, 1939, only four days after the IWP staff conference, Algren interviewed a Chicago prostitute for the Illinois Project. Like Bessie Jaffey's transcript, this interview, which Algren entitled, "When You Live Like I Done," is on file in the Library of Congress.[36]

In writing "Home and Goodnight," Algren remembered Botkin's "what is said" as well. That is, during his July 17, 1939, interview with the Chicago prostitute, she mentioned both Lifebuoy soap and a dice game called "26-game." Algren incorporated these references into "Home and Goodnight":[37]

"When You Live Like I Done"

- "You got to pay for the towels, for the music, for the lifebuoy,"[38]
- "They were arguing because he thought he had won a 26-game downstairs but the girl had cheated him and his wife hadn't been watching or something."[39]

"Home and Goodnight"

- "The girl in the little room smelling of Lifebuoy can say for the last time tonight,"[40]
- "And running a 26-game on North Clark Street"[41]

Algren was clearly influenced by both the Illinois Project's staff conference and the sessions he attended at the third American Writers' Congress. Years later, during a 1956 interview, Algren commented, "My most successful poetry, the lines people threw back at me years after they were written, were lines I never wrote. They were lines I heard, and repeated, usually by someone who never read and couldn't write."[42]

"Travelog," *Poetry*, November 1939, 76–77

The November 1939 issue of *Poetry* contains two poems by Algren. Besides "Home and Goodnight," this issue also includes "Travelog." In this poem Algren paints a bleak landscape of America:[43]

> Remember the darkened bus in the ruined town by the levee,
> The boarded windows and broken panes by the river,
> The abandoned feed-stores facing the moving Ohio.[44]

"This Table on Time Only," *Esquire*, March 1940, 78–79

"This Table on Time Only" tells the story of the murder of a man by at least three other men. It appears that the poem is based on a newspaper article that Algren read in the *Chicago Times* newspaper. The epigraph of the poem reads:

> "Skidmarks across the street from the 34th street
> wall of Comiskey Park indicate Piccioti was thrown from an
> auto going west. Three .25 calibre bullets fired at close range into
> the back of the neck...."
> —Item, *Chicago Daily Times.*[45]

With no sensationalism at all, Algren manages to convey not only the horror of the murder but also how Mr. Piccioti must have been feeling in the moments before he was shot:

> They stopped speaking softly between Wabash and State,
> And parked in the alley beneath the Congress Street station
> Until the groan of the El overhead could muffle the shot.
> He fainted once during that wait, and came to in a sweat.
> Just as the El overhead began slowing down toward the station.[46]

"How Long Blues," *Poetry*, September 1941, 309

The September 1941 issue of *Poetry* magazine includes both "How Long Blues" and "Local South" under the predictable caption, "Two Poems."

The title, "How Long Blues," refers to the 1928 song, "How Long— How Long Blues," by the Indianapolis pianist Leroy Carr.[47]

"How Long Blues" is not so much gloomy as it is melancholy. The poem tells the story of the last hours of a nightclub; it is closing the next day, as America has entered World War II. The bartender is joining an air platoon, and the "strip-tease number" has signed up to work for the USO. The bouncer has a bad eye, and so he will be deferred, at least for a while. All the employees are going their separate ways, and so the band is asked to play the song, "How Long Blues" over and over again. The last stanza explains why:

> To tell us the night is long, as long,
> As the long derisive rhythms of a rain
> That taps cold mockeries all night
> Against a lightless pane.[48]

Many of Algren's poems during this time are unrhymed free verse. This poem is not. Instead, with the exception of the last stanza, the rhyming scheme is AABB. "How Long Blues" is an excellent illustration of Algren's talents as a lyricist. It is a remarkable poem.[49] (Figure 12)

"Local South," *Poetry*, September 1941, 308–09

"Local South" is dark and gloomy; it asks, "What time will it be when the last El crashes?" as it imagines Chicago's cleaning ladies and cab drivers on the brink of some unspecified apocalypse.[50]

Figure 12: This Vocalion Records advertisement for the 1928 song, "How Long—How Long Blues," by Leroy Carr, appeared in the September 8, 1928, issue of *The Chicago Defender*. The song features Leroy Carr on vocals and piano and Francis "Scrapper" Blackwell on guitar. "How Long—How Long Blues" was Carr's breakthrough hit, and it inspired hundreds of later songs.

This advertisement reads, "Every lovin' man knows what it means to have his sweetie go away and leave him all alone. He gets to feelin' blue, disgusted and mean, wondering how long he'll have to wait for her to come back. That's just the way Leroy Carr feels when he tells you how he's waitin' down at the railroad station for his good woman."

Nelson Algren's poem, "How Long Blues," appears in the September 1941 issue of *Poetry* magazine. Two of the lines read: "So let's hear the *How Long Blues* once again,/Play it over and over while stirring your gin—"

"The Swede Was a Hard Guy," *Southern Review,* Spring 1942, 873–79

This is a prose poem about the "Black Sox"—eight Chicago White Sox baseball players, including Charles "Swede" Risberg and "Shoeless" Joe Jackson, who were banned from baseball after being accused of being paid off to intentionally lose the 1919 World Series to the Cincinnati Reds:[51]

> Here, on another fall afternoon,
> A Georgia millhand the kids called Shoeless Joe
> Pegged a runner out at the plate on his knees
> From against the far left-field stands.
> And never played again.
> Nor pegged another.[52]

"Epitaph: The Man with the Golden Arm,"
 Poetry, September 1947, 316–17

Most readers of Nelson Algren's books know that an epitaph for the doomed card dealer Frankie Machine appears at the end of Algren's acclaimed novel, *The Man with the Golden Arm* (1949). They may not know that this poem was published two years earlier in *Poetry* magazine:

> It's all in the wrist, with a deck or a cue,
> And Frankie Machine had the touch
> He had the touch, and a golden arm—[53]

"The Bride Below the Black Coiffure,"
 Rogue, July 1961, 30–31

Algren met French philosopher and author Simone de Beauvoir in 1947, and they immediately began a long-distance love affair, exchanging hundreds of letters until the relationship ended in 1964. In a letter to Algren dated August 1961, Beauvoir joked about a magazine that Algren sent her: "Yes, I got the nice 'Tiquetonne poem' in a strange magazine showing what a vicious man you are: I had to hide the pictures from the nice people coming to my nice place—are you not ashamed?" This "strange magazine" was the July 1961 issue of *Rogue*, a men's magazine, and the poem was, "The Bride Below the Black Coiffure." The first stanza reads:[54]

> There are sad little sights of Paris
> After Metro lights go out.
> There are strange flowers woven of rain
> That scatter like petals on the Rue Tiquetonne.[55]

Algren published a shorter and untitled version of "The Bride Below the Black Coiffure" in *Who Lost an American?* The poem was a preface to his account of his trips to Paris.[56]

"Afternoon in the Land of the Strange Light Sleep,"
 Cavalier, September 1962, 24–25, 27

In "Afternoon in the Land of the Strange Light Sleep," Algren writes of young people caught up in the throes of drug addiction.

During a 1955 interview, when Algren was asked, "Do you try to write a poetic prose?" he replied:

No. No, I'm not writing it, but so many people say things poetically, they say it for you in a way you never could. Some guy just coming out of jail might say, "I did it from bell to bell," or like the seventeen-year-old junkie, when the judge asked him what he did all day, he said, "Well, I find myself a doorway to lean against, and I take a fix, and then I lean, I just lean and dream." They always say things like that.[57]

Seven years later, Algren used the young man's words in "Afternoon in the Land of the Strange Light Sleep":

> "What do you do all the day?" I heard the judge ask the sixteen-year-old in Narcotics Court.
> "I lean," the boy replied, still adrift on a rain-blue cloud, "just lean.
> I find a hallway or washroom 'n' take a shot. Then I lean. Lean 'n' dream."
> An evening country where ten a.m. looks like five in the afternoon.
> Where purple jukes just lean 'n' dream.[58]

The editors of *Cavalier* called "Afternoon in the Land of the Strange Light Sleep" "a prose poem in a new dimension."[59]

"Tricks Out of Times Long Gone," *The Nation*, 22 September 1962, 162

Except for his famous prose poem, *Chicago: City on the Make* (1951), which is discussed in this book, Nelson Algren did not publish any poetry during the entire decade of the 1950s. He quickly changed that in the 1960s. The September 22, 1962, issue of *The Nation* magazine featured his haunting poem, "Tricks Out of Times Long Gone."[60]

In this poem Algren resurrects the people he had written about during his life as a novelist and a journalist—drifters, hookers, and winos. These people come back, "seeking chances lost":

> Tonight when chimneys race against the cold
> Tricks out of times long gone, forgotten marks
> Come seeking chances lost, and long-missed scores
> Faces once dear now nameless and bereft
> Hepghosts made of rain that softly try old doors
> Forever trying to get down one last bet.[61]

The poem was reprinted as the epilogue in *Who Lost an American?* An expanded version is the last item in *The Last Carousel*. Another version appears at the end of the third edition (1968) of *Chicago: City on the Make*. The first stanza of *The Last Carousel* version was read at Algren's funeral.[62]

But did Algren give Simone de Beauvoir a draft of this poem? After Beauvoir was invited to speak at a number of U.S. universities, she flew from France to New York in January 1947 to begin a four-month tour across America. She met Algren when she was in Chicago on a thirty-six-hour layover, and this encounter was the start of a love affair that continued after Beauvoir returned to France. She would periodically come to the United States, and she would stay at his Wabansia Avenue apartment. In 1949 he visited her in Paris, and in 1950 and 1951 she stayed with him at his cottage in Miller Beach, a small community on the southernmost shore of Lake Michigan that is within the municipal boundaries of Gary, Indiana.[63]

But Beauvoir also had a relationship with fellow philosopher Jean-Paul Sartre. Beauvoir met Sartre in July of 1929. A few months later, in October of that year, Beauvoir and Sartre made a pact of so-called "essential love" that allowed either party to have *contingent* affairs—relationships with other people while still remaining pledged to each other.[64]

Algren loved Beauvoir, but she was committed to Sartre, and she would not leave Paris and Sartre for America and Algren. In 1951 Algren wrote Beauvoir:[65]

> I don't regret a single one of the moments we have had together. But now I want a different kind of life, with a woman and a house of my own.... The disappointment I felt three years ago, when I began to realize that your life belonged to Paris and to Sartre, is an old one now, and it's become blunted by time.
> What I've tried to do since is to take my life back from you. My life means a lot to me, I don't like its belonging to someone so far off, someone I see only a few weeks every year... [ellipses in original].[66]

Algren remarried his ex-wife Amanda Kontowicz in 1953; the marriage triggered a long period of depression. They divorced in 1955. Algren wrote Beauvoir in December 1957, and in this Christmas note he expressed nostalgia for their life together and for the magic of his former Wabansia Avenue apartment that they had shared.[67]

Algren came back to Paris in 1960. By this time, he and Beauvoir were friends, not lovers. Algren biographer Bettina Drew writes that while he was there, he told Beauvoir that he had once found himself walking unthinkingly toward the Paris apartment they had lived in in 1949, as if his body were living in the past. At about this time in his life, he began imagining people from his days on Wabansia Avenue approaching him from the shadows. Algren wrote the poem, "Tricks Out of Times Long Gone" as a sad farewell to these people. This poem was first published in 1962. But could Algren have written this poem two years earlier in Paris, when he was lost in thoughts of his own "times long gone" with Beauvoir, walking towards their 1949 apartment?[68] (Figure 13)

While Algren was in Paris, Beauvoir and Sartre went to Brazil; Algren stayed behind. But while she was gone, he mailed her a poem. By the time she returned, he had left her apartment, but he had left her another poem. Could one of these poems have been an early draft of "Tricks Out of Times Long Gone," perhaps first composed in his mind while he was wandering

Figure 13: Nelson Algren biographer Bettina Drew writes that while Algren was in Paris in 1960, he told Simone de Beauvoir that he had once found himself walking unthinkingly toward the apartment they had shared in 1949, as if his body was living in the past. At about this time in his life, he began imagining people from his days on Chicago's Wabansia Avenue approaching him from the shadows.

Artist Marshall Philyaw has drawn this "fantasy picture" of Algren walking the streets of Paris while thinking of his earlier life on Wabansia Avenue.

the streets of Paris in 1960, later revised and eventually published two years later?[69]

If Algren did give Beauvoir a copy of "Trick Out of Times Long Gone," did he include in the poem a secret message to her? Consider the penultimate stanza:

> Upon the just-before-day bus I saw a woman,
> The only one who rode
> Look wanly out at streets she used to know—
> "And here I went"—"and there I slept"—"and there I rose"—
> Again by evening in a billboard's cold blue glow
> She came forever toward me
> Walking slow
> Saying *za za-za-zaza-za-zaza-za-zaza*
> Walking slow[70]

"Zaza" was the nickname of Elizabeth Mabille, Beauvoir's childhood best friend. *Mémoires d'une jeune fille rangée* (*Memoirs of a Dutiful Daughter*, published in 1958), is the first of four volumes of Beauvoir's autobiography. A significant portion of this volume concerns the friendship of Beauvoir and Zaza. Each of the four sections of the book ends with a reference to Zaza, and the book itself ends with her death. (Accounts differ; Zaza was either 20 or 22 years old when she died, possibly of meningitis or encephalitis.)[71]

Algren met Beauvoir in 1947. Surely by 1960 she would have told him of Zaza and their childhood friendship.[72]

Is Beauvoir the woman on the bus in "Tricks Out of Times Long Gone"? When Algren wrote her in December of 1957, he told her of his nostalgia for the magic of their shared past. Later, when Algren wrote this poem, was he still feeling nostalgic? Did he include Beauvoir and Zaza in this poem so that Beauvoir might read it and think of her own "times long gone" in Chicago and possibly even think nostalgic thoughts of him?[73]

The editors of *The Nation* buried "Tricks Out of Times Long Gone" at the end of the magazine. It should have been on the cover.

"Goodbye Lilies Hello Spring," *Zeitgeist* 1, No. 4 (Summer 1966): 50–51

In the late 1950s, Nelson Algren was unable to obtain an advance from a publisher so that he could finish his novel, *Entrapment*. This rejection by commercial publishers may have angered Algren. In 1959, the *Chicago Sun-Times* reported that when the National Book Awards committee asked Algren, "What has our prize, the NBA award, done for you?" he replied, "The purpose of this award appears to be to unify the publicity departments of the various publishers. If you are in touch with any person interested in purchasing the first plaque awarded by your committee, I should be pleased to dispose of it."[74]

Algren's possible resentment of commercial publishers may have resulted in him publishing some of his most original work in obscure literary magazines. In May of 1966 he spoke in East Lansing, Michigan, possibly at Michigan State University. *Zeitgeist* was an East Lansing literary magazine (now defunct) that appears to have been loosely affiliated with the university. Algren went to East Lansing "for a reading and discussion of his works as part of the *Zeitgeist* Profile Series."[75]

While he was in Michigan, it appears that he gave (or perhaps later mailed) *Zeitgeist* one of his poems. The Summer 1966 issue featured "Goodbye Lilies Hello Spring," a scathing attack on Simone de Beauvoir. Why was it scathing? Her book, *Force of Circumstance*, was published in early 1965, but excerpts appeared in the November 1964 and December 1964 issues of *Harper's Magazine*. *Force of Circumstance* would enrage Algren for the rest of his life. Not only did Algren discover that from the very beginning of his relationship with Beauvoir, Jean-Paul Sartre had always been her "first love"; he also learned that he was, in her words, a "problem," a "deviation," a "contingent love" and a "defect in our system." This is what Algren read in the November 1964 issue of *Harper's*:[76]

America became still closer to me when I became attached to Nelson Algren toward the end of my stay. Although I related this affair—very approximately—in *The Mandarins*, I return to it, not out of any taste for gossip, but in order to examine more closely a problem that in *The Prime of Life*, the second volume of my autobiography, I took to be too easily resolved: Is there any possible reconciliation between fidelity and freedom? And if so, at what price?[77]

There are many couples who conclude more or less the same pact as that of Sartre and myself: to maintain throughout all deviations from the main path a "certain fidelity."[78]

Sartre and I have been more ambitious; it has been our wish to experience "contingent loves"; but there is one question we have deliberately avoided: How would the third person feel about our arrangement? It often happened that the third person accommodated himself to it without difficulty; our union left plenty of room for loving friendships and fleeting affairs. But if the protagonist wanted more, then conflicts would break out.[79]

Although my understanding with Sartre has lasted for more than thirty years, it has not done so without some losses and upsets in which the "others" always suffered. This defect in our system manifested itself with particular acuity during the period I will relate next [in the December issue of *Harper's Magazine*].[80]

Algren would never see Beauvoir or talk to her again. He could not forgive her for using him, similar to how Ralph Bellamy and Don Ameche used Dan Aykroyd and Eddie Murphy in the 1983 film, *Trading Places*. Just as characters Randolph Duke and Mortimer Duke used Louis Winthorpe III and Billy Ray Valentine to test their theory of nature versus nurture, Beauvoir used Algren to test her theory—that one could have a secondary relationship outside a primary one. Algren could also not forgive Beauvoir for publicizing their affair with no concern for his own feelings.[81]

Beauvoir biographer Deirdre Bair writes that Algren spent the next several years castigating Beauvoir in reviews and articles and the rest of his life denouncing her to anyone who would listen. He grumbled in the December 28, 1964, issue of *Newsweek* that "I have the old-fashioned puritanical idea that some things are private. Sex doesn't get taken care of by literary sublimation." He wrote a devastating article in the May 1965 issue of *Harper's*. It was ostensibly a review of *Force of Circumstance*, but it was really a review of Beauvoir: "Anybody who can experience love contingently has a mind that has recently snapped. How can love be *contingent*? Contingent upon *what*?" [emphasis in original] Algren reviewed *Force of Circumstance* in *Ramparts* (October 1965), calling it "the most tedious chronicle of public snitchery since Joe Valachi sacrificed himself for television." (Joe Valachi was a Mafia hoodlum who became an informant; in 1963 Valachi testified against the Cosa Nostra in televised hearings.)[82]

And then Algren wrote "Goodbye Lilies Hello Spring," apparently in 1966. How harsh is it? The poem is reprinted below, exactly as it appears in *Zeitgeist*:

"GOODBYE LILIES HELLO SPRING"
for Simone de Beauvoir

That shaded stone where dead love rests
Rests best unhung by green
Lest a telephone ring and a voice come in
(Faintly as though on another line)
Crying *Wasn't it upsy and wasn't it down
And didn't they envy us all over town—*
Tell her you'll call back in an hour and a half
But never call back never call back never call back.
Spare the lilies; let grass go to seed
Lilies are dandy but what's better are weeds.

*I was like Héloise You were Abélard
On the paperback shelves it'll sell by the yard—
Avoid, avoid that shadowy plot*
And the old fraud below it who can't shut her mouth—
*O wasn't it magical O wasn't it tragical
Love like ours will never die out
(Providing I tell it the way it was not)—*

Is there no brickyard streaked by rain
Where nobody wanders to hear her complain
Where her bones can bog down under old streetcar stones
And no streetcar runs any more?
Wasn't it nice and the very best yet

It ought to rate me right up with Colette—
Find some old gas-main and jam her in square
She was explosive in her day: she won't explode in there.

Down in some basement below the bin
Where baby-rats drown when water creeps in
Straight down upside-down in the slag and the guck
Stuff the yammering humbug straight down in the muck—
Let her yack on forever way way down there
Then slam the door and jump up the stair—
Open the window and let in some air
Each April should teach us anew how to swing:
Saying Goodbye Lilies
Hello
Spring.[83]

The Nation had published "Tricks Out of Times Long Gone" just four years earlier. Did Algren first submit "Goodbye Lilies Hello Spring" to *The Nation*? Did the magazine decline publication, believing it to be too bitter and acerbic? Or did Algren deliberately thumb his nose at *The Nation* and the other national magazines and just turn the poem over to *Zeitgeist*, to be printed once and then never to be printed again?[84]

"Nobody Knows," *Saturday Review*, 3 September 1966, 15

In 1962 Nelson Algren decided to go on a three-month tour of the Far East. Algren booked passage on a freighter, the *Malaysia Mail*. He would board in Seattle, and the ship would travel to Japan, Korea, Hong Kong, Malaysia, India, Pakistan, and the Philippines. Ernest Hemingway had died in July 1961, and Algren had written an article on Hemingway that *The Nation* had published four months later. Algren now wanted to use this travel time to expand the article into a book. The ship pulled away from its Seattle port in June 1962.[85]

The *Malaysia Mail* returned to the United States in September. Although Algren went back to Chicago with an unfinished Hemingway manuscript and a stack of notes from his travels, he never wrote a book on Hemingway. He did write an article, however, entitled "Hemingway All the Way," that *Cavalier*, a men's magazine, published in February 1965. He also took his Hemingway manuscript, padded it with essays that he had written about his stops in various cities, and published it all in August 1965 as the travel book, *Notes from a Sea Diary: Hemingway All the Way*.[86]

In addition to his Hemingway article, Algren also wrote a poem. It is called, "Nobody Knows," and it appears that the poem was written after (or during) his 1962 visit to India. The poem is subtitled "Madras 1962."

Madras, also known as Chennai, is a city in India. The poem was published in a 1966 issue of *Saturday Review*. Although "Nobody Knows" is not featured in *Notes from a Sea Diary*, fragments of the poem are buried in one of the stories in *Sea Diary*.[87]

Unfortunately, the poem is hackneyed and trite, ending with this observation:

> All that we may now safely venture
> Is that at this time tomorrow
> There are going to be more people
> On The-Committee-For-Counting-Cats-In-Madras
> Than there are today.[88]

"The Cockeyed Hooker of Bugis Street," *Lillabulero* 1, No. 1 (Winter 1967): 24

"The Cockeyed Hooker of Bugis Street" was published in the first issue (Winter 1967) of *Lillabulero*, a North Carolina literary magazine. The name of the "cockeyed hooker" is Po-Tin. Algren had written an essay about her for his 1965 book, *Notes from a Sea Diary: Hemingway All the Way*.[89]

"The Country of Kai-Li," *Lillabulero* 1, No. 1 (Winter 1967): 24–25

The first issue of *Lillabulero* featured two poems. The second poem was "The Country of Kai-Li," a haunting poem about an Asian prostitute.[90]

"City on the Make," In *Law & Disorder: The Chicago Convention and Its Aftermath*, ed. Donald Myrus (Chicago: Privately printed, 1968), [11]

The 1968 Democratic National Convention was held during the last week of August at Chicago's International Amphitheatre. As President Lyndon B. Johnson had announced he would not seek reelection, Democratic Party delegates would select the party's 1968 presidential election nominee at the convention.[91]

Many student anti-war groups also came to the convention. Because the Democratic Party was the party of Lyndon Johnson, it seemed only appropriate that the anti-war movement would focus its anger about the Vietnam War on the Democrats. In addition, the convention was also the culmination of Eugene McCarthy's anti-war presidential campaign; his supporters would make their final stand on the convention floor. Finally, the anti-war movement was media savvy. The sheer number of reporters and television cameras that would be at the Amphitheatre made the convention almost irresistible to the students.[92]

Chicago Mayor Richard J. Daley intended to use the convention to showcase his and the city's achievements to the world. Instead, the convention became famous for the large number of hippies, Yippies, and other demonstrators that came to Chicago. It became infamous for the conduct of the Chicago Police Department. During the convention, policemen charged through crowds with clubs and indiscriminately beat demonstrators, bystanders, and news reporters.[93]

Donald Myrus and Burton Joseph managed to pull together more than a dozen contributors and publish *Law & Disorder: The Chicago Convention and Its Aftermath* sometime during the remaining months of 1968. Myrus writes that the unnumbered sixty-four-page magazine of articles and photographs "tells the story of the Chicago Convention as it was seen by those who were there, by those who felt or saw the aspirations and fear and who are disturbed about what the Chicago experience means to the continuation of American democracy."[94]

Nelson Algren was in Chicago at the time of the convention, and he was one of the contributors to the magazine. The "Copyright & Permissions" section of the magazine contains only this short statement concerning his contribution: "Nelson Algren article: Excerpted with permission of the author from *Chicago: City on the Make*, 3rd edition. Copyright © 1961, Nelson Algren."[95]

But this statement is incorrect. Algren's *Law & Disorder* article is not solely an excerpt from *Chicago: City on the Make*. It is an original piece of work, highlighted by a fifty-six-line original prose poem about the convention that essentially updates *Chicago: City on the Make* to 1968. The article also consists of parts of the Introduction to the 1961 edition of *Chicago: City on the Make* and also parts of chapters 1, 5, 6, and 7 of *Chicago: City on the Make*.[96]

Algren is direct and blunt in his criticism (if not castigation) of the City of Chicago and its police department. The first five lines of the new poem set its tone:

> What other city could show me eight
> armed cops
> Beating the living bejusus out of
> two defenseless winos
> In Living Color?[97]

Algren worked this new and untitled prose poem into the epilogue of the third edition of *Chicago: City on the Make*, which was also published in 1968. But otherwise, Algren never reprinted this work again. It does not appear in *The Last Carousel* (1973). Perhaps there is a reason. In the fifteenth line of the poem he uses the forbidden "F" word:[98]

> And busts the poet who says "f—" on
> a platform—[99]

There was no reason for Algren to do this. The use of the word is gratuitous; he just as easily could have said, "And busts the poet who shouts an obscenity on a platform." But by using this word, did Algren also bust himself?

Algren had not published any poetry since "Nobody Knows" two years earlier, and in that instance the editors of *Saturday Review* failed to list the poem in the "Table of Contents" of the magazine. Now, was history repeating itself? During the 1950s, some of Algren's best work appeared in magazines with limited circulation. Because of one word, were publishers reluctant to reprint this prose poem? With one word, did Algren doom himself to the one-time publication of one of his most original works, and then in an obscure regional magazine?[100]

"The Cockeyed Hooker of Bugis Street," *Chicago Tribune Magazine*, 8 October 1972, 30

"The Country of Kai-Li," *Chicago Tribune Magazine*, 8 October 1972, 29

"It Don't Matter How You Spell It," *Chicago Tribune Magazine*, 8 October 1972, 30

"Gentlemen: The Law is Present," *Chicago Tribune Magazine*, 8 October 1972, 29

"Ode to an Absconding Bookie," *Chicago Tribune Magazine*, 8 October 1972, 31

On October 8, 1972, the *Chicago Tribune* announced on the cover of its Sunday magazine: "Nelson Algren: Verses from Gritty City."[101] Nelson Algren had written some new poems.

One of the poems is a revision of "The Cockeyed Hooker of Bugis Street," which first appeared in *Lillabulero* in 1967. Bugis Street is a famous street in Singapore. Singapore is an island nation that is just off the southern tip of Malaysia in Southeast Asia. The *Malaysia Mail* stopped in

Singapore when Algren traveled to the Far East in 1962. It is possible that Algren visited Bugis Street and later wrote this poem.[102]

The *Tribune* version of "The Cockeyed Hooker of Bugis Street" is faintly similar to a few lines from the last chapter of *Chicago: City on the Make*:

Chicago: City on the Make:

> When chairs are stacked and glasses are turned and arc-lamps all are dimmed. By days when the wind bangs alley gates ajar and the sun goes by on the wind. By nights when the moon is an only child above the measured thunder of the cars, you may know Chicago's heart at last.[103]

"The Cockeyed Hooker of Bugis Street":

> When chairs are stacked and jukes are still
> Seller and sailor all have left
> And pimps have made a night of it
> Po-Tin herself at last finds rest
> Her cockeyed head upon her arm.[104]

"The Country of Kai-Li" is a revision of the poem that also originally appeared in *Lillabulero* in 1967. The poem was haunting before; it is even more so now, as Algren heart-breakingly contrasts Kai-Li's ancestral home to her present home, "the last room on the left":

> The country of Kai-Li is a high, cold land
> Rivers are made of snow-waters there....
> Now the country of Kai-Li is the last room on the left:
> The one with bars of yellow iron.[105]

"It Don't Matter How You Spell It" is about Frank Lloyd Wright, who "sure liked buildings." Algren writes that "what Frank Lloyd Wright thought made a city enduring was the height and the heft and the light and the depth of its buildings." Algren disagrees, claiming that "what Mr. Wright forgot was that a village of ragged tents pitched on the open prairie may be a city more enduring than a million-windowed metropolis rising a mile high upon foundations a mile deep in which nobody knows who he is."[106]

"Gentlemen: The Law is Present" contains courtroom scenes that are similar to the "show-up" or police "line-up" scenes in *Never Coming Morning* (1942) and *The Man with the Golden Arm* (1949):

> No, Your Honor.
> I had no intention of robbing that store.
> I was leaning against the window thinking of enlisting
>   in the Marines
> When the glass gave in.

> So I stepped inside to leave my name and address
> So I could make the damage good
> Before leaving the country with my outfit.
> I was looking for a paper and pencil in the cash register
> When these officers entered.[107]

"Ode to An Absconding Bookie" tells the story of "Sam the Jackal," a bookie who accepts a fifty-dollar bet on *Reckless Love* at odds of 44 to 1, but then takes off with the winnings:

> We were waiting where we always wait
> Beside the fifty-buck partition
> Exchanging self-congratulations
> While doing some additions
> And disdaining well-backed entries who find their strides too late—
> When it came to one and all of us
> That you were a little late yourself.
> Too late too late too late Sam the Jackal?[108]

Algren included a longer version of "Ode to An Absconding Bookie" in his 1973 collection, *The Last Carousel*. He never reprinted any of the other four poems after their 1972 *Chicago Tribune* publication.[109]

Conclusion

Although Nelson Algren was known first and foremost as a novelist, over the course of thirty-three years, he wrote and published twenty-three poems. Almost all of them are superb examples of Algren's poetic talents.

Notes

1. Richard Studing, "A Nelson Algren Checklist," *Twentieth Century Literature* 19, no. 1 (January 1973): 33; Kenneth G. McCollum, *Nelson Algren: A Checklist* (Detroit: Gale Research Co., 1973), 58–59; Martha Heasley Cox and Wayne Chatterton, *Nelson Algren* (Boston: Twayne, 1975), 152; Brooke Horvath, *Understanding Nelson Algren* (Columbia: University of South Carolina Press, 2005), 193; Matthew J. Bruccoli, *Nelson Algren: A Descriptive Bibliography* (Pittsburgh: University of Pittsburgh Press, 1985), 109–26 passim. Cox and Chatterton write that the poem, "Sentiment with Terror," appeared in the December 1939 issue of *Poetry*. This is not a poem; this is a book review. See Cox and Chatterton, *Nelson Algren*, 152.

2. Studs Terkel, introduction to Nelson Algren, *Chicago: City on the Make* (New York: McGraw-Hill, 1983), 5; Nelson Algren, "Afternoon in the Land of the Strange Light Sleep," *Cavalier*, September 1962, 25; Bettina Drew, *Nelson Algren: A Life on the Wild Side* (Austin: University of Texas Press, 1991), 240–41, 395; Nelson Algren, "Epilogue: Quais of Calcutta," in *Algren at Sea: Who Lost an American? & Notes from a Sea Diary–Travel Writings* (New York: Seven Stories Press, 2008), 461–62. Algren's poem to Simone de Beauvoir that he wrote in her copy of *Never Come Morning* has been reprinted; see Deirdre Bair, *Simone de Beauvoir: A Biography* (New York: Summit Books, 1990), 341, 648n44; Simone de

Beauvoir, *A Transatlantic Love Affair: Letters to Nelson Algren*, comp. and annot. by Sylvie Le Bon de Beauvoir (New York: New Press, 1998), 15; Carole Seymour-Jones, *A Dangerous Liaison: Simone de Beauvoir and Jean-Paul Sartre* (London: Century, 2008), 346.

3. Algren's last *Poetry* magazine poem was in the September 1947 issue, and his last *Poetry* book review appeared in the October 1944 issue. Edward E. Chielens, editor of *American Literary Magazines*, describes *Poetry* as "the longest-running, most influential little magazine ever published in America." Algren died on May 9, 1981. What is probably his last published book review was in the *Chicago Tribune* on April 26, 1981. Why did Algren stop writing for *Poetry*, when he was writing for other periodicals almost until the day he died? See Bruccoli, *Nelson Algren*, 111, 137, 180; Edward E. Chielens, ed., *American Literary Magazines: The Twentieth Century* (Westport, Conn.: Greenwood Press, 1992), 261; Horvath, *Understanding Nelson Algren*, 11; Nelson Algren, "Modern India Comes Alive in a Burst of Surrealism," review of *Midnight's Children*, by Salman Rushdie, *Chicago Tribune Book World*, 26 April 1981, 3. It does not appear that Algren stopped writing for *Poetry* because he had a poor relationship with the magazine. Algren's numerous letters to Ken McCollum indicate that Algren often dated his correspondence with only the month and day, omitting the year. In a typewritten letter written from West Palm Beach, Florida, dated only December 26 (but with "1961" added by hand), Algren wrote the following to his friend Herman Kogan: "Reason I was asked down here, it develops, is that J. Pat [J. Patrick Lannan, former chairman of the board of trustees of *Poetry* magazine] is thinking of giving Poetry a fresh shake and thinks I'm the right cat to shake it. It would pay $7500 a year without being full time, but I doubt I ought to take it just because it isn't full time. My answer was Gwendolyn Brooks." Nelson Algren to Herm[an Kogan], December 26 [1961], photocopy, author's collection; Paul Durica, "Back Page," *Poetry*, September 2012, [519].

4. Bruccoli, *Nelson Algren*, 126; [Editorial], *Lillabulero* no. 14 (Spring 1974), [i].

5. Drew, *Nelson Algren*, 299–300, 330–32; Cox and Chatterton, *Nelson Algren*, 138; Henry Kisor, "Nelson Algren, Hale and Salty at 64," *Chicago Daily News Panorama*, 27–28 October 1973, 2; Jan Herman, "Nelson Algren: The Angry Author," *Chicago Sun-Times Chicagostyle*, 21 January 1979, 9; Colin Asher, *Never a Lovely So Real: The Life and Work of Nelson Algren* (New York: W.W. Norton, 2019), 341, 381, 415, 452; "A Note on Our Contributors," *Zeitgeist* 1, no. 4 (Summer 1966): 94.

6. Bruccoli, *Nelson* Algren, 107, 109.

7. Jack Conroy and Nelson Algren, eds., *The New Anvil*, March 1939, 1; "Introducing *The New Anvil*," *The New Anvil*, March 1939, [3].

8. Horvath, *Understanding Nelson Algren*, 35.

9. Nelson Algren, "Makers of Music," *The New Anvil*, March 1939, 23. "Makers of Music" has been reprinted; see Jack Conroy and Curt Johnson, eds., *Writers in Revolt: The Anvil Anthology* (New York: Lawrence Hill, 1973), 209.

10. Drew, *Nelson Algren*, 103, 109–10; Douglas Wixson, "Jack Conroy and The East St. Louis Toughs," *New Letters* 57, no. 4 (Summer 1991): 33, 35, 45; Douglas Wixson, *Worker-Writer in America: Jack Conroy and the Tradition of Midwestern Literary Radicalism, 1898–1990* (Urbana: University of Illinois Press, 1994), 444, 571n79; Bruccoli, *Nelson Algren*, 109. A photograph of the front cover of the April–May 1939 issue of *The New Anvil* appears in Kenneth G. McCollum's book, *Nelson Algren: A Checklist*. This magazine was Algren's personal copy. Before Algren gave the magazine to McCollum, Algren circled the name, "Lawrence O'Fallon" that appears on the cover, drew a line from the circle, and then wrote "pseudonym for Algren" next to the line. McCollum, *Nelson Algren*, 58; Ken McCollum to Dick Bales, 2 January 2018. When Algren sent Ken McCollum his copy of the April–May 1939 issue of *The New Anvil*, Algren appeared to dismiss the writing of "Utility Magnate" under the "Lawrence O'Fallon" pseudonym. In his letter to McCollum, Algren casually referred to "an old *Anvil* in which I slipped in a poem about Sam Insull under a friend's name. It was supposed to be a comical deal I assume." See Nelson Algren to Ken McCollum, 30 July 1972, photocopy, author's collection.

11. "Notes on Contributors," *The New Anvil*, April-May 1939, 29.

12. Horvath, *Understanding Nelson Algren*, 35–36.

13. Lawrence O'Fallon [Nelson Algren], "Utility Magnate," *The New Anvil*, April-May 1939, 16.

14. O'Fallon [Algren], "Utility Magnate," 16–17; Forrest McDonald, *Insull* (Chicago: University of Chicago Press, 1962), 231, 243–44; Emmett Dedmon, *Fabulous Chicago* (New York: Random House, 1953), 326–28; Nelson Algren to Ken McCollum, 30 July 1972, photocopy, author's collection. Algren also refers to "old Sam Insull" in his prose poem, *Chicago: City on the Make*. See Nelson Algren, *Chicago: City on the Make*, 60th Anniversary Edition (Chicago: University of Chicago Press, 2011), 55, 121. "Utility Magnate" has been reprinted; see Nelson Algren, *Entrapment and other Writings*, eds. Brooke Horvath and Dan Simon (New York: Seven Stories Press, 2009), 53–55.

15. Piers Brendon, *The Dark Valley: A Panorama of the 1930s* (London: Jonathan Cape, 2000), 516–40 passim.

16. Brendon, *The Dark Valley*, 530–36; Stanley G. Payne, *A History of Fascism, 1914–1945* (Madison: University of Wisconsin Press, 1995), 242; Victor Bondi, ed., *American Decades 1930–1939* (Detroit: Gale, 1995), 20.

17. Nelson Algren, "Program for Appeasement," *The New Anvil*, June-July 1939, 12. "Program for Appeasement" has been reprinted in Conroy and Johnson, *Writers in Revolt*, 210–11.

18. James R. Grossman, Ann Durkin Keating, and Janice L. Reiff, eds., *The Encyclopedia of Chicago* (Chicago: University of Chicago Press, 2004), s.v. "Eastland"; see also Jay Bonansinga, *The Sinking of the Eastland: America's Forgotten Tragedy* (New York: Citadel Press, 2004); George W. Hilton, *Eastland: Legacy of the Titanic* (Stanford, Calif.: Stanford University Press, 1995); Grossman, Keating, and Reiff, *The Encyclopedia of Chicago*, s.v. "Memorial Day Massacre"; see also Michael Dennis, *The Memorial Day Massacre and the Movement for Industrial Democracy* (Palgrave Macmillan, 2010); Donald G. Sofchalk, "The Chicago Memorial Day Incident: An Episode of Mass Action," *Labor History* 6, no. 1 (Winter 1965): 3–43; Ron Grossman, "Republic Steel: Riot or Massacre?" in *Chicago Flashback: The People and Events That Shaped a City's History* (Chicago: Midway Books, 2017), [224]-227. Algren was born in 1909. Algren's mother took the young Algren to see the wreck of the *Eastland* in 1915. Twenty-four years later, Algren wrote about the *Eastland* disaster in "Program for Appeasement." See Drew, *Nelson Algren*, 13, 17.

19. Algren, *Chicago: City on the Make*, 2011, vii–viii, 75–76.

20. Grossman, Keating, and Reiff, *The Encyclopedia of Chicago*, s.v. "Federal Writers' Project"; H.E.F. Donohue, *Conversations with Nelson Algren* (New York: Hill and Wang, 1964), 64–66; Jerre Mangione, *The Dream and the Deal: The Federal Writers' Project 1935–1943* (Boston: Little Brown, 1972), 121, 123; Drew, *Nelson Algren*, 100; David A. Taylor, *Soul of a People: The WPA Writers' Project Uncovers Depression America* (Hoboken, N.J.: John Wiley & Sons, 2009), 49; *The WPA Guide to Illinois: The Federal Writers' Project Guide to 1930s Illinois* (New York: Pantheon Books, 1983), xvii; Scott Borchert, *Republic of Detours: How the New Deal Paid Broke Writers to Rediscover America* (New York: Farrar, Straus and Giroux, 2021), 115.

21. Drew, *Nelson Algren*, 116; Franklin Folsom, *Days of Anger, Days of Hope: A Memoir of the League of American Writers 1937–1942* (Niwot: University Press of Colorado, 1994), 333; Donald Ogden Stewart, ed., *Fighting Words* (New York: Harcourt, Brace, 1940), 7–11; Mangione, *The Dream and the Deal*, 270.

22. Stewart, *Fighting Words*, 11; Sara Rutkowski, "Nelson Algren's *Personalism*: The Influence of the Federal Writers' Project," *Studies in American Naturalism* 9, no. 2 (Winter 2014): 205, 222.

23. Stewart, *Fighting Words*, 13–14.

24. Stewart, *Fighting Words*, 7, 11; see also Mangione, *The Dream and the Deal*, 270–73; B.A. Botkin, "We Called It 'Living Lore,'" *New York Folklore Quarterly* 14, no. 3 (Autumn 1958): 199; reprint, "We Called It 'Living Lore,'" *Voices* 27, no. 3–4 (Fall–Winter 2001): 19. (The subsequent page reference is to the reprint edition.)

25. Stewart, *Fighting Words*, 9; Botkin, "We Called It 'Living Lore,'" *Voices*, 19.

26. Folsum, *Days of Anger, Days of Hope*, 333; Drew, *Nelson Algren*, 105; Bessie Jaffey, "Staff Conference in Industrial Folklore," 13 July 1939, *Folklore Project, Life Histories 1936–1939*, Box A707, Records of the United States Work Projects Administration, Manuscript Division, Library of Congress, Washington, D.C., 1.

27. William F. McDonald, *Federal Relief Administration and the Arts* ([Columbus]: Ohio State University Press, 1969), 715; Jaffey, "Staff Conference in Industrial Folklore," 1. For a general discussion of the "Living Lore Unit" of the New York City Writers' Project, see B.A. Botkin, "Living Lore on the New York City Writers' Project," *New York Folklore Quarterly* 2, no. 4 (November 1946): 252–263.

28. The quoted material from the transcript is very lightly edited.

29. Jaffey, "Staff Conference in Industrial Folklore," 1.

30. Jaffey, "Staff Conference in Industrial Folklore," 1.

31. Jaffey, "Staff Conference in Industrial Folklore," 1.

32. Rutkowski, "Nelson Algren's Personalism," 205, 222; Jaffey, "Staff Conference in Industrial Folklore," 2.

33. Horvath, *Understanding Nelson Algren*, 35.

34. Nelson Algren, "Home and Goodnight," *Poetry*, November 1939, 74.

35. Drew, *Nelson Algren*, 85–86.

36. Drew, *Nelson Algren*, 110, 385; Nelson Algren, "When You Live Like I Done," 17 July 1939, *Folklore Project, Life Histories 1936–1939*, Box A707, Records of the United States Work Projects Administration, Manuscript Division, Library of Congress, Washington, D.C.; Rutkowski, "Nelson Algren's Personalism," 207–08. Algren's interview is reprinted in Ann Banks' book, *First-Person America*. Banks writes that the prostitute's name was Ellen O'Connor. See Ann Banks, *First-Person America* (New York: Alfred A. Knopf, 1980), 177–80; see also Borchert, *Republic of Detours*, 144. It is assumed that the interview was had on July 17, 1939, because the transcript of the interview on file in the Library of Congress is date stamped "JUL 17 1939."

37. Bob Hughes, "The '26' Game and Its Girls Finally Run Out of Luck," *Chicago Tribune Magazine*, 16 March 1986, 10. When Algren was working for the Illinois Writers' Project, he would stay out late playing "26." See Drew, *Nelson Algren*, 111.

38. Algren, "When You Live Like I Done," 2.

39. Algren, "When You Live Like I Done," 6.

40. Algren, "Home and Goodnight," 75.

41. Algren, "Home and Goodnight," 74.

42. Cox and Chatterton, *Nelson Algren*, 133, 147n26. "Home and Goodnight" has been reprinted; see Algren, *Entrapment*, 55–56.

43. Horvath, *Understanding Nelson Algren*, 35.

44. Nelson Algren, "Travelog," *Poetry*, November 1939, 76. Algren incorporates portions of this poem in his short story, "Kingdom City to Cairo." See Nelson Algren, "Kingdom City to Cairo," in *The Neon Wilderness* (New York: Seven Stories Press, 1986), 184. "Travelog" has been reprinted; see Algren, *Entrapment*, 57–58.

45. Nelson Algren, "This Table on Time Only," *Esquire*, March 1940, 78. The ellipses in the text are in the original.

46. Algren, "This Table on Time Only," 79. The "el" is Chicago's elevated rapid transit system. See Grossman, Keating, and Reiff, *The Encyclopedia of Chicago*, s.v. "L." On October 12, 1939, Algren wrote Mr. Norman Corwin of the Columbia Broadcasting System, thanking Corwin for allowing him to use Corwin's name as a reference in an attempt to obtain a Guggenheim award. Algren then added, "I'm enclosing a modification of a poem, now in your hands, called Tag-Dance. This modification I've sold to *Esquire*." The poem bears the title, "This Table on Time Only." However, Algren has written along the top of the page, "Revision of 'Tag-Dance.'" The poem sent to Corwin is just slightly different from the poem that appears in *Esquire*. Furthermore, the differences are inconsequential, even meaningless. In the *Esquire* version, the killers abduct their victim from the Cherry Gardens nightclub, where Jerry Johnson's Royal Swingsters are playing a song. In the version sent to Corwin, the man is at the Merry Gardens nightclub, and Guy Lombardo's Royal Canadians are playing. See Nelson Algren to Norman Corwin, 12 October 1939, author's collection. The *Esquire* version of "This Table on Time Only" has been reprinted; see Algren, *Entrapment*, 58–60.

47. Elijah Wald, *Escaping the Delta: Robert Johnson and the Invention of the Blues* (New York: Amistad, 2005), 36. Algren would often refer to songs in his writing. For example, in

his short story, "A Holiday in Texas," he quotes lyrics from "Dreary Black Hills"; "Halle-lujah, I'm a Bum"; "Old Chisholm Trail"; and "The Comintern," which is the Communist anthem. The copyright page of *The Man with the Golden Arm* contains twenty-one lines of copyright information relating to the lyrics of the many songs he quotes in the book. See Horvath, *Understanding Nelson Algren*, 16–17, 161n7; Nelson Algren, *The Man with the Golden Arm*, eds. William J. Savage Jr., and Daniel Simon, 50th Anniversary Critical Edi-tion (New York: Seven Stories Press, [1999]), [iv].

48. Nelson Algren, "How Long Blues," *Poetry*, September 1941, 309; Horvath, *Under-standing Nelson Algren*, 34–35.

49. Horvath, *Understanding Nelson Algren*, 34.

50. Nelson Algren, "Local South," *Poetry*, September 1941, 308; Horvath, *Understand-ing Nelson Algren*, 34–35. "Local South" has been reprinted; see Nelson Algren, "Local South," in *Encore*, February 1942, 75; Nelson Algren, "Local South," in *Entrapment*, 60–61.

51. "The Swede Was a Hard Guy" was revised and published as "Ballet for Opening Day" in *The Last Carousel*. See Nelson Algren, "Ballet for Opening Day" in *The Last Carousel* (New York: Seven Stories Press, 1997), 268–98.

52. Nelson Algren, "The Swede Was a Hard Guy," *Southern Review*, Spring 1942, 874. "The Swede Was a Hard Guy" was reprinted in *Chicago* magazine. See Nelson Algren, "The Swede Was a Hard Guy," *Chicago*, June 1956, 30–34.

53. Nelson Algren, "Epitaph: The Man with the Golden Arm," *Poetry*, September 1947, 316; Nelson Algren, "Epitaph: The Man with the Golden Arm," *The Man with the Golden Arm*, [341]. "Epitaph" was also reprinted in *The Last Carousel*. See Algren, "Epitaph," in *The Last Carousel*, 225.

54. Beauvoir, *A Transatlantic Love Affair*, dust jacket, 9–10, 546.

55. Nelson Algren, "The Bride Below the Black Coiffure," *Rogue*, July 1961, 30.

56. Nelson Algren, "They're Hiding the Ham on the Pinball King," in *Algren at Sea*, 77–78. A version of this article, but without the poem, was reprinted; see Nelson Algren, "They're Hiding the Ham on the Pinball King, or, Some Came Stumbling," *Contact*, Sep-tember 1961, [101]–11. Algren is described in this issue of *Contact* as a contributing editor.

57. Malcolm Cowley, ed., "Nelson Algren," in *Writers at Work: The "Paris Review" Inter-views* (N.Y.: The Viking Press, 1958), 233, 246.

58. Algren, "Afternoon in the Land of the Strange Light Sleep," 25.

59. "Afternoon in the Land of the Strange Light Sleep" has been reprinted; see Algren, *Entrapment*, 215–18.

60. Nelson Algren, "Tricks Out of Times Long Gone," *The Nation*, 22 September 1962, 162; Bruccoli, *Nelson Algren*, 36, 112–16, 119.

61. Algren, "Tricks Out of Times Long Gone," *The Nation*, 162. In 1959 the *Chicago Sun-Times* hired Algren to write about the World Series. In his last and final article, Algren wrote: "I have seen the hep-ghosts of the rain before. I know who they are. They are ghosts of old-time buskers and long-gone hustlers that have been left here and there around town for haunting of bars and ball parks, to play make-believe World Series there after the squares have gone home." Algren recycled this paragraph of his article into the sec-ond stanza of "Tricks Out of Times Long Gone": "I think hep-people leave small ghosts behind/For haunting of winter ball parks and locked bars/That ghosts of oldtime hook-ers walk once more/That no ghost follows where a square has gone." See Algren, "Tricks Out of Times Long Gone," *The Nation*, 162; Nelson Algren, "Nelson Algren's Reflections: Hep-Ghosts of the Rain," *Chicago Sun-Times*, final home edition, 10 October 1959, 12. This article also appears in the "final edition" of the October 10, 1959, *Sun-Times*, but with a different title. See Nelson Algren, "Algren at Game 6: Shoeless Joe is Gone, Too," *Chicago Sun-Times*, final edition, 10 October 1959, sec. 2, 12.

62. Nelson Algren, *Epilogue*, in *Algren at Sea*, 267–68; Nelson Algren, "Tricks Out of Times Long Gone," in *The Last Carousel*, 429–35; Nelson Algren, *Chicago: City on the Make*, 3rd ed. (Oakland, Calif.: Angel Island Publications, [1968]), 146–48; Joe Pintauro, "Algren in Exile," *Chicago*, February 1988, 162.

63. Drew, *Nelson Algren*, 177–86, 204, 220–22, 232–33; Beauvoir, *A Transatlantic Love Affair*, 9, 11, 14, 434; Seymour-Jones, *A Dangerous Liaison*, 344–45, 354–55; Hazel Rowley,

Tête-à-Tête: Simone de Beauvoir and Jean-Paul Sartre (New York: HarperCollins, 2005), 198; Simone de Beauvoir, *America Day by Day* (Berkeley: University of California Press, 1999), xvii, 3, 94–96. Lake County, Indiana, land records indicate that Algren purchased this house on Forrest Avenue in Miller Beach in 1950. Algren was burdened by financial difficulties in the late 1950s, and he sold the home to his friend Dave Peltz in 1957. Algren was heavily in debt, and he received no money from the sale. See Art Shay, *Nelson Algren's Chicago* (Urbana: University of Illinois Press, 1988), xvi; "Save Novelist from Lagoon as Ice Breaks," *Chicago Daily Tribune*, 1 January 1957, pt. 1, 4; Lake County, Indiana, land records; Linda Simon and Jane Ammeson, *Images of America: Miller Beach* (Charleston, S.C.: Arcadia Publishing, 2012) 6, 7; Drew, *Nelson Algren*, 284–85, 295.

    64. Seymour-Jones, *A Dangerous Liaison*, 3–4, 68–69, 87–89; Bair, *Simone de Beauvoir*, 155–58; Drew, *Nelson Algren*, 207, 322; Serge Julienne-Caffié, "Variations on Triangular Relationships," in *Contingent Loves: Simone de Beauvoir and Sexuality*, ed. Melanie C. Hawthorne (Charlottesville: University Press of Virginia, 2000), 34.

    65. Bair, *Simone de Beauvoir*, 500–01.

    66. Simone de Beauvoir, *Force of Circumstance*, trans. Richard Howard (New York: G.P. Putnam's Sons, 1964), 250–51. Algren's letter to Beauvoir also appears in Drew, *Nelson Algren*, 234, and Bair, *Simone de Beauvoir*, 431. See also Beauvoir, *A Transatlantic Love Affair*, 442–46 passim.

    67. Beauvoir, *A Transatlantic Love Affair*, 478, 521, 526–27; Drew, *Nelson Algren*, 244–45; Mary Wisniewski, *Algren: A Life* (Chicago: Chicago Review Press, 2017), 240.

    68. Drew, *Nelson Algren*, 309–11; Bruccoli, *Nelson Algren*, 119.

    69. Drew, *Nelson Algren*, 308–311; Bair, *Simone de Beauvoir*, 479–482; Beauvoir, *A Transatlantic Love Affair*, 531–538.

    70. Algren, "Tricks Out of Times Long Gone," *The Nation*, 162.

    71. Elaine Marks, *Simone de Beauvoir: Encounters with Death* (New Brunswick, N.J.: Rutgers University Press, 1973), 36–37, 45–55; Deborah MacKeefe, "Zaza Mabille: Mission and Motive in Simone de Beauvoir's '*Mémoires*,'" *Contemporary Literature* 24, no. 2 (Summer 1983): 204, 217; Carol Ascher, *Simone de Beauvoir: A Life of Freedom* (Boston: Beacon Press, 1981), 186; Jean Leighton, *Simone de Beauvoir on Women* (Rutherford, N.J.: Fairleigh Dickinson University Press, 1975), 199.

    72. Beauvoir, *A Transatlantic Love Affair*, 9, 11.

    73. Beauvoir, *A Transatlantic Love Affair*, 527. On the other hand, is the reference to "za-za" in "Tricks Out of Times Long Gone" only just a coincidence? After all, *The Last Carousel* (1973), Algren's collection of short stories, articles, and poetry, was published nine years after Algren broke off his relationship with Beauvoir, yet he nonetheless refers to "za-za" in three of its stories. If "za-za" was truly a reference to Beauvoir's friend, why would Algren mention her in *The Last Carousel*, a post-Beauvoir book? No one knows the answer to that question, but there is precedent for Algren calmly referring to Beauvoir after their 1964 breakup. He wrote a diatribe-free article about John Paul Sartre and Beauvoir for the December 1980 issue of *Chicago* magazine. See Nelson Algren, "The Ryebread Trees of Spring," in *The Last Carousel*, 253; Nelson Algren, "The Moon of the Arfy Darfy," in *The Last Carousel*, 358–59; Nelson Algren, "Watch Out for Daddy," in *The Last Carousel*, 388–90; Beauvoir, *A Transatlantic Love Affair*, 10; Nelson Algren, "Last Rounds in Small Cafés: Remembrances of Jean-Paul Sartre and Simone de Beauvoir," *Chicago*, December 1980, 210–13, 237–38, 240.

    74. Drew, *Nelson Algren*, 284–85, 288, 291; [Irv Kupcinet], "Kup's Column," *Chicago Sun-Times*, 15 March 1959, 60.

    75. "A Note on Our Contributors," *Zeitgeist*, 94. For another example of a memorable contribution to a university magazine, see Nelson Algren, "Seven Feet Down and Creeping," *The New Orleans Review* 2, no. 1 (1970): 3–5.

    76. Simone de Beauvoir, "The Question of Fidelity," *Harper's Magazine*, November 1964, 57–64; Simone de Beauvoir, "An American Rendezvous: The Question of Fidelity, Part II," *Harper's Magazine*, December 1964, 111–14, 116, 119–20, 122; Nelson Algren, "Goodbye Lilies Hello Spring," *Zeitgeist* 1, no. 4 (Summer 1966): 50–51; "A Note on Our Contributors," *Zeitgeist*, 94.

77. Beauvoir, "The Question of Fidelity," 64; Beauvoir, *Force of Circumstance*, 124.
78. Beauvoir, "The Question of Fidelity," 64; Beauvoir, *Force of Circumstance*, 124.
79. Beauvoir, "The Question of Fidelity," 64; Beauvoir, *Force of Circumstance*, 125.
80. Beauvoir, "The Question of Fidelity," 64; Beauvoir, *Force of Circumstance*, 125.
81. Beauvoir, *Force of Circumstance*, 125; Drew, *Nelson Algren*, 322–23; Rowley, *Tête-à-Tête*, 301; Bair, *Simone de Beauvoir*, 419, 500; Seymour-Jones, *A Dangerous Liaison*, 458–59; Horvath, *Understanding Nelson Algren*, 159n18; W.J. Weatherby, "The Last Interview," in *The Devil's Stocking*, by Nelson Algren (New York: Arbor House Publishing, 1983), 10–11; "I Ain't Abelard," *Newsweek*, 28 December 1964, 59. In "The Last Interview" Algren refers to *Force of Circumstance* as *The Prime of Life*. This is incorrect; *The Prime of Life* was Beauvoir's 1960 autobiography. See Weatherby, "The Last Interview," 10.
82. Bair, *Simone de Beauvoir*, 500; "I Ain't Abelard," 59; Nelson Algren, "The Question of Simone de Beauvoir," review of *Force of Circumstance*, by Simone de Beauvoir, *Harper's Magazine*, May 1965, 136; Nelson Algren, "Simone à Go Go," review of *Force of Circumstance*, by Simone de Beauvoir, *Ramparts*, October 1965, 66; "The Smell of It," *Time*, 11 October 1963, 28.
83. Algren, "Goodbye Lilies Hello Spring," 50–51; see also Rowley, *Tête-à-Tête*, 304–05. This poem is not listed in Bruccoli's bibliography, and it is reprinted courtesy of Bernice S. Behar and the estate of Nelson Algren. Algren and Beauvoir must have joked in the past about her apparent excessive talking. In a letter dated March 17, 1948, she told him that the dentist was working on her jaw, and that "I think I'll be able to move it twice as quick as I used to do." She then added, "I am sure you'll appreciate it." On November 22, 1948, she wrote Algren of a newspaper asking her an abstract question. Rather than attempt to answer it, she admitted that "I gave my jaw a rest, as you say." See Beauvoir, *A Transatlantic Love Affair*, 183, 239. Algren ends his *Harper's* book review of *Force of Circumstance* with the italicized question, "*Will she ever quit talking?*" See Algren, "The Question of Simone de Beauvoir," 136. William Brevda claims that "in the real dark night of the soul," Algren turned his back on Beauvoir because he felt she had turned her back on him. See William Brevda, "The Rainbow Sign of Nelson Algren," *Texas Studies in Literature and Language* 44, no. 4 (Winter 2002): 408. See also William Brevda, *Signs of the Signs: The Literary Lights of Incandescence and Neon* (Lewisburg, Pa.: Bucknell University Press, 2011), 225.
Algren refers to "Colette" in this poem. He knew that Beauvoir admired the French author Colette, née Sidonie-Gabrielle Colette. On March 6, 1948, she wrote Algren: "I think you heard of Colette: she is the only really great woman writer in France, a really great writer." Ironically, Algren admired her as well. When Algren was researching the Rubin "Hurricane" Carter case, he gave author Linda Kay a typed reading list of twenty-four recommended books. Using a black marker, he wrote an additional item on the sheet of paper: "Everything by Colette." See Beauvoir, *A Transatlantic Love Affair*, 178, 180; Bair, *Simone de Beauvoir*, 90; Linda Kay, *The Reading List* (Lanham, Md.: 2005), 27–28; Elizabeth Richardson Viti, "Colette's Renée Néré: Simone de Beauvoir's Existential Heroine?," *French Forum* 21, no. 1 (1996): 79; Judith Thurman, *Secrets of the Flesh: A Life of Colette* (New York: Alfred A. Knopf, 1999), xii–xiii.
84. Bruccoli, *Nelson Algren*, 119.
85. Nelson Algren, "The Dye That Did Not Run," *The Nation*, 18 November 1961, 387–90; Drew, *Nelson Algren*, 314–15, 400; Asher, *Never a Lovely So Real*, 395, 398–401; Donohue, *Conversations with Nelson Algren*, 281.
86. Nelson Algren, "Hemingway All the Way," *Cavalier*, February 1965, 30–31; Asher, *Never a Lovely So Real*, 402, 417–19. It appears that Algren was promoting this Hemingway book as late as 1964. Algren reviewed a book by Hemingway for the June 1, 1964, issue of *The Nation* magazine. At the end of the review there is the comment, "Nelson Algren is presently writing a study of Hemingway to be published by G.P. Putnam's." A December 1964 *Newsweek* article about Algren and Simone de Beauvoir describes him as "currently working on a book about Hemingway." See "I Ain't Abelard," 59; Nelson Algren, "Who's Who at the Lost & Found," review of *A Moveable Feast*, by Ernest Hemingway, *The Nation*, 1 June 1964, 561.

87. Nelson Algren, "Nobody Knows," *Saturday Review*, 3 September 1966, 15; Nelson Algren, "The Quais of Calcutta," in *Algren at Sea*, 425–26. Perhaps *Saturday Review* added "Nobody Knows" as a last-minute space filler; the poem is not listed in the "Table of Contents" page of the magazine. See [Table of Contents], *Saturday Review*, 3 September 1966, 2.

88. Algren, "Nobody Knows," 15.

89. Nelson Algren, "The Cockeyed Hooker of Bugis Street," *Lillabulero* 1, no. 1 (Winter 1967): 24; Nelson Algren, "July 1st: 472 Cho-Ryang-Dong: A Parlor Once Purple Now Faded to Rose," in *Algren at Sea*, 299–308.

90. Nelson Algren, "The Country of Kai-Li," *Lillabulero* 1, no. 1 (Winter 1967): 24–25.

91. Adam Cohen and Elizabeth Taylor, *American Pharaoh: Mayor Richard J. Daley: His Battle for Chicago and the Nation* (Boston: Little, Brown, 2000), 447–51, 469–76.

92. Cohen and Taylor, *American Pharaoh*, 460.

93. Cohen and Taylor, *American Pharaoh*, 446, 471–81; Mike Royko, *Boss: Richard J. Daley of Chicago* (New York: E.P. Dutton, 1971), 181–87; Norman Mailer, *Miami and the Siege of Chicago: An Informal History of the Republican and Democratic Conventions of 1968* (New York: World Publishing, 1968), 166–73; Daniel Walker, *Rights in Conflict: Convention Week in Chicago August 25–29, 1968* (New York: E.P. Dutton, 1968), 1–11, 138–60.

94. Donald Myrus, ed., *Law & Disorder: The Chicago Convention and Its Aftermath* (Chicago: Privately printed, 1968), [1–2].

95. Drew, *Nelson Algren*, 334–35; Myrus, *Law & Disorder*, [2].

96. Nelson Algren, "City on the Make," in Myrus, *Law & Disorder*, [10–11]; Nelson Algren, *Chicago: City on the Make* (Sausalito, Calif.: Contact Editions, 1961), 9–11, 14, 16–17, 34–35, 44–45, 92–93, 95–96, 102–03, 112–13. Algren's 1968 untitled prose poem appears in *Law & Disorder* at the end of excerpts from Algren's prose poem, *Chicago: City on the Make*.

97. Algren, "City on the Make," in Myrus, *Law & Disorder*, [11].

98. Algren, *Chicago: City on the Make*, 3rd ed. [1968], [4], 122–23, 133–34; Bruccoli, *Nelson Algren*, 39.

99. Algren, "City on the Make," in Myrus, *Law & Disorder*, [11].

100. [Table of Contents], *Saturday Review*, 3 September 1966, 2.

101. Nelson Algren, "An Absconding Bookie and Four Other Poems," *Chicago Tribune Magazine*, 8 October 1972, 28–31. The title poem is actually called, "Ode to an Absconding Bookie."

102. Nelson Algren, "The Cockeyed Hooker of Bugis Street," *Chicago Tribune Magazine*, 8 October 1972, 30; Drew, *Nelson Algren*, 313–15; Asher, *Never a Lovely So Real*, 395, 398, 401–02.

103. Nelson Algren, *Chicago: City on the Make*, 2011, 72–73.

104. Algren, "The Cockeyed Hooker of Bugis Street," *Chicago Tribune Magazine*, 30.

105. Nelson Algren, "The Country of Kai-Li," *Chicago Tribune Magazine*, 8 October 1972, 29.

106. Nelson Algren, "It Don't Matter How You Spell It," *Chicago Tribune Magazine*, 8 October 1972, 30. Algren expresses a similar thought in his 1960 article, "Mafia of the Heart": "A hundred tents on the open prairie with one man's voice to be its conscience, would be a place more enduring than one with a double-tiered causeway making the longest right-hand turn into the highest skyscraper on the earth of Man." Nelson Algren, "Mafia of the Heart," *Contact*, October 1960, 15. See also his article, "Chicago III": "We have had men and women who knew that a city of a hundred tents, owning the voice of single man speaking for the conscience of those hundred tents, is a city more enduring than that which we are now building." Nelson Algren, "Chicago III: If I Can't Sell It I'll Keep Settin' on It; I Jest Won't Give It Away (Old Song)," in *Algren at Sea*, 226.

107. Nelson Algren, "Gentlemen: The Law is Present," *Chicago Tribune Magazine*, 8 October 1972, 29; Nelson Algren, *Never Come Morning* (New York: Seven Stories Press, 1996), 135–52; Algren, *The Man with the Golden Arm*, 185–97.

108. Nelson Algren, "Ode to an Absconding Bookie," *Chicago Tribune Magazine*, 8 October 1972, 31.

109. Nelson Algren, "Ode to an Absconding Bookie," in *The Last Carousel*, 311–13.

SELECTED BIBLIOGRAPHY

Algren, Nelson. "Afternoon in the Land of the Strange Light Sleep." *Cavalier*, September 1962, 24–25, 27.

Algren, Nelson. "Algren at Game 6: Shoeless Joe Is Gone, Too." *Chicago Sun-Times*, final edition, 10 October 1959, sec. 2, 12.

Algren, Nelson. *Algren at Sea: Who Lost an American? & Notes from a Sea Diary—Travel Writings*. New York: Seven Stories Press, 2008.

Algren, Nelson. "The Bride Below the Black Coiffure." *Rogue*, July 1961, 30–31.

Algren, Nelson. *Chicago: City on the Make*. Sausalito, Calif.: Contact Editions, 1961.

Algren, Nelson. *Chicago: City on the Make*. 3rd ed. Oakland, Calif.: Angel Island Publications, [1968].

Algren, Nelson. *Chicago: City on the Make*. New York: McGraw-Hill, 1983.

Algren, Nelson. *Chicago: City on the Make*, 60th Anniversary Edition. Chicago: University of Chicago Press, 2011.

Algren, Nelson. "City on the Make." In *Law & Disorder: The Chicago Convention and Its Aftermath*, ed. Donald Myrus (Chicago: Privately printed, 1968), [11].

Algren, Nelson. "The Cockeyed Hooker of Bugis Street." *Chicago Tribune Magazine*, 8 October 1972, 30.

Algren, Nelson. "The Cockeyed Hooker of Bugis Street." *Lillabulero* 1, no. 1 (Winter 1967): 24.

Algren, Nelson. "The Country of Kai-Li." *Chicago Tribune Magazine*, 8 October 1972, 29.

Algren, Nelson. "The Country of Kai-Li." *Lillabulero* 1, no. 1 (Winter 1967): 24–25.

Algren, Nelson. "The Dye That Did Not Run." *The Nation*, 18 November 1961, 387–90.

Algren, Nelson. *Entrapment and other Writings*. Edited by Brooke Horvath and Dan Simon. New York: Seven Stories Press, 2009.

Algren, Nelson. "Epitaph: The Man with the Golden Arm." *Poetry*, September 1947, 316–17.

Algren, Nelson. "Gentlemen: The Law is Present." *Chicago Tribune Magazine*, 8 October 1972, 29.

Algren, Nelson. "Goodbye Lilies Hello Spring." *Zeitgeist* 1, no. 4 (Summer 1966): 50–51.

Algren, Nelson. "Hemingway All the Way." *Cavalier*, February 1965, 30–31.

Algren, Nelson, to Herm[an Kogan], 26 December [1961], photocopy, author's collection.

Algren, Nelson. "Home and Goodnight." *Poetry*, November 1939, 74–76.

Algren, Nelson. "How Long Blues." *Poetry*, September 1941, 309.

Algren, Nelson. "It Don't Matter How You Spell It." *Chicago Tribune Magazine*, 8 October 1972, 30.

Algren, Nelson, to Ken McCollum, 30 July 1972, photocopy, author's collection.

Algren, Nelson. "Kingdom City to Cairo." In *The Neon Wilderness*, 179–87. New York: Seven Stories Press, 1986.

Algren, Nelson. *The Last Carousel*. New York: Seven Stories Press, 1997.

Algren, Nelson. "Last Rounds in Small Cafés: Remembrances of Jean-Paul Sartre and Simone de Beauvoir." *Chicago*, December 1980, 210–13, 237–38, 240.

Algren, Nelson. "Local South." *Encore*, February 1942, 75.

Algren, Nelson. "Local South." *Poetry*, September 1941, 308–09.

Algren, Nelson. "Mafia of the Heart." *Contact*, October 1960, [9], 11–15.

Algren, Nelson. "Makers of Music." *The New Anvil*, March 1939, 23.

Algren, Nelson. *The Man with the Golden Arm*, edited by William J. Savage, Jr., and Daniel Simon. 50th Anniversary Critical Edition. New York: Seven Stories Press, [1999].

Algren, Nelson. "Modern India Comes Alive in a Burst of Surrealism." Review of *Midnight's Children*, by Salman Rushdie. *Chicago Tribune Book World*, 26 April 1981, 7, 3.

Algren, Nelson. "Nelson Algren's Reflections: Hep-Ghosts of the Rain." *Chicago Sun-Times*, final home edition, 10 October 1959, 12.

Algren, Nelson. *Never Come Morning*. New York: Seven Stories Press, 1996.

Algren, Nelson. "Nobody Knows." *Saturday Review*, 3 September 1966, 15.

Algren, Nelson. "Ode to an Absconding Bookie." *Chicago Tribune Magazine*, 8 October 1972, 31.

Algren, Nelson. "Program for Appeasement." *The New Anvil*, June–July 1939, 12.

Algren, Nelson. "The Question of Simone de Beauvoir." Review of *Force of Circumstance*, by Simone de Beauvoir. *Harper's Magazine*, May 1965, 134, 136.

Algren, Nelson. "Simone à Go Go." Review of *Force of Circumstance*, by Simone de Beauvoir. *Ramparts*, October 1965, 65–67.

Algren, Nelson. "The Swede Was a Hard Guy." *Southern Review*, Spring 1942, 873–79.

Algren, Nelson. "They're Hiding the Ham on the Pinball King, or, Some Came Stumbling." *Contact*, September 1961, [101]-11.

Algren, Nelson. "This Table on Time Only." *Esquire*, March 1940, 78–79.

Algren, Nelson. "Travelog." *Poetry*, November 1939, 76–77.

Algren, Nelson. "Tricks Out of Times Long Gone." *The Nation*, 22 September 1962, 162.

[Algren, Nelson.] "Utility Magnate." *The New Anvil*, April–May 1939, 16–17.

Algren, Nelson. "When You Live Like I Done." 17 July 1939, *Folklore Project, Life Histories 1936–1939*, Box A707, Records of the United States Work Projects Administration, Manuscript Division, Library of Congress, Washington, D.C.

Algren, Nelson. "Who's Who at the Lost & Found." Review of *A Moveable Feast*, by Ernest Hemingway. *The Nation*, 1 June 1964, 560–61.

Asher, Colin. *Never a Lovely So Real: The Life and Work of Nelson Algren*. New York: W.W. Norton, 2019.

Bair, Deirdre. *Simone de Beauvoir: A Biography*. New York: Summit Books, 1990.

Banks, Ann. *First-Person America*. New York: Alfred A. Knopf, 1980.

Beauvoir, Simone de. *America Day by Day*. Berkeley: University of California Press, 1999.

Beauvoir, Simone de. "An American Rendezvous: The Question of Fidelity, Part II." *Harper's Magazine*, December 1964, 111–14, 116, 119–20, 122.

Beauvoir, Simone de. "The Question of Fidelity." *Harper's Magazine*, November 1964, 57–64.

Beauvoir, Simone de. *A Transatlantic Love Affair: Letters to Nelson Algren*. Comp. and annot. By Sylvie Le Bon de Beauvoir. New York: New Press, 1998.

Beauvoir, Simone de. *Force of Circumstance*. Translated by Richard Howard. New York: G.P. Putnam's Sons, 1964.

Bonansinga, Jay. *The Sinking of the Eastland: America's Forgotten Tragedy*. New York: Citadel Press, 2004.

Bondi, Victor, ed. *American Decades 1930–1939*. Detroit: Gale, 1995.

Borchert, Scott. *Republic of Detours: How the New Deal Paid Broke Writers to Rediscover America*. New York: Farrar, Straus and Giroux, 2021.

Botkin, B.A. "Living Lore on the New York City Writers' Project." *New York Folklore Quarterly* 2, no. 4 (November 1946): 252–63.

Botkin, B.A. "We Called It 'Living Lore.'" *New York Folklore Quarterly* 14, no. 3 (Autumn 1958): 189–201.

Botkin, B.A. "We Called It 'Living Lore.'" *Voices* 27, no. 3–4 (Fall-Winter 2001): 16–19.

Brendon, Piers. *The Dark Valley: A Panorama of the 1930s*. London: Jonathan Cape, 2000.

Brevda, William. *Signs of the Times: The Literary Lights of Incandescence and Neon*. Lewisburg, Pa.: Bucknell University Press, 2011.

Brevda, William. "The Rainbow Sign of Nelson Algren." *Texas Studies in Literature and Language* 44, no. 4 (Winter 2002): 393–413.

Bruccoli, Matthew J. *Nelson Algren: A Descriptive Bibliography*. Pittsburgh: University of Pittsburgh Press, 1985.

Chielens, Edward E. ed. *American Literary Magazines: The Twentieth Century*. Westport, Conn.: Greenwood Press, 1992.

Cohen, Adam, and Elizabeth Taylor. *American Pharaoh: Mayor Richard J. Daley: His Battle for Chicago and the Nation*. Boston: Little, Brown, 2000.

Conroy, Jack, and Curt Johnson, eds. *Writers in Revolt: The Anvil Anthology*. New York: Lawrence Hill, 1973.

Cowley, Malcolm, ed. "Nelson Algren." In *Writers at Work: The "Paris Review" Interviews*. N.Y.: The Viking Press, 1958, 233–49.

Cox, Martha Heasley, and Wayne Chatterton. *Nelson Algren*. Boston: Twayne, 1975.

Dedmon, Emmett. *Fabulous Chicago*. New York: Random House, 1953.

Dennis, Michael. *The Memorial Day Massacre and the Movement for Industrial Democracy*. Palgrave Macmillan, 2010.

Donohue, H.E.F. *Conversations with Nelson Algren*. New York: Hill and Wang, 1964.

Drew, Bettina. *Nelson Algren: A Life on the Wild Side*. Austin: University of Texas Press, 1991.

Durica, Paul. "Back Page." *Poetry*, September 2012, [519].

Folsom, Franklin. *Days of Anger, Days of Hope: A Memoir of the League of American Writers 1937–1942*. Niwot: University Press of Colorado, 1994.

Grossman, James R., Ann Durkin Keating, and Janice L. Reiff, eds. *The Encyclopedia of Chicago*. Chicago: University of Chicago Press, 2004.

Grossman, Ron. "Republic Steel: Riot or Massacre?" In *Chicago Flashback: The People and Events That Shaped a City's History*, [224]-227. Chicago: Midway Books, 2017.

Herman, Jan. "Nelson Algren: The Angry Author." *Chicago Sun-Times Chicagostyle*. 21 January 1979, 8–11.

Hilton, George W. *Eastland: Legacy of the Titanic*. Stanford, Calif.: Stanford University Press, 1995

Horvath, Brooke. *Understanding Nelson Algren*. Columbia: University of South Carolina Press, 2005.

Hughes, Bob. "The '26' Game and Its Girls Finally Run Out of Luck." *Chicago Tribune Magazine*, 16 March 1986, 10.

"I Ain't Abelard." *Newsweek*, 28 December 1964, 58–59.

Jaffey, Bessie. "Staff Conference in Industrial Folklore," 13 July 1939, *Folklore Project, Life Histories 1936–1939*, Box A707, Records of the United States Work Projects Administration, Manuscript Division, Library of Congress, Washington, D.C.

Kay, Linda. *The Reading List*. Lanham, Md.: Hamilton Books, 2005.

Kisor, Henry. "Nelson Algren, Hale and Salty at 64." *Chicago Daily News Panorama*, 27–28 October 1973, 2–3.

[Kupcinet, Irv]. "Kup's Column." *Chicago Sun-Times*, 15 March 1959, 60.

Mailer, Norman. *Miami and the Siege of Chicago: An Informal History of the Republican and Democratic Conventions of 1968*. New York: World Publishing, 1968.

Mangione, Jerre. *The Dream and the Deal: The Federal Writers' Project 1935–1943*. Boston: Little Brown, 1972.

McCollum, Kenneth G. *Nelson Algren: A Checklist*. Detroit: Gale Research Co., 1973.

McDonald, Forrest. *Insull*. Chicago: University of Chicago Press, 1962.

McDonald, William F. *Federal Relief Administration and the Arts*. [Columbus]: Ohio State University Press, 1969.

Myrus, Donald, ed. *Law & Disorder: The Chicago Convention and Its Aftermath*. Chicago: Privately printed, 1968.

O'Fallon, Laurence. [Algren, Nelson.] "Utility Magnate." *The New Anvil*, April–May 1939, 16–17.

Payne, Stanley G. *A History of Fascism, 1914–1945*. Madison: University of Wisconsin Press, 1995.

Pintauro, Joe. "Algren in Exile." *Chicago*, February 1988, 92–101, 156–63.

Rowley, Hazel. *Tête-à-Tête: Simone de Beauvoir and Jean-Paul Sartre*. New York: HarperCollins, 2005

Royko, Mike. *Boss: Richard J. Daley of Chicago*. New York: E.P. Dutton, 1971.

Rutkowski, Sara. "Nelson Algren's Personalism: The Influence of the Federal Writers' Project." *Studies in American Naturalism* 9, no. 2 (Winter 2014): 198–223.

"Save Novelist from Lagoon as Ice Breaks." *Chicago Daily Tribune*, 1 January 1957, pt. 1, 4.

Seymour-Jones, Carole. *A Dangerous Liaison: Simone de Beauvoir and Jean-Paul Sartre*. London: Century, 2008.

Shay, Art. *Nelson Algren's Chicago*. Urbana: University of Illinois Press, 1988.

Simon, Linda, and Jane Ammeson. *Images of America: Miller Beach*. Charleston, S.C.: Arcadia Publishing, 2012.

"The Smell of It." *Time*, 11 October 1963, 28.

Sofchalk, Donald G. "The Chicago Memorial Day Incident: An Episode of Mass Action." *Labor History* 6, no. 1 (Winter 1965): 3–43.

Stewart, Donald Ogden, ed. *Fighting Words*. New York: Harcourt, Brace, 1940.

Studing, Richard. "A Nelson Algren Checklist." *Twentieth Century Literature* 19, no. 1 (January 1973): 27–39.

Taylor, David A. *Soul of a People: The WPA Writers' Project Uncovers Depression America*. Hoboken, N.J.: John Wiley & Sons, 2009.

The WPA Guide to Illinois: The Federal Writers' Project Guide to 1930s Illinois. New York: Pantheon Books, 1983.

Wald, Elijah. *Escaping the Delta: Robert Johnson and the Invention of the Blues*. New York: Amistad, 2005

Walker, Daniel. *Rights in Conflict: Convention Week in Chicago August 25–29, 1968*. New York: E.P. Dutton, 1968.

Weatherby, W.J. "The Last Interview." In *The Devil's Stocking*, by Nelson Algren. New York: Arbor House, 1983.

Wisniewski, Mary. *Algren: A Life*. Chicago: Chicago Review Press, 2017.

Wixson, Douglas. "Jack Conroy and The East St. Louis Toughs." *New Letters* 57, no. 4 (Summer 1991): 29–57.

Wixson, Douglas. *Worker-Writer in America: Jack Conroy and the Tradition of Midwestern Literary Radicalism, 1898–1990*. Urbana: University of Illinois Press, 1994.

Nelson Algren and the Ethics
of Book Reviewing

Introduction

Bettina Drew writes in her biography, *Nelson Algren: A Life on the Wild Side*, that "Algren had always been a steady book reviewer." This observation is certainly true; indeed, if anything, it is probably an understatement. Matthew Bruccoli lists 236 reviews in his book, *Nelson Algren: A Descriptive Bibliography*, as supplemented by two addenda. These reviews were published over a period of forty-six years—between 1935 and 1981. The decade-by-decade breakdown of Nelson Algren's 236 published and Bruccoli-reported book reviews (together with Algren's 1935 review of *Annunciation*, by Meridel Le Sueur, which is unlisted in Bruccoli's bibliography) is as follows: 1930 through 1939 he published 5 reviews; 1940 through 1949 he published 83 reviews; 1950 through 1959 he published 52 reviews; 1960 through 1969 he published 32 reviews; 1970 through 1981, the year he died, he published 65 reviews, or a total of 237 known and published reviews.[1]

During these forty-six years, Algren's reviews appeared in publications as diverse as *Poetry*, the *Saturday Review*, *The Critic*, *The Nation*, and *Rolling Stone*. But ninety-one reviews—or 38 percent—were published in four Chicago newspapers: the *Chicago Sun*, the *Chicago Sun-Times*, the *Chicago Daily News*, and the *Chicago Tribune*.

Algren's reading tastes were eclectic, ranging from the works of contemporary novelists to a three-volume history of the Civil War. His favorite writers included Don DeLillo, John Cheever, and Joan Didion.[2]

Algren appreciated a good book review. After reading William Styron's *New York Times* review of James Blake's *The Joint*, Algren wrote in 1971: "If there's a better reviewer than Styron I don't know who it is unless it's Elizabeth Hardwick; until she gets too cerebral."[3]

Unlike Elizabeth Hardwick, Algren did not write reviews to be

Figure 14: Nelson Algren had a cat named Doubleday, named after the publisher of three of his books. Simone de Beauvoir, his erstwhile lover, told her biographer, Deirdre Bair, that "we were very much alike, Algren and I, except that he wanted children and he always had those damn cats." He drew a cat on the last page of his last book, *The Devil's Stocking.* When Burt Britton asked Algren to contribute a picture for Britton's book, *Self-Portrait: Book People Picture Themselves*, Algren drew a cat. When Algren signed a book, he often added a cat next to his signature. (See Figure 31.) It is, therefore, no surprise that his bookplate, shown here, features his drawing of a cat.

cerebral. He reviewed books for money. As he told a *Chicago Daily News* reporter in 1973:

> I live on book reviews and by giving talks.... I write for financial reasons. I don't figure I'm changing the world. Some people get a lot of laughs out of what I write, and that's good. I'm satisfied with this trade, which I do very easily—and because there's really nothing else I can do.[4]

Bettina Drew notes that Algren thought enough of his reviews to have all of them retyped as a seven-hundred-page collection.[5]

Although he was proud of his book reviews, this collection was never published as a separate volume of literary criticism. Should it have been? The writing of book reviews involves several principles or guidelines—perhaps even ethical standards. How did Nelson Algren (and his editors) address what might be called the "Ten Commandments of Book Reviewing"? Did they even follow them at all? If Algren's reviews fall short of the benchmark established by these principles, were these reviews even worthy of publication as a separate volume? This essay will address these questions.

These Ten Commandments are:

- One: The book reviewer should avoid words like "unforgettable" or "a masterpiece."[6]
- Two: A book review should consist of more than just a plot summary.[7]
- Three: The book reviewer should read (or at least familiarize himself with) some of the other works of the author.[8]
- Four: A book reviewer should be neutral and unbiased; alternatively, if the reviewer has any bias towards the author or the subject matter of the book, the reviewer should disclose this bias in his review.[9]
- Five: A book reviewer should not review a friend's book.[10]
- Six: A book reviewer should not review an enemy's book.[11]
- Seven: A book reviewer should not review a colleague's book.[12]
- Eight: A book reviewer should not review the book of an author who has criticized the reviewer's book.[13]
- Nine: A book reviewer should not attack the author personally.[14]
- Ten: A book reviewer should not use a book as a springboard for a personal essay.[15]

Algren published his first book review in 1935. This essay will focus on his later book reviews, beginning in 1947.[16]

First Principle: Avoid Hyperbole

Joseph Heller's war novel, *Catch-22*, was released in 1961 to generally mixed reviews. Some reviewers hedged their bets, including a "but" after their positive comments. For example:[17]

New York Times: "*Catch-22* has much passion, comic and fervent, but it gasps for want of craft and sensibility."[18]

Time: "Heller's talent is impressive, but it also is undisciplined, sometimes luring him into bogs of boring repetition."[19]

Nelson Algren reviewed *Catch-22* in the November 4, 1961, issue of *The Nation* magazine. His thoughts are not tempered by the word, "but." Instead, he is unabashedly enthusiastic about *Catch-22*, ending his review with this declaration:

This novel is not merely the best American novel to come out of World War II; it is the best American novel that has come out of anywhere in years.[20]

Algren continued to champion *Catch-22*. In June of 1962 he stated this in the *Chicago Daily News*: "Even though you know beforehand that a novel has failed by every measure of well-behaved letters, if you're paid for reviewing, you'll review it. That was the glum attitude in which I put myself to the chore of *Catch*—and found myself caught by a classic."[21]

Algren described *Catch-22* as "the best American novel" and "a classic." Did Algren go too far with these comments? William McPherson, who received the Pulitzer Prize for Distinguished Criticism in 1977, believes that to describe a book as "unforgettable" or "a masterpiece" is to say very little. On the other hand, he maintains that "to suggest how a book is put together, why it works or fails to work, to demonstrate its accuracy or reveal its errors, to bring some illuminating insight to the whole, is to say a great deal." Similarly, Gail Pool, author of *Faint Praise: The Plight of Book Reviewing in America*, claims that the reviewer should not make "a grand statement for all time," predicting a book's impact on "the future of literature," as this is just hype, not passion. A book reviewer's vision and perception of the worthiness and potential of a book is limited, and a book does not have to "change literature" to be good.[22]

In his essay, "'*Catch-22*': Twenty-Five Years Later," published in the University of Michigan's *Michigan Quarterly Review* in 1987, John W. Aldridge seems at first to echo McPherson and Pool. Aldridge writes that when Algren called *Catch-22* "the best American novel that has come out of anywhere in years," Algren "made what became perhaps the most famous pronouncement on a literary subject to be uttered since John O'Hara announced, on the front page of *The New York Times Book Review* back in 1950, that Hemingway was 'the outstanding author since the death of Shakespeare.'"[23]

But Aldridge also states in this article that Algren was "prophetically perceptive," and so it seems clear that Aldridge's remark was intended as praise and not as criticism. Indeed, the passage of time has proven Algren right. Twenty-five years after *Catch-22* was published, Aldridge describes the book as "a monumental artifact of contemporary American literature, almost as assured of longevity as the statues on Easter Island." The editors of *A "Catch-22" Casebook* (1973) write in the book's preface that "[we] feel, without reservation, that *Catch-22* is a masterpiece." Algren's review is the first entry in this casebook. (The contributors are not listed alphabetically.) Walter James Miller claims in *Modern Critical Interpretations: Joseph Heller's "Catch-22"* (2001) that "Joseph Heller is the greatest-selling writer of serious fiction in American history." Perhaps Nelson Algren was right and Gail Pool was wrong, at least in this instance. Pool maintains that the reviewer should not make "a grand statement for all time." But in this case, Algren's "grand statement" may have been prescience, not hype.[24]

Second Principle: Write More Than a Plot Summary

L.E. Sissman, former columnist for *The Atlantic*, wrote book reviews for *The New Yorker*. In the book, *Book Reviewing*, edited by Sylvia E. Kamerman, he lists several "moral imperatives" of book reviewing. One of them is that the book reviewer should never write a review that is "merely a plot summary and nothing more." Sissman maintains that "the reader of the review deserves a judgment, a rating, not simply a recapitulation." Writer and book reviewer Lynne Sharon Schwartz, also writing in *Book Reviewing*, similarly cautions that plot summaries "should be minimal." She suggests that if the book is nonfiction, the reviewer should discuss "the major issues and points" of the book. If it is fiction, the reviewer should comment on "the nature and interaction of the characters" of the novel.[25]

Algren often ignored both Sissman's imperative and Schwartz's advice. For example, all but the last two sentences of Algren's 1957 review of *The Magnificent Rube*, by Charles Samuels, is plot summary. Because the review consists of 99 lines of text, and all but eight lines are plot summary, 92 percent of the review is plot summary.[26]

Similarly, all but the last two sentences of his 1961 review of *The Coral Barrier*, by Pierre Gascar, is plot summary. This review consists of seventy-one lines of text, and all but five lines are plot summary. Therefore, 93 percent of the review is plot summary.[27]

Admittedly, however, Algren was often able to do wonders with those few lines. P. Albert Duhamel, former book review editor of *The Boston Herald American*, notes that comparing or contrasting a book with another book on the same subject can be "a very effective means of demonstrating why an opinion for or against a book is not just personal, subjective, or a matter of taste." As noted in the introduction to this essay, Algren read widely on a variety of subjects, including world literature, history, and contemporary novels. Consequently, he was often able to compare or contrast the book he was reviewing with another book that he had read.[28]

For example, the last paragraph—the non-summary part—of Algren's review of *The Magnificent Rube* is below. In just a few words Algren is able to describe the book and give his opinion of it, comparing it to John Lardner's 1951 book about the golden age of boxing:

> This is not so much the story of a man's life as it is a recap of the sports-world of the Twenties. Mr. Samuels reports it competently, though without the zest with which John Lardner invested it in his *White Hopes and Other Tigers*.[29]

Third Principle: Become Familiar with the Author's Other Writing

Gail Pool writes that "a reviewer can't become an instant expert, but he can bring an intelligent, informed perspective to a book if he has read, say, all the author's previous work, several other biographies of the figure whose latest biography he's reviewing, various travel accounts of whatever country is the subject of his review." Pool continues, though, with the observation that in her experience, book review editors do not require that reviewers do this background reading. She comments that editors might feel that it is inappropriate to require this additional reading in light of the relatively low compensation editors pay for book reviews and the tight time frame editors impose on the reviewer. She cautions, though, that "without this background reading, reviews tend to be not only uninformed and unsophisticated but also timid; reviewers who know that they don't really know enough to evaluate what they're reading are reluctant to be critical and instead are far more likely to be mildly praising or noncommittal."[30]

But Algren did this background reading. In 1988 Bettina Drew interviewed Sue McNear, a friend of Algren's. McNear (who was a fiction editor for *Playboy* when she knew Algren) told Drew: "I don't know anyone who read more. When he reviewed a book he would always go back and reread all of an author's work."[31]

Algren did more than this. In at least one instance he wrote an author and asked for background information that he could use in his review.

In 1964 he reviewed the American edition of Terry Southern's book, *Candy*, for *Life* magazine. (*Candy* is a novel about the sexual adventures of a young woman. Although not legally pornographic, the novel was controversial, and it was banned in some libraries and many bookstores.) In preparing for the review, Algren wrote Southern, asking for additional information.[32]

Book banning and controversy were clearly on Southern's mind when he responded to Algren's letter. Here are Southern's opening comments:

> Dear Nelson:
>
> LIFE MAG?!? Great Scott, that would certainly be a break for Can-baby if big Life mag gave her the green-light and family-fun stamp of okay! Anyway you can count on my cooperation in this attempt, only regretting my history is not less prosaic [maybe you can spice it up].[33]

Gail Pool writes that no editor has ever asked her to do background reading. She comments that no editor has ever asked her if she had done such reading. But Algren did it, and it appears that he did it routinely. And at least one time he even contacted an author and asked for additional information for his review—something that Gail Pool does not even mention in her book.[34] (Bracketed information in the original.)

Fourth Principle: Be Neutral and Unbiased

In 1934 James Henle, president of Vanguard Press, asked author James T. Farrell to review the manuscript of Algren's first book, *Somebody in Boots*. Farrell replied to Henle with a detailed, sixteen-page report, suggesting dozens of changes. It appears that Algren neither forgave nor forgot Farrell's critique, because Algren was very critical in his later reviews of Farrell's books. Farrell's biographer, Robert K. Landers, calls Algren a "tireless carper where Farrell was concerned." Is Landers correct in his assessment of Algren? Was Algren biased when he reviewed Farrell's books, or was Algren a severe but fair reviewer?[35]

An American Dream Girl and Other Stories, Ferrell's collection of twenty-one short stories, was published in 1950. Algren reviewed it for the *Saturday Review of Literature* in December of that year. In the second paragraph of his review, Algren refers to Farrell's "compassionless prose and belabored cataloging." A few paragraphs later, Algren goes in for the kill:[36]

> For there is a slovenliness in Farrell's use of words and a tastelessness about his prose that rob these stories of color and forward movement. If he wrote them in longhand it would be with the old-fashioned Palmer Method backhand-slant.[37]

Algren's review is harsh, exceptionally so. But is it any worse than an anonymous review in the *New Yorker* that includes this comment:

> There are twenty-one stories here, all concerned with lack of privilege in one form or another and all written in a berating tone that seems to nag for pity because it has not the spirit to command respect.[38]

Book Review Digest is a compendium of excerpts of book reviews of hundreds of books that are culled from hundreds of periodicals. When one reads the *Book Review Digest* reviews of *An American Dream Girl*—reviews originally published in newspapers like the *New York Times* and the *New York Herald Tribune*—a common conclusion is immediately apparent—the reviewers' enthusiasm for the book is lukewarm at best.[39]

Vanguard published Farrell's *The Face of Time* in 1953, and Algren again reviewed it in the *Saturday Review*. Although he did state that the book "could have been cut in half without losing a thing," he also admitted that "the present saga is easily the best written of Farrell's many novels. There is nothing faked here; every line of dialogue rings true."[40]

Was Algren neutral and unbiased in his reviews of Farrell's books? It appears that he was. Both Algren and other reviewers were critical of *An American Dream Girl*. Similarly, Algren (and other reviewers) liked *The Face of Time*.[41]

Although Algren may have been unbiased, Farrell's biographer may still have been right; Algren might have also been a "tireless carper." In writing that there was "a slovenliness in Farrell's use of words and a tastelessness about his prose" in his review of *An American Dream Girl*, Algren may have crossed the line. He may have gone from just reviewing Farrell's book to attacking Farrell personally.

Why would Algren do this? It is likely that he was still angry about Farrell's *Somebody in Boots* review. But he also may have been jealous of Farrell. Algren's review of *An American Dream Girl* appeared in the *Saturday Review of Literature* in 1950. By this time a picture of Farrell had appeared on the cover of this magazine twice—October 24, 1936, and May 18, 1946. By 1950, Algren had not been on the cover even once—indeed, Algren would never appear on the cover.[42]

Fifth Principle: Do Not Review a Friend's Book

L.E. Sissman's first "moral imperative" is: "Never review the work of a friend." The obvious reason is that book reviewers must be objective. They are expected to give their candid judgment about a book. Sissman warns that "if you know the man at all well, you become confused and diffident; your praise becomes fulsome, and you fail to convey the real merits and demerits of the book to the poor reader."[43]

Gail Pool also admonishes: "No reviewing books written by friends, or by friends of friends ... no personal relationships of any kind, and if in doubt, bow out." Yet Nelson Algren was somehow allowed (perhaps even encouraged) to review books written not only by his *acquaintances*, not only by his *friends*, but even books written by his *close friends*.[44]

Nelson Algren's Own Book of Lonesome Monsters was published in

76

Bruce Jay Friedman's <u>Stern</u> is not about Jewishness; it is about unjewishness:

When the Seder began, Uncle Sweets would take long difficult passages to himself, which gave him an opportunity to hit high notes galore, but soon Uncle Mackie would break in with great clamor, doing a series of heroic-sounding but clashing chants that seemed to have been developed outdoors in Arizona. Uncle Sweets would stop and say to him, "What the hell do you know? You shit in your hat in Phoenix." And Uncle Mackie would fly at him, saying, "I'll kick your two-bit ass through the window"....And thus the curtain would come down on another religious holiday.

The time when the East 10th Street kitchen was a sanctuary that returned, by evening, the dignity lost in the day's humiliations, is past: and all the greenery of suburbia cannot bring it back. Indeed, a task force of caterpillars ravage Stern's suburban greenery as if they had been sent, while his neighbors' gardens bloom unblighted. Who sends caterpillars?

...even with three years of Hebrew School under his belt Stern still felt a loner among the chanting sufferers at synagogues. After a while he began to think that you could never get to be one of the groaners through mere audience at Hebrew School. You probably had to pick it all up in Europe.

Figure 15: Nelson Algren wrote almost all of his book reviews in a "book summary/book review" format. However, he also wrote and published two "review essays." Both of these essays were published in 1964, and both of them were featured in *The Nation* magazine. Shown here is the first page of what appears to be an early draft of one of these essays, "The Radical Innocent." This page is numbered, indicating that Algren probably sold this manuscript at auction at his 1975 moving sale, when he was preparing to move from Chicago to New Jersey. This page also bears Algren's signature. The March 9, 1975, issue of the *Chicago Tribune* has a photograph of Algren signing a book. (*continued*)

1962. This collection of thirteen stories includes a story by Bruce Jay Friedman. In July of 1964 Algren stayed with Friedman and his family while they were vacationing on New York's Fire Island. At night Algren and Friedman would drink and talk about their careers. It is possible that these conversations led to Algren reviewing three of Friedman's books—*Stern* (1962), *Far from the City of Class* (1963), and *A Mother's Kisses* (1964) in one essay. This review was published in the September 21, 1964, issue of *The Nation* magazine.[45]

Algren and Friedman were friends, and Algren's *The Nation* review was favorable, but that relationship did not prevent Algren from criticizing Friedman's 1978 book, *The Lonely Guy's Book of Life* in a *Chicago Tribune* review: "Its attempt to be humorous is vitiated by the author's self-pity. Neither a novel nor a collection of stories, the book does nothing to sustain the unique humor of Friedman's previous work."[46]

Years later, Friedman commented about Algren and this review in a 1990 magazine article:

> In later years, he said of my book *The Lonely Guy* that I had become too interested in *things*. He was right—I hadn't done too well with people—but I felt he should have taken me aside and scolded me instead of doing it in front of half the world. He probably felt that he had loved me in print, so it was appropriate for him to hate me in print as well. He was probably right about that, too, but I pouted for a while nonetheless.[47]

In the fall of 1955 Terry Southern interviewed Algren in Greenwich Village for the *Paris Review* magazine. The men stayed in touch after the interview, and Algren became not only one of Southern's mentors, but also one of the earliest champions of his work. In his review of Southern's 1959 novel, *The Magic Christian*, Algren wrote that the book was "the most profoundly satiric and wildly comic account of our life and times in years." Algren described Southern as "an absolutely first-rate writer" in his 1964 *Life* magazine review of *Candy*. In a 1964 *The Nation* magazine essay, Algren declared that Southern wrote with "incisive perception."[48]

But in Algren's eyes, accolades (even from a mentor) for one book do not mean that the author gets a free pass for a mediocre book. Southern's *Blue Movie* was published in 1970. Algren described it as an "interminable, humorless and downright banal sequence of anecdotes."[49]

The caption reads, "Poet Nelson Algren gives out autographs Saturday to dozens of persons who crowded into his flat at 1958 W. Evergreen Av. for a sale of his personal possessions."

It appears that an unpublished essay, "The Chevalier of Vain Regrets," which is also numbered and signed and now owned by the Newberry Library in Chicago, was also sold at this auction. Who knows what other unpublished and unknown works were sold at Algren's moving sale?

Algren was aware of the problems of reviewing books written by friends. He once declined to review a book by author and activist Kay Boyle because he did not want to hurt their friendship if he did not like it. Although he did eventually review one of her books, *The Long Walk at San Francisco State and Other Essays* (1970), the review was innocuous, almost indifferent. In the review Algren writes about Kay Boyle and her "brilliant coverage, for the *New Yorker*, of the trial of Heinrich Baab, a small-time Eichmann, in the spring of 1950 at Frankfort." But this book is not about the trial of Heinrich Baab; it is about a 1968–69 student strike at San Francisco State College. In his apparent effort to be neutral and unbiased, Algren never comments about her book; he never *evaluates* it; he merely writes generally about student unrest at the college. Boyle may have "brilliantly covered" a trial in Frankfort, but Algren never describes her coverage of the student strike. Ultimately, his review is a disservice to both her and the reader.[50]

Book columnist B.A. Bergman observes that "many reviews mean little, for they are written by friends of the author, dripping glowing adjectives about the book's merits." Algren's review meant little, but for a different reason—it dripped nothing at all.[51]

Algren clearly gave Kay Boyle's book short shrift in his review. He made up for it, though, two years later, by dedicating his 1973 collection, *The Last Carousel*, "For Kay Boyle."[52]

Algren's review of James Blake's book, *The Joint*, is very similar to his review of Kay Boyle's book. Algren met Blake in 1948 at a Chicago nightclub called The Pink Poodle; Blake had been playing the piano in the band. After Blake was convicted of breaking and entering and petit larceny in 1950 and sentenced to serve two years in the Duval County jail in Jacksonville, Florida, Blake wrote Algren. The two began corresponding, with Algren encouraging Blake to keep writing. They continued to correspond after Blake was released from jail, and they continued to write each other after Blake was sentenced in 1954 to serve three years in the Florida State Prison in Raiford, Florida, for possession of marijuana.[53]

When Simone de Beauvoir was visiting Algren in Chicago, she saw a packet of Blake's letters. She sent them to Jean-Paul Sartre, who had them translated and published in *Les Temps modernes*, a French journal. Some of Blake's letters (dated 1951–52) were later published in the *Paris Review* in 1956. Other letters (dated 1956–57 and 1967) appeared in *Esquire* in 1970.[54]

George A. Plimpton, editor of the *Paris Review*, took Blake's letters to Doubleday & Company, a New York book publisher. The letters were written to Algren and other friends of Blake from 1951 to 1964. Doubleday published the letters (together with Blake's occasional commentary) in 1971 as the book entitled *The Joint*.[55]

Figure 16: In 1950 James Blake was convicted of breaking and entering and petit larceny. He was sentenced to serve two years in the Duval County jail in Jacksonville, Florida. In 1954 Blake was sentenced to serve three years in the Florida State Prison in Raiford, Florida, for possession of marijuana. While Blake was incarcerated, he corresponded with several people, including Nelson Algren. In 1971 Doubleday published these letters, plus Blake's commentary, in a book aptly titled, *The Joint.*

Algren's review of Blake's book appeared in the April 18, 1971, issue of the *Los Angeles Times.* The review featured this publicity photograph of Blake, taken by Doubleday employee Alex Gotfryd.

Algren included Blake's short story, "Day of the Alligator," in his 1962 book, *Nelson Algren's Own Book of Lonesome Monsters.*

Nelson Algren reviewed *The Joint* for the *Los Angeles Times.* Only the opening paragraphs and the last paragraph of Algren's article—it is more an article than a review—is a discussion of the book. The rest of the article consists of excerpts from a few letters and Algren's reminiscences of Blake.[56]

As indicated in one of the first paragraphs of this essay, William Styron also reviewed *The Joint.* Styron's review is thought-provoking and insightful. Secker & Warburg, a London publisher, released a British edition of *The Joint* in 1972. When one compares the two reviews, it is obvious why Styron's review was chosen as the introduction to this edition of *The Joint* and not Algren's article.[57]

Thankfully, Algren did not review all of his friends' books equally. Algren met Studs Terkel during their days with the Illinois Writers' Project, and Terkel remained one of Algren closest friends for the rest of his life. Algren reviewed Terkel's second book of oral history, *Hard Times: An Oral History of the Great Depression,* in 1970, the year before he reviewed Kay Boyle's book and James Blake's book. Although too much of the review is quoted material, Algren still manages to discuss the book, and at one point he even gently criticizes it:[58]

> This intuition has also lent impact to the studies of Oscar Lewis. But whereas Lewis will stick with a single personality until he obtains understanding in depth, Terkel takes it off the top of the tape and is off to the next sitting. This lends his work wider range than Lewis' but at some cost in characterization and depth. What saves his subjects from merging into a milling throng is the author's discernment of individuality.[59]

Algren reviewed Terkel's memoir, *Talking to Myself*, seven years later. Although seventy-three percent of the book is summary, Algren again does an excellent job of discussing the merits of Terkel's memoir.[60]

Algren and Terkel were friends with Mike Royko, a nationally syndicated Chicago newspaper columnist. In 1969 an editor from E.P. Dutton and Company, a New York publisher, approached Royko about writing a book about Richard J. Daley, then mayor of Chicago. Royko was reluctant at first, because writing a newspaper column left him little time to do anything else. But both Algren and Terkel urged him to do it, and Royko finally agreed, telling his editor at the *Chicago Daily News* that he would continue to write his usual five columns a week and that he would work on the book on the weekends.[61]

Boss: Richard J. Daley of Chicago was published in January of 1971, and it was an instant success, rising to number four on the *New York Times* best seller list in just a few weeks. Ignoring the maxim that "friends should not review the books of friends," *both* Algren and Terkel reviewed *Boss*. Terkel landed the *New York Times*; Algren had to settle for *The Critic*.[62]

Most of Algren's review is summary, but what remains is an enthusiastic but apparently still objective opinion of *Boss*:

> [What Royko has given us is] a tightly-stitched accounting of how a political machine, controlled by one man, may survive police scandals, court scandals, housing scandals, assassinations, riots, pollution, gerrymandering and kickbacks from the Assessor's office right up to the recent secret fix put in by Boss to retain a white segregationist as President of the School Board.[63]

On the other hand, Studs Terkel's review is devoid of any sense of objectivity. Terkel writes in his *New York Times* review that *Boss* is "a stunning portrait of a clod, his resistible rise, and fortuitousness; of that psychic frontier where the man leaves off and the machine begins." Terkel's final comment is caustic in its condemnation: "[Daley] attends mass each morning. It is the only time he genuflects."[64]

Algren and Terkel were both friends of Royko. Why are Algren's comments so radically different from Terkel's? It is possible that both Algren and Terkel had similar opinions of Daley, but while Terkel lacked

Figure 17: From left to right the men are Studs Terkel, Nelson Algren, and Mike Royko. The woman is unidentified. (This photograph is from the collection of Ken McCollum. When McCollum asked Algren who the woman was in the photo, Algren cryptically replied, "Just a friend.")

Mike Royko writes in the acknowledgments of his 1971 book about Chicago's mayor, *Boss: Richard J. Daley of Chicago*, that he was "grateful for the help of many knowledgeable Chicagoans in putting this book together." These people included Studs Terkel, "for talking me into it," and Nelson Algren. Terkel reviewed *Boss* for the *New York Times*, and Algren reviewed the book for the *Critic* magazine (*Chicago Sun-Times*/Chicago History Museum).

objectivity in his review, Algren managed to keep his objectivity in focus and his opinion in check.

Community activist Saul D. Alinsky also encouraged Royko to write the book, and Alinsky reviewed *Boss* for *The Nation* magazine. The last sentence of Alinsky's review is reminiscent of how Algren described Joseph Heller's *Catch-22*: "[*Boss*] is my nominee for the Pulitzer Prize in 1971."[65]

Boss was not universally acclaimed, however. Dr. Paul Kiniery of Loyola University, Chicago, reviewed *Boss* for *Best Sellers: The Semi-Monthly Book Review*, and he writes that *Boss* "is simply an extended attack on a public official; it does not deserve to be taken seriously by anyone interested in the history of Chicago." Perry L. Weed parses *Boss* in the

Saturday Review, and he concludes that "Royko's book is, in the final analysis, too personal, superficial, bitter, and simplistic."[66]

Andrew M. Greeley, professor of sociology at the University of Chicago, reviewed *Boss* for *Chicago History* magazine, and his review is unique in that he addresses some of the ethical issues addressed in this essay. Greeley writes that "*Boss* is a shallow, mean, vindictive book, as much an insult to the city of Chicago as it is a sweeping personal attack on the city's mayor." Greeley notes that both Algren and Terkel not only wrote favorable book reviews, but are also mentioned in the book's acknowledgments. Greeley adds:[67]

> It's an interesting little group. Mr. Terkel praises Mr. Algren on his radio program. Mr. Algren, in one of his earlier books, praises Mr. Royko. Mr. Royko thanks Mr. Algren and Mr. Terkel for their help in writing the book and they respond in kind by writing laudatory reviews. How all this fits the ethics of book reviewing remains problematic. One wonders how many times, for example, the *New York Times* gives a book for review to a man who is acknowledged in the introduction as having inspired it. One also wonders how many times someone mentioned in the introduction will accept a book for review.[68]

Actually, the ethical issues may be worse than what Greeley indicates in his review. Besides Algren and Terkel, Royko names nine other people in the acknowledgment section of his book. Two of these nine men are Saul Alinsky and Roy Fisher (Royko describes Fisher as "a good and kind boss"). Fisher wrote a book review of *Boss* for *The New Republic* in which he states that Royko "adds much to one's understanding of why urban politics is played as it is." Thus, four of the eleven people named in the book's acknowledgments (Algren, Terkel, Alinsky, and Fisher—three friends and a boss) wrote positive reviews of the book that were published in the mainstream press.[69]

Sixth Principle: Do Not Review an Enemy's Book

Just as B.A. Bergman indicates that a reviewer should not review a friend's book, he also recommends that one should not review the book of an enemy. Bergman's reasoning is simple and straightforward—the reviewer may criticize a book that deserves praise. It is possible that this is what happened when Algren reviewed Otto Preminger's memoir.[70]

In 1955 film director Otto Preminger asked Algren to come to California to write a screenplay of the movie version of Algren's novel, *The Man with the Golden Arm* (1949). Algren took the train to Los Angeles, and he met Preminger in Malibu. Unfortunately, the men did not get along, and Algren was in Hollywood only a few days before Preminger summarily dismissed him from the production. Algren was promised payment of one thousand dollars a week to write the screenplay; instead, he had to fight, through his agent, just to have his expenses paid. Furthermore, Algren felt that he had been cheated out of thousands of dollars for the sale of the *Golden Arm* movie rights to Preminger. Algren never forgot any of this, and he would write about it (and talk bitterly about it) for the rest of his life.[71]

"For the rest of his life" includes 1977, when Algren reviewed Preminger's book, *Preminger: An Autobiography*. It is a "tell-all" account of Preminger's career, with anecdotes of movie stars and the rich and famous.[72]

Algren describes the book as "an innocuous little memoir" in the first sentence of his review. He then recounts several of Preminger's stories about movie stars and the filming of Preminger's movies. Algren finishes the review by writing of his own trip to Hollywood and working with Preminger.[73]

Why did Algren devote forty-five percent of his review to his 1955 trip to Hollywood? Why did Algren include in his review the snide remark, "Preminger is a modest sort of fellow who has since made many films. The more films he makes the more reason he has to be modest." Why did Algren write only four words—"an innocuous little memoir"—as the sole description of and commentary about Preminger's book?[74]

It seems likely that Algren used his review as retribution against Preminger, not only for what happened in Hollywood, but also for what Preminger said in his autobiography. In his book Preminger discusses the filming of *The Man with the Golden Arm*. Preminger writes that Algren was "an amusing, intelligent man but he couldn't write dialogue or visualize scenes. He was purely a novelist, a storyteller. I had to get another writer, Walter Newman, to prepare the script." These remarks must have struck a nerve, as Algren mentions one of them in his review: "In this autobiography, Otto expresses the opinion that I 'could not visualize.' I find this curious. I never gave him a script."[75]

Twice-hurt by Preminger, Algren retaliated with comments such as, "The life of the common man has never filtered into Otto's brain and emotions; or into his talent such as he has." As described later in this essay, this was not the only time that Algren would use his typewriter as a club with which to attack his critics.[76]

Seventh Principle: Do Not Review a Colleague's Book

One should not review the book of a colleague, as there will always be the "appearance of impropriety" lurking between the lines—that is, the possibility that the reviewer has falsely inflated his evaluation of his co-worker's book. For example, Gail Pool writes that "in an issue of the *New York Observer*, Robert Gottlieb reviews a memoir by a former colleague, whose memories of Gottlieb, the reviewer tells us, are 'warm and generous.'" She adds that in return, Gottlieb thought that his ex-colleague's book was a "triumph."[77]

Algren did not have "colleagues" in the traditional sense. However, he wrote book reviews for newspapers and magazines; are the editors of these periodicals colleagues in the context of book reviewing ethics?

Editors and colleagues may be ethically equivalent, but this comparison is still not entirely satisfactory. The concern is the same with both colleagues and editors—has the reviewer given an honest opinion of the book, or is the review padded with false praise? The reasons for these concerns, however, are different. A reviewer may recommend the book of a colleague just because they have to work together; an honest but critical review might create workplace animosity. On the other hand, a book reviewer may fill his review of an editor's book with insincere accolades in hopes that the grateful editor will steer more book review assignments his way.

Fabulous Chicago, by Emmett Dedmon, was published in 1953. Algren reviewed this social history for *The Nation* magazine. Unlike Robert Gottlieb, Algren did *not* describe Dedmon's book as a "triumph." The best Algren could say about the book was that "*Fabulous Chicago* contains several anecdotes heretofore untold. But its chief justification is that it is illustrated so beautifully and bound so handsomely." Algren ended his review with two words of exceptionally faint praise: "Eminently lookable."[78]

In 1953 (the year *Fabulous Chicago* was published) Dedmon was the assistant Sunday editor for the *Chicago Sun-Times* newspaper. The last time Algren had reviewed a book for the *Sun-Times* prior to 1953 was 1950. Algren's review appeared in *The Nation* in February 1954. Was Algren looking for more reviewing assignments from the *Sun-Times* when he reviewed Dedmon's book? If so, he might have increased his chances by writing a more positive review of *Fabulous Chicago*. But he did not. Did Dedmon punish Algren by black-balling him from doing any more work for the *Sun-Times*? No, he did not. The *Sun-Times* printed an Algren book review in October 1954. In 1959 the Chicago White Sox won its first American League pennant in forty years. Dedmon, now the assistant managing editor of the *Sun-Times*, hired Algren to write a series of articles detailing (as stated in the newspaper) "his impressions of the World Series." (Algren, on the other hand, wrote that Dedmon hired him "to write human interest stuff from the grandstand.)[79]

Algren's *The Nation* review of February 13, 1954, featured two books—*Fabulous Chicago* and also *Big Bill of Chicago*, by Lloyd Wendt and

Herman Kogan. Wendt was the *Chicago Tribune*'s assistant Sunday editor, and Kogan was the book and drama critic for the *Chicago Sun-Times*. Herman Kogan was also Algren's friend. In 1961 Algren dedicated the second edition of his prose poem, *Chicago: City on the Make*, to Kogan and his wife.[80]

In 1954 both the weekend edition of the *Sun-Times* and the Sunday edition of the *Tribune* featured book reviews. Because Wendt and Kogan worked respectively for the *Tribune* and the *Sun-Times*, they might have been able to direct book review work to Algren. To muddy the ethical waters even more, one of the authors was Algren's friend. Did Algren take the bait? Did he, like Robert Gottlieb, call their book a "triumph"? No, he did not. Although Algren's review was positive, it certainly was not enthusiastic. If anything, Algren went out of his way to be evenhanded and understated in his review: *"Big Bill of Chicago* would read like a sprightly fantasy were it not for its dismaying application to the current hysteria. Eminently readable."[81]

Robert Cromie published his book, *The Great Chicago Fire*, in 1958. At that time, he was a reporter and feature writer for the *Chicago Tribune*. Algren wrote a favorable review of Cromie's book for the *Saturday Review*. (Algren called it a "rarity, a work of exhaustive research that reads as well as a good novel.") In 1958 Algren was reviewing books for the *Chicago Sun-Times*, but not for the *Chicago Tribune*. Did Algren write this review, hoping to get book review business from the *Tribune*? If so, his plan did not work; the *Tribune* did not publish an Algren book review until 1973. Admittedly, Cromie, still working for the *Tribune*, later devoted an entire column to Algren and his book, *Chicago: City on the Make*. Furthermore, Cromie's column was later reprinted as an advertisement for Algren's book. However, it is clear that Algren did not write a positive review of Cromie's book in exchange for Cromie writing an article about him, as Cromie's column about *City on the Make* did not appear in the *Tribune* until 1968, ten years after Algren's review of Cromie's book was published in the *Saturday Review*.[82]

Algren reviewed *The "Chicago Review" Anthology* for both the *Chicago Sun-Times* and *The Nation* magazine. Both reviews were favorable (though meandering and unfocused) and were published within one month of each other. Algren's review appeared in the *Chicago Sun-Times* on May 31, 1959. *The Nation* published his review (longer than but similar to the *Sun-Times* review) on June 27, 1959. In addition, Algren supplied original "advance praise" for the back of the dustjacket of the book that is not in either book review.[83]

David Ray was the editor of *The "Chicago Review" Anthology*. He interviewed Algren at his Chicago apartment, and the text of his interview, entitled, "A Talk on the Wild Side," appeared in the June 11, 1959, issue of *The Reporter* magazine, chronologically sandwiched between the dates of Algren's two book reviews. (Strangely, David Ray's interview was reprinted five years later in *Cavalcade*, a men's magazine.)[84]

Ray and Algren were both authors, and they both worked in related fields. They were, therefore, colleagues in the professional sense, and as noted above, there is always the possibility of the "appearance of impropriety" when one reviews the work of a colleague. In this case, the appearance is real, not possible. Did Algren agree to write not one but two favorable reviews of Ray's anthology (Algren called the book "a singular service to American letters" in both reviews), and did Algren agree to supply "advance praise" for the book, all in exchange for being interviewed by Ray for an article in a national magazine?[85]

Eighth Principle: Do Not Review the Book of an Author Who Has Criticized the Reviewer's Book

When a reviewer reviews the book of an author who has criticized the reviewer's book, there is always the chance that the book review may not be a balanced and unbiased evaluation of the book. Unfortunately, this is especially true with Algren's reviews of the books of his critics.[86]

In 1958 Edmund Fuller published *Man in Modern Fiction*. In this book he calls Nelson Algren, Saul Bellow, and Norman Mailer "the most vindictive writers working today; not the most humble, but the most arrogant; not the binders of the wounds of their fallen brothers, but the destroyers of the social order."[87]

In a 1981 interview, Algren admitted that he had a tendency of "sometimes being too quick to hit back." Algren hit Fuller back by reviewing *Man in Modern Fiction* in a review aptly titled, "Author Bites Critic." Algren reviewed not only Fuller's book but Fuller personally: "The tools of the critic's trade would seem to be lucidity of thought, liberality of spirit and a decent command of his native tongue. Fuller's thought is larded, his liberality befits a railroad dick anxious to make a pinch, and his English is ambiguous."[88]

In his *New York Times* review of Algren's novel, *A Walk on the Wild Side* (1956), Alfred Kazin writes (among other things) that the book has a "boozily artificial and contrived quality." Kazin later reprinted this review in *Contemporaries*, his 1962 collection of articles.[89]

Nelson Algren biographer Mary Wisniewski writes that Algren "used the reviewer's pulpit to take on his own critics." In Kazin's case, Algren's *modus operandi* was the same as with Fuller. Because Fuller criticized

Algren in *Man in Modern Fiction*, Algren took on Fuller by reviewing *Man in Modern Fiction*. Because Kazin criticized Algren's book in *Contemporaries*, Algren took on Kazin by reviewing *Contemporaries*. Again, as with Fuller, Algren attacks Kazin personally in his review: "Like Colonel Clevenger of *Catch-22*, this critic is a man who knows all there is to know about literature except how to enjoy it."[90]

Ninth Principle: Do Not Attack the Author Personally

Book reviewers should review books and not the authors of the books. When reviewers cross the line from harsh criticism of a book to personal criticism of an author, the reviewer risks a libel suit and being held legally accountable for his opinion. It appears that Algren was never sued for book review defamation. However, during the course of his book reviewing career (1935–1981), Algren attacked at least two authors personally and repeatedly in his reviews. Those authors are Simone de Beauvoir and Willard Motley.[91]

Simone de Beauvoir was probably the poster child of Algren-author animosity. Algren and Beauvoir met in 1947. They subsequently engaged in a "Transatlantic Love Affair" until 1964, when *Harper's Magazine* published excerpts of her book, *Force of Circumstance*. When Algren read these passages, he realized that Beauvoir and philosopher Jean-Paul Sartre had made a pact. They had agreed that they would be allowed to have "contingent loves," or relationships with other parties. However, these book excerpts revealed that Algren was never Beauvoir's "first love," only a second-place contingent love.[92]

Algren was enraged at this revelation, and this anger carried over into his book reviews. For the rest of his life, whenever Algren reviewed a book by Beauvoir (or even *about* Beauvoir), he would use the review to attack her personally.[93]

The English translation of *Force of Circumstance* was published in 1965, but the *Harper's* excerpts appeared in the November 1964 and December 1964 issues of the magazine. Algren retaliated immediately with a devastating article in the May 1965 issue of *Harper's*. The article was ostensibly a review of *Force of Circumstance*, but both the title—"The Question of Simone de Beauvoir"—and the text make it clear that this was an article about Beauvoir, not a review of her book. The first sentence of the second paragraph sets the tone:[94]

> No chronicler of our lives since Theodore Dreiser has combined so steadfast a passion for human justice with a dullness so asphyxiating as Mme. de Beauvoir.[95]

The October 1965 issue of *Ramparts* features another Algren article disguised as a *Force of Circumstance* review. The sarcastic essay is primarily a fantasy conversation between Algren and Beauvoir:

> "Sartre and I have been more ambitious. We seek to maintain through all deviations 'a certain fidelity.'"
> "Is that the same," I inquired eagerly, "as 'grabbing a quickie?'"[96]

In 1972 Algren reviewed Beauvoir's book, *The Coming of Age*, for the *Los Angeles Times*. Again, the review is about her, not about her book. For example:

> Nor is Madame content merely to present second-hand revelations. She must flatten the reader's nose against her blackboard, prod him with her 12-inch ruler and give him fair warning that, if he doesn't start shaping up into an adult immediately, she'll hold her breath until he does.[97]

Five years later Algren reviewed *Hearts and Minds: The Common Journey of Simone de Beauvoir and Jean-Paul Sartre*, by Axel Madsen. Surprisingly, the review is calm and balanced. For example, Algren writes that "the book is a comprehensive account of a couple who have, for 40 years, been consistently humane in their assessments of Western Civilization. Both have demonstrated enormous courage in facing down the French bourgeoisie."[98]

But even twelve years after the publication of *Force of Circumstance*, Algren cannot help getting one more dig in at Beauvoir:

> "When you see a man doing the work of an animal," Madame instructed me, "then you know you are in an undeveloped country."
> I had assumed that the man under the firewood had been Darryl Zanuck until she'd enlightened me.
> Madame's fiction is equally sententious. Strict attention must be paid because Madame knows.[99]

After a relationship that endured (if not lasted) seventeen years, Algren read in the November 1964 issue of *Harper's Magazine* that he was a "deviation from the main path" walked by Beauvoir and Sartre and a "defect" in their "system." In the December issue, he read passages from letters he had written her. It is, therefore, perhaps understandable why Algren lashed out at Beauvoir in his reviews. What is not so understandable, however, is Algren's treatment of Willard Motley.[100]

Algren and Motley worked together at the Illinois Writers' Project, and they were friends after the Project ended in 1943. But then Motley published *Knock on Any Door* four years later, and with the publication of that book, cracks began to form in their relationship.[101]

Knock on Any Door is the story of Nick Romano, an altar boy who grows up on the West Side of Chicago, falls in with the wrong crowd, gets sent to a juvenile home, spirals downward, and at twenty-one years of age, kills a policeman. (The dust jacket of the book refers to Romano as "the sensitive boy who dreamed of the stars and stumbled into a gutter.") In a 1949 interview with Harvey Breit, assistant editor of the *New York Times Book Review*, Algren comments about Motley and his book.[102]

> I had a funny thing with him. I was sitting in his place, drinking, and I felt uncomfortable because I knew I was going to bum-rap the book, because I knew I was going to bum-rap his book. I didn't like it. I finally told him I didn't know if it was all right to drink his whisky when I was going to bum-rap his book. Willard said "sure, drinking my whisky doesn't oblige you to like my book. You can express your disappointment in my work and still drink my whisky."[103]

Strangely, even though Algren told Motley that he was going to "bum-rap" *Knock on Any Door*, it appears that Algren's review of Motley's first book was never published. Equally peculiar is the fact that generally speaking, reviewers praised the book. Why did Algren feel the need to criticize *Knock on Any Door*?[104]

The answer is suggested in Horace R. Cayton's review of Motley's book:

> The drama of migrant peoples struggling against great odds has been told by many writers. James Farrell described it for the Irish, Nelson Algren for the Polish, Meyer Levin for the Jews, and Richard Wright for the Negroes. Now Willard Motley deals with the Italians.[105]

Cayton indicates that in writing *Knock on Any Door*, Motley was following the footsteps of men like Algren—that what Motley had written about the Italians was similar to what Algren had written about the Polish. And Cayton is right. Nick Romano being arrested and convicted for killing Riley the policeman is much like Bruno Bicek being arrested for killing the Greek in *Never Come Morning* (1942). Furthermore, the plots of both *Knock on Any Door* and *Never Come Morning* play out on the West Side of Chicago.[106]

Algren's intention to "bum-rap" *Knock on Any Door* suggests that Algren was not pleased with Motley sowing the literary field that Algren had plowed. Algren made that clear in his *Chicago Tribune* review of Motley's third novel, *Let No Man Write My Epitaph* (1958), a sequel to *Knock on Any Door*:[107]

> *Let No Man Write My Epitaph* is an account of two heroin-heads, mother and son. It might have been subtitled, "Stick Me, Mama, It's My Turn Now." ... The author creates a deceptive kind of excitement by calling warning to the reader—"Catch!"—and then ducks behind the backstop to look for the ball. In this

one Motley spends most of his time looking for the ball.... In the present effort, the author flies at times like Farrell, again like Wright, and then like Sandburg, but never in his own style. The result is a magpie's nest marking a kind of backward progress, since his first novel, from the derivative to the imitative. Why doesn't someone do a book about a legless Hercules? Maybe the movies will buy it.[108]

Motley's story of Nick Romano, Jr., and heroin addiction is certainly suggestive of Algren's novel, *The Man with the Golden Arm* (1949) and the morphine-addicted Frankie Machine. Reviewers for both the *New York Times* and *Time* magazine thought so as well, with the reviewer for *Time* writing, "What the book has to offer is the authenticity of setting and speech that recalls Nelson Algren's excursion into the same territory. Unfortunately, author Motley has not written another *Man with the Golden Arm*." Algren, by now incensed at Motley's *second* intrusion into his literary space, includes a sarcastic comment in his above *Chicago Tribune* review about writing a book about a "legless Hercules"—an obvious reference to the "half-giant" Achilles "Legless" Schmidt in Algren's 1956 novel, *A Walk on the Wild Side*.[109]

Motley responded to Algren's review with a "letter to the editor" of the *Tribune*, writing that the review "sounds somewhat like a child having a temper tantrum and as if he [Algren] feels he has a permanent lease on Chicago, so that no one but himself may write about it or about drug addiction." (Bracketed information in the original.) Admittedly, other reviewers besides Algren were critical of *Let No Man Write My Epitaph*, and other reviewers besides Algren noted the similarity between *Golden Arm* and *Epitaph*. Algren, however, crossed the line between legitimate criticism of the book and personal attack of its author. Motley recognized this, commenting about Algren in his letter, "If one of his novels were accidently published with my name on the cover, he wouldn't like the book."[110]

Motley died in 1965. A year later, his last novel, *Let Noon Be Fair*, was published posthumously. Even after Motley died, Algren criticized both Motley and his final book: "Motley's lack of any grasp of the economy of the world in which he lived forced him to depend upon degeneration for subject matter.... And nowhere in all of Motley's work is there either zest or joy."[111]

Iowa State University Press published *The Diaries of Willard Motley* in 1979. The *Chicago Tribune* undoubtedly assigned Algren to review the *book*, but instead, he reviewed *Motley*. Ever a recycler, Algren took a phrase from his Otto Preminger review and revised it to describe the deceased author: "Everybody liked Willard Motley. He was a modest sort of fellow who wrote a number of books and the more books he wrote the more reason he had for modesty." Algren finished off Motley with the final sentence: "As a literary figure, we now perceive, he does not even exist."[112]

Motley, of course, was not able to defend himself by writing another "letter to the editor," but two *Tribune* readers wrote letters to protest Algren's review. One of them complained that "Nelson Algren wielded a hatchet better than he did a pen" and that "his job on Willard Motley lifts assassination to an art."[113]

When asked about James T. Farrell's Chicago writing, Algren groused, "You just don't like to see somebody lousing up your neighborhood." It seems clear that Algren resented Motley for writing about what Algren had already claimed as his own (and exclusive) domain—the West Side of Chicago and the challenges (including drug addiction) that confront the denizens of that part of the city. Writer Jack Conroy agreed with this assessment. Jack Conroy biographer Douglas Wixson interviewed Conroy in 1986, and Wixson writes: "Conroy guessed that it was a turf problem with Algren: Motley's subject matter was uncomfortably close to Algren's own." But Conroy thought that it was more than just a turf war. Wixson continues:

Figure 18: In June of 1936, Jack Conroy, beset with financial problems, moved from his home in Moberly, Missouri, to St. Louis to work for the Missouri Writers' Project. He first stayed in a louse-infested hotel, but then he moved to a run-down mansion nicknamed "The Kremlin." The building, divided into apartments, was on the corner of Franklin and Grand avenues. This photograph by Wayne Barker, circa 1936, is of Conroy in his "Kremlin" apartment (Jack Conroy Papers, The Newberry Library, Chicago).

"[Conroy guessed that] Algren sought to distance himself from Motley, particularly when literary naturalism began to fall into critical disfavor."[114]

Or maybe it was simply jealousy. Algren writes in *The Man with the Golden Arm* of drug addiction being a monkey on the back of Frankie Machine. Perhaps a green-eyed monster was on Algren's back. Two weeks after *Knock on Any Door* was released, it had sold 47,000 copies. The September 30, 1947, issue of *Look* magazine featured an eleven-page "picture dramatization" of the book, using excerpts of the novel and photographs of people from the Maxwell Street–West Madison Street Chicago neighborhood. From December 15, 1947, to January 20, 1948, King Features Syndicate ran a newspaper comic strip based on *Knock on Any Door*, telling Nick Romano's story in three panels per installment. The strip included brief excerpts from the book. Columbia Pictures made a 1949 movie based on the novel, featuring Humphrey Bogart as Nick Romano's attorney.[115]

The comparison of Motley to Algren is both sad and inescapable:

- Motley's first novel sold 47,000 copies in the first two weeks of publication. Algren's first novel sold only 762 copies in the first *year* of publication.[116]
- Motley's book was featured in a 1947 photo spread in *Look* magazine. Algren's scheduled 1950 picture story in *Life* magazine was cancelled in favor of a photo essay about life in a Mexican prison.[117]
- In 1949 Columbia Pictures made a movie based on *Knock on Any Door*. In 1955 United Artists released a movie based on *The Man with the Golden Arm*. However, it appears that Algren was not paid all of the money he was contractually owed for the sale of the movie rights to film director Otto Preminger.[118]

Algren scholar James R. Giles describes Algren as "an unjustly neglected writer clearly jealous of successful rivals." In his 1949 interview with Algren, Harvey Breit referred to Motley as "a writer who had done without money for a long time and who, a few years ago, had hit the jackpot with *Knock on Any Door*." It is possible that jealousy of Motley's early success fueled the meanness of Algren's reviews.[119]

Although Algren was critical of Motley's third novel, *Let No Man Write My Epitaph*, the story of mother and son heroin addicts, Algren liked *The Golden Spike*, Hal Ellson's book about a young drug addict. Writing in the *Saturday Review*, Algren described the book as "the straightest story on addiction yet to be done up in a fiction package, and one considerably more authentic than most of what has been marketed, by TV and *Harper's*, as fact." Algren may have praised *The Golden Spike* because Ellson's book is set in New York City, not Chicago, and so there was no turf problem. With the territoriality issue out of the way, Algren was free to write that the book was "authentic." Ellson was a recreational therapist at a Manhattan city hospital, working with troubled youths. Ellson comments: "I saw all kinds of mixed up and crazy things at that job, and I took my notebook everywhere I went. I made lots of notes, and a lot of the stuff in my books was just writing down what these young people said." Algren could certainly appreciate this, as Algren also recorded dialogue and anecdotes in notebooks while researching *The Man with the Golden Arm*.[120]

Tenth Principle: Do Not Use a Book as a Springboard for a Personal Essay

In early 1974 *Esquire* magazine offered Algren $1,250 for an article about boxer Rubin "Hurricane" Carter, who had been convicted of triple murder in 1967. At first Algren thought that Carter was guilty, but as he studied the case, he became convinced that Carter was innocent and that the boxer's conviction had been a serious miscarriage of justice. *Esquire* rejected Algren's article about Carter in the summer of 1974, but by then that probably did not matter to Algren. He needed a project and publicizing the plight of "Hurricane" Carter was it.[121]

In her essay, "Book Reviewing at the Local Level," professional book reviewer Jan Frazer admonishes aspiring reviewers: "Never use a book as a springboard for an elaborate personal essay on a subject close to your heart. Your review should be about the book, so the reader can determine whether or not it is a book he wants to read." But Algren did not heed Frazer's advice. Carter's book, *The Sixteenth Round*, was released in 1974, the same year that *Esquire* rejected Algren's article, and Algren did what Frazer said the reviewer should not do when Algren ostensibly reviewed Carter's book for the *Los Angeles Times*.[122]

In his alleged review for the *Times*, Algren did not review Carter's book. He did not even summarize the book. Instead, Algren reviewed and summarized Carter's trial (at times using information not contained in the book) and wrote an essay publicizing the Carter case and the likelihood of Carter's innocence. In writing this article, Algren was not a book reviewer; instead, he was Carter's publicist.[123]

Conclusion

During the time period covered by this essay (1947–1979), Nelson Algren broke almost all of the Ten Commandments of book reviewing.

This is not as bad as it appears, however. Even though he reviewed the books of his friends and his colleagues, these reviews were surprisingly unbiased. But as Algren admitted a few weeks before he died, he had a tendency of "sometimes being too quick to hit back." This was markedly evident in the reviews of the books of his enemy (Otto Preminger), his critic (Alfred Kazin), his imitator (Willard Motley), and of course, his former lover (Simone de Beauvoir).[124]

One cannot discount, however, the possible agreement, if not conspiracy, of his editors. This is especially apparent in his *Harper's Magazine* review of Beauvoir's book, *Force of Circumstance*. Excerpts of this book were published in *Harper's*. After reading that he was a "deviation" and a "defect" in the November 1964 issue of *Harper's*, and after seeing intimate portions of his letters to Beauvoir reprinted in the December 1964 issue of the magazine, is there any wonder that he retaliated in his May 1965 *Harper's* review of her book? Were the editors of *Harper's* surprised at his rage, or did they ask him to review the book, *expecting* an outpouring of vitriol? Were they intentionally *complicit* in his breaking of the Ninth Commandment?[125]

In his essay, "The Function of a Book Editor," Larry Swindell observes that a common weakness of many negative book reviews is an unjustified attack on the author. He maintains that "this is something that must always be deleted from a review. The book editor, functioning as an editor, does not rewrite or distort what the reviewer has presented, but he most certainly can cut." But the editors at *Harper's* did not cut. Were they afraid of Algren, or did they conclude that the vented spleen of a famous writer now spurned lover sells magazines? Possibly the latter; in 1963 *Harper's* had a circulation of about 260,000 with an annual deficit averaging about $125,000 to $150,000. By 1967 the circulation had risen to 276,638, but the annual deficit was still at $150,000. Is it any wonder that the *Harper's* editors trumpeted "Nelson Algren on Simone de Beauvoir" in a banner headline across the cover of the May 1965 issue?[126]

Although Algren broke most of the Ten Commandments, he somehow managed to rise above the wreckage. Over a period of forty-six years (1935–1981), he wrote and published 237 reviews, and many of them are quite good. Algren had his book reviews retyped as a seven-hundred-page collection. Do they deserve to be published as a separate volume of literary criticism? No, they do not. Too many of them consist of not enough review and either too much summary or too much quoted material. A seven-hundred-page book? No. But a two-hundred-and-fifty page book of the annotated "greatest hits" of his book reviews would be a worthwhile project.[127]

Gail Pool writes in her book, *Faint Praise: The Plight of Book Reviewing in America*:

[Book reviewing] guidelines should of course take in ethics, explicitly defining the kinds of relationships that aren't acceptable or allowed: no reviewing books written by friends, or by friends of friends, or by enemies—no personal relationships of any kind, and if in doubt, bow out.[128]

But Algren did not bow out. On page 126 of Jerre Mangione's book, *The Dream and the Deal: The Federal Writers' Project, 1935-1943*, there is a photograph of four men standing in a group. Perhaps this photograph should appear in any compilation of Algren's book reviews as silent testimony to the fact that even though Algren ignored the advice of Gail Pool and did not bow out, he often managed to make it work.[129]

The picture is not dated. The caption states merely that it was taken "sometime after the Project ended." The men are smiling and enjoying a drink. They are obviously acquaintances, friends, or colleagues. But what is the significance of this photograph? Three of these men are Jack Conroy, Emmett Dedmon, and Willard Motley, and between 1935 and 1981, Nelson Algren, the fourth man in the picture, reviewed the books of all three of the other men.[130]

NOTES

1. Bettina Drew, *Nelson Algren: A Life on the Wild Side* (Austin: University of Texas Press, 1991), 341; Matthew J. Bruccoli, *Nelson Algren: A Descriptive Bibliography* (Pittsburgh: University of Pittsburgh Press, 1985), 135–58; Matthew J. Bruccoli, "Addenda to Bruccoli, *Nelson Algren*," *The Papers of the Bibliographical Society of America*, September 1988, 369; Robert A. Tibbetts, "Further Addenda to Bruccoli, *Nelson Algren*," *The Papers of the Bibliographical Society of America*, June 1989, 215–17. Beginning in 1958, Algren would sometimes revise or reprint a review and publish it with a new title and in a different periodical. These revised and reprinted reviews are not included in this total of 237 published reviews. See Bruccoli, *Nelson Algren*, 149, 150, 157. Algren started reviewing movies in 1970. His four movie reviews, as reported by Bruccoli, are also not included in this total figure. See Bruccoli, *Nelson Algren*, 154, 155, 156.

2. Drew, *Nelson Algren*, 341–42.

3. Drew, *Nelson Algren*, 341, 402, 414; William Styron, review of *The Joint*, by James Blake, *New York Times Book Review*, 25 April 1971, 1, 10, 12.

4. Henry Kisor, "Nelson Algren, Hale and Salty at 64," *Chicago Daily News Panorama*, 27–28 October 1973, 2; see also Drew, *Nelson Algren*, 342; Jan Herman, "Nelson Algren: The Angry Author," *Chicago Sun-Times Chicagostyle*, 21 January 1979, 9; H.E.F. Donohue, *Conversations with Nelson Algren* (New York: Hill and Wang, 1964), 202–03.

5. Drew, *A Life on the Wild Side*, 341.

6. William McPherson, "The Book Reviewer's Craft," in *Book Reviewing*, ed. Sylvia E. Kamerman (Boston: The Writer, 1978), 72; Gail Pool, *Faint Praise: The Plight of Book Reviewing in America*. (Columbia: University of Missouri Press, 2007), 80, 137.

7. Sylvia E. Kamerman, foreword to Kamerman, *Book Reviewing*, viii–ix; Doris Grumbach, "A Review of the Craft of Reviewing," in Kamerman, *Book Reviewing*, 20; Lynne Sharon Schwartz, "The Making of a Reviewer," in Kamerman, *Book Reviewing*, 40; McPherson, "The Book Reviewer's Craft," in Kamerman, *Book Reviewing*, 70; L.E. Sissman, "Reviewer's Dues," in Kamerman, *Book Reviewing*, 123.

8. Grumbach, "A Review of the Craft of Reviewing," in Kamerman, *Book Reviewing*,

17–18; Herbert A. Kenny, "The Basics of Book Reviewing," in Kamerman, *Book Reviewing*, 85; Poole, *Faint Praise*, 56–57, 133.

9. Poole, *Faint Praise*, 50, 61–62; Robert Hauptman, *Authorial Ethics: How Writers Abuse Their Calling* (Lanham, Md.: Lexington Books, 2013), 14; Kamerman, foreword to Kamerman, *Book Reviewing*, vi–vii; Robert Kirsch, "The Importance of Book Reviewing," in Kamerman, *Book Reviewing*, 4–5; Kenny, "The Basics of Book Reviewing," in Kamerman, *Book Reviewing*, 85–86; P. Albert Duhamel, "The Structure of a Book Review," in Kamerman, *Book Reviewing*, 145–46.

10. Pool, *Faint Praise*, 62, 100, 137; Grumbach, "A Review of the Craft of Reviewing," in Kamerman, *Book Reviewing*, 24–25; B.A. Bergman, "Do's and Don'ts of Book Reviewing," in Kamerman, *Book Reviewing*, 30; Schwartz, "The Making of a Reviewer," in Kamerman, *Book Reviewing*, 49; McPherson, "The Book Reviewer's Craft," in Kamerman, *Book Reviewing*, 70–71; Sissman, "Reviewer's Dues," in Kamerman, *Book Reviewing*, 120.

11. Grumbach, "A Review of the Craft of Reviewing," in Kamerman, *Book Reviewing*, 24–25; Bergman, "Do's and Don'ts of Book Reviewing," in Kamerman, *Book Reviewing*, 30; McPherson, "The Book Reviewer's Craft," in Kamerman, *Book Reviewing*, 70–71; Sissman, "Reviewer's Dues," in Kamerman, *Book Reviewing*, 120–21; Pool, *Faint Praise*, 137.

12. Pool, *Faint Praise*, 50, 51, 137.

13. Pool, *Faint Praise*, 50, 51; Hauptman, *Authorial Ethics*, 14–15.

14. Hauptman, *Authorial Ethics*, 14–15; Kamerman, foreword to Kamerman, *Book Reviewing*, vi; Larry Swindell, "The Function of a Book Editor," in Kamerman, *Book Reviewing*, 82; Pool, *Faint Praise*, 67–72; Gillian Dooley, "True or False? The Role of Ethics in Book Reviewing," *Australian Humanities Review*, no. 60 (November 2016): 129, 132–33.

15. Grumbach, "A Review of the Craft of Reviewing," in Kamerman, *Book Reviewing*, 24–25; Jan Frazer, "Book Reviewing at the Local Level," in Kamerman, *Book Reviewing*, 107.

16. Bruccoli, *Nelson Algren*, 135.

17. Tracy Daugherty, *Just One Catch: A Biography of Joseph Heller* (New York: St. Martin's Press, 2011), 225–26; Dorothy P. Davison, ed., *The Book Review Digest: Fifty-Eighth Annual Cumulation, March 1962 to February 1963 Inclusive* (New York: H.W. Wilson, 1963), 534–35.

18. Richard G. Stern, "Bombers Away," review of *Catch-22*, by Joseph Heller, *New York Times Book Review*, 22 October 1961, 50.

19. "Good Soldier Yossarian," review of *Catch-22*, by Joseph Heller, *Time*, 27 October 1961, 98.

20. Nelson Algren, "The Catch," review of *Catch-22*, by Joseph Heller, *The Nation*, 4 November 1961, 358.

21. Daugherty, *Just One Catch*, 231; Nelson Algren, "*Catch-22*: A Happy Reappraisal," *Chicago Daily News*, 23 June 1962, 18; Van Allen Bradley, "Novelist Algren Campaigns for Neglected Book," *Chicago Daily News*, 23 June 1962, 18. In the 1950s and 1960s, Algren's opinion about a book could influence book sales. By Thanksgiving of 1961, *Catch-22* was popular on the East Coast but had not yet gained national attention. Algren's June 23, 1962, *Chicago Daily News* article spurred interest in the novel throughout the Midwest. See Daugherty, *Just One Catch*, 228–231. Algren's opinion mattered, even without a published book review. It appears that Algren never formally reviewed Ray Bradbury's book, *Fahrenheit 451*, for publication, even though Ballantine Books Senior Editor Stanley Kauffmann had sent him an advance copy in early September of 1953. Algren did, however, send a letter to Kauffmann, praising the book, and this September 30, 1953, letter was incorporated into Ballantine's fall 1953 advertising campaign." Ray Bradbury, *Fahrenheit 451*, 60th Anniversary Edition (New York: Simon & Schuster, 2013), 215.

22. McPherson, "The Book Reviewer's Craft," in Kamerman, *Book Reviewing*, 68, 72; Pool, *Faint Praise*, 80, 137.

23. John W. Aldridge, "*Catch-22*: Twenty-Five Years Later," *Michigan Quarterly Review* 26, no. 2 (Spring 1987): 380; reprint, John W. Aldridge, "*Catch-22*: Twenty-Five Years Later," in *Classics and Contemporaries* (Columbia: University of Missouri Press, 1992), 144–51. (The subsequent page reference is to the original article.)

24. Aldridge, "*Catch-22*," 379–80; Frederick Kiley and Walter McDonald, preface to *A "Catch-22" Casebook* (New York: Thomas Y. Crowell, 1973), v, 3–5; Walter James Miller, "Joseph Heller's Fiction," in *Modern Critical Interpretations: Joseph Heller's "Catch-22*," ed. Harold Bloom (Philadelphia: Chelsea House, 2001), 133. Algren continued to praise *Catch-22* years after it was published. In 1973 he wrote, "There must be a gene of poetry in a book to make it a classic. *Catch* possesses that gene." See Nelson Algren, "The Best Novels of World War II," *The Critic*, January–February 1973, 77; reprinted, "The Six Best Novels of World War II, and Why Five Died," *Intellectual Digest*, April 1973, 69. After attending a party in New York City, Algren told his friend Art Shay, "Great party. Joe Heller says my review of *Catch-22* made a lot of dough for him. All I called it was the best novel to come out of this or any war.... No lie, give or take *War and Peace*." See Art Shay, *Album for an Age: Unconventional Words and Pictures from the Twentieth Century* (Chicago: Ivan R. Dee, 2000), 93. (Ellipses in the original) In return, Algren scholar James R. Giles suggests that Algren's book, *A Walk on the Wild Side*, influenced Heller. See James R. Giles, *Confronting the Horror: The Novels of Nelson Algren* (Kent, Ohio: Kent State University Press, 1989), 8, 77, 82; see also Barbara Eckstein, *Sustaining New Orleans: Literature, Local Memory, and the Fate of a City* (New York: Routledge, 2006), 81. Algren did not let the success of *Catch-22* influence his review of Heller's second novel, *Something Happened*. Algren panned the book, writing, "Neither the black hilarity nor the tragic laughter of *Catch-22* is caught in *Something Happened*." See Nelson Algren, review of *Something Happened*, by Joseph Heller, *The Critic*, October–November–December, 1974, 91; Daugherty, *Just One Catch*, 525. Algren included one of Heller's stories as the lead story in his 1962 book, *Nelson Algren's Own Book of Lonesome Monsters*. See Joseph Heller, "World Full of Great Cities," in *Nelson Algren's Own Book of Lonesome Monsters*, ed. Nelson Algren (New York: Lancer Books, 1962), 11–23.

25. Sissman, "Reviewer's Dues," in Kamerman, *Book Reviewing*, 119, 120, 123; Schwartz, "The Making of a Reviewer," in Kamerman, *Book Reviewing*, 38, 40.

26. Nelson Algren, "The Stars Were for Hocking," review of *The Magnificent Rube: The Life and Gaudy Times of Tex Rickard*, by Charles Samuels, *New York Times Book Review*, 12 May 1957, 7.

27. Nelson Algren, "Shared Corruption," review of *The Coral Barrier*, by Pierre Gascar, *The Nation*, 20 May 1961, 443.

28. Duhamel, "The Structure of a Book Review," in Kamerman, *Book Reviewing*, 142, 144; Drew, *Nelson Algren*, 341.

29. Algren, "The Stars Were for Hocking," 7.

30. Poole, *Faint Praise*, 56–57.

31. Drew, *Nelson Algren*, 340–41, 402.

32. Niles Southern and Brooke Allen, eds., *Yours in Haste and Adoration: Selected Letters of Terry Southern* (New York: Antibookclub, 2015), 173; Terry Southern and Mason Hoffenberg, *Candy* (New York: G.P. Putnam's Sons, 1964); Nelson Algren, "Un-American Idea: Sex Can Be Funny," review of *Candy*, by Terry Southern and Mason Hoffenberg, *Life*, 8 May 1964, 8.

33. Southern and Allen, *Yours in Haste and Adoration*, 173.

34. Poole, *Faint Praise*, 56. As discussed later in the text, after Southern interviewed Algren in 1955, the two men stayed in touch, and Algren became not only a mentor of Southern but also one of the earliest champions of Southern's works. It is possible that Algren asked Southern for this additional information so that he could showcase Southern in his review and portray both him and his book in the best possible light.

35. Drew, *Nelson Algren*, 54, 75–84; Robert K. Landers, *An Honest Writer: The Life and Times of James T. Farrell* (San Francisco: Encounter Books, 2004), 206–07, 339. Robert K. Landers calls Algren a "tireless carper where Farrell was concerned," but Algren wrote only four known published reviews of Farrell's books. Two are discussed in this essay; the other two are Nelson Algren, review of *Judgment Day*, by James T. Farrell, *The Windsor Quarterly* 3, no. 1 (Fall 1935): 83–84, and Nelson Algren, "A World We Never Saw," review of *The Short Stories of James T. Farrell*, by James T. Farrell, *The Beacon* (November 1937), 20–21.

36. James T. Farrell, *An American Dream Girl and Other Stories* (New York: Vanguard Press, 1950); Nelson Algren, "Case Studies of Dreams," review of *An American Dream Girl*, by James T. Farrell, *The Saturday Review of Literature*, 9 December 1950, 16.

37. Algren, "Case Studies of Dreams," 16.

38. "Briefly Noted: *An American Dream Girl and Other Stories*," review of *An American Dream Girl and Other Stories*, by James T. Farrell, *The New Yorker*, 18 November 1950, 168.

39. Mertice M. James and Dorothy P. Davison, eds., *The Book Review Digest: Forty-Sixth Annual Cumulation, March 1950 to February 1951 Inclusive* (New York: H.W. Wilson, 1951), 295–96.

40. Nelson Algren, "New Chicago Cantos," review of *The Face of Time*, by James T. Farrell, *The Saturday Review*, 14 November 1953, 29.

41. James and Davison, *The Book Review Digest: Forty-Sixth Annual Cumulation*, 295–96; Mertice M. James and Dorothy P. Davison, eds., *The Book Review Digest: Forty-Ninth Annual Cumulation, March 1953 to February 1954 Inclusive* (New York: H.W. Wilson, 1954), 306.

42. Giles, *Confronting the Horror*, 87; Drew, *Nelson Algren*, 356–57.

43. Bergman, "Do's and Don'ts of Book Reviewing," in Kamerman, *Book Reviewing*, 30; Sissman, "Reviewer's Dues," in Kamerman, *Book Reviewing*, 120.

44. Pool, *Faint Praise*, 137. From the very beginning of his book reviewing career, Algren violated Sissman's and Poole's warnings about reviewing books of friends and acquaintances. Algren met writer Jack Conroy at a conference in Chicago in 1934, and they became friends almost immediately. Algren's review of Conroy's second book, *A World to Win*, was published in *The Windsor Quarterly* a year later. Matthew Bruccoli lists Algren's book reviews in chronological order in his book, *Nelson Algren: A Descriptive Bibliography*. Algren's review of *A World to Win* is the first review in Bruccoli's bibliography. In the 1930s Algren worked with poet Margaret Walker at the Illinois office of the Federal Writers' Project. Algren helped her write her poem, "For My People." This poem appears in her book, *For My People*, which was published in 1942. Algren reviewed her book in the February 1943 issue of *Poetry* magazine. This review is number thirteen in Bruccoli's bibliography. Algren also worked with Sam Ross at the Project, and Algren reviewed Ross's book for the *Chicago Sun-Times* in 1948. In all three reviews, Algren failed to mention his employment connection with the authors. See Bruccoli, *Nelson Algren*, 135–36, 142; Douglas Wixson, *Worker-Writer in America: Jack Conroy and the Tradition of Midwestern Literary Radicalism, 1898–1990* (Urbana: University of Illinois Press, 1994), 377–79; Jerre Mangione, *The Dream and the Deal: The Federal Writers' Project 1935–1943* (Boston: Little Brown, 1972), 119–24; Nelson Algren, review of *A World to Win*, by Jack Conroy, *The Windsor Quarterly* 3, no. 1 (Fall 1935): 73; Nelson Algren, "A Social Poet," review of *For My People*, by Margaret Walker, *Poetry*, February 1943, 634–36; Margaret Walker, *For My People* (New Haven, Conn: Yale University Press, 1942), 13–14; Liesl Olson, *Chicago Renaissance: Literature and Art in the Midwest Metropolis* (New Haven, Conn.: Yale University Press, 2017), 241–42; Nelson Algren, "Success Measured in Distance from 12th St. to Wilson Ave.," review of *Someday, Boy*, by Sam Ross, *Chicago Sun-Times Book Week*, 11 April 1948, 6X.

45. Bruce Jay Friedman, "Show Biz Connections," in *Nelson Algren's Own Book of Lonesome Monsters*, ed. Nelson Algren (New York: Lancer Books, 1962), 34–43; Colin Asher, *Never a Lovely So Real: The Life and Work of Nelson Algren* (New York: W.W. Norton, 2019), 410–12; Bruce Jay Friedman, "Algren and Shaw," *Smart*, January-February 1990, 24; reprinted, Bruce Jay Friedman, "Algren and Shaw," in *Even the Rhinos Were Nymphos* (Chicago: University of Chicago Press, 2000), 27 (subsequent references are to the original article); Nelson Algren, "The Radical Innocent," *The Nation*, 21 September 1964, 142–43.

46. Nelson Algren, "A Lone Wolf Crying in His Beer," review of *The Lonely Guy's Book of Life*, by Bruce Jay Friedman, *Chicago Tribune Book World*, 12 November 1978, 11; Asher, *Never a Lovely So Real*, 410; Drew, *Nelson Algren*, 321; Friedman, "Algren and Shaw," 24.

47. Friedman, "Algren and Shaw," 24.

48. Alston Anderson and Terry Southern, "Nelson Algren," *The Paris Review*, no. 11 (Winter 1955): 36–58; reprint; Alston Anderson and Terry Southern, "Nelson Algren," in *Writers at Work: The "Paris Review" Interviews*, ed. Malcolm Cowley (New York: The

Viking Press, 1958), 233; Lee Hill, *A Grand Guy: The Art and Life of Terry Southern* (New York: HarperCollins, 2001), 63–64; Nelson Algren, "Making It Hot," review of *The Magic Christian*, by Terry Southern, *The Nation*, 27 February 1960, 193; Nelson Algren, "Wild Times of Big Spender–This Baby Packs a Satire," review of *The Magic Christian*, by Terry Southern, *Chicago Sun-Times Book Week*, 21 February 1960, 4; Algren, "Un-American Idea: Sex Can Be Funny," 8; Nelson Algren, "The Donkeyman by Twilight," *The Nation*, 18 May 1964, 509.

49. Nelson Algren, "A Guy Who Got Wiped," review of *Blue Movie*, by Terry Southern, *Chicago Free Press* 1, no. 8 (16 November 1970): 33.

50. Drew, *Nelson Algren*, 332; Mary Wisniewski, *Algren: A Life* (Chicago: Chicago Review Press, 2017), 285; Nelson Algren, review of *The Long Walk at San Francisco State*, by Kay Boyle, *The Critic*, July–August 1971, 68–69; Duhamel, "The Structure of a Book Review," in Kamerman, *Book Reviewing*, 145.

51. Bergman, "Do's and Don'ts of Book Reviewing," in Kamerman, *Book Reviewing*, 30.

52. Nelson Algren, *The Last Carousel* (New York: G.P. Putnam's Sons, 1973), [v].

53. James Blake, *The Joint* (Garden City, N.Y.: Doubleday, 1971), [13]-14, 25–26, 50–51, [55], 62, 64–65, [381]; Nelson Algren, "*The Joint*: Fresh Approach to Where Man Takes Flight," review of *The Joint*, by James Blake, *Los Angeles Times Calendar*, 18 April 1971, 1, 26–27; Styron, review of *The Joint*, 1.

54. Blake, *The Joint*, [381]; James Blake, "Letters from an American Prisoner," *The Paris Review*, no. 13 (Summer 1956): 8–44; "Letters from James Blake: Southern Con, American Author," *Esquire*, August 1970, 76–79, 143.

55. [Masthead], *The Paris Review*, no. 52 (Summer 1971): [7]; Blake, *The Joint*, [13]-15, 64–70, 80–82, [171], 377–79, [381]; "James Blake, Pianist Who Wrote *Joint*, Letters from Prison," *New York Times*, 20 February 1979, sec. D, 15; Styron, review of *The Joint*, 1. After *The Joint* was published, the *Paris Review* again featured some of Blake's letters. See James Blake, The Happy Islanders," *The Paris Review*, no. 52 (Summer 1971): 101–27.

56. Algren, "*The Joint*," 1, 26–27.

57. William Styron, introduction to *The Joint*, by James Blake (London: Secker & Warburg, 1972), 7–11.

58. Drew, *Nelson Algren*, 101, 109, 134, 311–12, 324, 370; Nelson Algren, "Imaginary Pockets," review of *Hard Times: An Oral History of the Great Depression*, by Studs Terkel, *The Nation*, 30 March 1970, 376, 378; Mangione, *The Dream and the Deal*, 123, 127, 128.

59. Algren, "Imaginary Pockets," 378.

60. Nelson Algren, "Studs Terkel: The Survival of One of the Fittest," review of *Talking to Myself*, by Studs Terkel, *Los Angeles Times Book Review*, 10 April 1977, 1, 7–8.

61. Wisniewski, *Algren*, 281; F. Richard Ciccone, *Royko: A Life in Print* (New York: PublicAffairs, 2001), 147, 156–61. Mike Royko had at least four columns about Algren. Two of them were published in the 1960s; a third column, a posthumous tribute to Algren, was published four days after Algren died. Royko wrote another posthumous column several months later. See Mike Royko, "A Small-Print Burglar Hustles Nelson Algren," *Chicago Daily News*, 7 June 1966, 3; Mike Royko, "Nelson Algren Takes Dim View of Girl Scribblers," *Chicago Daily News*, 22 March 1967, 3; Mike Royko, "Algren's Golden Pen," *Chicago Sun-Times*, 13 May 1981, 2; Mike Royko, "Algren Paved the Way, *Chicago Sun-Times*, 2 October 1981, 2. "A Small-Print Burglar Hustles Nelson Algren" is primarily a letter that Algren wrote Royko. "Nelson Algren Takes Dim View of Girl Scribblers" was not written by Royko. Instead, Algren wrote it as a guest columnist.

62. Ciccone, *Royko*, 160; Nelson Algren, review of *Boss: Richard J. Daley of Chicago*, by Mike Royko, *The Critic*, May–June 1971, 72–75; Studs Terkel, review of *Boss: Richard J. Daley of Chicago*, by Mike Royko, *New York Times Book Review*, 4 April 1971, 46–47.

63. Algren, review of *Boss*, 73–74.

64. Ciccone, *Royko*, 108, 156, 158; Terkel, review of *Boss*, 46, 47.

65. Ciccone, *Royko*, 156, 158; Algren, "The Catch," 358; Saul D. Alinsky, "Life in the Second City," review of *Boss: Richard J. Daley of Chicago*, by Mike Royko, *The Nation*, 19 April 1971, 508.

66. Paul Kiniery, Ph.D., review of *Boss: Richard J. Daley of Chicago*, by Mike Royko, *Best*

Figure 19: Legendary Chicago book seller Stuart Brent, owner of the equally legendary book store, The Seven Stairs, was an ardent fan of Nelson Algren and his book, *The Neon Wilderness* (1947). Brent would periodically hold parties at his store to promote the book. One month he would call the event Algren's birthday, another month, the birthday of the publication of the book, and still another month, the birthday of the book itself. Brent writes in his autobiography, *The Seven Stairs*, that his friend Ira Blitzsten once remarked that "he didn't want Nelson to autograph his copy as he wanted the distinction of being the only person in Chicago with an unsigned copy."

It appears that this picture was taken at one of these parties. The group gathered around the cake includes two colleagues from Algren's days with the Illinois Writers' Project—Studs Terkel and Jack Conroy. From left to right are Studs Terkel, Robert Parrish, Stephen Spender, Stuart Brent, Jack Conroy, and Nelson Algren (Chicago History Museum, ICHi-092993).

Sellers: The Semi-Monthly Book Review 33, no. 1 (1 April 1971): 11; Perry L. Weed, "Second Thoughts on Mayor Daley," review of *Boss: Richard J. Daley of Chicago*, by Mike Royko, *The Saturday Review*, 24 April 1971, 29.

67.   Andrew M. Greeley, "Another Look at Mike Royko's *Boss*," review of *Boss: Richard J. Daley of Chicago*, by Mike Royko, *Chicago History* 1, no. 4 (Fall 1971): 250–51.

68.   Greeley, "Another Look at Mike Royko's *Boss*," 251.

69.   Roy M. Fisher, "He Made It," review of *Boss: Richard J. Daley of Chicago*, by Mike Royko, *The New Republic*, 17 April 1971, 28. Professor Carlo Rotella maintains that Royko pays homage to Algren in chapter 6 of *Boss*. Rotella observes that chapter 6 of *Boss* begins with the line, "The desk sergeant was drunk." Similarly, *The Man with the Golden Arm* begins with the sentence, "The captain never drank." Rotella writes: "It may seem an innocuous resonance, but for a writer who publicly places himself in Algren's debt, 'The captain never drank' has the referential heft of 'Call me Ishmael': one does not casually echo

the opening. The corrupt captain provides the template for the corrupt sergeant, much as Algren provided a template of Chicago writing for Royko." See Carlo Rotella, *October Cities: The Redevelopment of Urban Literature* (Berkeley: University of California Press, 1998), 335–36n24.

70. Bergman, "Do's and Don'ts of Book Reviewing," in Kamerman, *Book Reviewing*, 30.

71. Drew, *Nelson Algren*, 211, 213–14, 219, 260–65, 271, 283, 298, 308, 329, 342–43, 370; Nelson Algren, "Otto Preminger's Strange Suspenjers," in *Focus Media*, eds. Jess Ritter and Grover Lewis (San Francisco: Chandler Publishing, 1972), 10–18; reprint, Nelson Algren, "But Most of All, I Remember Otto," *Chicago Sun-Times Midwest Magazine*, 21 May 1972, 16–17, 22, 24; see also Nelson Algren, "Otto Preminger's Strange Suspenjers," in *The Last Carousel* (New York: Seven Stories Press, 1997), 21–36; Nelson Algren, "Shlepker, or White Goddess Say You Not Go That Part of Forest," *Cavalier*, February 1963, 12–14, 84–89. In February, 1955, Algren wrote a letter to Preminger in a vain attempt to mock and hurt him. The letter was later reprinted by Stuart Brent in his book, *The Seven Stairs*. See Stuart Brent, *The Seven Stairs* (Boston: Houghton Mifflin, 1962), 47–48; Drew, *Nelson Algren*, 262–63; Wixson, *Worker-Writer in America*, 469–70.

72. Otto Preminger, *Preminger: An Autobiography* (Garden City, N.Y.: Doubleday, 1977), dust jacket.

73. Nelson Algren, "Otto Preminger: Man with the Golden Prerogative," review of *Preminger: An Autobiography*, by Otto Preminger, *Los Angeles Times West View*, 15 May 1977, 3.

74. Algren, "Otto Preminger," 3.

75. Preminger, *Preminger*, 111; Algren, "Otto Preminger," 3.

76. Algren, "Otto Preminger," 3. The editors of the *Los Angeles Times* must have felt that Algren's review was sufficiently inflammatory that Preminger's side of the story needed to be told. A sidebar article appears on the same page of the newspaper as Algren's review. It is entitled "The View from Preminger's Side," and it consists of several paragraphs from Preminger's book wherein Preminger tells of working with Algren. See "The View from Preminger's Side," *Los Angeles Times West View*, 15 May 1977, 3.

77. Pool, *Faint Praise*, 50.

78. Nelson Algren, "City Against Itself," review of *Big Bill of Chicago*, by Lloyd Wendt and Herman Kogan and *Fabulous Chicago*, by Emmett Dedmon, *The Nation*, 13 February 1954, 135–36.

79. Emmett Dedmon, *Fabulous Chicago* (New York: Random House, 1953), dust jacket; Bruccoli, *Nelson Algren*, 145–47; "Emmett Dedmon, 65; Led 2 Chicago Papers," *New York Times*, 21 September 1983, sec. D, 27; Nelson Algren, "Early Chicago Journalism," *Chicago Free Press* 1, no. 3 (12 October 1970): 28; revised, Nelson Algren, "Different Clowns for Different Towns," in *The Last Carousel*, Seven Stories Press, 258; Nelson Algren, "Nelson Algren Writes Impressions of Series," *Chicago Sun-Times*," final edition, 2 October 1959, sec. 1, 5; Nelson Algren, "Algren Writes of Roses and Hits," *Chicago Sun-Times*, final edition, 3 October 1959, 5; Nelson Algren, "Nelson Algren's Reflections: Hep-Ghosts of the Rain," *Chicago Sun-Times*, final home edition, 10 October 1959, 12. This article also appears in the "final edition" of the October 10, 1959, *Sun-Times*, but with a different title. See Nelson Algren, "Algren at Game 6: Shoeless Joe is Gone, Too," *Chicago Sun-Times*, final edition, 10 October 1959, sec. 2, 12.

80. Algren, "City Against Itself," 135–36; Lloyd Wendt and Herman Kogan, *Big Bill of Chicago* (Indianapolis: Bobbs-Merrill, 1953), dust jacket; Drew, *Nelson Algren*, 271; Nelson Algren, *Chicago: City on the Make* (Sausalito, Calif.: Contact Editions, 1961, [5]; Bruccoli, *Nelson Algren*, 39.

81. Algren, "City Against Itself," 135; Pool, *Faint Praise*, 50.

82. Robert Cromie, *The Great Chicago Fire* (New York: McGraw-Hill, 1958), x, dust jacket; Nelson Algren, "Fabulous Firetrap," book review of *The Great Chicago Fire*, by Robert Cromie, *Saturday Review*, 22 November 1958, 35–36; Bruccoli, *Nelson Algren*, 148–49, 155, 170; Robert Cromie, "Cromie Looks at Authors and Books: Algren's 'Finksville' Has Another Name," *Chicago Tribune*, 16 February 1968, sec. 1, 23; Kenneth G. McCollum, *Nelson Algren: A Checklist* (Detroit: Gale Research, 1973), 23–24.

83. Nelson Algren, *"Chicago Review* in an Anthology," review of *The "Chicago Review"* *Anthology,* ed. David Ray, *Chicago Sun-Times Book Week,* 31 May 1959, 4; Nelson Algren, "No Lorgnette for Bessie," review of *The "Chicago Review" Anthology,* ed. David Ray, *The Nation,* 27 June 1959, 580–81; David Ray, ed., *The "Chicago Review" Anthology* (Chicago: University of Chicago Press, 1959), dust jacket.

84. David Ray, "A Talk on the Wild Side," *The Reporter,* June 11, 1959, 31–33; reprint, David Ray, "A Talk on the Wild Side: A *Cavalcade* Interview with Nelson Algren," *Cavalcade,* July 1964, 52–55; Ray, *The "Chicago Review" Anthology,* dust jacket.

85. Algren, *"Chicago Review* in an Anthology," 4; Algren, "No Lorgnette for Bessie," 581; David Ray, *The Endless Search: A Memoir* (Brooklyn: Soft Skull Press, 2003), 295; Ray, *The "Chicago Review" Anthology,* dust jacket.

86. Hauptman, *Authorial Ethics,* 14–15.

87. Edmund Fuller, *Man in Modern Fiction: Some Minority Opinions on Contemporary American Writing* (New York: Random House, 1958), 43–44.

88. Barbara Delatiner, "Algren Entering the East End Ring," *New York Times Long Island Weekly,* 26 April 1981, 15; Nelson Algren, "Author Bites Critic," review of *Man in Modern Fiction,* by Edmund Fuller, *The Nation,* 2 August 1958, 58. Robert Hauptman, author of *Authorial Ethics: How Writers Abuse Their Calling,* would probably maintain that Algren should not have written this review. Hauptman comments that "ignorant, careless, foolish, or vindictive reviewers may abuse their power." Hauptman believes that "if one chooses to publish and disseminate work, he or she must be willing to accept legitimate criticism." See Hauptman, *Authorial Ethics,* 14–15.

89. Alfred Kazin, "Some People Passing By," review of *A Walk on the Wild Side,* by Nelson Algren, *The New York Times Book Review,* 20 May 1956, 4; Alfred Kazin, "Nelson Algren on the Wild Side," in *Contemporaries* (Boston: Little, Brown, 1962), 183–85.

90. Wisniewski, *Algren,* 254; Nelson Algren, "Ride on an Elephant," review of *Contemporaries,* by Alfred Kazin, *The Nation,* 19 May 1962, 450; Bettina Drew similarly notes that for Algren, "a review could nicely serve the revenge motive." See Drew, *Nelson Algren,* 342.

91. Bruccoli, *Nelson Algren,* 135; Tibbetts, "Further Addenda to Bruccoli," 217; Pool, *Faint Praise,* 67–72.

92. Drew, *Nelson Algren,* 177–78, 322–24; Simone de Beauvoir, *A Transatlantic Love Affair: Letters to Nelson Algren,* comp. and annot. By Sylvie Le Bon de Beauvoir (New York: New Press, 1998), 6–12.

93. Deirdre Bair, *Simone de Beauvoir: A Biography* (New York: Summit Books, 1990), 500.

94. Drew, *Nelson Algren,* 322; Beauvoir, *A Transatlantic Love Affair,* 7; Simone de Beauvoir, "The Question of Fidelity," *Harper's Magazine,* November 1964, 57–64; Simone de Beauvoir, "An American Rendezvous: The Question of Fidelity, Part II," *Harper's Magazine,* December 1964, 111–114, 116, 119–20, 122; Nelson Algren, "The Question of Simone de Beauvoir," review of *Force of Circumstance,* by Simone de Beauvoir, *Harper's Magazine,* May 1965, 134, 136.

95. Algren, "The Question of Simone de Beauvoir," 134. Again, Robert Hauptman would undoubtedly condemn Algren's review. He writes in *Authorial Ethics: How Writers Abuse Their Calling,* that "no one should have to suffer the false accusations of the ill-informed or the abusive or hateful rantings of their enemies." See Hauptman, *Authorial Ethics,* 15.

96. Nelson Algren, "Simone à Go Go," review of *Force of Circumstance,* by Simone de Beauvoir, *Ramparts,* October 1965, 65.

97. Nelson Algren, "How to Break Silence Conspiracy Over Old Age," review of *The Coming of Age,* by Simone de Beauvoir, *Los Angeles Times Book Review,* 25 June 1972, 1, 13.

98. Nelson Algren, "Courage, Gossip, and Politics," review of *Hearts and Minds: The Common Journey of Simone de Beauvoir and Jean-Paul Sartre,* by Axel Madsen, *Chicago Tribune Book World,* 9 October 1977, 4.

99. Algren, "Courage, Gossip, and Politics," 4.

100. Beauvoir, "The Question of Fidelity," 64; Beauvoir, "An American Rendezvous," 114, 116, 122; Beauvoir, *A Transatlantic Love Affair,* 9–10.

101. Mangione, *The Dream and the Deal,* 121, 126, 348, 369; Willard Motley, "Voice of

the Reader: An Author Protests," *Chicago Tribune Magazine of Books*, 1 February 1959, 11; Harvey Breit, "Talk with Nelson Algren," *New York Times Book Review*, 2 October 1949, 33; reprint, Harvey Breit, "Nelson Algren," in *The Writer Observed* (Cleveland: World Publishing, 1956), 86–87. (Subsequent page references are to the original article.)

102. Beauvoir, *A Transatlantic Love Affair*, 9; Drew, *Nelson Algren*, 204–08; Breit, "Talk with Nelson Algren," 33; Breit, *The Writer Observed*, dust jacket; Orville Prescott, "Books of the Times," review of *Knock on Any Door*, by Willard Motley, *New York Times*, 5 May 1947, 21; Willard Motley, *Knock on Any Door* (New York: D. Appleton-Century, 1947), 3–4, 27–28, 187–98, 311–20, 324–27, 453, 467, dust jacket; Rick Kogan, "Remembering the Forgotten Willard Motley," *Chicago Tribune*, 5 April 2015, sec. 4, 6.

103. Breit, "Talk with Nelson Algren," 33.

104. Bruccoli, *Nelson Algren*, 139–41; Breit, "Talk with Nelson Algren," 33; Mertice M. James and Dorothy Brown, eds., *The Book Review Digest: Forty-Third Annual Cumulation, March 1947 to February 1948 Inclusive* (New York: H.W. Wilson, 1948), 654–55.

105. Horace R. Cayton, "A Terrifying Cross Section of Chicago," review of *Knock on Any Door*, by Willard Motley, *Chicago Tribune Magazine of Books*, 4 May 1947, 3.

106. Nelson Algren, *Never Come Morning* (New York: Seven Stories Press, 1996), 11, 74–75, 282–84; Motley, *Knock on Any Door*, 111–12.

107. Robert E. Fleming, *Willard Motley* (Boston: Twayne Publishers, 1978), 95.

108. Nelson Algren, "Motley Novel Tackles the Dope Problem," review of *Let No Man Write My Epitaph*, by Willard Motley, *Chicago Tribune Magazine of Books*, 17 August 1958, 1–2. Algren also reviewed this book for *The Nation*. In *The Nation* review he questioned the realism and authenticity of Motley's depiction of drug addiction and America's drug problem: "This novel was plucked, not from those corners where the traffic is plied, but off the national paperback clothesline as it stretches, drug store to drug store, coast to coast." See Nelson Algren, "Epitaph Writ in Syrup," review of *Let No Man Write My Epitaph*, by Willard Motley, *The Nation*, 16 August 1958, 78.

109. "The Wire Recorder Ear," review of *Let No Man Write My Epitaph*, by Willard Motley, *Time*, 11 August 1958, 74; David Dempsey, "Skid Row Revisited," review of *Let No Man Write My Epitaph*, by Willard Motley, *New York Times Book Review*, 10 August 1958, 18; Nelson Algren, *A Walk on the Wild Side* (N.p.: Thunder's Mouth Press, 1990), 266–69, 338–40. Algren also wrote about the legless "professional strong man" Railroad Shorty in the story, *The Face on the Barroom Floor*. See Nelson Algren, "The Face on the Barroom Floor," in *The Neon Wilderness* (New York: Seven Stories Press, 1986), 130, 133; Nelson Algren, "The Face on the Barroom Floor," *The American Mercury* (January 1947), 26–35; Martha Heasley Cox and Wayne Chatterton, *Nelson Algren* (Boston: Twayne, 1975), 86–88.

110. Motley, "An Author Protests," 11; Wixson, *Worker-Writer in America*, 477; Dorothy P. Davison, ed., *The Book Review Digest: Fifty-Fourth Annual Cumulation, March 1958 to February 1959 Inclusive* (New York: H.W. Wilson, 1959), 782; Dooley, "True or False?," 133. Douglas Wixson comments that Algren's "savage" review of *Let No Man Write My Epitaph* "stung the sensitive black writer who had been a colleague of Algren's on the Illinois Writers' Project." See Wixson, *Worker-Writer in America*, 477, 578n17. It appears that Motley was not asked to respond to Algren's review of *Let No Man Write My Epitaph*. Instead, he wrote a letter to the newspaper. This was not the case in 1976, when Algren reviewed *City Dogs*, by William Brashler, for the *Chicago Daily News*. Algren was so critical of this book about a seamy Chicago North Side neighborhood that the newspaper invited Brashler to comment on Algren's review. Henry Kisor of the *Daily News* writes: "With customary acuteness Algren has kicked *City Dogs* smartly in the ribs: Its people, he writes, lack any chance for redemption and therefore cannot be real. This very judgment raises the question whether Algren and Brashler perhaps have such different views of society and humanity that the other side also ought to be heard. Should an author be afforded a chance to defend his book side by side with the review itself? It's unusual, but not unheard of. So Brashler's reaction to the review was invited." See Nelson Algren, "Uptown's Underside: A Grim Novel," review of *City Dogs*, by William Brashler, *Chicago Daily News Panorama*, 10–11 January 1976, 6; Henry Kisor, "Clashing Visions: Brashler's Reply," *Chicago Daily News Panorama*, 10–11 January 1976, 6.

111. Fleming, *Willard Motley*, [14]; Nelson Algren, "The Trouble at Gringo Gulch," review of *Let Noon Be Fair*, by Willard Motley, *New York Herald Tribune Book Week*, 6 March 1966, 15.

112. Nelson Algren, "Motley: He Was an 'Invisible Man' among Black Writers," review of *The Diaries of Willard Motley*, ed. Jerome Klinkowitz, *Chicago Tribune Book World*, 25 February 1979, 1; Algren, "Otto Preminger," 3.

113. "Letters," *Chicago Tribune Book World*, 11 March 1979, 2.

114. Wixson, *Worker-Writer in America*, 578n17; Arthur Shay, "Author on the Make: Nelson Algren's Bittersweet Affair with Chicago," *Chicago Tribune Magazine*, 14 September 1986, 39; Alson J. Smith, *Chicago's Left Bank* (Chicago: Henry Regnery Co., 1953), 247–48. Studs Terkel compares Algren's and Farrell's writing styles in his memoirs: "James T. Farrell was among the first to have captured the argot of Chicago streets, South Side Irish. He caught the language, the idiom, that Chicagoesque quality. But Nelson went a step beyond; there was a lyricism to his writing, a poetic aspect." See Studs Terkel, *Touch and Go: A Memoir* (New York: The New Press, 2007), 198.

115. Nelson Algren, *The Man with the Golden Arm*, eds. William J. Savage Jr., and Daniel Simon, 50th Anniversary Critical Edition (New York: Seven Stories Press, [1999]), 57–61; Fleming, *Willard Motley*, 61; "Knock on Any Door," *Look*, 30 September 1947, 21–31.

116. Fleming, *Willard Motley*, 61; Drew, *Nelson Algren*, 86–87.

117. Fleming, *Willard Motley*, 61; "Knock on Any Door," *Look*, 21–31; Drew, *Nelson Algren*, 211–212, 218–19; "The Black Palace," *Life*, 3 April 1950, 106–115; Shay, "Author on the Make," 32.

118. Fleming, *Willard Motley*, 61; Preminger, *Preminger*, 113, 197; Drew, *Nelson Algren*, 271.

119. Giles, *Confronting the Horror*, 87; Breit, "Talk with Nelson Algren," 33. See also Drew, *Nelson Algren*, 356–57; Fleming, *Willard Motley*, 119. Douglas Wixson writes at some length about Algren's bitterness during the latter half of the 1950s. Wixson indicates that this was due to Algren's sale of the film rights for *The Man with the Golden Arm* to movie producer Bob Roberts, who then sold them (for probably much more money) to film director Otto Preminger. Wixson comments that his bitterness was also fueled by the negative reviews of Algren's novel, *A Walk on the Wild Side* (1956). Wixson suggests that Algren's bitterness tainted his review of *Let No Man Write My Epitaph*. See Wixson, *Worker-Writer in America*, 468–72. The December 1963 issue of *Rogue* featured interviews with Algren, Motley, and Harper Lee. There was no panel discussion, instead, the interviews were separate, and so there was no interaction between Algren and Motley. See Bob Ellison, "Three Best-Selling Authors: Conversations," *Rogue*, December 1963, 20–24, 78–79.

120. Drew, *Nelson Algren*, 127–28; Lee Server, "Ellson, Hal," in *Encyclopedia of Pulp Fiction Writers* (New York: Checkmark Books, 2002), 89; Nelson Algren, "Spoon-fed Universe," review of *The Golden Spike*, by Hal Ellson, *The Saturday Review*, 6 December 1952, 35; Anderson and Southern, "Nelson Algren," *The Paris Review*, 46–47; reprint, Anderson and Southern, "Nelson Algren," in *Writers at Work*, 240.

121. Drew, *Nelson Algren*, 350–52.

122. Rubin "Hurricane" Carter, *The Sixteenth Round: From Number 1 Contender to # 45472* (Toronto: Penguin Canada, 1974), [iv]; Frazer, "Book Reviewing at the Local Level," in Kamerman, *Book Reviewing*, 107; Nelson Algren, "Hurricane Carter Awaits Bell," review of *The Sixteenth Round: From Number One Contender to # 45472*, by Rubin "Hurricane" Carter, *Los Angeles Times Calendar*, 28 July 1974, 60–61.

123. It appears that Algren used Hurricane Carter's trial transcript in writing his quasi-review of Carter's book. Carter recounts the testimony of Sergeant Capter in *The Sixteenth Round*: "'I had no reason actually to take them to headquarters,' answered the veteran sergeant. 'I figured I'd bring them to the scene of the crime because they're only suspects,' he said. And that's what put us in jail—bringing us to the scene. Following Capter's testimony, there was a long line of cop witnesses coming and going, all testifying to some small detail of what they had performed in their lines of duty." Algren relates the same testimony in his review, but Algren continues with additional testimony

not contained in *The Sixteenth Round*: "'I figured I'd bring them back to the scene of the crime,' the arresting officer explained later in court, 'as they were only suspects. I had no reason actually to take them to headquarters. I asked Bello (the white man who'd warned off the woman) to look at Carter's white 1966 Dodge. He told me that that was the car.' 'Did he walk right up and look at it?' 'No. He stood right there.'" Carter, *The Sixteenth Round*, 290; Algren, "Hurricane Carter Awaits Bell," 60; Drew, *Nelson Algren*, 355–56.

124. Delatiner, "Algren Entering the East End Ring," 15.

125. Beauvoir, "The Question of Fidelity," 64; Beauvoir, "An American Rendezvous," 114, 116, 122; Algren, "The Question of Simone de Beauvoir," 134, 136.

126. Swindell, "The Function of a Book Editor," in Kamerman, *Book Reviewing*, 82; Sissman, "Reviewer's Dues," in Kamerman, *Book Reviewing*, 120–21; Jack Bales, *Willie Morris: An Exhaustive Annotated Bibliography and a Biography* (Jefferson, N.C.: McFarland, 2006), 41; Willie Morris, *New York Days* (Boston: Little, Brown, 1993), 21, 30, 80–81.

127. Drew, *Nelson Algren*, 341; Bruccoli, *Nelson Algren*, 135–58; Bruccoli, "Addenda to Bruccoli," 369; Tibbetts, "Further Addenda to Bruccoli," 215–17. Some of Algren's later reviews might have to be excluded from his "greatest hits." Mary Wisniewski writes that many of the book reviews Algren submitted to the *Chicago Tribune* during the 1970s "needed a lot of editing." See Wisniewski, *Algren*, 282–85.

128. Pool, *Faint Praise*, 137.

129. Mangione, *The Dream and the Deal*, 126.

130. Mangione, *The Dream and the Deal*, 126; Bruccoli, *Nelson Algren*, 135, 147, 149, 157.

Selected Bibliography

Aldridge, John W. "*Catch-22*: Twenty-Five Years Later." In *Classics and Contemporaries*, 144–51. Columbia: University of Missouri Press, 1992.

Aldridge, John W. "*Catch-22*: Twenty-Five Years Later." *Michigan Quarterly Review* 26, no. 2 (Spring 1987): 379–86.

Algren, Nelson. "Algren at Game 6: Shoeless Joe is Gone, Too." *Chicago Sun-Times*, final edition, 10 October 1959, sec. 2, 12.

Algren, Nelson. "Algren Writes of Roses and Hits." *Chicago Sun-Times*, final edition, 3 October 1959, 5.

Algren, Nelson. *America Eats*. Iowa City: University of Iowa Press, 1992.

Algren, Nelson. "Author Bites Critic." Review of *Man in Modern Fiction*, by Edmund Fuller. *The Nation*, 2 August 1958, 57–58.

Algren, Nelson. "The Best Novels of World War II." *The Critic*, January–February 1973, 74–77.

Algren, Nelson. "Bitter Physics of the Deprived." Review of *Duke*, by Hal Ellson. *The Saturday Review*, 4 July 1953, 20–21.

Algren, Nelson. "But Most of All, I Remember Otto." *Chicago Sun-Times Midwest Magazine*, 21 May 1972, 16–17, 22, 24.

Algren, Nelson. "Case Studies of Dreams." Review of *An American Dream Girl*, by James T. Farrell. *The Saturday Review of Literature*, 9 December 1950, 16.

Algren, Nelson. "The Catch." Review of *Catch-22*, by Joseph Heller. *The Nation*, 4 November 1961, 357–58.

Algren, Nelson. "*Catch-22*: A Happy Reappraisal." *Chicago Daily News*, 23 June 1962, 18.

Algren, Nelson. *Chicago: City on the Make*. Sausalito, Calif.: Contact Editions, 1961.

Algren, Nelson. "*Chicago Review* in an Anthology." Review of *The "Chicago Review" Anthology*. Edited by David Ray. *Chicago Sun-Times Book Week*, 31 May 1959, 4.

Algren, Nelson. "City Against Itself." Review of *Big Bill of Chicago*, by Lloyd Wendt and Herman Kogan and *Fabulous Chicago*, by Emmett Dedmon. *The Nation*, 13 February 1954, 135–36.

Algren, Nelson. "Courage, Gossip, and Politics." Review of *Hearts and Minds: The Common Journey of Simone de Beauvoir and Jean-Paul Sartre*, by Axel Madsen. *Chicago Tribune Book World*, 9 October 1977, 1, 4.

Algren, Nelson. "The Donkeyman by Twilight." *The Nation*, 18 May 1964, 509–12.

Algren, Nelson. "Early Chicago Journalism." *Chicago Free Press* 1, no. 3 (12 October 1970): 28–30.

Algren, Nelson. "Epitaph Writ in Syrup." Review of *Let No Man Write My Epitaph*, by Willard Motley. *The Nation*, 16 August 1958, 78.

Algren, Nelson. "Fabulous Firetrap." Review of *The Great Chicago Fire*, by Robert Cromie. *Saturday Review*, 22 November 1958, 35–36.

Algren, Nelson. "A Guy Who Got Wiped." Review of *Blue Movie*, by Terry Southern. *Chicago Free Press* 1, no. 8 (16 November 1970): 32–33.

Algren, Nelson. "How to Break Silence Conspiracy Over Old Age." Review of *The Coming of Age*, by Simone de Beauvoir. *Los Angeles Times Book Review*, 25 June 1972, 1, 13, 15.

Algren, Nelson. "Hurricane Carter Awaits Bell." Review of *The Sixteenth Round: From Number One Contender to # 45472*, by Rubin "Hurricane" Carter. *Los Angeles Times Calendar*, 28 July 1974, 60–61.

Algren, Nelson. "Imaginary Pockets." Review of *Hard Times: An Oral History of the Great Depression*, by Studs Terkel. *The Nation*, 30 March 1970, 376, 378.

Algren, Nelson. "*The Joint*: Fresh Approach to Where Man Takes Flight." Review of *The Joint*, by James Blake. *Los Angeles Times Calendar*, 18 April 1971, 1, 26–27.

Algren, Nelson. "Jungle of Tenements." Review of *The Pecking Order*, by Mark Kennedy. *The Saturday Review*, 6 June 1953, 16.

Algren, Nelson. *The Last Carousel*. New York: G.P. Putnam's Sons, 1973.

Algren, Nelson. *The Last Carousel*. New York: Seven Stories Press, 1997.

Algren, Nelson. "A Lone Wolf Crying in His Beer." Review of *The Lonely Guy's Book of Life*, by Bruce Jay Friedman. *Chicago Tribune Book World*, 12 November 1978, 11.

Algren, Nelson. "Making It Hot." Review of *The Magic Christian*, by Terry Southern. *The Nation*, 27 February 1960, 192–93.

Algren, Nelson. *The Man with the Golden Arm*. Edited by William J. Savage, Jr., and Daniel Simon. 50th Anniversary Critical Edition. New York: Seven Stories Press, [1999].

Algren, Nelson. "Motley: He Was an 'Invisible Man' among Black Writers." Review of *The Diaries of Willard Motley*. Edited by Jerome Klinkowitz. *Chicago Tribune Book World*, 25 February 1979, 1.

Algren, Nelson. "Motley Novel Tackles the Dope Problem." Review of *Let No Man Write My Epitaph*. *Chicago Tribune Magazine of Books*, 17 August 1958, 1–2.

Algren, Nelson. "Nelson Algren Writes Impressions of Series." *Chicago Sun-Times*, final edition, 2 October 1959, sec. 1, 5.

Algren, Nelson. "Nelson Algren's Reflections: Hep-Ghosts of the Rain." *Chicago Sun-Times*, final home edition, 10 October 1959, 12.

Algren, Nelson. *Never Come Morning*. New York: Seven Stories Press, 1996.

Algren, Nelson. "New Chicago Cantos." Review of *The Face of Time*, by James T. Farrell. *The Saturday Review*, 14 November 1953, 29.

Algren, Nelson. "No Lorgnette for Bessie." Review of *The "Chicago Review" Anthology*. Edited by David Ray. *The Nation*, 27 June 1959, 580–81.

Algren, Nelson. "Otto Preminger: Man with the Golden Prerogative." Review of *Preminger: An Autobiography*, by Otto Preminger, *Los Angeles Times West View*, 15 May 1977, 3.

Algren, Nelson. "Otto Preminger's Strange Suspenjers." In *Focus Media*, edited by Jess Ritter and Grover Lewis, 10–18. San Francisco: Chandler Publishing, 1972.

Algren, Nelson. "The Question of Simone de Beauvoir." Review of *Force of Circumstance*, by Simone de Beauvoir. *Harper's Magazine*, May 1965, 134, 136.

Algren, Nelson. "The Radical Innocent." *The Nation*, 21 September 1964, 142–43.

Algren, Nelson. "Record of a Sure Hand." Review of *The Golden Watch*, by Albert Halper. *The Saturday Review*, 7 March 1953, 27–28.

Algren, Nelson. Review of *Boss: Richard J. Daley of Chicago*, by Mike Royko. *The Critic*, May–June 1971, 72–75.

Algren, Nelson. Review of *Judgment Day*, by James T. Farrell. *The Windsor Quarterly* 3, no. 1 (Fall 1935): 83–84.

Algren, Nelson. Review of *The Long Walk at San Francisco State*, by Kay Boyle. *The Critic*, July–August 1971, 68–69.

Algren, Nelson. Review of *Something Happened*, by Joseph Heller. *The Critic*, October–November–December 1974, 90–91.

Algren, Nelson. Review of *A World to Win*, by Jack Conroy. *The Windsor Quarterly* 3, no. 1 (Fall 1935): 73.

Algren, Nelson. "Ride on an Elephant." Review of *Contemporaries*, by Alfred Kazin. *The Nation*, 19 May 1962, 449–50.

Algren, Nelson. "Shared Corruption." Review of *The Coral Barrier*, by Pierre Gascar. *The Nation*, 20 May 1961, 443.

Algren, Nelson. "Shlepker, or White Goddess Say You Not Go That Part of Forest." *Cavalier*, February 1963, 12–14, 84–89.

Algren, Nelson. "Simone à Go Go." Review of *Force of Circumstance*, by Simone de Beauvoir. *Ramparts*, October 1965, 65–67.

Algren, Nelson. "The Six Best Novels of World War II, and Why Five Died." *Intellectual Digest*, April 1973, 68–69.

Algren, Nelson. "A Social Poet." Review of *For My People*, by Margaret Walker. *Poetry*, February 1943, 634–36.

Algren, Nelson. "Spoon-fed Universe." Review of *The Golden Spike*, by Hal Ellson. *The Saturday Review*, 6 December 1952, 35.

Algren, Nelson. "The Stars Were for Hocking." Review of *The Magnificent Rube: The Life and Gaudy Times of Tex Rickard*, by Charles Samuels. *New York Times Book Review*, 12 May 1957, 7.

Algren, Nelson. "Studs Terkel: The Survival of One of the Fittest." Review of *Talking to Myself*, by Studs Terkel. *Los Angeles Times Book Review*, 10 April 1977, 1, 7–8.

Algren, Nelson. "Success Measured in Distance from 12th St. to Wilson Ave." Review of *Someday, Boy*, by Sam Ross. *Chicago Sun-Times Book Week*, 11 April 1948, 6X.

Algren, Nelson. "The Trouble at Gringo Gulch." Review of *Let Noon Be Fair*, by Willard Motley. *New York Herald Tribune Book Week*, 6 March 1966, 5, 15.

Algren, Nelson. "Un-American Idea: Sex Can Be Funny." Review of *Candy*, by Terry Southern and Mason Hoffenberg. *Life*, 8 May 1964, 8.

Algren, Nelson. "Uptown's Underside: A Grim Novel." Review of *City Dogs*, by William Brashler. *Chicago Daily News Panorama*, 10–11 January 1976, 6.

Algren, Nelson. *A Walk on the Wild Side*. N.p.: Thunder's Mouth Press, 1990.

Algren, Nelson. "Wild Times of Big Spender—This Baby Packs a Satire." Review of *The Magic Christian*, by Terry Southern. *Chicago Sun-Times Book Week*, 21 February 1960, 4.

Algren, Nelson. "A World We Never Saw." Review of *The Short Stories of James T. Farrell*, by James T. Farrell. *The Beacon*, November 1937, 20–21.

Alinsky, Saul D. "Life in the Second City." Review of *Boss: Richard J. Daley of Chicago*, by Mike Royko. *The Nation*, 19 April 1971, 507–08.

Anderson, Alston, and Terry Southern. "Nelson Algren." *The Paris Review*, no. 11 (Winter 1955): 36–58.

Anderson, Alston, and Terry Southern. "Nelson Algren." In *Writers at Work: The "Paris Review" Interviews*, edited by Malcolm Cowley, 231–49. New York: Viking Press, 1958.

Asher, Colin. *Never a Lovely So Real: The Life and Work of Nelson Algren*. New York: W.W. Norton, 2019.

Bair, Deirdre. *Simone de Beauvoir: A Biography*. New York: Summit Books, 1990.

Bales, Jack. *Willie Morris: An Exhaustive Annotated Bibliography and a Biography*. Jefferson, N.C.: McFarland, 2006.

Beauvoir, Simone de. "An American Rendezvous: The Question of Fidelity, Part II." *Harper's Magazine*, December 1964, 111–14, 116, 119–20, 122.

Beauvoir, Simone de. "The Question of Fidelity." *Harper's Magazine*, November 1964, 57–64.

Beauvoir, Simone de. *A Transatlantic Love Affair: Letters to Nelson Algren*. Comp. and annot. by Sylvie Le Bon de Beauvoir. New York: New Press, 1998.

"The Black Palace." *Life*, 3 April 1950, 106–115.

Blake, James. "The Happy Islanders." *The Paris Review*, no. 52 (Summer 1971): 101–27.

Blake, James. *The Joint*. Garden City, N.Y.: Doubleday, 1971.

Blake, James. "Letters from an American Prisoner." *The Paris Review*, no. 13 (Summer 1956): 8–44.

Bradbury, Ray. *Fahrenheit 451*. 60th Anniversary Edition. New York: Simon & Schuster, 2013.

Bradley, Van Allen. "Novelist Algren Campaigns for Neglected Book." *Chicago Daily News*, 23 June 1962, 18.

Breit, Harvey. "Nelson Algren." In *The Writer Observed*, 85–87. Cleveland: World Publishing, 1956.

Breit, Harvey. "Talk with Nelson Algren." *New York Times Book Review*. 2 October 1949, 33.

Brent, Stuart. *The Seven Stairs*. Boston: Houghton Mifflin, 1962.

"Briefly Noted: *An American Dream Girl and Other Stories*." Review of *An American Dream Girl and Other Stories*, by James T. Farrell. *The New Yorker*, 18 November 1950, 168.

Bruccoli, Matthew J. "Addenda to Bruccoli, *Nelson Algren*." *The Papers of the Bibliographical Society of America*, September 1988, 367–69.

Bruccoli, Matthew J. *Nelson Algren: A Descriptive Bibliography*. Pittsburgh: University of Pittsburgh Press, 1985.

Carter, Rubin "Hurricane." *The Sixteenth Round: From Number 1 Contender to # 45472*. Toronto: Penguin Canada, 1974.

Cayton, Horace R. "A Terrifying Cross Section of Chicago." Review of *Knock on Any Door*, by Willard Motley. *Chicago Tribune Magazine of Books*, 4 May 1947, 3.

Ciccone, F. Richard. *Royko: A Life in Print*. New York: PublicAffairs, 2001.

Cox, Martha Heasley, and Wayne Chatterton. *Nelson Algren*. Boston: Twayne, 1975.

Cromie, Robert. *The Great Chicago Fire*. New York: McGraw-Hill, 1958.

Cromie, Robert. "Cromie Looks at Authors and Books: Algren's 'Finksville' Has Another Name." *Chicago Tribune*, 16 February 1968, sec. 1, 23.

Daugherty, Tracy. *Just One Catch: A Biography of Joseph Heller*. New York: St. Martin's Press, 2011.

Davison, Dorothy P., ed. *The Book Review Digest: Fifty-Fourth Annual Cumulation, March 1958 to February 1959 Inclusive*. New York: H.W. Wilson, 1959.

Davison, Dorothy P., ed. *The Book Review Digest: Fifty-Eighth Annual Cumulation, March 1962 to February 1963 Inclusive*. New York: H.W. Wilson, 1963.

Dedmon, Emmett. *Fabulous Chicago*. New York: Random House, 1953.

Delatiner, Barbara. "Algren Entering the East End Ring." *New York Times Long Island Weekly*, 26 April 1981, 15.

Dempsey, David. "Skid Row Revisited." Review of *Let No Man Write My Epitaph*, by Willard Motley. *New York Times Book Review*, 10 August 1958, 18.

Donohue, H.E.F. *Conversations with Nelson Algren*. New York: Hill and Wang, 1964.

Dooley, Gillian. "True or False? The Role of Ethics in Book Reviewing." *Australian Humanities Review*, no. 60 (November 2016): 127–40.

Drew, Bettina. *Nelson Algren: A Life on the Wild Side*. Austin: University of Texas Press, 1991.

Eckstein, Barbara. *Sustaining New Orleans: Literature, Local Memory, and the Fate of a City*. New York: Routledge, 2006.

Ellison, Bob. "Three Best-Selling Authors: Conversations." *Rogue*, December 1963, 20–24, 78–79.

"Emmett Dedmon, 65; Led 2 Chicago Papers." *New York Times*, 21 September 1983, sec. D, 27.

Farrell, James T. *An American Dream Girl and Other Stories*. New York: Vanguard Press, 1950.

Fisher, Roy M. "He Made It." Review of *Boss: Richard J. Daley of Chicago*, by Mike Royko. *The New Republic*, 17 April 1971, 28–29.

Fleming, Robert E. *Willard Motley*. Boston: Twayne Publishers, 1978.

Friedman, Bruce Jay. "Algren and Shaw." *Smart*, January–February 1990, 24.

Friedman, Bruce Jay. *Even the Rhinos Were Nymphos*. Chicago: University of Chicago Press, 2000.

Friedman, Bruce Jay. "Show Biz Connections." In *Nelson Algren's Own Book of Lonesome Monsters*, edited by Nelson Algren, 34–43. New York: Lancer Books, 1962.

Fuller, Edmund. *Man in Modern Fiction: Some Minority Opinions on Contemporary American Writing*. New York: Random House, 1958.

Giles, James R. *Confronting the Horror: The Novels of Nelson Algren*. Kent, Ohio: Kent State University Press, 1989.

"Good Soldier Yossarian." Review of *Catch-22*, by Joseph Heller. *Time*, 27 October 1961, 97–98.

Greeley, Andrew M. "Another Look at Mike Royko's *Boss*," by Mike Royko. *Chicago History* 1, no. 4 (Fall 1971): 250–51.

Hauptman, Robert. *Authorial Ethics: How Writers Abuse Their Calling*. Lanham, Md.: Lexington Books, 2013.

Heller, Joseph. "World Full of Great Cities." In *Nelson Algren's Own Book of Lonesome Monsters*, edited by Nelson Algren, 11–23. New York: Lancer Books, 1962.

Herman, Jan. "Nelson Algren: The Angry Author." *Chicago Sun-Times Chicagostyle*. 21 January 1979, 8–11.

Hill, Lee. *A Grand Guy: The Art and Life of Terry Southern*. New York: HarperCollins, 2001.

"James Blake, Pianist Who Wrote *Joint*, Letters from Prison." *New York Times*, 20 February 1979, sec. D, 15.

James, Mertice M. and Dorothy Brown, eds. *The Book Review Digest: Forty-Third Annual Cumulation, March 1947 to February 1948 Inclusive*. New York: H.W. Wilson, 1948.

James, Mertice M., and Dorothy P. Davison, eds. *The Book Review Digest: Forty-Ninth Annual Cumulation, March 1953 to February 1954 Inclusive*. New York: H.W. Wilson, 1954.

James, Mertice M., and Dorothy P. Davison, eds. *The Book Review Digest: Forty-Sixth Annual Cumulation, March 1950 to February 1951 Inclusive*. New York: H.W. Wilson, 1951.

Kamerman, Sylvia E., ed. *Book Reviewing*. Boston: The Writer, 1978.

Kazin, Alfred. "Nelson Algren on the Wild Side." In *Contemporaries*, 183–85. Boston: Little, Brown, 1962.

Kazin, Alfred. "Some People Passing By." Review of *A Walk on the Wild Side*, by Nelson Algren. *The New York Times Book Review*, 20 May 1956, 4, 24.

Kiley, Frederick, and Walter McDonald, eds. *A "Catch-22" Casebook*. New York: Thomas Y. Crowell, 1973.

Kiniery, Paul, Ph.D. Review of *Boss: Richard J. Daley of Chicago*, by Mike Royko. *Best Sellers: The Semi-Monthly Book Review* 33, no. 1 (1 April 1971): 10–11.

Kisor, Henry. "Clashing Visions: Brashler's Reply." *Chicago Daily News Panorama*, 10–11 January 1976, 6, 8.

Kisor, Henry. "Nelson Algren, Hale and Salty at 64." *Chicago Daily News Panorama*, 27–28 October 1973, 2–3.

"Knock on Any Door." *Look*, 30 September 1947, 21–31.

Kogan, Rick. "Remembering the Forgotten Willard Motley." *Chicago Tribune*, 5 April 2015, sec. 4, 6.

Landers, Robert K. *An Honest Writer: The Life and Times of James T. Farrell*. San Francisco: Encounter Books, 2004.

"Letters." *Chicago Tribune Book World*, 11 March 1979, 2.

"Letters from James Blake: Southern Con, American Author." *Esquire*, August 1970, 76–79, 143.

Mangione, Jerre. *The Dream and the Deal: The Federal Writers' Project 1935–1943*. Boston: Little Brown, 1972.

McCollum, Kenneth G. *Nelson Algren: A Checklist*. Detroit: Gale Research, 1973.

Miller, Walter James. "Joseph Heller's Fiction." In *Modern Critical Interpretations: Joseph Heller's "Catch-22,"* edited by Harold Bloom, 133–40. Philadelphia: Chelsea House, 2001.

Morris, Willie. *New York Days*. Boston: Little, Brown, 1993.

Motley, Willard. *Knock on Any Door*. New York: D. Appleton-Century, 1947.

Motley, Willard. "Voice of the Reader: An Author Protests." *Chicago Tribune Magazine of Books*, 1 February 1959, 11.

Olson, Liesl. *Chicago Renaissance: Literature and Art in the Midwest Metropolis*. New Haven, Conn.: Yale University Press, 2017.

Pool, Gail. *Faint Praise: The Plight of Book Reviewing in America*. Columbia: University of Missouri Press, 2007.

Preminger, Otto. *Preminger: An Autobiography*. Garden City, N.Y.: Doubleday, 1977.

Prescott, Orville. "Books of the Times." Review of *Knock on Any Door*, by Willard Motley. *New York Times*, 5 May 1947, 21.

Randolph, Eleanor. "Algren's House Sale Not Quite a Best Seller." *Chicago Tribune*, 9 March 1975, sec. 1, 10.

Ray, David, ed. *The "Chicago Review" Anthology*. Chicago: University of Chicago Press, 1959.

Ray, David. *The Endless Search: A Memoir*. Brooklyn: Soft Skull Press, 2003.

Ray, David. "A Talk on the Wild Side: A *Cavalcade* Interview with Nelson Algren." *Cavalcade*. July 1964, 52–55.

Ray, David. "A Talk on the Wild Side." *The Reporter*, 11 June 1959, 31–33.

Royko, Mike. "Algren Paved the Way." *Chicago Sun-Times*, 2 October 1981, 2.

Royko, Mike. "Algren's Golden Pen." *Chicago Sun-Times*, 13 May 1981, 2.

Royko, Mike. "Nelson Algren Takes Dim View of Girl Scribblers." *Chicago Daily News*, 22 March 1967, 3.

Royko, Mike. "A Small-Print Burglar Hustles Nelson Algren." *Chicago Daily News*, 7 June 1966, 3.

Server, Lee. "Ellson, Hal." In *Encyclopedia of Pulp Fiction Writers*. New York: Checkmark Books, 2002, 88–89.

Shay, Art. *Album for an Age: Unconventional Words and Pictures from the Twentieth Century*. Chicago: Ivan R. Dee, 2000.

Shay, Arthur. "Author on the Make: Nelson Algren's Bittersweet Affair with Chicago." *Chicago Tribune Magazine*, 14 September 1986, 10–12, 14–17, 32, 39.

Smith, Alson J. *Chicago's Left Bank*. Chicago: Henry Regnery Co., 1953.

Soll, Rick. "Nelson Algren Bids Final Farewell." *Chicago Tribune*, 10 March 1975, sec. 1, 2.

Southern, Niles, and Brooke Allen, eds. *Yours in Haste and Adoration: Selected Letters of Terry Southern*. New York: Antibookclub, 2015.

Southern, Terry, and Mason Hoffenberg. *Candy*. New York: G.P. Putnam's Sons, 1964.

Stern, Richard G. "Bombers Away." Review of *Catch-22*, by Joseph Heller. *New York Times Book Review*, 22 October 1961, 50.

Styron, William. Introduction to *The Joint*, by James Blake, 7–11. London: Secker & Warburg, 1972.

Styron, William. Review of *The Joint*, by James Blake. *New York Times Book Review*, 25 April 1971, 1, 10, 12.

Terkel, Studs. Review of *Boss: Richard J. Daley of Chicago*, by Mike Royko. *New York Times Book Review*, 4 April 1971, 46–47.

Terkel, Studs. *Touch and Go: A Memoir*. New York: The New Press, 2007.

Tibbetts, Robert A. "Further Addenda to Bruccoli, *Nelson Algren*." *The Papers of the Bibliographical Society of America*, June 1989, 214–17.

"The View from Preminger's Side." *Los Angeles Times West View*. 15 May 1977, 3.

Walker, Margaret. *For My People*. New Haven, Conn: Yale University Press, 1942.

Weed, Perry L. "Second Thoughts on Mayor Daley." Review of *Boss: Richard J. Daley of Chicago*, by Mike Royko. *The Saturday Review*, 24 April 1971, 29.

Wendt, Lloyd, and Herman Kogan. *Big Bill of Chicago*. Indianapolis: Bobbs-Merrill, 1953.

"The Wire Recorder Ear." Review of *Let No Man Write My Epitaph*, by Willard Motley. *Time*, 11 August 1958, 74.

Wixson, Douglas. *Worker-Writer in America: Jack Conroy and the Tradition of Midwestern Literary Radicalism, 1898–1990*. Urbana: University of Illinois Press, 1994.

Book Introductions

Introduction

Nelson Algren has written novels, short stories, poetry, non-fiction, and even book reviews. He has written introductions to several of his own books. It appears, however, that he has written only four book introductions to other writers' books, and the circumstances surrounding two of the four introductions are rather unusual.[1]

F.S.C.

The 1963 novel, *F.S.C.*, by Con Sellers, is the story of one man coping with an all-intrusive federal government. The book is a combination of *Tarzan of the Apes* and *Atlas Shrugged*. Algren begins his introduction on the back cover with this statement: "Had George Orwell thought more about Tarzan and less about Stalin, *F.S.C.* is the novel he would have written instead of *1984*."[2]

F.S.C. was reissued in 1974 by a different publisher with the title, *Mr. Tomorrow*. Algren's introduction does not appear in this edition. However, the back cover of this 1974 version also bears Algren's 1963 back cover statement.[3]

Erik Dorn

In 1963 the University of Chicago Press republished Ben Hecht's 1921 book, *Erik Dorn*, as the third book in its "Chicago in Fiction" series. Algren wrote the introduction, which was entitled, "A Thousand and One Afternoons in Nada."[4]

Hecht did not read what Algren wrote until after the book was released. Three thousand, five hundred copies were printed with Algren's introduction, which included such comments as, "for no American yet has written a novel this good yet this bad. This is the one work of serious literature we have that by the same token stands as a literary hoax."[5]

Figure 20: In 1963 the University of Chicago Press republished Ben Hecht's 1921 book, *Erik Dorn*. Nelson Algren was asked to write the book's introduction. Algren's introduction included such unusual comments as, "for no American yet has written a novel this good yet this bad. This is the one work of serious literature we have that by the same token stands as a literary hoax."

This angered Hecht, and he responded by refusing to attend a cocktail party sponsored by the publisher. Algren, however, *did* attend the party. As shown in this photograph, he is the center of attention, and he is obviously enjoying himself (Photograph © Ernest Anheuser—USA TODAY NETWORK).

Hecht was angry, and he responded by refusing to attend a cocktail party sponsored by the publisher and by telling a reporter that Algren had "a Beverly Hillbilly kind of intellectuality." Herb Lyon, a *Chicago Tribune* gossip columnist, breathlessly described the animosity between the two authors:[6]

The red-hot feud between noted Chicago authors Ben Hecht and Nelson Algren caused Hecht to cancel out of Carter Davidson's At Random show Saturday night. Ben, irked by Algren's foreword to a re-issue of his novel, *Erik Dorn*, (from the U. of Chicago Press) snapped "Not me, not on the same panel with Algren!" Algren issued a challenge to Ben to show up and "hash it out!" Ben refused![7]

Could Algren have had an ulterior motive in writing his disparaging introduction to Hecht's book? Possibly. Hecht was an uncredited screenwriter for the two movies that were made of Algren's novels—*The Man with the Golden Arm* (1949) and *A Walk on the Wild Side* (1956). Algren hated the way Frank Sinatra played Frankie Machine in Otto Preminger's 1955 film adaptation of *Golden Arm*. Algren realized too late that he sold the film rights to *Wild Side* for one-third their value, and he later disavowed any connection to the 1962 movie version of his novel.[8]

In a 1970 interview, Algren said:

> The reviewer in *The Nation* put it best when he said the book [*The Man with the Golden Arm*] was written out of respect and the movie was made out of contempt. So after seeing it I didn't bother to see the other movie [*A Walk on the Wild Side*]. I heard it was nothing like the book anyway.[9]

As discussed in this book's essay, "Nelson Algren and the Ethics of Book Reviewing," Algren would sometimes use his role as book reviewer to (in his words) "hit back" at his critics and perceived enemies. Perhaps Algren knew that Hecht worked on the screenplays for these two movies. The *Walk on the Wild Side* movie came out only a year before *Erik Dorn* was republished. Perhaps Algren let his feelings about these two films prejudice his writing of the introduction to *Erik Dorn*.[10]

Next Time Is for Life

Algren wrote at least one other questionable book introduction. Frank Sandiford, writing under the pseudonym, "Paul Warren," is the author of the 1953 book, *Next Time Is for Life*. Sandiford writes:[11]

> When my book was being seriously considered by Dell, Knox Burger, the editor, asked Nelson if he would write a foreword. I gave him a carbon of my manuscript and a few days later his wife Amanda showed up with it. Inside was a copy of his letter to Knox. In a single-spaced letter, using both sides of the page, he wrote of *Next Time Is for Life* with such vitriol that Knox later said, "It was so abusive that I wondered what was wrong with Nelson Algren."[12]

Dell published the book without Algren's foreword. Instead, when the book was released in 1953, the back cover included the statement, "Foreword by Erle Stanley Gardner." Advance praise by Erle Stanley Garner ran across the book's front cover.[13]

Gardner is probably best known as the author of the Perry Mason books. The first Mason book, *The Case of the Velvet Claws*, was published in 1933.

Figure 21: Nelson Algren is in his second-floor apartment at 1523 West Wabansia Avenue in Chicago. The book on the top shelf of Algren's book case is *A Jew
in Love*, by Ben Hecht. As discussed in the text, Algren wrote the introduction
to the 1963 edition of Hecht's book, *Erik Dorn*.

A close look at a larger print of this photograph reveals the words "Sophie"
and "Sparrow" on the sheet of paper in Algren's right hand. This indicates that
Algren is typing the manuscript of his 1949 novel, *The Man with the Golden
Arm*. (Sophie was the wife of Frankie Machine, the book's title character, a card
dealer and amateur drummer. Solly "Sparrow" Saltskin was Frankie's friend)
(photograph by Art Shay, courtesy Richard Shay and Victor Armendariz).

The True Story of Bonnie and Clyde

In 1968 Signet Books released *The True Story of Bonnie and Clyde*.
Algren's three-part introduction meanders across fifteen pages and is
reprinted in *The Last Carousel* (1973) as "After the Buffalo."[14]

Conclusion

Nelson Algren was paid $1,000 to write the introduction to *Erik Dorn* and then proceeded to call the book a "literary hoax." Both *F.S.C.* and *The True Story of Bonnie and Clyde* are potboilers. It appears that Algren looked at writing book introductions merely as a source of revenue. Why else would he lend his name to two books of dubious literary quality?[15]

But on the other hand, if Algren viewed writing book introductions as merely an income stream, why didn't he write more of them? As described in this book's essay, "Nelson Algren and the Ethics of Book Reviewing," from 1935 until he died in 1981, Algren wrote and published 237 book reviews. In 1973 he told an interviewer, "I live on book reviews and by giving talks." Why didn't he also live on writing book introductions? Why did he write only three published book introductions? Perhaps writing book reviews was easier and more financially lucrative than writing book introductions. On the other hand, perhaps after reading Algren's three introductions, or perhaps after hearing about what happened to Ben Hecht and Frank Sandiford, people stopped asking Algren to write introductions.[16]

NOTES

1. Matthew J. Bruccoli, *Nelson Algren: A Descriptive Bibliography* (Pittsburgh: University of Pittsburgh Press, 1985), 100–102.

2. Nelson Algren, introduction to *F.S.C.*, by Con Sellers (Chicago: Novel Books, 1963), back cover, [1–2].

3. Con Sellers, *Mr. Tomorrow* (N.p.: Papillon Books, 1974), back cover. Perhaps Algren wrote this introduction as a favor to Paul Neimark. Neimark also wrote an introduction to *F.S.C.* Neimark was the editor-in-chief of *Men's Digest*. Novel Books, the publisher of *F.S.C.*, also published *Men's Digest*. Algren wrote a book review of *F.S.C.* for *Men's Digest*. Neimark was also the editor of the 1957 magazine, *The Race for Space!* Algren wrote an article for *The Race for Space!* See Nelson Algren, Review of *F.S.C.*, by Con Sellers, *The Annual Edition of The Men's Digest*, no. 49 [1963]: 52; Nelson Algren, "Ain't Nobody on My Side?," in *The Race for Space!*, ed. Paul G. Neimark (Chicago: Camerarts Publishing Co., 1957), 13; Paul Neimark, introduction to *F.S.C.*, by Con Sellers, [1, 3].

4. Nelson Algren, "A Thousand and One Afternoons in Nada," introduction to *Erik Dorn*, by Ben Hecht (Chicago: University of Chicago Press, 1963), vii–xvii; Hecht, *Erik Dorn*, [iv], dust jacket. Algren obviously took the title of his introduction from the title of Hecht's 1922 book, *A Thousand and One Afternoons in Chicago*.

5. Algren, "A Thousand and One Afternoons in Nada," x; Mary Wisniewski, *Algren: A Life* (Chicago: Chicago Review Press, 2017), 257; Austin C. Wehrwein, "Hecht Attacks Algren Preface," *New York Times*, 21 November 1963, 36.

6. Wehrwein, "Hecht Attacks Algren Preface," 36.

7. Herb Lyon, "Tower Ticker," *Chicago Tribune*, 21 November 1963, sec. 1, 18; see also Wehrwein, "Hecht Attacks Algren Preface," 36; Jan Herman, "The Paradox of Ben Hecht," *Chicago Quarterly Review*, no. 17 (2014): 62–63; Bettina Drew, *Nelson Algren: A Life on the Wild Side* (Austin: University of Texas Press, 1989), 320. Parenthetical publisher information in the text is in the original.

8. William MacAdams, *Ben Hecht: The Man Behind the Legend* (New York: Charles

Scribner's Sons,1990), 271, 282, 327, 329–30; H.E.F. Donohue, *Conversations with Nelson Algren* (New York: Hill and Wang, 1964), 123–25; Art Shay, *Nelson Algren's Chicago* (Urbana: University of Illinois Press, 1988), xv; Colin Asher, *Never a Lovely So Real: The Life and Work of Nelson Algren* (New York: W.W. Norton, 2019), 403; Drew, *Nelson Algren*, 289–90.

    9. Irwin Saltz, "Nelson Algren on the Make," *Chicagoland Magazine*, May 1970, 26.

    10. MacAdams, *Ben Hecht*, 329; Mary Wisniewski, "Nelson Algren and Polonia's Revenge," *Chicago History* 42, no. 1 (Winter 2018): 55; Hecht, *Erik Dorn*, [iv]; Barbara Delatiner, "Algren Entering the East End Ring," *New York Times Long Island Weekly*, 26 April 1981, 15.

    11. Paul Warren, *Next Time Is for Life* (New York: Dell Publishing Co., 1953).

    12. Frank Sandiford, "My Main Man," *New Letters* 57, no. 4 (Summer 1991): 21; Douglas Wixson, *Worker-Writer in America: Jack Conroy and the Tradition of Midwestern Literary Radicalism, 1898-1990* (Urbana: University of Illinois Press, 1994), 470.

    13. Wixson, *Worker-Writer in America*, 576n69; Erle Stanley Gardner, foreword to *Next Time Is for Life*, by Paul Warren, [4–5]; Warren, *Next Time Is for Life*, front cover, back cover.

    14. Nelson Algren, introduction to *The True Story of Bonnie & Clyde*, comp. and ed. By Jane I. Fortune (New York: Signet, 1968), v–xix; Nelson Algren, "After the Buffalo," in *The Last Carousel* (New York: Seven Stories Press, 1997), 164–177.

    15. Wisniewski, *Algren: A Life*, 257; Algren, "A Thousand and One Afternoons in Nada," x.

    16. Henry Kisor, "Nelson Algren, Hale and Salty at 64," *Chicago Daily News Panorama*, 27–28 October 1973, 2; Bruccoli, *Nelson Algren*, 135–58; Matthew J. Bruccoli, "Addenda to Bruccoli, *Nelson Algren*," *The Papers of the Bibliographical Society of America*, September 1988, 367–69; Robert A. Tibbetts, "Further Addenda to Bruccoli, *Nelson Algren*," *The Papers of the Bibliographical Society of America*, June 1989, 214–17.

Selected Bibliography

Algren, Nelson. Introduction to *F.S.C.*, by Con Sellers, back cover, [1–2]. Chicago: Novel Books, 1963.

Algren, Nelson. Introduction to *The True Story of Bonnie & Clyde*. Compiled and edited by Jane I. Fortune, v–xix. New York: Signet, 1968.

Algren, Nelson. "Ain't Nobody on My Side?" In *The Race for Space!*, edited by Paul G. Neimark, 13. Chicago: Camerarts Publishing Co., 1957.

Algren, Nelson. *The Last Carousel*. New York: Seven Stories Press, 1997.

Algren, Nelson. Review of *F.S.C.*, by Con Sellers. *The Annual Edition of The Men's Digest*, no. 49 [1963]: 52.

Algren, Nelson. "A Thousand and One Afternoons in Nada." Introduction to *Erik Dorn*, by Ben Hecht, vii–xvii. Chicago: University of Chicago Press, 1963.

Asher, Colin. *Never a Lovely So Real: The Life and Work of Nelson Algren*. New York: W.W. Norton, 2019.

Bruccoli, Matthew J. "Addenda to Bruccoli, *Nelson Algren*." *The Papers of the Bibliographical Society of America*, September 1988, 367–69.

Bruccoli, Matthew J. *Nelson Algren: A Descriptive Bibliography*. Pittsburgh: University of Pittsburgh Press, 1985.

Delatiner, Barbara. "Algren Entering the East End Ring." *New York Times Long Island Weekly*, 26 April 1981, 15.

Donohue, H.E.F. *Conversations with Nelson Algren*. New York: Hill and Wang, 1964.

Drew, Bettina. *Nelson Algren: A Life on the Wild Side*. Austin: University of Texas Press, 1989.

Herman, Jan. "The Paradox of Ben Hecht." *Chicago Quarterly Review*, no. 17 (2014): 59–69.

Kisor, Henry. "Nelson Algren, Hale and Salty at 64." *Chicago Daily News Panorama*, 27–28 October 1973, 2–3.

Lyon, Herb. "Tower Ticker." *Chicago Tribune*, 21 November 1963, sec. 1, 18.

MacAdams, William. *Ben Hecht: The Man Behind the Legend*. New York: Charles Scribner's Sons, 1990.

Neimark, Paul. Introduction to *F.S.C.*, by Con Sellers, [1, 3]. Chicago: Novel Books, 1963.

Saltz, Irwin. "Nelson Algren on the Make." *Chicagoland Magazine*, May 1970, 24–27.

Sandiford, Frank. "My Main Man." *New Letters* 57, no. 4 (Summer 1991): 11–27.

Sellers, Con. *Mr. Tomorrow*. N.p.: Papillon Books, 1974.

Shay, Art. *Nelson Algren's Chicago*. Urbana: University of Illinois Press, 1988.

Tibbetts, Robert A. "Further Addenda to Bruccoli, *Nelson Algren*." *The Papers of the Bibliographical Society of America*, June 1989, 214–17.

Warren, Paul. *Next Time Is for Life*. New York: Dell Publishing Co., 1953.

Wehrwein, Austin C. "Hecht Attacks Algren Preface." *New York Times*, 21 November 1963, 36.

Wisniewski, Mary. *Algren: A Life*. Chicago: Chicago Review Press, 2017.

Wisniewski, Mary. "Nelson Algren and Polonia's Revenge." *Chicago History* 42, no. 1 (Winter 2018): 44–59.

Wixson, Douglas. *Worker-Writer in America: Jack Conroy and the Tradition of Midwestern Literary Radicalism, 1898–1990*. Urbana: University of Illinois Press, 1994.

PART THREE

Special Interests

Chicago White Sox Literature

Introduction

Nelson Algren was a passionate fan of the Chicago White Sox, and he wrote about this baseball team throughout his writing career. Algren once said, "I live on book reviews and by giving talks," and during these talks he would sometimes stop speaking about writing and books and instead talk about the Sox. This essay is an attempt to document and describe Algren's White Sox literary output, placing his baseball articles, stories, and poems within the context of Algren's life and the lives of his contemporaries.[1]

Nelson Algren was born in Detroit in 1909. In 1913 his family moved to Chicago, to the city's South Side. Comiskey Park and the Chicago White Sox were also in this part of the city, and he spent his childhood idolizing the

JOE JACKSON
RIGHT FIELD
CHICAGO "WHITE SOX" A. L.

Figure 22: This baseball card of "Shoeless" Joe Jackson is number 15 of the 1920–1921 W514 baseball card set. This set of 120 cards contains seven of the eight "Black Sox" players. The only "Black Sox" player missing is Fred McMullin.

Nelson Algren reminisces in *The Neon Wilderness* (1947) that "I remember trading an entire strip of ten to get just one of Joe Jackson." The Jackson card he traded for would have looked like the card pictured here.

Sox. He even gave himself the nickname, "Swede," in honor of his favorite player, Charles "Swede" Risberg, the team's shortstop.[2]

In 1919 Risberg and the rest of the White Sox played in the World Series, eight baseball games that will be forever tainted by the infamous Black Sox Scandal—when the Chicago White Sox lost to the Cincinnati Reds. Eight Chicago players, including Risberg and the legendary "Shoeless" Joe Jackson, were later accused of being paid off to intentionally lose games in what baseball historians call the "Big Fix." Risberg and the rest of the players were indicted by a grand jury in 1920, and they went to trial in 1921. Although all of the men were acquitted, they were immediately banned for life from organized baseball by newly appointed baseball commissioner Kenesaw Mountain Landis, a federal judge.[3]

"The Swede Was a Hard Guy"

Matthew J. Bruccoli's book, *Nelson Algren: A Descriptive Bibliography*, indicates that Algren's first published work was a 1933 magazine story. Only nine years later, the *Southern Review*, the literary journal of Louisiana State University, featured Algren's poem about the Black Sox entitled, "The Swede Was a Hard Guy."[4]

Daniel A. Nathan, author of *Saying It's So: A Cultural History of the Black Sox Scandal*, describes the poem as "a mournful, nostalgic lament" for the eight banished players. The poem ends with Algren urging the reader to simply forget the Black Sox:[5]

> Forget Chase and Lefty Williams and little Nemo Liebold
> And do not be remembering the most natural man ever to wear spiked shoes.
> The canniest fielder and the longest hitter,
> The good, easy nature who could run with Carey or field with Harry Hooper.
> Who squatted on his heels,
> In a uniform muddied at both knees,
> Till the bleacher shadows grew long behind him....
>
> For Shoeless Joe is gone, long gone,
> A long yellow grass-blade between his teeth
> And the bleacher-shadows behind him.
>
> And a lefthander's wind blows by, blows by,
> Like a wind blowing always away from home.[6]

The "Swede" in Algren's poem is an obvious reference to shortstop Charles "Swede" Risberg. But what is the significance and origin of the poem's title—"The Swede Was a Hard Guy"?[7]

"Shoeless" Joe Jackson testified before a grand jury about a month before the eight players were indicted. A portion of a *Chicago Tribune* article of September 29, 1920—the day after Jackson testified—bears the caption, "Jackson's Story," and it begins, "Joe Jackson last night described his confession to the grand jury as follows": Jackson's statement ends with these words:[8]

> Now Risberg threatens to bump me off if I squawk. That's why I had all the bailiffs with me when I left the grand jury room this afternoon. I'm not under arrest yet, and I've got the idea that after what I told them, old Joe Jackson isn't going to jail. But I'm not going to get far from my protectors until this blows over. Swede's a hard guy.[9]

It appears that Algren read this 1920 *Tribune* article before writing "The Swede Was a Hard Guy." The poem was reprinted in the June 1956 issue of *Chicago* magazine, and in the editors' introductory comments, they write: "Algren has missed few opening days at Comiskey Park since 1920, and after he had become an adult fan, he decided to find out more about the Black Sox scandal. He read the contemporary newspaper accounts at the library and did some other research."[10]

In a 1979 *Tribune* story, Algren commented about both this phrase and his poem:

> On the stand, on a charge of conspiracy, Jackson attempted to explain how he had gotten into the gamblers' big fix to throw the World Series of 1919 to the Cincinnati Reds. He had been forced, he said, by threats from Swede Risberg. "The Swede," Jackson told reporters, "was a hard guy." In a blank verse poem written sometime in the '40s, I had used Jackson's phrase for a title.[11]

Jackson may not have been the first to describe Risberg as a "hard guy." The April 3, 1920, *Chicago Tribune* featured a column, "In the Wake of the News," that contained several paragraphs of commentary on the White Sox lineup for the coming season. This column, written months before Jackson testified, included a few sentences about Risberg:

> The other arrangement will call for Swede Risberg at first. The Swede has the natural build for the job and can field well enough. Of course, he'd have to learn a bit more about scooping 'em in and reaching for the tall ones without losing the sack. In addition, he's a "hard guy" on the field, which is to say he is not the kind to back up when the other fellows come in with spikes high or resort to other shady tactics [quotation marks in the original].[12]

Perhaps the anonymous *Tribune* scribe who claims that Risberg is a "'hard guy' on the field" is referring to an incident that occurred less than two years earlier. Tim Hornbaker, author of *Turning the Black Sox White: The Misunderstood Legacy of Charles A. Comiskey*, explains what happened:

> While in California working for a shipbuilding company in late 1918, Risberg played on the company's ball team to earn a little extra money. A close play

started an argument with an official that quickly got out of hand, and he ended up knocking umpire Jakey Baumgardner out with a single punch. His actions earned him an indefinite suspension, but it didn't matter because within a few months, he was back with Chicago—and all was forgotten. However, the incident added to Risberg's reputation, and to this day is often recited as an example of his fierce attitude and physicality.[13]

The Neon Wilderness

Nelson Algren wrote about the White Sox in his 1947 collection of short stories, *The Neon Wilderness*. In "A Lot You Got to Holler," he reminisces about his childhood and trading "ten-for-a-penny pictures of baseball players."[14]

> I remember trading an entire strip of ten to get just one of Joe Jackson. And a month later, when Jackson had been kicked out of organized baseball, I had to give one of him, one of Buck Weaver, and two Happy Felschs just to get one Ray Schalk—who'd been on the original strip I'd traded for Shoeless Joe in the first place.[15]

Chicago: City on the Make

Algren's memorable book-length prose poem, *Chicago: City on the Make*, was published in 1951. In chapter 3, entitled "The Silver-Colored Yesterday," the author tells how the Black Sox Scandal affected his childhood.[16]

Algren and his family moved from Chicago's South Side to North Troy Street, on the city's Northwest Side, in 1920. Algren notes that "Troy Street led, like all Northside streets—and alleys too—directly to the alien bleachers of Wrigley Field." Young Algren was now, like Robert A. Heinlein's Valentine Michael Smith, a "Stranger in a Strange Land"—a White Sox fan in the alien land of the Chicago Cubs.[17]

On the day the family moved across town, neighborhood boys stopped eleven-year-old Algren in front of his new house and asked him, "Who's yer fayvrut player?" When Algren replied, "Swede Risberg," he was told, "It got to be a National Leaguer." Algren then comments, "So that's how the wind was blowing." He was eventually allowed to play baseball with his interrogators, but he was relegated to right field.[18]

That was probably the spring of 1920. A few months later, on Tuesday, September 28, two White Sox players, pitcher Eddie Cicotte and outfielder "Shoeless" Joe Jackson, told a grand jury of their participation in the Black

Sox Scandal. On October 22, 1920, the grand jury indicted eight players—including "Swede" Risberg. The indictments charged conspiracy to commit an illegal act.[19]

Risberg was indicted in 1920—and Algren had told his teammates that Risberg was his favorite player. As Algren relates in *Chicago: City on the Make* (referring to either the Red Scare of 1919 or the Cold War anti-communist witch hunts), "The Black Sox were the Reds of that October and mine was the guilt of association." Algren writes that after Risberg and the other players were charged, the neighborhood boys, now a "Committee" (an obvious reference to the House Committee on Un-American Activities, or HUAC, which in 1947 had begun investigating the motion picture industry for possible links between Hollywood and the Communist party) asked Algren accusingly, "What kind of American *are* you anyhow?" They then added, "No wonder you're always in right field where nothin' ever comes—nobody could trust you in center" (emphasis in original).[20]

Crushed into submission, Algren describes his response with one more allusion to HUAC and the anti-communist fervor of the Cold War—the naming of names:

Figure 23: **This strip of five cards is from the 1920–1921 W514 baseball card set. Nelson Algren writes in** *Chicago: City on the Make* **(1951) of a boy "who had a paying thing going, for weekdays, in the resale of colored paper-picture strips of major-league players. He bought them ten for a penny and resold them to us for two." The baseball cards he is referring to were these W514 cards. There were 120 cards in this set. These cards were sold by local grocers, "5 & 10 cent" stores, and ice cream parlors. The W514 (as designated in the American Card Catalog) card set is a so-called "strip" set. That is, these cards were issued to stores in strips of ten cards. Buyers of a strip could then cut apart the cards, guided by the vertical dotted lines that separated each player on the strip. This strip of five cards is numbered 11–15. It is likely that someone originally bought a strip of ten cards, numbered 11 through 20, and then cut off this strip of five cards. The players on this strip are Cactus Cravath, Pat Moran, Dick Rudolph, Arthur Fletcher, and Joe Jackson.**

"We all make mistakes, fellas," I broke at last. "We all goof off, we're all human...." Choked with guilt and penitence.... I pleaded to be allowed, with all my grievous faults, to go along with the gang.... "Can I keep my job if I bum-rap some people for you?"[21]

"The Silver-Colored Yesterday" has been reprinted in the books, *Baseball: A Literary Anthology, The Fireside Book of Baseball,* and *The New Baseball Reader.* It also appears in *Sport Literate* magazine.[22]

Algren refers to the White Sox in two other chapters of *Chicago: City on the Make.* In chapter 5 Algren mentions a non–Black Sox player—Charlie Robertson, who pitched a perfect game on April 30, 1922. In the last chapter, Algren reminisces one more time about Joe Jackson, the legendary Black Sox outfielder: "Shoeless Joe, who lost his honor and his job, is remembered now more fondly here, when stands are packed and a striped sun burns across them, than old Comiskey, who salvaged his own."[23]

Chicago Sun-Times *Articles About the 1959 World Series*

On September 22, 1959, the Chicago White Sox won the American League pennant by beating the Cleveland Indians. The forty-year drought was over; the White Sox were going to the World Series. In a few days Chicago's South Siders would battle the National League champion, the Los Angeles Dodgers. But it was more than baseball—The White Sox would be able to finally exorcize the demons of 1919 and the Black Sox Scandal.[24]

Emmett Dedmon of the *Chicago Sun-Times* newspaper hired Nelson Algren to write "human interest stuff from the grandstand" during the series. Algren would eventually write three articles for the *Sun-Times.*[25]

Algren begins the first article, written after the first game, with a reference to the Black Sox Scandal of forty years ago:

There was an October 40 Octobers gone, when a lamplighter on a Pathfinder bicycle, carrying a torch across his handle bars, came down South Park Av. between 71st and 72d every evening and the White Sox were going to whip Cincinnati.[26]

Although there are a few subsequent references to the 1919 team in this inaugural account, Algren also writes of the baseball memories of his youth:

I walked from 71st to 35th one Sunday afternoon. Outside Sox park, mounted police were trying to keep a mob of locked-out fans from crashing the center-field fence, which was then wooden. Inside the park Eddie Cicotte was pitching to Ruth. The crush of the mob swept police, horses and myself onto the field and I scampered into the centerfield bleachers. I've been in the center-field bleachers ever since.

The papers described the incident as RIOT AT SOX PARK! Overnight I became the kid who not only had survived a riot but had seen Cicotte strike out Ruth. I was made: my existence was recognized by the world of men. I had had adventure and had survived the world where men played catch. My name in that world was "Swede."[27]

The Sox routed the Dodgers 11–0 in the first game, and so it is proba-bly not surprising that Algren barely mentions the Black Sox in his second article, written after the second game, which the Sox lost 4–3. Instead, he humorously relates his observations of the people around him:[28]

A woman just showing the first signs of mileage sat beside me, wearing blue corduroy, with a cardboard horn as big as herself in her lap. But it lay there so disconsolately, I figured someone else must have put it there.... One of Bill Veeck's rose-bearing ushers came past and handed Blue Corduroy a rose. She took it gently, put it in her lap—and then, as if suddenly getting the full impact of the thing, stood up and blew like Harry James and blew a chorus of "The Battle Hymn of the Republic" then sat down abashed at her boldness.[29]

As historian Bill Savage observes in his article, "The '59 White Sox in Literature: Haunted by Ghosts of the Black Sox," the sense of "wistful mel-ancholy" from Algren's first story had now evaporated.[30]

Unfortunately, the Series continued with the Dodgers winning the third and fourth games. Although the Sox won Game 5, the Dodgers won the sixth game in Chicago, and with that victory, the Dodgers also won the World Series. It is not surprising that both the Black Sox and Algren's mel-ancholy return in the author's third and final article.[31]

Algren begins by writing about the past. He describes how his father smoked Father & Son cigars. He recalls how his mother spoke of the lake steamer *Chicora*, which went down in the ice off of South Haven, Michi-gan. But then, he adds:[32]

Yet that was only my mother's past, my father's past, my uncle Henry's past and had nothing real, I knew, to do with me. Nothing really had anything to do with me until I was 10-going-on-11. Then on the last afternoon of summer I saw Shoeless Joe Jackson leave his glove in left field, walk toward the darkening stands and never come back for his glove.
And my own past had begun.[33]

Algren concludes his final article by evoking the spirits of this past:

I have seen the ghosts of blue-moon hustlers leaping drunk below the all-night billboard lights.
Yesterday evening, when the crowd was gone and I stood up at last to leave, I saw the shade of Shoeless Joe.

He was walking toward the darkening stands, and he'd left his glove behind.[34]

Bill Savage comments about Algren's final remarks in "The '59 White Sox in Literature":

> For Algren, the sadness of a World Series defeat was best expressed by connecting back to the sorrow of not just the defeat, but the betrayal, of 1919. The tragic past isn't dead; it isn't even past.[35]

Daniel A. Nathan writes about Algren's sadness from a similar perspective in *Saying It's So: A Cultural History of the Black Sox Scandal*:

> Haunted by Jackson's ghost—which W.P. Kinsella would resurrect in his novel *Shoeless Joe* (1982)—and his own past, Algren left Comiskey Park as a light drizzle fell, his body and spirit dampened.[36]

Who Lost an American?

Who Lost an American? was published in 1963. This book, together with *Notes from a Sea Diary* (1965), were the two so-called "travel books" that Nelson Algren published in the mid–1960s.[37]

Who Lost an American? has four chapters about Chicago. They are entitled Chicago I, Chicago II, Chicago III, and Chicago IV. None of these chapters contain anything about the Black Sox. In the essay in Chicago III, however, Algren devotes a few paragraphs to the White Sox of the 1920s and the 1930s. In a manner completely at odds with his gentle observations of "Blue Corduroy" at the 1959 World Series, Algren sarcastically comments about some of the players:[38]

> One season a pitcher called Bullfrog Bill Dietrich won seven games while losing only thirteen. The next season he won four while losing only six—it became plain that if he had been allowed to pitch twice as often he would have won eight while losing only twelve.... Our heroes were Banana-Nose Bonura, who never lost a ball in the sun because his nose would get in the way instead; of Moe Berg, the only backstop in the majors with a Ph.D.; and of Great-Man Shires, whose biggest asset was a right hook to the jaw.[39]

The Last Carousel

Years after the 1959 World Series, Algren revised his three *Chicago Sun-Times* articles and combined them into one story, "Go! Go! Go! Forty Years Ago." It was published in *The Last Carousel*, Algren's 1973 collection of short stories and poetry.[40]

The Last Carousel also features "Ballet for Opening Day: The Swede Was a Hard Guy." In writing this piece, Algren took his *Southern Review* poem and substantially reworked it into a combination of short story and poetry.[41]

Examples of the nature and extent of these revisions are shown below:

The Southern Review, "The Swede Was a Hard Guy"

Let thirty-two ushers defend this dust
Till the last of the iron-throated boys gets through the last far gate.
Let a single typewriter be clacking derisively.
Let a lefthander's wind be blowing away from home.[42]

The Last Carousel, "Ballet for Opening Day"

Yet a left-hander's wind keeps blowing this way then that
Around an abandoned ball park
Always blowing away from home.
And if a single typewriter keeps clacking derisively
High in the press-box
It's only the ghost of a high-collared Hoosier:
There's nobody in the press-box tonight.[43]

The Southern Review, "The Swede Was a Hard Guy"

Gandil finally phoned a judge:
"I'm an honest man."
"I know you are not." The judge hung up.
"I'll be right over," Gandil phoned back,
And explained in the judge's chambers:
"I got to get in on the ground floor
"But I got to be awful careful, too.
"Faber and Collins and Schalk weren't in. Jackson just ain't caught on.
"I got to be careful now."
"You've been fairly careless to date," suggested the judge—
"Why the sudden caution?"
It took a moment to answer that.
Then:
"The Swede is a hard guy."[44]

The Last Carousel, "Ballet for Opening Day"

Jackson finally phoned one Judge MacDonald. "I'm an honest man," he told the judge.
"I know you are not," MacDonald assured him, and hung up.
"I'll be right over," Jackson phoned back; and explained himself in chambers:
"Faber and Collins and Kerr and Schalk weren't in. I got to be careful now."
"You've been fairly careless to date," the judge pointed out—"why the sudden caution?"
It took Jackson a minute of thought to answer that:
"The Swede is a hard guy."[45]

Eliot Asinof writes about the Black Sox in his 1963 book, *Eight Men Out*. Both Asinof and Algren appear to pay homage to each other's works. Scattered throughout Asinof's non-fictional account of the "Big Fix" are lines from the *Southern Review*'s "The Swede Was a Hard Guy." Similarly, "Ballet for Opening Day" begins with a long quotation from *Eight Men Out*.[46]

"We Never Made It to the White Sox Game"

"We Never Made It to the White Sox Game" is a tribute to fellow writer James T. Farrell. The *Chicago Tribune* published it in its "Book World" section eleven days after Farrell's death.[47]

Farrell, like Algren, grew up a White Sox fan. Both of them were profoundly affected by the Black Sox scandal. Algren wrote poetry, articles, and a book chapter about it during his literary career. Farrell wrote two baseball books; the first, *My Baseball Diary* (1957) is a collection of more than two dozen essays, including "I Remember the Black Sox" and "Buck Weaver's Last Interview," the latter being a story about the post-1921 years of the Black Sox's third baseman. Farrell's other baseball book, *Dreaming Baseball* (2007), is a posthumously published novel about the Black Sox scandal.[48]

For much of Algren's life, Algren did not like Farrell, nor did he like his writing style. Algren's ill will goes back to the publication of Algren's first book, *Somebody in Boots*, by Vanguard Press. After Algren submitted the manuscript in 1934, Vanguard President James Henle asked Farrell to review it. (Vanguard published Farrell's "Studs Lonigan Triology" in 1935.) Farrell described the book as being in "very bad shape," and he sent Henle a detailed, sixteen-page report suggesting almost fifty pages of changes. Algren biographer Bettina Drew writes that "Algren was stung by the criticism and angry." She notes that Algren, though upset, agreed to most of the suggested changes, "saving his rancor for Farrell."[49]

And Algren *did* save his rancor—for years. In 1947 Algren met Simone de Beauvoir, a French writer and intellectual. They began a passionate but long distant relationship that lasted until 1964. In 1949 de Beauvoir wrote Algren wherein she commented on Algren's feelings towards Farrell:[50]

> Honey, I got your nice letter. It was sweet to read it on my little balcony, looking at the blue sea. I always like the stories about Farrell, he seems the worst kind of conceited, dull worth-nothing writer you could find in USA or France![51]

In a 1973 interview, Algren said, "James T. Farrell is another one. He got goofy pretty early, you know, and he was never a very good writer to begin with."[52]

But "We Never Made It to the White Sox Game" indicates that not only had Algren's resentment towards Farrell faded in recent years, he had also begun to respect Farrell as a writer:

> And [Farrell's] achievement was enduring: He took the naturalism of Stephen Crane and Theodore Dreiser, and Studs Lonigan made it new. For thousands upon thousands of young men, then in their late teens or early 20s, Studs Lonigan afforded an impact which, 50 years later, they still feel.

Farrell did something else: He is one of the very few writers who changed readers' lives. Dickens did this, and Hemingway. Faulkner and Fitzgerald have no such effect. Studs Lonigan affected multitudes.[53]

Algren reveals in what the *Tribune* calls his "valedictory" that when he reviewed Farrell's book, *The Death of Nora Ryan*, for the *Los Angeles Times* in 1978, he hoped that somehow Farrell would see the review and acknowledge it. If Farrell saw it, he would invite Farrell to see the White Sox play.[54]

But the *Los Angeles Times* never published the review. It appears that Farrell never saw it. Algren writes in this *Tribune* article (appropriately entitled, "We Never Made It to the White Sox Game") that "I was still trying to figure out some way of approaching Farrell in order to see the White Sox with him when the bad news came [of Farrell's death].[55]

105
SWEDE RISBERG
SHORT STOP
CHICAGO "WHITE SOX" A. L.

Figure 24: When Nelson Algren was growing up on the North Side of Chicago, "Swede" Risberg was his favorite baseball player.

This baseball card of "Swede" Risberg is from the famous 1920–1921 W514 baseball card set. These cards measured 1⅜ inches by 2½ inches in size and featured rather crude painted portraits of the players. The cardstock is stiff paper; it is not the cardboard of the baseball cards of later years.

If Algren owned a "Swede" Risberg card, it undoubtedly looked like the card pictured here.

"So Long, Swede Risberg"

The July 1981 issue of *Chicago* magazine featured "So Long, Swede Risberg," a sympathetic and humanizing story of the 1919 Black Sox players.[56]

In this article, Nelson Algren emphasizes the essential goodness of the players by contrasting them with White Sox owner Charles Comiskey. To Algren, the saga of the Black Sox was truly black and white; the players were the Good Guys and Comiskey was the Bad Guy. In *Eight Men Out* Eliot Asinof writes that Comiskey was a "cheap, stingy tyrant," adding that Comiskey's ballplayers "were the best and were paid as poorly as the worst." In "So Long, Swede Risberg," Algren brings forward this description of Comiskey by quoting pitcher Eddie Cicotte as saying, "Comiskey throws money around like manhole covers."[57]

And so long, Nelson Algren, who died on May 9, 1981. Algren probably never saw "So Long, Swede Risberg" in print. The article appeared in the July 1981 issue of *Chicago* magazine, and so it is likely that he died before this issue was published and on magazine racks.[58]

"So Long, Swede Risberg" has been reprinted in the book, *Best Sport Stories 1982* and in the Algren collection, *Entrapment and Other Writing*.[59]

Ballet for Opening Day: The Swede Was a Hard Guy (*Sherwin Beach Press, Limited Edition*)

In 2002 Sherwin Beach Press, a Chicago publisher, issued an "extremely limited edition" of fifty copies of *Ballet for Opening Day: The Swede Was a Hard Guy*.[60]

The deluxe edition of the November 2002 issue of *Parenthesis: The Journal of the Fine Press Book Association*, included a box of assorted ephemera from various publishers. One of the twelve items was a sample page from this Sherwin Beach Press limited edition book.[61]

Final Observations

On October 7, 1920 (more than two weeks before the final Black Sox indictments were handed down on October 22), the *Sporting News*, then commonly referred to as "Baseball's Bible," ran photographs of the eight players under the headline, "FIX THESE FACES IN YOUR MEMORY." The caption includes these words:[62]

> These are the White Sox players who committed the astounding and contemptible crime of selling out the baseball world in the 1919 World Series.... Some of the eight have been great stars in their day, but they will be remembered from now on only for the depths of depravity to which they could sink.[63]

Baseball commissioner Kenesaw Mountain Landis worked hard in the years immediately following the Black Sox players' acquittal—and their subsequent banishment from America's pastime—"to restore some much-needed integrity and order to the game." Unfortunately, Landis was kept busy during those years overseeing a variety of (mostly minor) baseball scandals. Publicity concerning these incidents only served to help maintain the otherwise receding Black Sox memories in America's consciousness.[64]

FIX THESE FACES IN YOUR MEMORY

"CHICK" GANDIL

"HAP" FELSCH

JOE JACKSON

EDDIE CICOTTE

CLAUDE WILLIAMS

FRED McMULLIN

"SWEDE" RISBERG

"BUCK" WEAVER

EIGHT MEN CHARGED WITH SELLING OUT BASEBALL

Figure 25: The October 7, 1920, issue of the *Sporting News* featured this picture of the eight Chicago White Sox players who were accused of intentionally losing games during the 1919 World Series. These eight "Black Sox" players include "Shoeless" Joe Jackson and Charles "Swede" Risberg. The eight men were indicted by a grand jury on October 22, 1920, and although they were acquitted at trial on August 2, 1921, they were banished from baseball for life by baseball commissioner Kenesaw Mountain Landis immediately after their acquittal.

F. Scott Fitzgerald refers to the scandal in *The Great Gatsby* (1925). After Nick Carraway, the narrator in what has been called "the great American novel," learns that gambler Meyer Wolfshiem—Jay Gatsby's mysterious benefactor—was "the man who fixed the World's Series back in 1919," Carraway reflects:[65]

The idea staggered me. I remembered of course that the World's Series had been fixed in 1919 but if I had thought of it at all I would have thought of it as a thing that merely *happened*, the end of some inevitable chain. It never occurred to me that one man could start to play with the faith of fifty million people—with the single-mindedness of a burglar blowing a safe [emphasis in original].[66]

Daniel A. Nathan writes that "for some readers, the scene reverberates throughout the novel, for it is one of the earliest indicators that the dashing Gatsby is not what he appears to be. Thereafter his underworld connections undermine his legitimacy and taint him." John Lauricella goes even further, claiming in "The Black Sox Signature Baseball in *The Great Gatsby*" that "the moment is so well-known and so strongly characteristic of Nick and Gatsby that it may be read as the novel's signature scene."[67]

Fitzgerald published *The Great Gatsby* only a few years after the trial ended. By making the "Big Fix" part of the novel's "signature scene," Fitzgerald helped to preserve the Black Sox in America's collective memories in the years immediately following 1921.[68]

But if literature can *preserve* memories, can literature *rehabilitate* them as well? And if so, then what about Nelson Algren? Does he have a place in this reassessment process? Because "So Long, Swede Risberg" was published in the July 1981 issue of *Chicago* magazine, it appears that this article kept the Black Sox scandal alive in Americans' minds even after Algren's death. But was there a redemptive effect to Algren's writing as well? For example, did his 1942 *Southern Review* poem soften the nation's image of these banned players? Are the Eight Men no longer Out?

The answers to all of these questions may be "yes." Not only does Nathan believe that literature can maintain otherwise receding memories, he also contends that Algren's writings served to "reinscribe"—that is, to "reevaluate" and then "reimprint" or "reimpress" the events of 1919–21 in the minds of Algren's readers. Nathan comments, for example, that "Algren used the Black Sox as a way of reconnecting with the past—sometimes nostalgically, sometimes with a more critical perspective—and thus in a small way he helped reinscribe the event and its participants in America's collective memories."[69]

For example, consider "The Swede Was a Hard Guy," published in the *Southern Review* twenty-one years after the Black Sox players were expelled from baseball. Nathan refers to the poem's "unmistakable sympathy for the banished ballplayers, who are described as lambs being led to a shearing." Nathan maintains that the poem "poignantly reinscribes Jackson, Weaver, and the rest in American collective memories."[70]

Bill Savage agrees with Nathan's assessment of the restorative qualities of Algren's writing. Savage comments that "in his prose and poetry about the Black Sox, Algren may perhaps have begun the rehabilitation of Shoeless Joe Jackson, from criminal to redemptive hero in *Field of Dreams*.[71]

Savage points to Algren's "childhood defense of Shoeless Joe" in "The Silver-Colored Yesterday" as an example of Jackson's conversion from Bad Guy to Good Guy:

> Out of the welter of accusations, half denials and sudden silences a single fact drifted down: that Shoeless Joe Jackson couldn't play bad baseball even if he were trying to. He hit .375 in that series and played errorless ball, doing everything a major-leaguer could to win.[72]

Savage also notes that Algren's 1959 *Sun-Times* articles "continued to depict the Black Sox as tragic victims rather than criminals."[73]

Other writers have taken this rehabilitating process even further. Consider, for example, Bernard Malamud's novel *The Natural*, published in 1952, and W.P. Kinsella's 1982 book *Shoeless Joe*, on which the 1989 film *Field of Dreams* was based. But although these two authors may have used literary rehabilitation on a grander scale and to a greater degree, Algren was surely the first writer to "resurrect and reinscribe" the memory of the Black Sox Scandal.[74]

Conclusion

From a 1942 poem in a literary journal to a 1981 final farewell to a boyhood hero in a Midwestern magazine, Nelson Algren's writing about the Chicago White Sox spanned thirty-nine years. Almost all of his White Sox articles, stories, and poems were devoted to the Black Sox Scandal. Is there a reason why Algren committed so many pages to the "Big Fix"?

At the beginning of Algren's 1941 short story, "Biceps," there appears the following quotation from Walt Whitman's poetry collection, *Leaves of Grass*:

> *I feel I am one of them—*
> I belong to those convicts and prostitutes myself,
> And henceforth I will not deny them—
> For how can I deny myself?[75]

It is easy to simply conclude that because Algren had cast his lot with the downtrodden from the very beginning of his career, he would naturally side with these eight outcasts.

But such a statement is perhaps a bit simplistic. Yes, it was inevitable that Algren would spend almost forty years writing about Shoeless Joe, "Swede" Risberg, *et al.* But *why* is that so?

In *Chicago: City on the Make*, Nelson Algren writes these words:

I submit that literature is made upon any occasion that a challenge is put to the legal apparatus by conscience in touch with humanity.[76]

So why did Nelson Algren write about Eight Men Out? Because Algren was a writer of literature. Surely describing the struggles of eight men who were acquitted in court but still banned from baseball falls within Algren's definition of literature.

NOTES

1. Kermit Joyce, "Nelson Algren: The Unbeat Poet," *On the QT*, December 1959, 24; Henry Kisor, "Nelson Algren, Hale and Salty at 64," *Chicago Daily News Panorama*, 27–28 October 1973, 2.

2. Bettina Drew, *Nelson Algren: A Life on the Wild Side* (Austin: University of Texas Press, 1991), 13–14, 18; Eliot Asinof, *Eight Men Out: The Black Sox and the 1919 World Series* (New York: Holt, Rinehart & Winston, 1963), 20; Curt Smith, "Comiskey Park," in *Go-Go to Glory: The 1959 Chicago White Sox*, ed. Don Zminda (Skokie, Ill.: ACTA Publications, 2009), 7; Nelson Algren, *Chicago: City on the Make*, 60th anniversary edition (Chicago: University of Chicago Press, 2011), 33–34. All subsequent citations to *Chicago: City on the Make* are to this 2011 edition unless otherwise noted. The title of this book has been abbreviated to "*City on the Make*" throughout these endnotes.

3. Asinof, *Eight Men Out*, 15–20, 112–19, 225, 239, 272–73; "Indicts Three More in Baseball Fixing," *New York Times*, 23 October 1920, 4; William F. Lamb, *Black Sox in the Courtroom: The Grand Jury, Criminal Trial and Civil Litigation* (Jefferson, N.C.: McFarland, 2013), 20, 82, 85, 113, 144–45. For references to the term, the "Big Fix," see, e.g., Daniel A. Nathan, *Saying It's So: A Cultural History of the Black Sox Scandal* (Urbana: University of Illinois Press, 2003), 6, 68, and Gene Carney, *Burying the Black Sox: How Baseball's Cover-Up of the 1919 World Series Fix Almost Succeeded* (Washington, D.C.: Potomac Books, 2006), xiv, 219.

4. Matthew J. Bruccoli, *Nelson Algren: A Descriptive Bibliography* (Pittsburgh: University of Pittsburgh Press, 1985),107, 110; Nelson Algren, "The Swede Was a Hard Guy," *Southern Review*, Spring 1942, 873–79; Nathan, *Saying It's So*, 82–83.

5. Nathan, *Saying It's So*, 82.

6. Algren, "The Swede Was a Hard Guy," *Southern Review*, 878–79.

7. Asinof, *Eight Men Out*, 20.

8. Asinof, *Eight Men Out*, 175, 178, 209; Lamb, *Black Sox in the Courtroom*, 48–57; "Indicts Three More in Baseball Fixing," 4; "'We Threw World Series.' Cicotte, Jackson, Admit," *Chicago Daily Tribune*, 29 September 1920, 2.

9. "We Threw World Series," 2. The *Chicago Daily Journal* reported Jackson making a similar statement. See "Letter Holds Death Threat," *Chicago Daily Journal*, 29 September 1920, 2. See also Lamb, *Black Sox in the Courtroom*, 52–57; Carney, *Burying the Black Sox*, 119–25.

10. Nelson Algren, "The Swede Was a Hard Guy," *Chicago*, June 1956, 30–34.

11. Nelson Algren, "We Never Made It to the White Sox Game," *Chicago Tribune Book World*, 2 September 1979, sec. 7, 3.

12. "In the Wake of the News," *Chicago Daily Tribune*, 3 April 1920, 13.

13. Tim Hornbaker, *Turning the Black Sox White: The Misunderstood Legacy of Charles A. Comiskey* (New York: Sports Publishing, 2014), 268. Algren writes colorfully about this altercation between Risberg and the hapless umpire in the July 1981 issue of *Chicago* magazine: "The Swede was a hard guy. He took to fighting as easily as he did to baseball and occasionally confused these crafts. At Oakland he'd protested a third strike simply by stepping up to an umpire and knocking him cold with a short chop to his jaw. 'Call *that* a third strike,' he'd commented while the other umpire was trying to bring his colleague back to

life. And walked back to the dugout in disgust." (emphasis in original) See Nelson Algren, "So Long, Swede Risberg," *Chicago*, July 1981, 138. Baseball historians Kelly Boyer Sagert and Rod Nelson write that "Risberg managed to survive in Chicago by adopting a tough veneer that led to frequent fisticuffs and a reputation for toughness, excitability, and stand-offishness." See Kelly Boyer Sagert and Rod Nelson, "Swede Risberg," in *Scandal on the South Side: The 1919 Chicago White Sox*, ed. Jacob Pomrenke (Phoenix: Society for American Baseball Research, 2015), 171.

14. Nelson Algren, "A Lot You Got to Holler," in Nelson Algren, *The Neon Wilderness* (New York: Seven Stories Press, 1986), 110.

15. Algren, "A Lot You Got to Holler," 110.

16. Chapter 3 of *Chicago: City on the Make*, entitled "The Silver-Colored Yesterday," seems strangely out of place with the rest of the book. In the book's introduction (first written for the 1983 edition), Studs Terkel calls *City on the Make* a "singular prose poem," but "The Silver-Colored Yesterday" is clearly more prose than poem. Van Allen Bradley writes in his review of this book that "[Algren] loses his poetic way for a chapter to discuss the Black Sox scandal of 1919." See Studs Terkel, introduction to *Chicago: City on the Make*, by Nelson Algren (New York: McGraw-Hill, 1983), 8; Van Allen Bradley, "Algren's '*Chicago*': A Work of Genius and Poetic Vision," review of *Chicago: City on the Make*, by Nelson Algren, *Chicago Daily News*, 24 October 1951, sec. 2, 36.

17. Drew, *Nelson Algren*, 19; Algren, *City on the Make*, 34. Bettina Drew writes that the Algren family moved to the northwest side of Chicago in the spring of 1921, but the clues to the timeline of Algren's early life that Algren mentions in *Chicago: City on the Make*, together with the timeline of the grand jury indictments and the trial, suggest that his family may have moved to Chicago's northwest side in 1920 and not 1921. See Drew, *Nelson Algren*, 13, 19; Algren, *City on the Make*, 34–36; Robert I. Goler, "Black Sox," *Chicago History*, 17, nos. 3 and 4 (Fall and Winter 1988–89): 60; "Indicts Three More in Baseball Fixing," 4. Valentine Michael Smith was the main character in Robert A. Heinlein's 1961 science fiction novel, *Stranger in a Strange Land*.

18. Algren, *City on the Make*, 34–36.

19. Asinof, *Eight Men Out*, 168–78, 225; "We Threw World Series," 1–2; "Indicts Three More in Baseball Fixing," 4. All eight ballplayers had been previously indicted, but the indictments "were revoted to overcome legal technicalities" and the October 22 indictments were handed down "to guard against any irregularities that might have been found in the first bills." See "Indicts Three More in Baseball Fixing," 4; "Baseball Jury Indicts Burns, Chase and Attel," *Chicago Daily Tribune*, 23 October 1920, 17.

20. Algren, *City on the Make*, 35–37, 116–18; Nathan, *Saying It's So*, 83; Ellen Schrecker, *The Age of McCarthyism: A Brief History with Documents*, 2nd ed. (Boston: Bedford/St. Martin's, 2002), 229.

21. Algren, *City on the Make*, 38. On February 9, 1950, Senator Joseph McCarthy told a Republican women's club that he had a list of 205 people who were known to the Secretary of State as being members of the Communist Party and who were still making and shaping the policy of the State Department. McCarthy's baseless allegations would eventually become a four-year witch hunt of intimidation and state-coerced conformity that came to be called McCarthyism. *Chicago: City on the Make* was not published until October 1951, and so it is likely that Algren was aware of Joe McCarthy and McCarthyism when he wrote these sentences for *City on the Make*. See Victor S. Navasky, *Naming Names* (New York: Penguin Books, 1980), 23; Bruccoli, *Nelson Algren*, 37. For a detailed discussion of the various aspects of McCarthyism in "The Silver-Colored Yesterday," see Andrew Hazucha, "Nelson Algren's Chicago: The Black Sox Scandal, McCarthyism, and the Truth about Cubs Fans," in *Baseball/Literature/Culture: Essays, 2002–2003*, ed. Peter Carino (Jefferson, N.C.: McFarland, 2004), 49–59. The entities that most typified the anti-Communist climate of the late 1940s and the 1950s were congressional investigating committees. HUAC was the oldest and most influential of these committees. HUAC and these committees would interrogate people at public hearings. Algren asks in the text, "Can I keep my job if I bum-rap some people for you?" The naming of names was central to these hearings. See Schrecker, *The Age of McCarthyism*, 63, 64, 65; Ellen Schrecker, *Many Are the Crimes: McCarthyism*

in America (Princeton, N.J.: Princeton University Press, 1998), 285, 329–30; Larry Dane Brimner, *Blacklisted! Hollywood, The Cold War, and the First Amendment* (Honesdale, Pa.: Calkins Creek, 2018), 119–22; see generally Victor S. Navasky, *Naming Names*.

22. Nelson Algren, "The Silver-Colored Yesterday," in *Baseball: A Literary Anthology*, ed. Nicholas Dawidoff (New York: Library of America, 2002), 227–233; Nelson Algren, "The Silver-Colored Yesterday," in *The Fireside Book of Baseball*, ed. Charles Einstein (New York: Simon and Schuster, 1956), 2–5; Nelson Algren, "The Silver-Colored Yesterday," in *The New Baseball Reader: More Favorites from the Fireside Books of Baseball*, ed. Charles Einstein (New York: Viking, 1991), 1–7; Nelson Algren, "The Silver-Colored Yesterday," *Sport Literate* 3, no. 1 (1999): 88–97.

23. Algren, *City on the Make*, 54–55, 73; Richard C. Lindberg, *Total White Sox: The Definitive Encyclopedia of the Chicago White Sox* (Chicago: Triumph Books, 2011), 482. "Old Comiskey" is a reference to White Sox owner Charles Comiskey.

24. R.J. Lesch, "1959 Season Review," in Zminda, *Go-Go to Glory*, 218–19; R.J. Lesch, "1959 World Series," in Zminda, *Go-Go to Glory*, 220–21; Nathan, *Saying It's So*, 102–03; Hornbaker, *Turning the Black Sox White*, 352.

25. Nelson Algren, "Early Chicago Journalism," *Chicago Free Press* 1, no. 3 (12 October 1970): 28; Nelson Algren, "Different Clowns for Different Towns," in *The Last Carousel* (New York: Seven Stories Press, 1997), 258.

26. Nelson Algren, "Nelson Algren Writes Impressions of Series," *Chicago Sun-Times*, final edition, 2 October 1959, sec. 1, 5.

27. Algren, "Nelson Algren Writes Impressions of Series," sec. 1, 5.

28. Lindberg, *Total White Sox*, 578.

29. Lesch, "1959 World Series," 221; Nelson Algren, "Algren Writes of Roses and Hits," *Chicago Sun-Times*, final edition, 3 October 1959, 5.

30. Bill Savage, "The '59 White Sox in Literature: Haunted by Ghosts of the Black Sox," in Zminda, *Go-Go to Glory*, 234.

31. Lesch, "1959 World Series," 227; Savage, "The '59 White Sox in Literature," 234; Lindberg, *Total White Sox*, 579–81; Charles N. Billington, *Comiskey Park's Last World Series: A History of the 1959 Chicago White Sox* (Jefferson, N.C.: McFarland, 2019), 172–77.

32. "Nelson Algren, "Nelson Algren's Reflections: Hep-Ghosts of the Rain," *Chicago Sun-Times*, final home edition, 10 October 1959, 12.

33. Algren, "Nelson Algren's Reflections,"12. This article also appears in the final edition of the October 10, 1959, *Sun-Times*, but with a different title. See Nelson Algren, "Algren at Game 6: Shoeless Joe is Gone, Too," *Chicago Sun-Times*, final edition, 10 October 1959, sec. 2, 12. Algren mentions his uncle and the sinking of the *Chicora* in the essay, "The Night-Colored Rider" from his book, *Who Lost an American?* and in the essay, "Everything Inside is a Penny" from his book, *The Last Carousel*. However, in these essays the uncle is referred to as "Uncle Theodore" and not "Uncle Henry." See Nelson Algren, "Chicago I: The Night-Colored Rider," in Nelson Algren, *Algren at Sea: Who Lost an American? & Notes from a Sea Diary–Travel Writings* (New York: Seven Stories Press, 2008), 183–84; Nelson Algren, "Everything Inside for a Penny," in *The Last Carousel*, 237–38. See also H.E.F. Donohue, *Conversations with Nelson Algren* (New York: Hill and Wang, 1964), 4–5; Algren, *City on the Make*, 55, 75–76, 121. The *Chicora* sank on January 21, 1895, while navigating the ice fields between Milwaukee, Wisconsin and St. Joseph, Michigan. See William Ratigan, *Great Lakes Shipwrecks & Survivals*, revised edition (Grand Rapids, Mich.: Wm. B. Eerdmans Publishing, 1977), 242–43.

34. Algren, "Nelson Algren's Reflections,"12.

35. Savage, "The '59 White Sox in Literature," 234.

36. Nathan, *Saying It's So*, 103.

37. Bruccoli, *Nelson Algren*, 59, 73; Drew, *Nelson Algren*, 328.

38. Nelson Algren, "Chicago III: If I Can't Sell It I'll Keep Settin' on It; I Jest Won't Give It Away (Old Song)," in *Algren at Sea*, 211.

39. Algren, "Chicago III," in *Algren at Sea*, 211. Algren writes about these White Sox players: Bill "Bullfrog" Dietrich, pitcher; Henry "Banana Nose" Bonura, first baseman; Morris "Moe" Berg, catcher; and Art "The Great" Shires, third baseman. See Lindberg, *Total White Sox*, 156, 158, 179–80, 285–86.

40. Nelson Algren, "Go! Go! Go! Forty Years Ago," in *The Last Carousel*, 262–67.

41. Nelson Algren, "Ballet for Opening Day: The Swede Was a Hard Guy," in *The Last Carousel*, 268–98.

42. Algren, "The Swede Was a Hard Guy," *Southern Review*, 879.

43. Algren, "Ballet for Opening Day," in *The Last Carousel*, 298.

44. Algren, "The Swede Was a Hard Guy," *Southern Review*, 877.

45. Algren, "Ballet for Opening Day," in *The Last Carousel*, 295.

46. Asinof, *Eight Men Out*, 126, [277], 279, 286, 293; Algren, "Ballet for Opening Day," in *The Last Carousel*, 268.

47. Algren, "We Never Made It to the White Sox Game," 3.

48. James T. Farrell, *My Baseball Diary* (New York: A.S. Barnes, 1957), 99–108, 173–86; James T. Farrell, *Dreaming Baseball* (Kent, Ohio: Kent State University Press, 2007), v–vii; Nathan, *Saying It's So*, 101–02; Robert K. Landers, *An Honest Writer: The Life and Times of James T. Farrell* (San Francisco: Encounter Books, 2004), 41. For a discussion of the White Sox writings of Algren and Farrell (and also Ring Lardner), see James Hawking, "Stories of the White Sox: Farrell, Lardner, and Algren," in *The National Pastime: North Side, South Side, All Around the Town: Baseball in Chicago*, ed. Stuart Shea (Phoenix: The Society for American Baseball Research, 2015), 78–80.

49. Drew, *Nelson Algren*, 48, 53–55, 75, 82–86; Landers, *An Honest Writer*, 206–07; Colin Asher, *Never a Lovely So Real: The Life and Work of Nelson Algren* (New York: W.W. Norton, 2019), 85–87, 98, 106–07; James T. Farrell, *Studs Lonigan: A Trilogy* (New York: Vanguard Press, 1935).

50. Simone de Beauvoir, *A Transatlantic Love Affair: Letters to Nelson Algren*, comp. and annot. by Sylvie Le Bon de Beauvoir (New York: New Press, 1998), 9–10.

51. Beauvoir, *A Transatlantic Love Affair*, 272, 389, 490.

52. Tom Fitzpatrick, "Some Blunt but Not Unkind Words from Nelson Algren," *Chicago Sun-Times*, 26 March 1973, 14.

53. Algren, "We Never Made It to the White Sox Game," 3.

54. Algren, "We Never Made It to the White Sox Game," 3.

55. Algren, "We Never Made It to the White Sox Game," 3. It appears that Algren's review of *The Death of Nora Ryan* was never published in any newspaper or magazine. It is not listed in Matthew Bruccoli's book, *Nelson Algren: A Descriptive Bibliography* or its two addenda.

56. Algren, "So Long, Swede Risberg," 138–41, 158.

57. Asinof, *Eight Men Out*, 15, 20; Algren, "So Long, Swede Risberg," 138–39. Bob Hoie soundly refutes the claim that Charles Comiskey was tightfisted. See Bob Hoie, "1919 Baseball Salaries and the Mythically Underpaid Chicago White Sox," *Base Ball: A Journal of the Early Game*, Spring 2012, 17–34. See also Hornbaker, *Turning the Black Sox White*, 341–53; William Lamb, "Jury Nullification and the Not Guilty Verdicts in the Black Sox Case," *Baseball Research Journal* 44, no. 2 (Fall 2015): 56n39. On the other hand, in 1956 first baseman Arnold "Chick" Gandil claimed that Comiskey was "a sarcastic, belittling man who was the tightest owner in baseball." See Arnold (Chick) Gandil and Melvin Durslag, "This is My Story of the Black Sox Series," *Sports Illustrated*, 17 September 1956, 62.

58. Brooke Horvath, *Understanding Nelson Algren* (Columbia: University of South Carolina Press, 2005), 150. For the story of Nelson Algren's last year (spent in Sag Harbor, Long Island, New York), see Joe Pintauro, "Algren in Exile," *Chicago*, February 1988, 93–101, 156–163.

59. Nelson Algren, "So Long, Swede Risberg," in *Best Sports Stories 1982*, eds. *The Sporting News* and Edward Ehre (New York: E.P. Dutton, 1982), 46–54; Nelson Algren, "So Long, Swede Risberg," in Nelson Algren, *Entrapment and other Writings*, eds. Brooke Horvath and Dan Simon (New York: Seven Stories Press, 2009), 281–92.

60. This information is from promotional material for the Sherwin Beach Press limited edition.

61. *Parenthesis: The Journal of The Fine Press Book Association*, deluxe edition, no. 7 (November 2002).

62. "Fix These Faces in Your Memory," *Sporting News*, 7 October 1920, 2. After Joe Jackson and Eddie Cicotte testified before the grand jury on September 28, 1920, Charles

Comiskey immediately suspended all of the Black Sox players; this suspension was three weeks before the grand jury issued final indictments on October 22, 1920. See Nathan, *Saying It's So*, 63; Asinof, *Eight Men Out*, 179; "We Threw World Series," 1–2.

63. Nathan, *Saying It's So*, 58, 236n1; "Indicts Three More in Baseball Fixing," 4.

64. Nathan, *Saying It's So*, 59, 62–67.

65. Nathan, *Saying It's So*, 67–69.

66. F. Scott Fitzgerald, *The Great Gatsby* (New York: Collier Books, 1992), xi, xii, 78.

67. Nathan, *Saying It's So*, 67–68, 238n49; John A. Lauricella, "The Black Sox Signature Baseball in 'The Great Gatsby,'" *Aethlon: The Journal of Sport Literature* 10, no. 1 (Fall 1992): 86.

68. Nathan, *Saying It's So*, 67–69.

69. Nathan, *Saying It's So*, 81–84.

70. Nathan, *Saying It's So*, 48–51, 82; Asinof, *Eight Men Out*, 273.

71. Savage, "The '59 White Sox in Literature," 234. Gene Carney writes that Nathan "brilliantly puts the writings of Nelson Algren in context. The story was trying to fade away, but supporters of Buck Weaver and Joe Jackson kept agitating for justice. The country had new heroes—Ruth, DiMaggio, Williams, Musial—and 'unwittingly, these men induced Black Sox amnesia.'" See Carney, *Burying the Black Sox*, 282; see also Greg Couch, "The Inside Story," *Chicago Sun-Times*, 28 June 2000, 146.

72. Savage, "The '59 White Sox in Literature," 234; Algren, *City on the Make*, 38. Nathan agrees with Savage's assessment of "The Silver-Colored Yesterday." Nathan writes that this chapter from *Chicago: City on the Make* "resurrected and reinscribed the memory of the scandal for many readers, and probably introduced the event to many others." See Nathan, *Saying It's So*, 83.

73. Savage, "The '59 White Sox in Literature," 234.

74. Savage, "The '59 White Sox in Literature," 234; Nathan, *Saying It's So*, 83–84, 92–99, 154–57, 173–77; Bernard Malamud, *The Natural* (New York: Harcourt Brace, 1952); W.P. Kinsella, *Shoeless Joe* (Boston: Houghton Mifflin, 1982). "The Natural" (the movie) came out in 1984. See Nathan, *Saying It's So*, 170–73.

75. Nelson Algren, "Biceps," *Southern Review* 6, no. 4 (Spring 1941): 713.

76. Algren, *City on the Make*, 81. Algren's statement about literature is in the afterword of the 60th anniversary edition of *City on the Make*. The afterword originally appeared as the introduction to the second edition of *City on the Make*, published in 1961. See Algren, *City on the Make*, 127; Nelson Algren, *Chicago: City on the Make* (Sausalito, Calif.: Contact Editions, 1961), 9. For more information about the various editions of *Chicago: City on the Make*, see this book's essay, "The Writing of *Chicago: City on the Make*."

Selected Bibliography

Algren, Nelson. "Algren at Game 6: Shoeless Joe Is Gone, Too." *Chicago Sun-Times*, final edition, 10 October 1959, sec. 2, 12.

Algren, Nelson. *Algren at Sea: Who Lost an American? & Notes from a Sea Diary—Travel Writings*. New York: Seven Stories Press, 2008.

Algren, Nelson. "Algren Writes of Roses and Hits." *Chicago Sun-Times*, final edition, 3 October 1959, 5.

Algren, Nelson. "Biceps." *Southern Review* 6, no. 4 (Spring 1941): 713–28.

Algren, Nelson. *Chicago: City on the Make*. Sausalito, Calif.: Contact Editions, 1961.

Algren, Nelson. *Chicago: City on the Make*. New York: McGraw-Hill, 1983.

Algren, Nelson. *Chicago: City on the Make*. 60th anniversary edition. Chicago: University of Chicago Press, 2011.

Algren, Nelson. "Early Chicago Journalism." *Chicago Free Press* 1, no. 3 (12 October 1970): 28–30.

Algren, Nelson. *Entrapment and other Writings*. Edited by Brooke Horvath and Dan Simon. New York: Seven Stories Press, 2009.

Algren, Nelson. *The Last Carousel.* New York: Seven Stories Press, 1997.

Algren, Nelson. "Nelson Algren Writes Impression of Series." *Chicago Sun-Times*, final edition, 2 October 1959, sec. 1, 5.

Algren, Nelson. "Nelson Algren's Reflections: Hep-Ghosts of the Rain." *Chicago Sun-Times*, final home edition, 10 October 1959, 12.

Algren, Nelson. *The Neon Wilderness.* New York: Seven Stories Press, 1986.

Algren, Nelson. "The Silver-Colored Yesterday." In *Baseball: A Literary Anthology.* Edited by Nicholas Dawidoff, 227–33. New York: The Library of America, 2002.

Algren, Nelson. "The Silver-Colored Yesterday." In *The Fireside Book of Baseball*, 2–5. New York: Simon and Schuster, 1956.

Algren, Nelson. "The Silver-Colored Yesterday." In *The New Baseball Reader: More Favorites from The Fireside Books of Baseball.* Edited by Charles Einstein, 1–7. New York: Viking, 1991.

Algren, Nelson. "The Silver-Colored Yesterday." *Sport Literate* 3, no. 1 (1999): 88–97.

Algren, Nelson. "So Long, Swede Risberg." In *Best Sports Stories 1982*, eds. *The Sporting News* and Edward Ehre, 46–54. New York: E.P. Dutton, 1982.

Algren, Nelson. "So Long, Swede Risberg." *Chicago*, July 1981, 138–41, 158.

Algren, Nelson. "The Swede Was a Hard Guy." *Chicago*, June 1956, 30–34.

Algren, Nelson. "The Swede Was a Hard Guy." *Southern Review*, Spring 1942, 873–79.

Algren, Nelson. "We Never Made It to the White Sox Game." *Chicago Tribune Book World*, 2 September 1979, 3.

Asher, Colin. *Never a Lovely So Real: The Life and Work of Nelson Algren.* New York: W.W. Norton, 2019.

Asinof, Eliot. *Eight Men Out: The Black Sox and the 1919 World Series.* New York: Holt, Rinehart & Winston, 1963.

"Baseball Jury Indicts Burns, Chase and Attel." *Chicago Daily Tribune*, 23 October 1920, 17.

Beauvoir, Simone de. *A Transatlantic Love Affair: Letters to Nelson Algren.* Compiled and annotated by Sylvie Le Bon de Beauvoir. New York: New Press, 1998.

Billington, Charles N. *Comiskey Park's Last World Series: A History of the 1959 Chicago White Sox.* Jefferson, N.C.: McFarland, 2019.

Bradley, Van Allen. "Algren's 'Chicago': A Work of Genius and Poetic Vision." Review of *Chicago: City on the Make*, by Nelson Algren. *Chicago Daily News*, 24 October 1951, sec. 2, 36.

Brimner, Larry Dane. *Blacklisted! Hollywood, The Cold War, and the First Amendment.* Honesdale, Pa.: Calkins Creek, 2018.

Bruccoli, Matthew J. *Nelson Algren: A Descriptive Bibliography.* Pittsburgh: University of Pittsburgh Press, 1985.

Carney, Gene. *Burying the Black Sox: How Baseball's Cover-Up of the 1919 World Series Fix Almost Succeeded.* Washington, D.C.: Potomac Books, 2006.

Couch, Greg. "The Inside Story." *Chicago Sun-Times*, 28 June 2000, 146.

Donohue, H.E.F. *Conversations with Nelson Algren.* New York: Hill and Wang, 1964.

Drew, Bettina. *Nelson Algren: A Life on the Wild Side.* Austin: University of Texas Press, 1991.

Fitzgerald, F. Scott. *The Great Gatsby.* New York: Collier Books, 1992.

Fitzpatrick, Tom. "Some Blunt but Not Unkind Words from Nelson Algren." *Chicago Sun-Times*, 26 March 1973, 14.

"Fix These Faces in Your Memory." *Sporting News*, 7 October 1920, 2.

Gandil, Arnold (Chick), and Melvin Durslag. "This is My Story of the Black Sox Series." *Sports Illustrated*, 17 September 1956, 62, 64–70.

Goler, Robert I. "Black Sox." *Chicago History*, 17, nos. 3 and 4 (Fall and Winter 1988–89): 42–69.

Hawking, James. "Stories of the White Sox: Farrell, Lardner, and Algren." In *The National Pastime: North Side, South Side, All Around the Town: Baseball in Chicago.* Edited by Stuart Shea, 78–80. Phoenix: The Society for American Baseball Research, 2015.

Hazucha, Andrew. "Nelson Algren's Chicago: The Black Sox Scandal, McCarthyism, and the Truth about Cubs Fans." In *Baseball/Literature/Culture: Essays, 2002–2003.* Edited by Peter Carino, 49–59. Jefferson, N.C.: McFarland, 2004.

Hoie, Bob. "1919 Baseball Salaries and the Mythically Underpaid Chicago White Sox." *Base Ball: A Journal of the Early Game*, Spring 2012, 17–34.

Hornbaker, Tim. *Turning the Black Sox White: The Misunderstood Legacy of Charles A. Comiskey*. New York: Sports Publishing, 2014.

Horvath, Brooke. *Understanding Nelson Algren*. Columbia: University of South Carolina Press, 2005.

"In the Wake of the News." *Chicago Daily Tribune*, 3 April 1920, 13.

"Indicts Three More in Baseball Fixing." *New York Times*, 23 October 1920, 4.

Joyce, Kermit. "Nelson Algren: The Unbeat Poet." *On the QT*, December 1959, 22–25, 44–45.

Kisor, Henry. "Nelson Algren, Hale and Salty at 64." *Chicago Daily News Panorama*, 27–28 October 1973, 2–3.

Lamb, William F. *Black Sox in the Courtroom: The Grand Jury, Criminal Trial and Civil Litigation*. Jefferson, N.C.: McFarland, 2013.

Lamb, William. "Jury Nullification and the Not Guilty Verdicts in the Black Sox Case." *Baseball Research Journal* 44, no. 2 (Fall 2015): 47–56.

Landers, Robert K. *An Honest Writer: The Life and Times of James T. Farrell*. San Francisco: Encounter Books, 2004.

Lauricella, John A. "The Black Sox Signature Baseball in 'The Great Gatsby.'" *Aethlon: The Journal of Sport Literature* 10, no. 1 (Fall 1992): 83–98.

Lesch, R.J. "1959 Season Review." In *Go-Go to Glory: The 1959 Chicago White Sox*. Edited by Don Zminda, 206–19. Skokie, Ill.: ACTA Publications, 2009.

Lesch, R.J. "1959 World Series." In *Go-Go to Glory: The 1959 Chicago White Sox*. Edited by Don Zminda, 220–28. Skokie, Ill.: ACTA Publications, 2009.

"Letter Holds Death Threat." *Chicago Daily Journal*, 29 September 1920, 2.

Lindberg, Richard C. *Total White Sox: The Definitive Encyclopedia of the Chicago White Sox*. Chicago: Triumph Books, 2011.

Nathan, Daniel A. *Saying It's So: A Cultural History of the Black Sox Scandal*. Urbana: University of Illinois Press, 2003.

Navasky, Victor S. *Naming Names*. New York: Penguin Books, 1980.

Parenthesis: The Journal of the Fine Press Book Association, deluxe edition, no. 7 (November 2002).

Pintauro, Joe. "Algren in Exile." *Chicago*, February 1988, 92–101, 156–63.

Sagert, Kelly Boyer, and Rod Nelson. "Swede Risberg." In *Scandal on the South Side: The 1919 Chicago White Sox*. Edited by Jacob Pomrenke, 171–76. Phoenix: Society for American Baseball Research, 2015.

Savage, Bill. "The '59 White Sox in Literature: Haunted by Ghosts of the Black Sox." In *Go-Go to Glory: The 1959 Chicago White Sox*. Edited by Don Zminda, 233–34. Skokie, Ill.: ACTA Publications, 2009.

Schrecker, Ellen. *The Age of McCarthyism: A Brief History with Documents*, 2nd ed. Boston: Bedford/St. Martin's, 2002.

Schrecker, Ellen. *Many Are the Crimes: McCarthyism in America*. Princeton, N.J.: Princeton University Press, 1998.

Smith, Curt. "Comiskey Park." In *Go-Go to Glory: The 1959 Chicago White Sox*. Edited by Don Zminda, 7–10. Skokie, Ill.: ACTA Publications, 2009.

"'We Threw World Series.' Cicotte, Jackson, Admit." *Chicago Daily Tribune*, 29 September 1920, 1–2.

The Writing of *Chicago:*
City on the Make

Introduction

In his seven-page introduction to the 1983 edition of Nelson Algren's book, *Chicago: City on the Make*, Studs Terkel writes that "in this slender classic, first published in 1951 and, ever since, bounced around like a ping-pong ball, Algren tells us all we need to know about passion, heaven, hell. And a city." Although Algren tells us all about the City of Chicago, Terkel never tells the reader anything about the book. Terkel never discloses, for example, the backstory of *City on the Make*. He does not explain how Algren came to write this "slender classic." Terkel's omission was undoubtedly deliberate; it would not have been appropriate to relate in his introduction how *City on the Make* evolved from what Algren described as a "hack-and-patch" article published in *Holiday* magazine into a book that has been reprinted six times since its 1951 publication.[1]

Studs Terkel died in 2008. It is time to fill in the gaps. This essay will recount the history of the writing of *City on the Make*. It will show how Algren was influenced by other poets in the writing of this prose poem, and it will detail how Algren left his own individual touches on this work. It will also describe the various editions of this book.

This article is probably the most comprehensive discussion and analysis of *City on the Make* ever written. It is *not*, however, intended to offer a deeper understanding of the book. Several authors have already discussed this. Consider, for example, the following:

- In his book, *October Cities: The Redevelopment of Urban Literature*, Carlo Rotella maintains that *City on the Make* is an illustration of Chicago's decline as an industrial city.[2]
- Caroline Gottschalk-Druschke examines *City on the Make* in her essay, "The City That Turned the White Sox Black: Post-World War

II Chicago Boosterism and the Negation of Nelson Algren." She writes that "Rotella's interpretation is missing a certain layer of understanding. Algren included enough triumphant aspects of his city to necessitate a more-balanced reading of the text itself." She adds that "while Algren chronicled the decline of the ethnic urban village, he placed that decline in the context of a larger Chicago history."[3]

- Brooke Horvath discusses all of Algren's books in his work, *Understanding Nelson Algren*. In the section on *City on the Make*, Horvath describes Algren's book as "a diagnosis of American ills circa 1951."[4]

Figure 26: This photograph of Studs Terkel, circa 1960, was taken by photographer Stephen Deutch, who also took the pictures for the third edition of Nelson Algren's prose poem, *Chicago: City on the Make* (1968). Beginning in the mid–1960s, Algren would inexplicably end relationships with such friends as Max Geismar, Jack Conroy, Dave Peltz, John Clellon Holmes, and Bruce Jay Friedman. Studs Terkel (and also newspaper columnist Mike Royko) seems to have been one of the few close friends who was spared. In a 1986 interview, Terkel told Algren biographer Bettina Drew that "I kept my distance and we didn't break off" (Chicago History Museum, ICHi-065438, Stephen Deutch, photographer).

- In his essay, "The Radical Tradition of Algren's *Chicago: City on the Make*," James A. Lewin writes that "the underlying thesis of the whole cryptic essay is a passionate argument for the homeless."[5]
- Ian Peddie claims in his article, "Poles Apart? Ethnicity, Race, Class, and Nelson Algren" that *City on the Make* is "far more than a tale of industrial decline. Algren's lament is also a requiem for the decline in class sensibility that produced some of Chicago's greatest moments and many of its greatest heroes."[6]
- Sara Rutkoski notes in her essay, "Nelson Algren's *Personalism*," that Algren "derides the city's history of crime and corruption" in *City on the Make*. At the same time, the book is "a deeply personal essay that weaves its way through Algren's inner world, from his childhood recollections of the 1919 Black Sox scandal to his present experience of longing and loss."[7]

Part One: The History of Chicago: City on the Make

In the Beginning: *Holiday*

What essentially evolved into *Chicago: City on the Make* started out as a magazine article. Louis F.V. Mercier and Harry Sions, editors of *Holiday*, a travel magazine, wanted to publish a special Chicago issue, and they contacted (probably in the spring of 1950) photographer and Algren friend Art Shay and asked Shay to recommend "a good Chicago writer." Shay gave the men Nelson Algren's phone number. When they called Algren, he jokingly told Mercier and Sions to check his literary credentials with Carl Sandburg, who was then, according to Shay, "strumming his guitar and raising goats on his farm in North Carolina." Sandburg gave his approval and the magazine project was finalized. Algren would be paid $2,000 to write an essay about Chicago.[8]

Algren biographer Bettina Drew comments that Algren intended to write a "highly personalized essay." She writes that Algren viewed Chicago as a city "whose heart beat in its slums, a city with two faces—one for the haves and one for the have-nots." Unfortunately, this dualistic (and cynical) perspective was completely at odds with Sions' concern about offending, as Shay describes, "advertisers or the municipal powers who could discourage advertisers from buying space in an issue that knocked Chicago."[9]

Algren worked on this essay through the fall of 1950 and into the winter of 1950–51. Algren probably submitted it to *Holiday* in the first quarter of 1951. Drew notes that although the editors liked its originality, Algren's unique perspective of Chicago "wasn't exactly what they'd had in mind." In early May of 1951 *Holiday* sent Algren an edited proof copy, edited (most likely) to soften his views. Algren was given a week to make changes, but as he worked furiously, *Holiday* published its own edited copy titled "One Man's Chicago" without waiting for his revision.[10]

A *Holiday* editor, no doubt hoping to appease an angry Algren, wrote the author on May 24, 1951: "Don't let any of this trouble you, because we are still enormously pleased with your piece … and distinctly proud to have it in *Holiday*."[11]

Although this editor's tone might have been unctuous, Algren's reply three days later was anything but:

I'd be less disappointed were you more honest.…

To restore meaning and order to that piece, more than a week was actually required.… And because my concern over the piece was deep, and the limitations of which you advised me were sufficiently sharp, I was pleased to be able to bring it to life again within the promised time. If your taste is really so lacking or your timing so poor that you will publish the hack-and-patch version anyway, all I can say is that you're a sorry sort of operator indeed.

Nor do I feel that being well-paid, which I have been, justifies either the capriciousness of your action or the smugness of the letter with which you cap it. I've been served up with cheap flattery without swooning before this; but have never till now seen so much of it so densely packed.[12]

After *Holiday*: The Publication
of *Chicago: City on the Make*

In 1949 Doubleday published Algren's novel, *The Man with the Golden Arm*. A grim but powerful story of poverty, drug addiction, and hopelessness, the book was an immediate bestseller. Doubleday editor Ken McCormick, hoping to capitalize on the success of *Golden Arm*, suggested that Doubleday release "One Man's Chicago" in book form in time for the 1951 Christmas season. Algren loved the idea. His essay would be published as he had intended.[13]

The essay would be published, but not as "One Man's Chicago." Art Shay recounts the provenance of the book's eventual title, *Chicago: City on the Make*, in his own book, *Nelson Algren's Chicago*:

The title for the book that came of the article was born in my 1949 Pontiac around Hammond, Indiana, as I drove Algren and Doubleday's editor in chief, Ken McCormick, to Algren's house at Miller Beach. (Algren, pondering the title, said, "I've always thought of Chicago as a hustler's city." McCormick said, "Yes, it's a tough, working-class city, a sort of city on the make, a ..." I interrupted: "That's it," I said. "That's the title.")[14]

Chicago: City on the Make was released on October 18, 1951, to decidedly mixed reviews. Six days after the book was published, Van Allen Bradley of the *Chicago Daily News* exclaimed it was "a work of genius and absolutely the greatest piece of writing contemporary Chicago has produced." Emmett Dedmon, book and drama critic for the *Chicago Sun-Times*, stated that "the qualities of Nelson Algren's prose essay on Chicago are those of fine poetry." On the other hand, Alfred C. Ames of the *Chicago Tribune* sniffed that the book is "unpleasant, unlikely to please any who are not masochists, and is definitely an ugly, highly scented object." Budd Schulberg of the *New York Times* took a middle-of-the-road approach:[15]

[Algren's] profile of Chicago has depth if not breadth; by ordinary standards it is an unfair picture of the city, and therein lies its strength. About as unflattering as a Goya portrait of nobility, its degree of distortion is a measure of its creative impact.[16]

Figure 27: In 1950, Nelson Algren purchased this cottage in Miller Beach, Indiana. It is on Forrest Avenue (now Forest Avenue) where the road dead-ends into Marquette Park. The small house is at the end of a cul-de-sac, and he paid $15,000 for it. According to legend, Algren installed the oversized mailbox shown on the left side of the picture so that he could mail and receive manuscripts. Unfortunately, financial problems forced him to sell the house to his friend, Dave Peltz, in 1957 (photograph by George A. Rogge, co-founder [with Sue Rutsen] of the Nelson Algren Museum of Miller Beach).

Part Two: *The Influence of Other Writers on* Chicago: City on the Make

Bettina Drew describes the essay that became *Chicago: City on the Make* as "a prose poem: slangy, down-to-earth, and utterly original." But just how "original" is it? Scholarship undertaken years after her biography was published indicates that *City on the Make* bears the influence of at least two other writers.[17]

Jeff McMahon is responsible for this scholarship. In 2002 McMahon submitted a thesis entitled "The Secret Faces of Inscrutable Poets in Nelson Algren's *Chicago: City on the Make*" in partial fulfillment of a University of Chicago Master of Arts degree. McMahon wrote an article about his Algren research that was published a year later in *Newcity*, a Chicago newspaper. In these two works McMahon describes how these "inscrutable poets" left their fingerprints on the pages of *City on the Make*.[18]

The Influence of Carl Sandburg—
His Poem *Chicago*

The original 1951 edition of *Chicago: City on the Make* contains no introduction or preface, no afterword or epilogue, in which Algren might have acknowledged a person's assistance in writing the book. There are no footnotes or endnotes on any of the book's pages where Algren might have credited another writer's work. However, in a *Tribune* article written in 1947—four years before *City on the Make* was published—Algren telegraphed a harbinger of the identity of two men who clearly influenced him in the writing of his prose poem.

In this short article, "Laughter in Jars—Not as Sandburg Wrote of It," Algren decries the decline of Chicago since 1914—the year that *Poetry* magazine published Carl Sandburg's famous poem, *Chicago*.[19]

In his thesis McMahon uses this *Tribune* article to illustrate the many ways that Sandburg's poetry—especially *Chicago*—influenced Algren in the writing of *City on the Make*.

For example, McMahon notes that Algren begins "Laughter in Jars" by quoting two lines from Sandburg's *Chicago*:

> Under the terrible burden of destiny laughing as a young man laughs,
> Laughing even as an ignorant fighter laughs who never lost a battle.[20]

McMahon examines these lines, together with the following words from the same famous poem:

> City of the Big Shoulders.... Flinging magnetic curses amid the toil of piling job on job, here is a tall bold slugger set vivid against the little soft cities.[21]

McMahon similarly looks at Algren's description of "Uncle Johnson" in *City on the Make*:

> Uncle had never learned to fall down. He'd reel, lurch, bleed, bellow and bawl until the bartender would break the thing up at last.... Then a spot of color would touch his cheeks and he'd break out into that terrible lament ... to show us all he'd won again.[22]

By comparing the poetry of Sandburg to the prose poetry of Algren, McMahon is able to draw conclusions about the imagery created by the two writers:

> Sandburg describes Chicago in generic human forms: a worker with big shoulders, a laughing fighter, a tall bold slugger. Algren incarnates those forms with detail; he gives them faces. Sandburg's slugger thus becomes Uncle Johnson, a punch-drunk bar fighter too dumb to fall down.[23]

McMahon offers other examples of Sandburg's influence on the writing of *City on the Make*. Consider this line from *Chicago*:

And they tell me you are crooked and I answer: Yes, it is true I have seen the gunman kill and go free to kill again.[24]

Another gunman who killed and went free to kill again was "Terrible" Tommy O'Connor. Convicted of murdering a policeman in 1921, O'Connor was sentenced to death. But just days before his scheduled hanging, he broke out of the Cook County jail, never to be seen again.[25]

In *City on the Make* Algren memorializes O'Connor in words reminiscent of Sandburg's:

Terrible Tommy O'Connor was never a hero till he walked past the hangman and out the door and never came back any more.[26]

Sandburg's influence is even apparent in *City on the Make*'s dedication. As described below, each edition of Algren's book is dedicated to a different person. Algren dedicated the original 1951 edition "for Carl Sandburg."[27]

Nelson Algren pays homage to Sandburg throughout *City on the Make* by either mentioning him by name or by referring to him as the "white-haired poet." For example:

"City of the big shoulders" was how the white-haired poet put it.[28]

Chicago was the "City of the Big Shoulders" in Sandburg's *Chicago*. Sandburg also mentions "Laughing the stormy, husky, brawling laughter of Youth" in this poem. In *City on the Make* Algren combines both images—"big shoulders" and "laughing"—with his description, "heavy-shouldered laugher":[29]

They have builded a heavy-shouldered laugher here who went to work too young.[30]

Sandburg observes in *Chicago* that "I have seen your painted women under the gas lamps luring the farm boys." Algren writes in *City on the Make*: "Yet on nights when, under all the arc-lamps, the little men of the rain come running...."[31]

Sandburg mentions "the heart of the people" in his poem. Algren does this as well in *City on the Make*: "For the masses who do the city's labor also keep the city's heart." In fact, Algren refers to Chicago's heart throughout his book.[32]

The Influence of Carl Sandburg— Other Poetry

McMahon notes that other Sandburg poems besides *Chicago* influenced Algren in the writing of *City on the Make*. Below are lines from two of Sandburg's poems, followed by similar lines from *City on the Make*.[33]

McMahon refers to Sandburg's poem, *And This Will Be All?*

> Sandburg:
> And this will be all?
> And the gates will never open again?
> And the dust and the wind will play around the rusty door hinges
>   and the songs of October moan.[34]
> Algren:
> By days when the wind bangs alley gates ajar and the sun goes by
> on the wind.[35]

McMahon also mentions Sandburg's poem, *Halsted Street Car*:

> Sandburg:
> Come you, cartoonists,
> Hang on a strap with me here
> At seven o'clock in the morning
> On a Halsted street car.[36]
>
> Algren:
> Cruising down Milwaukee Avenue on any Loop-bound trolley on
>   any weekday morning, the straphangers to Success who keep the
>   factories and the ginmills running stand reading the papers.[37]

The Influence of Ben Maddow (David Wolff)

In "Laughter in Jars—Not as Sandburg Wrote of It," Nelson Algren alludes to "the words of another contributor" to *Poetry* magazine as he quotes several lines of a poem. McMahon writes in his 2003 *Newcity* article, "Nelson Algren's Secret: The True Story Behind *City on the Make*," that when he first sees these lines of poetry, "I hear already the echoes from *City on the Make*." But Algren does not identify this "contributor" to *Poetry*. Who is this person? McMahon's quest to identify this poet is detailed in his 2003 *Newcity* article.[38]

McMahon discovers the name of the poet in *The Neon Wilderness*, Algren's 1947 collection of short stories. The epigraph to this book consists of two stanzas of poetry, followed by the poem's title and a man's name. These twelve lines are different from those in the *Tribune* article, but that does not matter. McMahon writes that "the style is unmistakable, and the mystery poet now has a name—David Wolff."[39]

These twelve lines of poetry appear on unnumbered page 9 of *The Neon Wilderness*. On the fourth page of the book there is the statement, "The verses quoted on page 9 are reprinted by permission of *Poetry: A Magazine of Verse*." McMahon not only has a name and the title of the poem, he also has a publisher. Looking through the index of *Poetry* at the University of Chicago's Regenstein Library, he finds Wolff's poem, *The City*, in the January 1940 issue. McMahon also finds a library catalog reference—"Wolff, David. See also Maddow, Ben." McMahon discovers that "David Wolff" is a pseudonym for "Ben Maddow."[40]

It is possible that Algren and Maddow knew each other. Both Algren and Maddow were members of the League of American Writers, and both of them attended the second American Writers' Congress in 1937. In the months prior to the bombing of Pearl Harbor, the League actively engaged in anti-war efforts. Maddow organized a two-hour program where people read anti-war poems by Algren and other writers.[41]

Besides the similarities between the poetry in the "Laughter in Jars" article and the poetry in *The Neon Wilderness* epigraph, McMahon also discovered similarities between *City on the Make* and *The City*. As alluded to earlier, a sense of "duality" permeates *City on the Make*. For example, Algren writes in *City on the Make* that Chicago "forever keeps two faces, one for winners and one for losers; one for hustlers and one for squares." Algren also refers to Chicago as "a Jekyll-and-Hyde sort of burg." McMahon comments that "Algren exploits this duality by developing characters whose proudest efforts in the City on the Lake are betrayed by the City on the Make."[42]

But McMahon observes that this duality is also present in Ben Maddow's poem, *The City*. For example:

> None spoke, but waited to watch the discolored twins drawn forth, wrapped on the bed, together, born to the extremes of neglect ... still ignorant of desire, the double wilderness.... I heard the derision and the girls' duet of laughter of two who stopped before me.... Between the inner and the outer face, between the cold palm and the incestuous mind.[43]

McMahon also describes the obvious similarities between lines in *The City* and passages from *City on the Make*. For example:[44]

Comparison Number One

Algren:
And one for midnight subway watches when stations swing past like ferris wheels of light, yet leave the moving window wet with rain or tears.[45]

Maddow:
I, who all night restive in the unsleeping rain, awoke and saw the windows covered with tears.[46]

Comparison Number Two

Algren:
Now it's the place where we do as we're told, praise poison ... and applaud the artist, hanging for sale beside his work, with an ancestral glee.[47]

Maddow:
Where the painter hangs for sale beside his work ... he who can feign desire, praise poison, or hang by his teeth, lives well.[48]

Algren:
The high broken horizon of its towers overlooks this inland sea.[49]
Maddow:
Children of the cold sun and the broken horizon.[50]

Part Three: Nelson Algren Leaves His Own Marks on Chicago: City on the Make

Although Nelson Algren was influenced by the poetry of Carl Sandburg and Ben Maddow in writing *Chicago: City on the Make*, he also left his own independent and indelible marks on this prose poem.

Poetic License:
Revising White Sox History

Nelson Algren never lets Chicago's history get in the way of telling a great story. Consider this passage from *City on the Make*:

> For there's a left-hander's wind moving down Thirty-fifth, rolling the summer's last straw kelly across second into center, where fell the winning single of the first winning Comiskey team in thirty-two seasons.[51]

Algren wrote *City on the Make* in 1951. 1951 less thirty-two baseball seasons is 1919, the year of the Black Sox Scandal. Algren is suggesting in this sentence that the White Sox, Chicago's American League professional baseball team, did not have a winning season from 1919 until 1951.[52]

This is not true. Richard C. Lindberg, author of *Total White Sox: The Definitive Encyclopedia of the Chicago White Sox*, points out that the White Sox had winning seasons in 1925, 1926, 1936, 1937, 1939, 1940, and 1943.[53]

Could Algren have simply been mistaken? This is doubtful. Algren was a passionate White Sox fan. He devotes an entire chapter of *City on the Make* (chapter 3) to the Black Sox scandal. It is more likely that Algren embellished the truth to highlight the White Sox's memorable 1951 season. 1951 was a year that Lindberg calls "a remarkable, unforgettable year—truly the turning point in the sagging White Sox fortunes."[54]

Poetic License:
Revising Chicago Cubs History

Algren loved the White Sox, and he disliked the Chicago Cubs, the city's National League professional baseball team. This animosity (and his

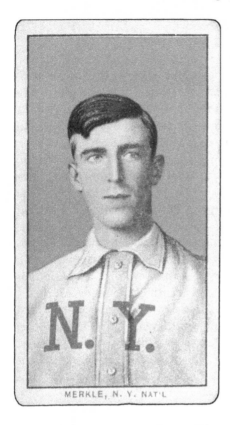
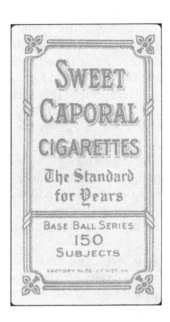

MERKLE, N. Y. NAT'L

Figure 28: "Merkle's Boner," one of the more famous events in baseball history, is named after New York Giants baseball player Fred Merkle. Pictured here is the front and back of Fred Merkle's 1909 baseball card. This card, like the famous Honus Wagner baseball card, is a "Sweet Caporal Cigarettes" tobacco card.

rewriting of Chicago Cubs history) is evident in the following phrase in which Algren describes the City of Chicago:[55]

> Town of the classic boners and the All-Time All-American bums.... Where somebody is always forgetting to touch second.[56]

In this passage Algren is referring to the infamous baseball mishap called "Merkle's Boner."[57]

What baseball historian Cait Murphy calls "baseball's most controversial game" took place on September 23, 1908. The Chicago Cubs played the New York Giants at the Polo Grounds in New York. The two teams were vying for the National League pennant. The Giants were at bat. It was the bottom of the ninth inning, there were two men out, and the score was tied, one to one. Harry "Moose" McCormick was on third base, and Fred Merkle was the runner on first base.[58]

When the Giant shortstop, Al Bridwell, hit a single, Moose McCormick ran for home. The Giants had apparently won the game, and jubilant Giant fans poured onto the field even while Merkle was heading for second base. Merkle was also convinced that the game was over, and so he never touched the base; he ran for the clubhouse instead. Cubs second baseman Johnny Evers noticed that Merkle never touched second. Evers knew that if he could get the ball and touch second base himself, Bridwell's winning run would be canceled by the force-out at second. Evers managed to get the ball and touch the base.[59]

Both teams claimed victory. Harry C. Pulliam, the league president, eventually voided the Giant run and declared the game a tie, to be replayed at the end of the season if the two teams were tied with no clear winner.[60]

And the two teams were tied at the end of the regular season. On October 8, 1908, a playoff game was held at the New York Polo Grounds. The Cubs won the game, the pennant, and eventually, the World Series.[61]

So where is the Cubs revisionist history in Algren's description of Chicago? Algren calls Chicago the "town of the classic boners." However, both games took place in New York. He refers to Chicago as being the town "where somebody is always forgetting to touch second," but it was a Giants player, not a Cubs player, who failed to touch second base, and at the time, second base was in New York, not Chicago.[62]

Revising Carl Sandburg's Legacy

Nelson Algren probably loved Carl Sandburg as much as he loved the White Sox, and so it is understandable that Algren would attempt to rewrite and revise Sandburg's literary legacy in *City on the Make*. Consider this passage:[63]

> "The slums take their revenge," the white-haired poet warned us thirty-two American League seasons and Lord-Knows-How-Many-Swindles-Ago. "Always somehow or other their retribution can be figured in any community."[64]

By doing the math—1951 less 32 American League seasons is again 1919—Algren is suggesting in this paragraph that Sandburg (the white-haired poet) wrote the phrase, "The slums take their revenge" during the 1919 Chicago Race Riots.[65]

Algren never actually *states* in *City on the Make* that Sandburg said this in 1919 during the riots. However, he clears up any ambiguity in his travel book, *Who Lost an American?* (1963) when he writes: "[The City of

Chicago] has not yet understood the simple truth told by a poet during the South Side race riots: 'The slums take their revenge.'"[66]

It is almost certain, however, that Sandburg never wrote "The slums take their revenge" during the 1919 Chicago riots. In the first part of July 1919, Sandburg was assigned to write a series of newspaper articles for the *Chicago Daily News*. Sandburg's articles were later published in book form in November of that year as *The Chicago Race Riots July, 1919*. The words, "The slums take their revenge" do not appear in this reprinted compilation of articles.[67]

But some of Sandburg's *Daily News* articles on the riots were not reprinted for this book. Is it possible that Sandburg made this statement in one of these other articles that was published during the riots?[68]

Did the *Daily News* publish such an article containing these words during the riots? When did the riots begin and end? William M. Tuttle, Jr., author of *Race Riot: Chicago in the Red Summer of 1919*, notes that Chicago suffered minor racial incidents in April, May, and early June of 1919, but that "it was not until the murder of two black men on the evening of June 21 that racial hatred leaped to fever pitch, and that the plummeting faith of blacks in the police struck bottom."[69]

Racial hatred did not stop on June 21. On Sunday afternoon, July 27, 1919, Eugene Williams and four other teenage black youths went swimming in Lake Michigan near 26th Street. They untied a raft and, kicking in the water, began propelling the raft south—towards the beach at 29th Street. Defying the unwritten law that designated the 29th Street beach as exclusively white, several blacks had earlier walked onto the beach, which resulted in a rock throwing melee between blacks and whites. As the raft passed the breakwater near 26th Street, a white man standing on the end of the breakwater began hurling rocks at Williams and the others. (It is not clear if the man was throwing rocks in angry retaliation against the perceived black intrusion at 29th Street.) Regardless, Williams was struck on the forehead, knocked unconscious, and drowned. The killing sparked two weeks of rioting. The state militia was eventually called out, and it (plus a "cooling rain") helped to quell the violence.[70]

Tuttle maintains that "the withdrawal of the state militia [on August 9] officially terminated the rioting of the past fourteen days." Algren maintains that Sandburg wrote, "The slums take their revenge" during the 1919 race riots; that would be sometime between July 27 and August 9. But a careful review of the *Chicago Daily News* from June 21 (the day two black men were murdered) through August 12 (three days after the withdrawal of the militia) does not reveal any article in which Sandburg writes these words.[71]

Although Sandburg did not write, "The slums take their revenge" during the 1919 riots, he *did* make this statement. He did so, however, more

The color line has reached the north.

Figure 29: This cartoon by famed cartoonist John T. McCutcheon appeared on page 1 of the July 29, 1919, issue of the *Chicago Tribune*, two days after Eugene Williams and four other teenage black youths went swimming in Lake Michigan near 26th Street, untied a raft, and, kicking in the water, propelled the raft towards 29th Street. The cartoon is captioned, "The color line has reached the north." The caption is an allegory. The rope in the water does not just symbolize the "whites only" 29th Street beach invisible line of segregation. Rather, it also represents the divide and tensions between blacks and whites in the northern states because of the Great Migration of blacks to the North in the years before 1919.

than twenty years later. In 1942 Sandburg wrote the following in a newspaper article, which was later reprinted in his 1943 book, *Home Front Memo*:

> The slums get their revenge, always somehow or other their retribution can be figured in any community, whether the slums are Negro ratholes such as those presented in *Native Son* by the Negro novelist Richard Wright, or slums of Polish white folk over the Northwest Side of Chicago, with an unforgettable and reeking house of vice, as reported in the novel *Never Come Morning* by the Scandinavian Nelson Allgren [sic].[72]

Algren was obviously influenced by Sandburg. It is reasonable to suggest that Algren read *Home Front Memo* when it was published in 1943. After all, Sandburg was complimentary towards Algren in the 1942 newspaper article that is reprinted in this book, even *if* Sandburg misspelled Algren's name.

In fact, it is possible that Algren owned *Home Front Memo* at the time he wrote *City on the Make*. After Algren died in 1981, Ohio State University purchased his personal library, which totaled over twelve hundred volumes at the time of his death. A search of Ohio State's Algren collection indicates that although Algren owned several books by Carl Sandburg, *Home Front Memo* is not one of these twelve hundred books. However, Algren might have owned it but then sold it during his 1975 house sale when he was preparing to move to New Jersey. Trunk Line, an Oak Park, Illinois, company, handled this sale of Algren's belongings. The company promoted the sale in a two-page typewritten advertisement. Among the items listed for sale in the advertisement are: "Some of Mr. Algren's personal library."[73]

While Algren was writing *City on the Make*, it is likely that Algren remembered what Sandburg wrote, probably read the article again in Sandburg's book, and decided to quote it (almost verbatim) in his book. But Sandburg wrote, "The slums get their revenge" during the beginning of World War II, a time that does not automatically connote an era of troubled black-and-white race relations. Perhaps Algren wanted to use Sandburg's phrase in *City on the Make*, but he wanted to enhance the circumstances as to when Sandburg wrote these words. By changing the year from 1942 to 1919, Algren was able to colorfully connect the phrase to the Chicago riots of that year.[74]

Nelson Algren as Literary Recycler

Nelson Algren was the ultimate recycler, often incorporating parts and passages from his older books and stories into newer ones. For example, compare the first sentence of Algren's 1942 poem, "The Swede Was a Hard Guy" to a sentence from the last chapter of *City on the Make*:

"The Swede Was a Hard Guy" (1942):
  There's a lefthander's wind coming down Thirty-Fifth
  Rolling the summer's last straw Kelly across second into center.[75]

City on the Make (1951):
  For there's a left-hander's wind moving down Thirty-fifth, rolling the summer's last straw kelly across second into center.[76]

Incredibly, Algren was even able to take phrases from *City on the Make* and later weave them into a 1954 book review of two books of Chicago history—*Big Bill of Chicago*, by Lloyd Wendt and Herman Kogan, and *Fabulous Chicago*, by Emmett Dedmon. The book review is entitled, "City Against Itself":

City on the Make (1951):
  You'll know it's the place built out of Man's ceaseless failure to overcome himself. Out of Man's endless war against himself we build our successes as well as our failures. Making it the city of all cities most like Man himself—loneliest creation of all this very old poor earth.[77]

"City Against Itself" (1954):
  And the city itself remains constant only in its ceaseless failure to overcome itself. Like man, it is engaged against itself. Like man, it builds its failures as well as its successes out of that engagement. It is left, like man, the loneliest thing in creation.[78]

Part Four: *The Various Editions of* Chicago: City on the Make

In the years since *City on the Make* was first published in 1951, the book has been reissued in six subsequent editions by various publishers. All editions of the book are described in the following pages.

Almost every edition has a different dedication, and the dedication appears immediately after the bibliographic information of each book.

- Algren, Nelson. *Chicago: City on the Make.* Garden City, New York: Doubleday & Co., 1951. (The 1951 Doubleday edition)

Dedication:
For Carl Sandburg

This book contains an epigraph; it is a portion of the poem, "Epilogue," by Charles Baudelaire:

> With heart at rest I climbed the citadel's
> Steep height, and saw the city as from a tower,
> Hospital, brothel, prison, and such hells,
> Where evil comes up softly like a flower ...
>
> Whether thou sleep, with heavy vapors full,
> Sodden with day, or new appareled, stand
> In gold-laced veils of evening beautiful,
>
> I love thee, infamous city! (ellipses in the original).[79]

This 1951 edition was issued in two printings. The first printing is a stated first edition on the copyright page. The second printing is identical to the first printing, except that it does not contain the words, "First Edition," on the copyright page.[80]

- Algren, Nelson. *Chicago: City on the Make.* Sausalito, California: Contact Editions, 1961. (The 1961 Contact edition)

Dedication:
For Herman and Marilou Kogan[81]

Matthew J. Bruccoli identifies this book as the second edition.[82]

This edition contains a twenty-seven-page introduction by Algren entitled, "The People of These Parts: A Survey of Modern Mid-American Letters." The epigraph of this introduction is from what Algren calls, "Notes on the condition of the city of Damascus from the tenth of August to the eighth of September in the year 1184." The epigraph, however, is actually from the book, *The Travels of Ibn Jubayr.* The words, "Notes on the condition of the city of Damascus...." merely appear at the top of a chapter in *The Travels of Ibn Jubayr.* This 1961 Contact edition epigraph reads as follows:[83]

> The people of these parts address each other as Mulai (Lord) and Sayyid (Sir), and use the expressions "Your servant" and "Your Excellency." When one meets another, instead of giving the ordinary greeting, he says respectfully, "Here is your slave" or "Here is your servant at your service." These make presents of honorifics to each other. Gravity with them is a fabulous affair.[84]

The first words of Algren's introduction are his often-quoted statement:

> "What is Literature?" Jean-Paul Sartre once asked in a small volume bearing that title.
> I submit that literature is made upon any occasion that a challenge is put to the legal apparatus by a conscience in touch with humanity.[85]

Algren's introduction to this 1961 edition is dated May 1961.

The Charles Baudelaire epigraph from the 1951 Doubleday edition appears after this introduction.

The back cover contains this statement: "*Chicago: City on the Make* was first published in 1952 [sic]. Its appearance divided Chicago into two almost-armed camps." Following these two sentences are short excerpts from book reviews of *City on the Make*, both pro and con.[86]

- Algren, Nelson. *Chicago: City on the Make.* 3rd ed. Oakland, California: Angel Island Publications, [1968]. (The 1968 Angel Island edition)

Dedication:
For Joan Baez
A conscience in touch with humanity

Although the copyright page suggests that this book was published in 1961, Matthew J. Bruccoli writes that the book was released in 1968. This copyright page indicates that this book is the third edition, and that is correct. This book contains the same epigraph and introduction as the 1961 Contact edition. The Charles Baudelaire epigraph from the 1951 Doubleday edition again appears immediately after the introduction.[87]

This edition also contains an epilogue. The writing of this epilogue is a fascinating story, and it is wonderfully detailed in an article by Robert Cromie in the February 16, 1968, issue of the *Chicago Tribune.*[88]

Cromie writes that "some months ago" Nelson Algren was asked by Angel Island Press to write some new material for a proposed third edition of *City on the Make*, an edition that would also include several photographs by photographer Stephen Deutch. Algren wrote the epilogue, calling it, "Ode to Lower Finksville." Later, though, after the publisher had

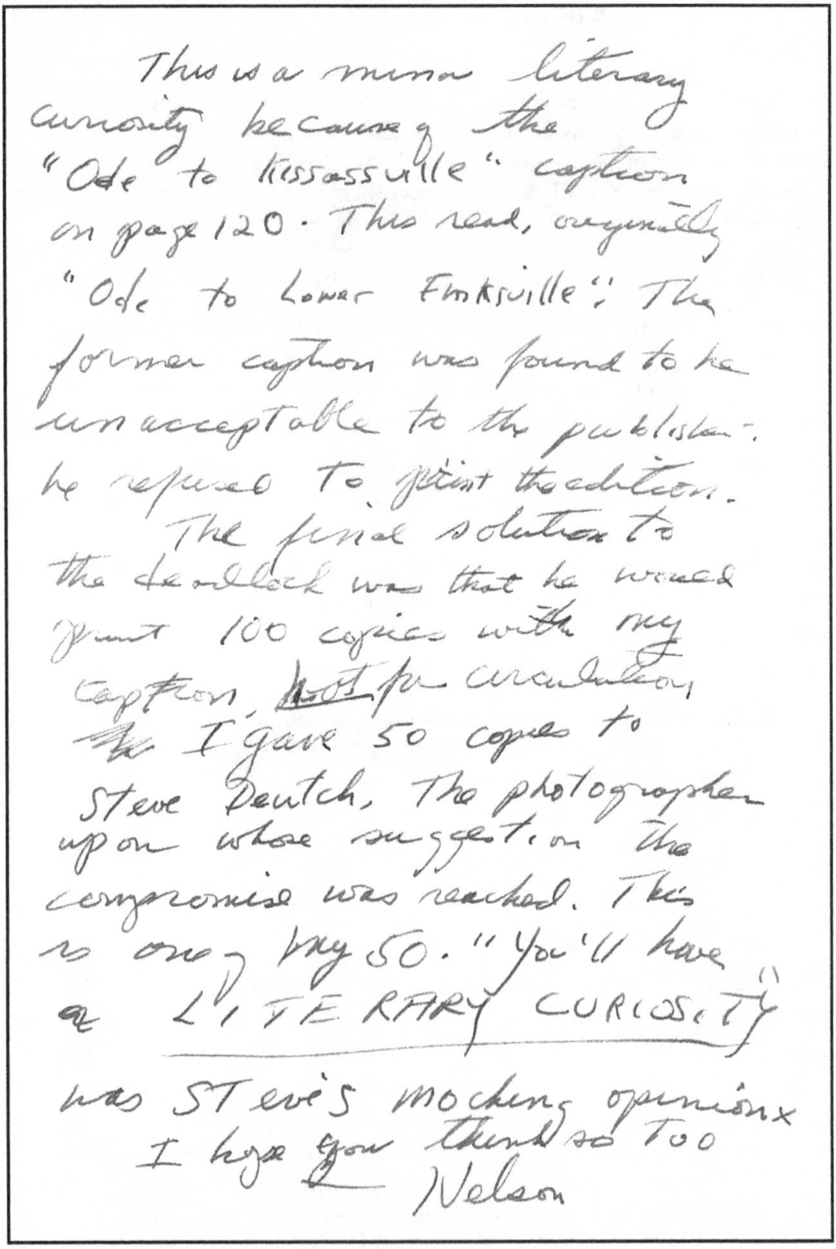

This is a minor literary curiosity because of the "Ode to Kissassville" caption on page 120. This read, originally, "Ode to Lower Finksville." The former caption was found to be unacceptable to the publisher. he refused to print the edition.

The final solution to the deadlock was that he would print 100 copies with my caption, not for circulation, the I gave 50 copies to Steve Deutch, The photographer upon whose suggestion the compromise was reached. This is one, My 50." You'll have a LITERARY CURIOSITY was STeve's mocking opinion. I hope you think so too

Nelson

Figure 30: Angel Island Publications printed one hundred copies of the 1968 third edition of *Chicago: City on the Make*, with "Ode to Kissassville or: Gone on the Arfy-Darfy" as the title of the epilogue. Robert Cromie explains the provenance of this title in the February 16, 1968, issue of the *(continued)*

sent out several hundred advertisements, announcing the new edition, Algren decided that he wanted to change the title of the epilogue to, "Ode to Kissassville or: Gone on the Arfy-Darfy."[89]

Algren had written the epilogue to continue his feud with Maggie Daly, a Chicago newspaper columnist, who had written a column about Algren being arrested after police found marijuana in a car in which he was a passenger. Cromie writes that Arthur Inman, the chairman of the publisher's board of directors, felt that Algren should not be allowed to use "that kind of language ... to promote his own private vendetta."[90]

Neither Algren nor Inman would budge. Finally, Algren telephoned Stephen Deutch, who suggested a compromise to Algren:

> There's not really so much difference between the two titles. Tell them to print 100 copies and send them on to you and you can do whatever you want with them. Then they can change the title and print the rest of the book.[91]

The two Angel Island editions (including epilogues) are identical except for the titles of the epilogues, buried on page 120 of both versions. The pagination of both versions of the epilogue is identical.

Arthur Inman probably never knew it, but Algren won this battle with the publisher. Inman obviously objected to the word, "Kissassville," as he believed that Algren should not use "that kind of language" in this 1968 edition. But Algren *did* use that kind of language in the book. On page 129, about one-third of the way through both versions of the twenty-nine-page epilogue, Algren writes a sentence obviously directed at Maggie Daly:[92]

> The very next afternoon I hurried to report my findings
> To The Magnificent Mile Marching Society
> & Kissassville Lady-Kolumnists' Band.[93]

It gets worse. As described in this book's essay, "Poetry," Algren integrated a portion of an untitled poem from *Law & Disorder* into this epilogue. This poem contains the forbidden "f-word." Both versions of the

Chicago Tribune. In one of these one hundred copies of the book, Nelson Algren wrote his own explanation:

"This is a minor literary curiosity because of the 'Ode to Kissassville' caption on page 120. This read, originally 'Ode to Lower Finksville.' The former caption was found to be unacceptable to the publisher—he refused to print the edition. The final solution to the deadlock was that he would print 100 copies with my caption, not for circulation. I gave 50 copies to Steve Deutch, the photographer upon whose suggestion the compromise was reached. This is one of my 50. 'You'll have a LITERARY CURIOSITY' was Steve's mocking opinion. I hope you think so too.—Nelson"

Stephen Deutch was the photographer who took the pictures for this third edition of *Chicago: City on the Make.*

epilogue (see page 123 of the 1968 Angel Island edition of *City on the Make*, at the top of the fourth page of each epilogue) contain this word.[94]

This epilogue essentially updates *City on the Make* to 1968. But also hidden in the last few pages of the epilogue is another poem that surely represents some of Algren's best work. The poem begins:

> Again that hour when taxies are deadheading home
> Before the trolley-buses start to run
> And snowdreams in a lace of mist drift down
> And paving-flares makes shadows on old walls.[95]

The poem is untitled in this epilogue, but a shorter version with different wording was published six years earlier in the September 22, 1962, issue of *The Nation* under the title, "Tricks Out of Times Long Gone." The poem appeared again a year later in Algren's book, *Who Lost an American?* and once more in his 1973 book, *The Last Carousel*. The words were revised again in *The Last Carousel*, and the poem is much longer than the earlier pieces, but the title is the same. Bettina Drew describes "Tricks Out of Times Long Gone" as "elegiac" and "a farewell poem to the lost." It was certainly appropriate that the first stanza of *The Last Carousel* version of this poem was read at Algren's funeral.[96]

Algren again mines Sandburg's *Chicago* in the epilogue to the 1968 edition of *City on the Make*:

> Sandburg:
> Come and show me another city with lifted head singing so proud
>   to be alive and coarse and strong and cunning.
> Flinging magnetic curses.[97]

> Algren:
> Come and show me another city
> So coarse and strong and cunning
> Flinging magnetic curses.[98]

- Algren, Nelson. *Chicago: City on the Make*. New York: McGraw-Hill, 1983. (The 1983 McGraw-Hill edition)

Dedication:
This is for Nelson Algren

Algren died in 1981. The dedication of this 1983 edition, the first posthumous edition, was obviously written to honor Algren.

Both versions of Algren's infamous 1968 epilogue are deleted from this edition. They do not appear in any other subsequent editions of *City on the Make*.

Charles Baudelaire's epigraph from the 1951 Doubleday edition is the epigraph of this edition.

Algren's introduction entitled, "The People of These Parts: A Survey of Modern Mid-American Letters," and the epigraph of this introduction, the "Notes on the condition of the city of Damascus" from the 1968 Angel Island edition, are now the afterword of this 1983 McGraw-Hill edition.

Studs Terkel writes a new introduction to this 1983 McGraw-Hill edition. Terkel begins this introduction with a reference to Charles Baudelaire's epigraph:[99]

> *I love thee, infamous city! Baudelaire's perverse ode to Paris is reflected in Nelson Algren's bardic salute to Chicago.*[100]

- Algren, Nelson. *Chicago: City on the Make*. Chicago: University of Chicago Press, 1987. (The 1987 University of Chicago edition)

Dedication:
This is for Nelson Algren

There is no noticeable difference between this edition and the 1983 McGraw-Hill edition. That is, both Terkel's 1983 introduction and the epigraph from Baudelaire appear again in this 1987 University of Chicago edition. Algren's former introduction entitled, "The People of These Parts: A Survey of Modern Mid-American Letters" and the epigraph from the "Notes on the condition of the city of Damascus" again compose the afterword of this 1987 edition.

- Algren, Nelson. *Chicago: City on the Make*. Chicago: University of Chicago Press, 2001. (The 2001 University of Chicago edition)

Dedication:
To Chicago
with the Socratic imperative: Know yourself

The front cover of this book indicates that it is the "50th anniversary edition" and that the book is "newly annotated."

This 2001 edition is highlighted with extensive annotations by David Schmittgens and Bill Savage. The book contains a new preface written by both annotators.

The epigraph, introduction, and the afterword are the same as the 1987 University of Chicago edition.

This 2001 University of Chicago edition contains a "Publishing History" that briefly discusses the various editions of this book. The two annotators also include an extensive bibliography of published texts that they used in their annotation research. The bibliography is divided into two categories. The first group consists of books that were available to Algren when he wrote *City on the Make*. The second group contains reference material that was published after *City on the Make* was released in 1951.

- Algren, Nelson. *Chicago: City on the Make*. Chicago: University of Chicago Press, 2011. (The 2011 University of Chicago edition)

Dedication:
To Chicago
with the Socratic imperative: Know yourself

A statement on the cover of this book proclaims that it is the "60th anniversary edition."

A few old photographs, none of them of Algren, are scattered throughout this 2011 reissue. Otherwise, there is no difference between this 2011 University of Chicago edition and the 2001 University of Chicago edition.

Part Five: Nelson Algren's Secret Revision of Chicago: City on the Make

Nelson Algren once secretly revised *City on the Make* by adding material to two post–1951 editions.

The following is from chapter 4 of the 1951 Doubleday edition:

1951 Doubleday edition:

Make your own little list. Of the streets you mustn't live on, the hotels where you can't register, the offices you can't work in and the unions you can never join. Make a good long list and have it typed in triplicate. Send one copy off to Senator Douglas and one to King Levinsky.

The King and the Senator are equally concerned.

You can belong to New Orleans.[101]

But note how Algren added material to the 1961 Contact edition:

1961 Contact edition:

Make your own little list. Of the streets you mustn't live on, the hotels where you can't register, the offices you can't work in and the unions you can never join.

Which would make a sort of jungle-sense, like this part of the forest is mine because it has the biggest banana trees and I'm white and you aint—Only how do you start thinking like somebody black when you're a full-grown man who grew up thinking white? What country is there for a white man that isn't white?

That's about the time you get that creepy kind of feeling, as though a man doesn't have to vanish just to be gone.

You can belong to New Orleans.[102]

This added material also appears in the 1968 Angel Island edition, but it was deleted (after Algren died) from the 1983 McGraw-Hill edition and all subsequent editions.

Part Six: Chicago: City on the Make in Other Publications

Portions of *City on the Make* have been reprinted in other publications:

- Chapter 1, "The Hustlers," appears in the book, *The Art of the Essay*, edited by Leslie Fiedler.[103]
- In honor of the 1983 edition of *City on the Make* and Studs Terkel's new introduction to this edition, a portion of chapter 1, all of chapter 4, all of chapter 6, a portion of chapter 7, together with Terkel's new introduction, are reprinted in the May 1983 issue of *Chicago* magazine. This reprint includes Algren's "secretly revised" chapter 4, as described in this essay.[104]
- Chapter, 3, "The Silver-Colored Yesterday," has been reprinted in the books, *Baseball: A Literary Anthology*, *The Fireside Book of Baseball*, and *The New Baseball Reader*. It also appears in *Sport Literate* magazine.[105]
- Chapter 4, "Love is for Barflies," as it originally appeared in the 1951 Doubleday edition, was reprinted in issue number 16 of *Rosebud* magazine.[106]
- Chapter 4, "Love is for Barflies," as it appeared in the 1961 Contact edition, was reprinted in the June 1982 issue of the Italian magazine, *Frigidaire*.[107]
- Chapter 6, "No More Giants," appears in two editions of the book, *Chicago Stories: Tales of the City*.[108]
- Chapter 7, "Nobody Knows Where O'Connor Went," appears in the books, *Smokestacks & Skyscrapers: An Anthology of Chicago Writing* and *The Party Train: A Collection of North American Prose Poetry*.[109]
- Parts of chapters 1, 5, 6, and 7 and parts of the Introduction and Epilogue to the 1968 Angel Island edition appear in the magazine, *Law & Disorder: The Chicago Convention and Its Aftermath*.[110]

Martha Heasley Cox and Wayne Chatterton write in their biobibliography, *Nelson Algren*, that an excerpt from *City on the Make* appears in the March 1958 issue of *The Kiwanis Magazine*.[111]

Conclusion

A few days after Nelson Algren died, famed Chicago newspaper columnist Mike Royko wrote a tribute to Algren. In his column, called

"Algren's Golden Pen," Royko praised *City on the Make* as "a wonderful prose poem about Chicago."[112]

And it *is* a wonderful poem, which is why the book is still in print, and which is why publishers have issued new editions of this book, years after it was originally published in 1951.

This essay, "The Writing of *Chicago: City on the Make*," begins with Studs Terkel's introduction to the 1983 edition. It is only appropriate that this essay ends the same way—by quoting a portion of this introduction:

> Maybe Nelson Algren's horses always ran out of the money. Maybe his luck at the poker table was never that good. Maybe he was never endowed by a university. Still, he may have had good reason to shuffle along, a laughing winner. And maybe it is for this small work, as much as for his novels and short stories, he will be remembered.[113]

Notes

1. Bettina Drew, *Nelson Algren: A Life on the Wild Side* (Austin: University of Texas Press, 1991), 231–32, 394; Studs Terkel, introduction to *Chicago: City on the Make*, by Nelson Algren (New York: McGraw-Hill, 1983), 2. Note that the title of this book, *Chicago: City on the Make*, has been abbreviated to "*City on the Make*" throughout this essay.

2. Carlo Rotella, *October Cities: The Redevelopment of Urban Literature* (Berkeley: University of California Press, 1998), 22–25.

3. Caroline Gottschalk-Druschke, "The City That Turned the White Sox Black: Post-World War II Chicago Boosterism and the Negation of Nelson Algren," in *Nelson Algren: A Collection of Critical Essays*, ed. Robert Ward (Madison, N.J.: Fairleigh Dickinson University Press, 2007), 123–24.

4. Brooke Horvath, *Understanding Nelson Algren* (Columbia: University of South Carolina Press, 2005), 89.

5. James A. Lewin, "The Radical Tradition of Algren's *Chicago: City on the Make*," in *MidAmerica XIX: The Yearbook of the Society for the Study of Midwestern Literature*, ed. David D. Anderson (East Lansing: The Midwestern Press, Michigan State University, 1992), 106.

6. Ian Peddie, "Poles Apart? Ethnicity, Race, Class, and Nelson Algren," *Modern Fiction Studies* 47 (Spring 2001): 140.

7. Sara Rutkowski, "Nelson Algren's *Personalism*: The Influence of the Federal Writers' Project," *Studies in American Naturalism* 9, no. 2 (Winter 2014): 217, 219.

8. Art Shay, *Nelson Algren's Chicago* (Urbana: University of Illinois Press, 1988), xiii; Drew, *Nelson Algren*, 220, 225.

9. Shay, *Nelson Algren's Chicago*, xiii; Drew, *Nelson Algren*, 226.

10. Drew, *Nelson Algren*, 220, 226, 231, 394; Nelson Algren, "One Man's Chicago," *Holiday*, October 1951, 72–73+.

11. Drew, *Nelson Algren*, 231, 394.

12. Drew, *Nelson Algren*, 231–32, 394.

13. Drew, *Nelson Algren*, 170, 199–202, 209–10, 231–32; Matthew J. Bruccoli, *Nelson Algren: A Descriptive Bibliography* (Pittsburgh: University of Pittsburgh Press, 1985), 25.

14. Shay, *Nelson Algren's Chicago*, xiii. The parenthetical information in the text is in the original.

15. Bruccoli, *Nelson Algren*, 37; Van Allen Bradley, "Algren's *Chicago*: A Work of Genius and Poetic Vision," review of *Chicago: City on the Make*, by Nelson Algren, *Chicago Daily News*, 24 October 1951, sec. 2, 36; Emmett Dedmon, "Hustling Metropolis," review of

Chicago: City on the Make, by Nelson Algren, *Saturday Review*, 8 December 1951, 17; Alfred C. Ames, "Algren Pens a Distorted, Partial Story of Chicago," review of *Chicago: City on the Make*, by Nelson Algren, *Chicago Tribune Magazine of Books*, 21 October 1951, 5.

16. Budd Schulberg, "Heartbeat of a City," review of *Chicago: City on the Make*, by Nelson Algren, *New York Times Book Review*, 21 October 1951, 3. For other comments and reviews, see "Books in Brief," review of *Chicago: City on the Make*," by Nelson Algren, *The Nation*, 10 November 1951, 409; George Bluestone, "Nelson Algren," *Western Review*, Autumn 1957, 39–40. When Algren wrote the introduction to the second edition of *Chicago: City on the Make* that was published in 1961, he clearly remembered Alfred C. Ames' vitriolic *Tribune* review and Ames' description of *Chicago: City on the Make* as a "highly scented object." Algren writes in this introduction: "'A book unlikely to please anyone but masochists—definitely a highly-scented object,' a busy little object who didn't smell too sweet himself typed busily away at *The Tribune*: the job of assistant travel editor was open." See Nelson Algren, *Chicago: City on the Make* (Sausalito, Calif.: Contact Editions, 1961), 15. Martha Heasley Cox and Wayne Chatterton, authors of an Algren biobibliography, claim that "the book has never been popular in Chicago." This statement seems dubious. Their book was published in 1975, and by this time *City on the Make* had been reissued twice, in 1961 and in 1968. See Martha Heasley Cox and Wayne Chatterton, *Nelson Algren* (Boston: Twayne, 1975), [10], 31.

In a new introduction to the second edition of *Chicago: City on the Make*, Algren writes that "'A Case For Ra(n)t Control' was the clever caption of the editorial with which *The Chicago Daily News* greeted the present essay, followed by a serious demand for 'revocation of the author's poetic license'; whatever that may mean." However, both an historian from the Chicago History Museum and I have pored over microfilmed issues of this newspaper, and we have been unable to locate this editorial. Over the years other writers have referred to this "A Case For Ra(n)t Control" *Chicago Daily News* editorial, but never with a citation to the actual editorial. See Algren, *Chicago: City on the Make*, Contact Editions, 1961, 15.

17. Drew, *Nelson Algren*, 226.

18. See Jeff McMahon, "The Secret Faces of Inscrutable Poets in Nelson Algren's *Chicago: City on the Make*," (master's thesis, University of Chicago, 2002), https://pdfs. semanticscholar.org/c3f7/71695e76605d23469cb21f0174132510f5ec.pdf, accessed 28 July 2020; see also Jeff McMahon, "Nelson Algren's Secret: The True Story Behind *City on the Make*," *Newcity*, 30 January 2003, 5–7; reprint, Jeff McMahon, "Nelson Algren's Secret Muse," http://home.uchicago.edu/~jmcmahon/Education6.html, accessed 28 July 2020. McMahon's quest to identify Algren's unnamed "secret muse" is fully detailed in the above *Newcity* article. Because "Nelson Algren's Secret Muse," the Internet version of this *Newcity* article, has no page numbers, citations to this article are to "Nelson Algren's Secret: The True Story Behind *City on the Make*," the published *Newcity* article.

19. Nelson Algren, "Laughter in Jars–Not as Sandburg Wrote of It," *Chicago Sun Book Week*, 20 July 1947, 2; McMahon, "The Secret Faces," 47; Carl Sandburg, "Chicago," in "Chicago Poems," *Poetry*, March 1914, 191–92.

20. Algren, "Laughter in Jars," 2; McMahon, "The Secret Faces," 19, 47. Algren incorrectly quotes Sandburg by omitting a word. The line from *Chicago* reads, "Laughing even as an ignorant fighter laughs who *has* never lost a battle." See Carl Sandburg, "Chicago" in *Chicago Poems* (New York: Henry Holt, 1916), 4. All subsequent citations to Sandburg's "Chicago" are to this 1916 book and not to the 1914 version of *Poetry* magazine.

21. McMahon, "The Secret Faces," 14–15, 44; Sandburg, "Chicago" in *Chicago Poems*, 3.

22. McMahon, "The Secret Faces," 13–14; Nelson Algren, *Chicago: City on the Make*, 60th anniversary edition (Chicago: University of Chicago Press, 2011), 32–33. All subsequent citations to *Chicago: City on the Make* are to this 2011 edition unless otherwise noted.

23. McMahon, "The Secret Faces," 14–15. See also Algren, *City on the Make*, 74: "The big town is getting something of Uncle Johnson's fixed look, like that of a fighter working beyond his strength and knowing it. 'Laughing even as an ignorant fighter laughs, who has never lost a battle,' the white-haired Poet wrote before his hair turned white." Cox and Chatterton write of Algren looking back at the "1930-1950 Chicago scene" in 1969

and Algren acknowledging Sandburg's influence: "Other than Sandburg, I never felt any impact from [Sherwood] Anderson, [James] Farrell, [Theodore] Dreiser or any of the others." See Cox and Chatterton, *Nelson Algren*, 27; McMahon, "The Secret Faces," 12.

24. McMahon, "The Secret Faces," 44; Sandburg, "Chicago" in *Chicago Poems*, 3.

25. Richard C. Lindberg, *To Serve and Collect: Chicago Politics and Police Corruption from the Lager Beer Riot to the Summerdale Scandal, 1855-1960* (Carbondale: Southern Illinois University Press, 1991), 219-25.

26. Algren, *City on the Make*, 57, see also *City on the Make*, 30, 74, 75; McMahon, "The Secret Faces," 14-16.

27. McMahon, "The Secret Faces," 12; Nelson Algren, Chicago: *City on the Make* (Garden City, N.Y.: Doubleday, 1951), [7].

28. Algren, *City on the Make*, 62; see also *City on the Make*, 52, 54, 67, 74; McMahon, "The Secret Faces," 12.

29. Sandburg, "Chicago" in *Chicago Poems*, 3, 4; McMahon, "The Secret Faces," 15-16.

30. Algren, *City on the Make*, 48, 119.

31. Algren, *City on the Make*, 49; McMahon, "The Secret Faces," 17; Sandburg, "Chicago" in *Chicago Poems*, 3.

32. Algren, *City on the Make*, 68, see also *City on the Make*, 26, 39, 48, 49, 68, 69, 73, 76, 77; Sandburg, "Chicago" in *Chicago Poems*, 4; McMahon, "The Secret Faces," 33-34.

33. McMahon, "The Secret Faces," 19n29.

34. Carl Sandburg, "And This Will Be All," *Complete Poems* (New York: Harcourt Brace & World, 1950), 200.

35. Algren, *City on the Make*, 72-73.

36. Sandburg, "Halsted Street Car," *Complete Poems*, 6.

37. Algren, *City on the Make*, 44. Algren also refers to people "straphanging toward the Loop" in his novel, *Never Come Morning*. See Nelson Algren, *Never Come Morning* (New York: Seven Stories Press, 1996), 215. See also Algren's 1939 poem, "Makers of Music," where he refers to, "Straphangers to Success on the last Shopper's Special." See Nelson Algren, "Makers of Music," *The New Anvil*, March 1939, 23; McMahon, "The Secret Faces," 19n29. In the foreword to *The Devil's Stocking*, Herbert Mitgang suggests that *City on the Make* "bears a strong resemblance to Sandburg's own Depression prose-poem, 'The People, Yes.'" See Herbert Mitgang, foreword to *The Devil's Stocking*, by Nelson Algren (New York: Arbor House Publishing, 1983), 2; Sandburg, "The People, Yes," *Complete Poems*, [437]-617.

38. McMahon, "Nelson Algren's Secret," 5; McMahon, "The Secret Faces," 22-27, 47; Algren, "Laughter in Jars," 2.

39. McMahon, "Nelson Algren's Secret," 5; McMahon, "The Secret Faces," 23; Nelson Algren, *The Neon Wilderness* (Garden City, N.Y.: Doubleday, 1947), [9].

40. Algren, *The Neon Wilderness*, [4], [9]; McMahon, "Nelson Algren's Secret," 5, 6; McMahon, "The Secret Faces," 22; David Wolff, "The City," *Poetry*, January 1940, 169-75. Maddow's poem, "The City," appears, with very slight changes, in his 1991 book of poetry. See Ben Maddow, "The City," in *A False Autobiography: Poems: 1940-1990* (Carmel, Calif.: Other Shore Press, 1991), 33-37; McMahon, "The Secret Faces," 25n40.

41. Douglas Wixson, *Worker-Writer in America: Jack Conroy and the Tradition of Midwestern Literary Radicalism, 1898-1990* (Urbana: University of Illinois Press, 1994), 435; Franklin Folsom, *Days of Anger, Days of Hope: A Memoir of the League of American Writers 1937-1942* (Niwot: University Press of Colorado, 1994), 192-93, 265-66, 304.

42. Algren, *City on the Make*, 23, 66; McMahon, "The Secret Faces," 25; McMahon, "Nelson Algren's Secret," 6; Gottschalk-Druschke, "The City That Turned the White Sox Black," 117. Chicago author Studs Terkel writes of this dualism in his own prose poem, *Chicago*. See Studs Terkel, *Chicago* (New York: Pantheon Books, 1986), 11-13.

43. McMahon, "The Secret Faces," 25, 45-46; Wolff, "The City," *Poetry*, 170, 172, 175.

44. McMahon, "The Secret Faces," 24; McMahon, "Nelson Algren's Secret," 6.

45. Algren, *City on the Make*, 23-24.

46. Wolff, "The City," *Poetry*, 169.

47. Algren, *City on the Make*, 52.

48. Wolff, "The City," *Poetry*, 171, 174.

49. Algren, *City on the Make*, 48.

50. Wolff, "The City," *Poetry*, 169.

51. Algren, *City on the Make*, 73–74.

52. The Black Sox are discussed in this book's essay, "Chicago White Sox Literature."

53. Richard C. Lindberg, *Total White Sox: The Definitive Encyclopedia of the Chicago White Sox* (Chicago: Triumph Books, 2011), 23–61 passim.

54. Lindberg, *Total White Sox*, 61.

55. Andrew Hazucha, "Nelson Algren's Chicago: The Black Sox Scandal, McCarthyism, and the Truth about Cubs Fans," in *Baseball/Literature/Culture: Essays, 2002–2003*, ed. Peter Carino (Jefferson, N.C.: McFarland, 2004), 56–58.

56. Algren, *City on the Make*, 65. How much did Algren dislike the Cubs? As noted earlier, a sense of duality runs through *City on the Make*. In chapter 2 of *City on the Make* Algren writes: "Chicago ... forever keeps two faces.... One for the White Sox and none for the Cubs." See Algren, *City on the Make*, 23–24.

57. Algren, *City on the Make*, 125.

58. Geoffrey C. Ward, *Baseball: An Illustrated History* (New York: Alfred A. Knopf, 2010), 92; Cait Murphy, *Crazy '08: How a Cast of Cranks, Rogues, Boneheads, and Magnates Created the Greatest Year in Baseball History* (New York: Smithsonian Books, 2007), [177], 186.

59. Murphy, *Crazy '08*, 189–91; Ward, *Baseball: An Illustrated History*, 92–93.

60. Murphy, *Crazy '08*, 193–98, 244–45, 253–55; Ward, *Baseball: An Illustrated History*, 93.

61. Murphy, *Crazy '08*, [257]-73 passim; Ward, *Baseball: An Illustrated History*, 93–95.

62. Algren, *City on the Make*, 125, Murphy, *Crazy '08*, [177], 190–95, 258–59.

63. Drew, *Nelson Algren*, 51.

64. Algren, *City on the Make*, 67; see also *City on the Make*, 75.

65. Algren, *City on the Make*, 62; James R. Grossman, Ann Durkin Keating, and Janice L. Reiff, eds., *The Encyclopedia of Chicago* (Chicago: University of Chicago Press, 2004), s.v. "Race Riots."

66. Nelson Algren, "Chicago III: If I Can't Sell It I'll Keep Settin' on It; I Jest Won't Give It Away (Old Song)" in *Algren at Sea: Who Lost an American? & Notes from a Sea Diary-Travel Writings*, Seven Stories Press (New York: Seven Stories Press, 2008), 212.

67. Carl Sandburg, *The Chicago Race Riots July, 1919* (New York: Harcourt, Brace and World, 1969), ix, 6.

68. Although the following published newspaper articles both include a Sandburg byline, they do not appear in *The Chicago Race Riots July, 1919*: Carl Sandburg, "Says Lax Conditions Caused Race Riots," *Chicago Daily News*, 28 July 1919, box score edition, 1; Carl Sandburg, "Negroes Not Leaving Chicago for South," *Chicago Daily News*, 7 August 1919, home edition, 6.

69. William M. Tuttle Jr., *Race Riot: Chicago in the Red Summer of 1919* (New York: Atheneum, 1970), 4–10, 54–55, 64, 236.

70. Tuttle, *Race Riot*, 4–10, 54–55; Sandburg, *The Chicago Race Riots July, 1919*, 3.

71. Tuttle, *Race Riot*, 64. The words, "The slums take their revenge...." do not appear in Tuttle's book.

72. Carl Sandburg, *Home Front Memo* (New York: Harcourt, Brace, 1943), [47], 205.

73. Elva Griffith, "The Nelson Algren Archive at the Ohio State University Libraries," in *Nelson Algren: A Collection of Critical Essays*, ed. Robert Ward (Madison, N.J.: Fairleigh Dickinson University Press, 2007), 175–78; Trunk Line, undated advertisement, author's collection; Eleanor Randolph, "Algren's House Sale Not Quite a Best Seller," *Chicago Tribune*, 9 March 1975, sec. 1, 10; Drew, *Nelson Algren*, 352–55; Jolie L. Braun, the Ohio State University Libraries, to Dick Bales, 30 August 2021. After Algren eventually moved to Sag Harbor, New York, a bookstore opened up near his house. Bettina Drew writes, "Algren went in and started poking around. 'You call this a bookshop?' he barked. 'I got more books than this in my bedroom.'" See Drew, *Nelson Algren*, 372; Joe Pintauro, "Algren in Exile," *Chicago*, February 1988, 93–101.

74. Brooke Horvath describes Algren's writing of *City on the Make*: "Points are made not via reasoned argument or facts but through charged language, poetic imagery. On issues such as Algren writes about here, emotional appeals and poetry are more persuasive than facts or rational argument." See Horvath, *Understanding Nelson Algren*, 91. Bettina Drew observes in her biography that "many of [Algren's] stories were based on incidents from his past, or tales told to him by others, or ideas gleaned from written sources, all filtered through his tremendous imagination." See Drew, *Nelson Algren*, 341. Algren used "The slums take their revenge" phrase again in 1974: "'The slums take their revenge,' was how Carl Sandburg put it fifty American League seasons gone. 'Always somehow or other their retribution can be figured in any community.'" Nelson Algren, "A Walk on the Mild Side Costs the Soul Plenty," *New York Times*, 20 April 1974, 31. This time, however, Algren failed the math test. 1974 less fifty American league seasons is 1924, not 1919.

75. Nelson Algren, "The Swede Was a Hard Guy," *Southern Review*, Spring 1942, 873.

76. Algren, *City on the Make*, 73–74.

77. Algren, *City on the Make*, 73.

78. Nelson Algren, "City Against Itself," review of *Big Bill of Chicago*, by Lloyd Wendt and Herman Kogan and *Fabulous Chicago*, by Emmett Dedmon, *The Nation*, 13 February 1954, 135–36.

79. Algren, *Chicago: City on the Make*, 1951 Doubleday edition, [9]; T.R. Smith, ed., *Baudelaire: His Prose and Poetry* (New York: Boni and Liveright, 1919), 58. The poem, "Epilogue," appears as an epilogue in the 1861 edition of Baudelaire's book, *Flowers of Evil*. The city Baudelaire is referring to in the poem is Paris. See Claire Ortiz Hill, *The Roots and Flowers of Evil in Baudelaire, Nietzsche, and Hitler* (Peru, Ill.: Open Court Publishing, 2006), 77; Algren, *City on the Make*, 2, 107. Why did Algren choose a poem by Charles Baudelaire as an epigraph? Bettina Drew writes that Algren "was enthralled by Baudelaire." See Drew, *Nelson Algren*, 104.

80. Bruccoli, *Nelson Algren*, 37.

81. Herman and Marilew Kogan were friends of Algren. In a 2014 *Chicago Tribune* article, their son, Rick Kogan, writes that Algren "dedicated the second edition of the paperback version of *Chicago: City on the Make* … to my parents, Herman and Marilew Kogan, misspelling my mother's name." See Rick Kogan, "2 Movies Try to Unravel the Mystery that is Algren," *Chicago Tribune*, 19 October 2014, sec. 4, 9.

82. Bruccoli, *Nelson Algren*, 39.

83. Algren, *Chicago: City on the Make*, 1961 Contact edition, [8]-35; *The Travels of Ibn Jubayr: Being the Chronicle of a Mediaeval Spanish Moor Concerning His Journey to the Egypt of Saladin, the Holy Cities of Arabia, Baghdad the City of the Caliphs, the Latin Kingdom of Jerusalem, and the Norman Kingdom of Sicily*, 2011 edition, trans. R.J.C. Broadhurst (New Delhi: Goodword Books, 2011), 295, 309.

84. Algren, *Chicago: City on the Make*, 1961 Contact edition, [8]; *The Travels of Ibn Jubayr*, 295, 309. Algren's epigraph reads, "*These* make presents…." However, *The Travels of Ibn Jubayr* indicates that the sentence should read, "*They* make presents…." See *The Travels of Ibn Jubayr*, 309. The parenthetical words in the text are in the original.

This epigraph from *The Travels of Ibn Jubayr* is also an epigraph in Algren's essay, "If You Got the Bread You Walk," which appears in his 1963 book, *Who Lost an American?* The typographical error, "*These* make presents," has been corrected in the epigraph in "If You Got the Bread You Walk." Also, the "If You Got the Bread You Walk" epigraph includes several additional sentences from *The Travels of Ibn Jubayr*. See Algren, "Chicago II: If You Got the Bread You Walk," in *Algren at Sea*, 201; *The Travels of Ibn Jubayr*, 309-10.

85. Algren, *Chicago: City on the Make*, 1961 Contact edition, 9. See Jean-Paul Sartre, *What Is Literature?* (New York: Harper & Row, 1965).

86. This statement as to the year of publication is incorrect. *Chicago: City on the Make* was first published in 1951. See Bruccoli, *Nelson Algren*, 36.

87. Bruccoli, *Nelson Algren*, 39.

88. Robert Cromie, "Cromie Looks at Authors and Books: Algren's 'Finksville' Has Another Name," *Chicago Tribune*, 16 February 1968, sec. 1, 23. Kenneth G. McCollum writes that Cromie's newspaper article was reprinted as an advertisement for *Chicago:*

City on the Make. See Kenneth G. McCollum, *Nelson Algren: A Checklist* (Detroit: Gale Research, 1973), 24.

89. Cromie, "Cromie Looks at Authors and Books," sec. 1, 23. "Gone on the Arfy-Darfy" is a term that Algren used throughout the latter part of his writing career. The term, "on the arfy-darfy," is defined in *Cassell's Dictionary of Slang* as "wandering the roads as a hobo." The dictionary entry indicates that Algren may have coined this term himself and that the S[tandard E[nglish] synonym is the "Artful Dodger," a character in the Charles Dickens novel, *Oliver Twist.* The following is the exact entry in *Cassell's Dictionary of Slang*: "on the arfy-darfy *phr.* [1960s] wandering the roads as a hobo. [? A nonce-coinage by Nelson Algren (1909–81). ? SE *artful dodger*]" See Jonathon Green, ed., *Cassell's Dictionary of Slang* (London: Cassell & Co, 2000), s.v. "on the arfy-darfy." Algren elaborates on this definition in his 1973 collection, *The Last Carousel.* See Nelson Algren, "Previous Days," in *The Last Carousel* (New York: Seven Stories Press, 1997), 219.

90. Cromie, "Cromie Looks at Authors and Books," sec. 1, 23; Nelson Algren, *Chicago: City on the Make,* 3rd ed. (Oakland, Calif.: Angel Island Publications, [1968]), 134; F. Richard Ciccone, *Royko: A Life in Print* (New York: PublicAffairs, 2001), 132; Jan Herman, "Nelson Algren: The Angry Author," *Chicago Sun-Times Chicagostyle,* 21 January 1979, 11; Drew, *Nelson Algren,* 334; Mike Royko, "Nelson Algren Takes Dim View of Girl Scribblers," *Chicago Daily News,* 22 March 1967, 3; Robert Cromie, "Algren Had His Code, and It Got Him Arrested," *Chicago Tribune Book World,* 17 May 1981, 1, 6; Algren, "Chicago III: If I Can't Sell It I'll Keep Settin' on It," in *Algren at Sea,* 220–21; Nelson Algren, "Different Clowns for Different Towns," in *The Last Carousel,* 257–61. Although Mike Royko's name appears at the head of his March 22, 1967, newspaper column that is cited in this note, Algren was a guest columnist, and Algren wrote almost all of the column. Royko wrote only a brief introduction.

91. Cromie, "Cromie Looks at Authors and Books," sec. 1, 23.

92. Cromie, "Cromie Looks at Authors and Books," sec. 1, 23.

93. Algren, *Chicago: City on the Make,* 1968 Angel Island edition, 129.

94. Nelson Algren, "City on the Make," in *Law & Disorder: The Chicago Convention and Its Aftermath,* ed. Donald Myrus (Chicago: privately printed, 1968), [10–11]; Algren, *Chicago: City on the Make,* 1968 Angel Island edition, 123.

95. Algren, *Chicago: City on the Make,* 1968 Angel Island edition, 146.

96. Drew, *Nelson Algren,* 376; Nelson Algren, "Tricks Out of Times Long Gone," *The Nation,* 22 September 1962, 162; Algren, *Chicago: City on the Make,* 1968 Angel Island edition, 146–48; Nelson Algren, "Tricks Out of Times Long Gone," in *Algren at Sea,* 267–68; Nelson Algren, "Tricks Out of Times Long Gone," in *The Last Carousel,* 429–35; Joe Pintauro, "Algren in Exile," *Chicago,* February 1988, 162.

97. Sandburg, "Chicago" in *Chicago Poems,* 3.

98. Algren, *Chicago: City on the Make,* 1968 Angel Island edition, 122.

99. A variation of Terkel's introduction had earlier appeared in his memoir, *Talking to Myself.* Furthermore, Terkel writes in his memoir that this variation had also been published in *Chicago* magazine. See Studs Terkel, "Glasses," in *Talking to Myself: A Memoir of My Times* (New York: Pantheon Books, 1973), [iv], 225–32. Versions have also appeared in other Algren books besides *Chicago: City on the Make.* See Studs Terkel, "Afterword," in Nelson Algren, *The Neon Wilderness* (N.p.: Writers and Readers Publishing, 1986), 287–93; Studs Terkel, "Glasses," in Nelson Algren, *The Man with the Golden Arm:* 50th Anniversary Critical Edition (New York: Seven Stories Press, [1999]), 371–75; Studs Terkel, "An Appreciation of Nelson Algren," in Nelson Algren, *The Man with the Golden Arm* (Cambridge, Mass.: Robert Bentley, 1978) x- xiv; Studs Terkel, "Nelson Algren: An Appreciation" in McCollum, *Nelson Algren: A Checklist,* 1–4.

100. Terkel, introduction to Algren, *Chicago: City on the Make,* 1983 McGraw-Hill edition, 2.

101. Algren, *Chicago: City on the Make,* 1951 Doubleday edition, 57. King Levinsky was a Chicago boxer, and Algren wrote an article about him that appeared in the October 5, 1970, issue of the *Chicago Free Press.* See Nelson Algren, "A Ticket to Biro-Bidjan," *Chicago Free Press* 1, no. 2 (5 October 1970): 37–38. For further details, see this book's essay, "The

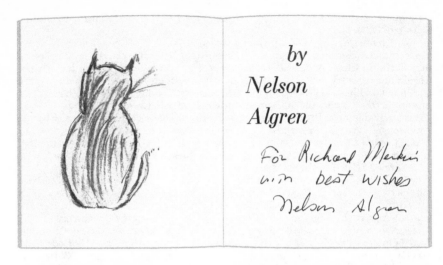

by

Nelson

Algren

For Richard Merkin
with best wishes
Nelson Algren

Figure 31: Nelson Algren and painter and illustrator Richard Merkin were friends. Merkin wrote the introduction to an anthology of three of Algren's books that was published in 1993 by the Quality Paperback Book Club. Merkin was also friends with artist Peter Blake. Blake and his wife Jann Haworth designed the cover of the Beatles' *Sgt. Pepper's Lonely Hearts Club Band* record album, and they added Merkin to the album cover. Merkin is in the back row on the cover, right of center, wearing a large hat, between Fred Astaire and a Vargas girl.

Algren loved cats, and when he autographed a book, he would sometimes include a drawing of a cat. Algren added a multi-colored cat to this Merkin-inscribed "Ode to Kissassville" version of the 1968 edition of *Chicago: City on the Make.*

Merkin writes in his introduction to the Quality Paperback Book Club anthology that after he sent Algren a "Swede" Risberg collage, Algren sent Merkin "an outlawed printing of *Chicago: City on the Make* which included a long poem, first titled 'Ode to Kissassville,' then changed, regrettably." The book that Algren signed and that is pictured here is undoubtedly the book that Merkin refers to in his introduction.

Chicago Free Press Era." Senator Douglas was Senator Paul Douglas, the Democratic U.S. Senator from Illinois. See Algren, *City on the Make*, 119.

102. Algren, *Chicago: City on the Make*, 1961 Contact edition, 83.

103. Nelson Algren, "The Hustlers," in *The Art of the Essay*, ed. Leslie Fiedler (New York: Thomas Y. Crowell Co., 1958), 145–48; Nelson Algren, "The Hustlers," in *The Art of the Essay*, 2nd ed., ed. Leslie Fiedler (New York: Thomas Y. Crowell Co., 1969), 99–103.

104. Nelson Algren, "Chicago: City on the Make," *Chicago*, May 1983, 2, 146–153.

105. Nelson Algren, "The Silver-Colored Yesterday," in *Baseball: A Literary Anthology*, ed. Nicholas Dawidoff (New York: Library of America, 2002), 227–233; Nelson Algren, "The Silver-Colored Yesterday," in *The Fireside Book of Baseball*, ed. Charles Einstein (New York: Simon and Schuster, 1956), 2–5; Nelson Algren, "The Silver-Colored Yesterday," in *The New Baseball Reader: More Favorites from the Fireside Books of Baseball*, ed. Charles Einstein (New York: Viking, 1991), 1–7; Nelson Algren, "The Silver-Colored Yesterday," *Sport Literate* 3, no. 1 (1999): 88–97.

106. Nelson Algren, "Love is for Barflies," *Rosebud*, no. 16 (1999): 115–18.

107. Nelson Algren, "Chicago: City on the Make," *Frigidaire*, June 1982, 31–33.

108. Nelson Algren, "Chicago: City on the Make," in *Chicago Stories: Tales of the City*, ed. John Miller and Genevieve Anderson (San Francisco: Chronicle Books, 1993), 139–45; Nelson Algren, "Chicago: City on the Make," in *Chicago Stories: Tales of the City*, ed. John Miller and Genevieve Anderson (San Francisco: Chronicle Books, [2003]),139–45.

109. Nelson Algren, "Chicago: City on the Make," in *Smokestacks & Skyscrapers: An Anthology of Chicago Writing*, ed. David Starkey and Richard Guzman (Chicago: Wild Onion Books, 1999), 207–10; Nelson Algren, "Nobody Knows Where O'Connor Went," in *The Party Train: A Collection of North American Prose Poetry*, ed. Robert Alexander, Mark Vinz, and C.W. Truesdale (Minneapolis: New Rivers Press, 1996), 47–50.

110. Algren, "City on the Make," in Myrus, *Law & Disorder*, [10–11].

111. Cox and Chatterton, *Nelson Algren*, 154; Nelson Algren, "The Poet's Chicago," *The Kiwanis Magazine*, March 1958, 24–25.

112. Mike Royko, "Algren's Golden Pen," 2. Mike Royko's column has been reprinted; see Mike Royko, "Algren's Golden Pen," in Nelson Algren, *The Man with the Golden Arm*: 50th Anniversary Critical Edition (New York: Seven Stories Press, [1999]), 363–65.

113. Terkel, introduction to Algren, *Chicago: City on the Make*, 1983 McGraw-Hill edition, 7.

Selected Bibliography

Algren, Nelson. *Algren at Sea: Who Lost an American? & Notes from a Sea Diary—Travel Writings*. New York: Seven Stories Press, 2008.

Algren, Nelson. *Chicago: City on the Make*. Garden City, N.Y.: Doubleday, 1951.

Algren, Nelson. *Chicago: City on the Make*. Sausalito, Calif.: Contact Editions, 1961.

Algren, Nelson. *Chicago: City on the Make*. 3rd ed. Oakland, Calif.: Angel Island Publications, [1968].

Algren, Nelson. *Chicago: City on the Make*. New York: McGraw-Hill, 1983.

Algren, Nelson. *Chicago: City on the Make*. Chicago: University of Chicago Press, 1987.

Algren, Nelson. *Chicago: City on the Make*. 50th anniversary edition. Chicago: University of Chicago Press, 2001.

Algren, Nelson. *Chicago: City on the Make*. 60th anniversary edition. Chicago: University of Chicago Press, 2011.

Algren, Nelson. "Chicago: City on the Make," *Chicago*, May 1983, 2, 146–153.

Algren, Nelson. "City Against Itself." Review of *Big Bill of Chicago*, by Lloyd Wendt and Herman Kogan and *Fabulous Chicago*, by Emmett Dedmon. *The Nation*, 13 February 1954, 135–36.

Algren, Nelson. *The Last Carousel*. New York: Seven Stories Press, 1997.

Algren, Nelson. "Laughter in Jars—Not as Sandburg Wrote of It." *Chicago Sun Book Week*, 20 July 1947, 2.

Algren, Nelson. "Makers of Music." *The New Anvil*, March 1939, 23.

Algren, Nelson. *The Neon Wilderness*. Garden City, N.Y.: Doubleday, 1947.

Algren, Nelson. *Never Come Morning*. New York: Seven Stories Press, 1996.

Algren, Nelson. "One Man's Chicago." *Holiday*, October 1951, 72–73+.

Algren, Nelson. "The Swede Was a Hard Guy." *Southern Review*, Spring 1942, 873–79.

Algren, Nelson. "Tricks Out of Times Long Gone." *The Nation*, 22 September 1962, 162.

Algren, Nelson. "A Walk on the Mild Side Costs the Soul Plenty." *New York Times*, 20 April 1974, 31.

Ames, Alfred C. "Algren Pens a Distorted, Partial Story of Chicago." Review of *Chicago: City on the Make*, by Nelson Algren. *Chicago Tribune Magazine of Books*, 21 October 1951, 5.

Bluestone, George. "Nelson Algren." *Western Review*, Autumn 1957, 27–44.

"Books in Brief." Review of *Chicago: City on the Make*, by Nelson Algren. *The Nation*, 10 November 1951, 408–09.

Bradley, Van Allen. "Algren's *Chicago*: A Work of Genius and Poetic Vision." Review of *Chicago: City on the Make*, by Nelson Algren. *Chicago Daily News*, 24 October 1951, sec. 2, 36.

Bruccoli, Matthew J. *Nelson Algren: A Descriptive Bibliography*. Pittsburgh: University of Pittsburgh Press, 1985.

Ciccone, F. Richard. *Royko: A Life in Print*. New York: PublicAffairs, 2001.

Cox, Martha Heasley, and Wayne Chatterton. *Nelson Algren*. Boston: Twayne, 1975.

Cromie, Robert. "Algren Had His Code, and It Got Him Arrested." *Chicago Tribune Book World*, 17 May 1981, 1, 6.

Cromie, Robert. "Cromie Looks at Authors and Books: Algren's 'Finksville' Has Another Name." *Chicago Tribune*, 16 February 1968, sec. 1, 23.

Dedmon, Emmett. "Hustling Metropolis." Review of *Chicago: City on the Make*, by Nelson Algren. *Saturday Review*, 8 December 1951, 17.

Drew, Bettina. *Nelson Algren: A Life on the Wild Side*. Austin: University of Texas Press, 1991.

Folsom, Franklin. *Days of Anger, Days of Hope: A Memoir of the League of American Writers 1937–1942*. Niwot: University Press of Colorado, 1994.

Gottschalk-Druschke, Caroline. "The City That Turned the White Sox Black: Post-World War II Chicago Boosterism and the Negation of Nelson Algren." In *Nelson Algren: A Collection of Critical Essays*, edited by Robert Ward, 115–25. Madison, N.J.: Fairleigh Dickinson University Press, 2007.

Griffith, Elva. "The Nelson Algren Archive at the Ohio State University Libraries." In *Nelson Algren: A Collection of Critical Essays*, edited by Robert Ward, 173–79. Madison, N.J.: Fairleigh Dickinson University Press, 2007.

Grossman, James R., Ann Durkin Keating, and Janice L. Reiff, eds. *The Encyclopedia of Chicago*. Chicago: University of Chicago Press, 2004.

Hazucha, Andrew. "Nelson Algren's Chicago: The Black Sox Scandal, McCarthyism, and the Truth about Cubs Fans." In *Baseball/Literature/Culture: Essays, 2002–2003*, edited by Peter Carino, 49–59. Jefferson, N.C.: McFarland, 2004.

Herman, Jan. "Nelson Algren: The Angry Author." *Chicago Sun-Times Chicagostyle*. 21 January 1979, 8–11.

Hill, Claire Ortiz. *The Roots and Flowers of Evil in Baudelaire, Nietzsche, and Hitler*. Peru, Ill.: Open Court Publishing, 2006.

Horvath, Brooke. *Understanding Nelson Algren*. Columbia: University of South Carolina Press, 2005.

Kogan, Rick. "2 Movies Try to Unravel the Mystery that is Algren." *Chicago Tribune*, 19 October 2014, sec. 4, 9.

Lewin, James. A. "The Radical Tradition of Algren's *Chicago: City on the Make*." In *Mid-America XIX: The Yearbook of the Society for the Study of Midwestern Literature*, edited by David D. Anderson, 106–15. East Lansing: The Midwestern Press, Michigan State University, 1992.

Lindberg, Richard C. *To Serve and Collect: Chicago Politics and Police Corruption from the Lager Beer Riot to the Summerdale Scandal, 1855–1960*. Carbondale: Southern Illinois University Press, 1991.

Lindberg, Richard C. *Total White Sox: The Definitive Encyclopedia of the Chicago White Sox*. Chicago: Triumph Books, 2011.

Maddow, Ben. "The City." In *A False Autobiography: Poems: 1940–1990*, 33–37. Carmel, Calif.: Other Shore Press, 1991.

McCollum, Kenneth G. *Nelson Algren: A Checklist*. Detroit: Gale Research, 1973.

McMahon, Jeff. "Nelson Algren's Secret: The True Story Behind *City on the Make*." *Newcity*, 30 January 2003, 5–7.

McMahon, Jeff. "Nelson Algren's Secret Muse." http://home.uchicago.edu/~jmcmahon/Education6.html, accessed 28 July 2020.

McMahon, Jeff. "The Secret Faces of Inscrutable Poets in Nelson Algren's *Chicago: City on the Make*." Master's thesis, University of Chicago, 2002. https://pdfs.semanticscholar.org/c3f7/71695e76605d23469cb21f0174132510f5ec.pdf, accessed 28 July 2020.

Mitgang, Herbert. Foreword to *The Devil's Stocking*, by Nelson Algren, [1]-5. New York: Arbor House Publishing, 1983.

Murphy, Cait. *Crazy '08: How a Cast of Cranks, Rogues, Boneheads, and Magnates Created the Greatest Year in Baseball History*. New York: Smithsonian Books, 2007.

Myrus, Donald, ed. *Law & Disorder: The Chicago Convention and Its Aftermath*. Chicago: Privately printed, 1968.

Peddie, Ian. "Poles Apart? Ethnicity, Race, Class, and Nelson Algren." *Modern Fiction Studies* 47 (Spring 2001): 118–44.

Pintauro, Joe. "Algren in Exile." *Chicago*, February 1988, 92–101, 156–63.

Rotella, Carlo. *October Cities: The Redevelopment of Urban Literature*. Berkeley: University of California Press, 1998.

Royko, Mike. "Algren's Golden Pen." *Chicago Sun-Times*, 13 May 1981, 2.

Royko, Mike. "Algren's Golden Pen." In *The Man with the Golden Arm*, 50th Anniversary Critical Edition, by Nelson Algren, 363–65. New York: Seven Stories Press, [1999].

Royko, Mike. "Nelson Algren Takes Dim View of Girl Scribblers." *Chicago Daily News*, 22 March 1967, 3.

Rutkowski, Sara. "Nelson Algren's *Personalism*: The Influence of the Federal Writers' Project." *Studies in American Naturalism* 9, no. 2 (Winter 2014): 198–223.

Sandburg, Carl. "Chicago." In "Chicago Poems." *Poetry*, March 1914, 191–92.

Sandburg, Carl. *Chicago Poems*. New York: Henry Holt, 1916.

Sandburg, Carl. *The Chicago Race Riots July, 1919*. New York: Harcourt, Brace and World, 1969.

Sandburg, Carl. *Complete Poems*. New York: Harcourt Brace & World, 1950.

Sandburg, Carl. *Home Front Memo*. New York: Harcourt, Brace, 1943.

Sandburg, Carl. "Negroes Not Leaving Chicago for South." *Chicago Daily News*, 7 August 1919, home edition, 6.

Sandburg, Carl. "Says Lax Conditions Caused Race Riots." *Chicago Daily News*, 28 July 1919, box score edition, 1.

Schulberg, Budd. "Heartbeat of a City." Review of *Chicago: City on the Make*, by Nelson Algren. *New York Times Book Review*, 21 October 1951, 3.

Shay, Art. *Nelson Algren's Chicago*. Urbana: University of Illinois Press, 1988.

Smith, T.R., ed. *Baudelaire: His Prose and Poetry*. New York: Boni and Liveright, 1919.

Terkel, Studs. "Afterword." In *The Neon Wilderness*, by Nelson Algren, 287–93. N.p.: Writers and Readers Publishing, 1986.

Terkel, Studs. "An Appreciation of Nelson Algren." In *The Man with the Golden Arm*, by Nelson Algren, x–xiv. Cambridge, Mass.: Robert Bentley, 1978.

Terkel, Studs. *Chicago*. New York: Pantheon Books, 1986.

Terkel, Studs. "Glasses." In *Talking to Myself: A Memoir of My Times*, 225–32. New York: Pantheon Books, 1973.

Terkel, Studs. "Glasses." In *The Man with the Golden Arm*, 50th Anniversary Critical Edition, by Nelson Algren, 371–75. New York: Seven Stories Press, [1999].

Terkel, Studs. "Nelson Algren: An Appreciation." In *Nelson Algren: A Checklist*, by Kenneth G. McCollum, 1–4. Detroit: Gale Research, 1973.

The Travels of Ibn Jubayr: Being the Chronicle of a Mediaeval Spanish Moor Concerning His Journey to the Egypt of Saladin, the Holy Cities of Arabia, Baghdad the City of the Caliphs, the Latin Kingdom of Jerusalem, and the Norman Kingdom of Sicily. 2011 edition. Translated by R.J.C. Broadhurst. New Delhi: Goodword Books, 2011.

Tuttle, William M., Jr. *Race Riot: Chicago in the Red Summer of 1919*. New York: Atheneum, 1970.

Ward, Geoffrey C. *Baseball: An Illustrated History*. New York: Alfred A. Knopf, 2010.

Wixson, Douglas. *Worker-Writer in America: Jack Conroy and the Tradition of Midwestern Literary Radicalism, 1898–1990*. Urbana: University of Illinois Press, 1994.

Wolff, David. "The City." *Poetry*, January 1940, 169–75.

Boxing Short Stories
and Other Works

Introduction

Nelson Algren was a boxing fan all his life. After he saw lightweight champion Barney Ross win a fight in the summer of 1927, Algren had a pair of boxing gloves tattooed on his arm. In 1939, while working for the Illinois Writers' Project, he interviewed Davey Day, a professional boxer. Forty years later, Algren told a newspaper reporter, "If I could make a living in the fight game hanging around a gym, I'd love that." In 1986, five years after Algren died, his friend Art Shay reminisced: "Among Algren's other dreams: 'owning' a boxer, 'like [writer] Budd Schulberg does,' and being at ringside for the fights."[1]

Algren wrote about the sport in his two novels, *The Devil's Stocking* and *Never Come Morning*. In his book, *Confronting the Horror: The Novels of Nelson Algren*, James R. Giles comments about the final fight scene in *Never Come Morning*:

> The fight sequence, in which Lefty battles a black boxer named Tucker, is perhaps the best scene of its kind in American literature. Algren understands the science of boxing, as well as the ugly blood lust of fight fans.[2]

Similarly, Martha Heasley Cox and Wayne Chatterton write in their biobibliography, *Nelson Algren*:

> Some idea of Algren's eye for detail and his sense of the dramatic in prize-fighting tactics may be gained through the following anecdote: In a sedate cocktail lounge of the Palmer House in Chicago, while describing a championship heavyweight prize fight to the co-authors of this study, Algren stood beside the table and pantomimed a full sequence of actions leading to a knockout.[3]

Algren's short stories about boxing appear in numerous anthologies. These are listed in Appendix A.

Nelson Algren's boxing short stories are listed below, together with other boxing-related items.

NOTES

1. Nelson Algren, Interview, Davey Day, 3 April 1939, "Industrial Folklore of Chicago," *Folklore Project, Life Histories 1936–1939*, Box A707, Records of the United States Work Projects Administration, Manuscript Division, Library of Congress, Washington, D.C.; Jan Herman, "Nelson Algren: The Angry Author," *Chicago Sun-Times Chicagostyle*, 21 January 1979, 11; Bettina Drew, *Nelson Algren: A Life on the Wild Side* (Austin: University of Texas Press, 1991), 355; Nelson Algren, review of *No Man Stands Alone: The True Story of Barney Ross*, by Barney Ross and Martin Abramson, *New York Times Book Review*, 8 December 1957, 17; Arthur Shay, "Author on the Make: Nelson Algren's Bittersweet Affair with Chicago," *Chicago Tribune Magazine*, 14 September 1986, 14; Brooke Horvath, *Understanding Nelson Algren* (Columbia: University of South Carolina Press, 2005), 142; Mary Wisniewski, *Algren: A Life* (Chicago: Chicago Review Press, 2017), 100; Sean Curtin and J.J. Johnston, *Chicago Amateur Boxing* (Charleston, N.C.: Arcadia, 2006), 14; J.J. Johnston and Sean Curtin, *Chicago Boxing* (Charleston, S.C.: Arcadia, 2005), 64–65.

2. James R. Giles, *Confronting the Horror: The Novels of Nelson Algren* (Kent, Ohio: Kent State University Press, 1989), 53–54; Nelson Algren, *Never Come Morning* (New York: Seven Stories Press, 1996), 260–80; see also Chris Vials, *Realism for the Masses: Aesthetics, Popular Front Pluralism, and U.S. Culture, 1935–1947* (Jackson: University Press of Mississippi, 2009), 26–31.

3. Martha Heasley Cox and Wayne Chatterton, *Nelson Algren* (Boston: Twayne, 1975), 146n22. For a discussion of Algren's stories about boxing, see Cox and Chatterton, *Nelson Algren*, 53–54.

4. See also Nelson Algren, *He Swung and He Missed* (Mankato, Minn.: Creative Education, 1993).

5. Algren never published his boxing story, "The Lightless Room," written in about 1939. A "clean, finished" copy was found in the Algren archives at Ohio State University, and as noted in the text, it was published in *Entrapment and Other Writings*. See Nelson Algren, *Entrapment and other Writings*, eds. Brooke Horvath and Dan Simon (New York: Seven Stories Press, 2009), 12, 15, 19. As also noted in the text, this boxing story appears in *Granta*.

6. See also Nelson Algren, "Home and Goodnight," in *Entrapment*, 55–56.

7. See also Nelson Algren, "Single Exit," in *Entrapment*, 77–85.

SHORT STORIES AND ARTICLES

"Depend on Aunt Elly," *The Neon Wilderness*.

"Million Dollar Brainstorm," *The Neon Wilderness*.

"Biceps," *Southern Review*, Spring 1941, 713–28; reprinted as "A Bottle of Milk for Mother," *The Neon Wilderness*.

"He Swung and He Missed," *The American Mercury*, July 1942, 57–63; reprinted in *The Neon Wilderness*.[4]

"Home to Shawneetown," *The Atlantic Monthly*, August 1968, 41–47; revised as "Dark Came Early in That Country," *The Last Carousel*.

"A Ticket to Biro-Bidjan," *Chicago Free Press* 1, no. 2 (5 October 1970): 37–38.

"No Cumshaw, No Rickshaw," (Part II), *Holiday* (November 1971), 44–47, 77, 80; reprinted in *The Last Carousel*.

"The Lightless Room" in *Entrapment and other Writings*, eds. Brooke Horvath and Dan Simon (New York: Seven Stories Press, 2009), 41–52; see also "The Lightless Room," *Granta*, no. 108 (Autumn 2009): 71–83.[5]

OTHER WORKS

References to boxing appear in the following works by Nelson Algren:

"June 27th: Lions, Lionesses, Deadbone Crunchers," *Notes from a Sea Diary: Hemingway All the Way.*

"Hemingway Himself," *Notes from a Sea Diary: Hemingway All the Way.*

"Ballet for Opening Day: The Swede Was a Hard Guy," *The Last Carousel.*

"Chicago IV: The Irishman in the Grotto, the Man in the Iron Suit, and the Girl in Gravity-Z: The *Playboy* Magazine Story or Mr. Peepers as Don Juan," *Who Lost an American?*

"Home and Goodnight," *Poetry* (November 1939), 74–76.[6]

"Single Exit," in *Cross Section 1947: A Collection of New American Writing*, ed. Edwin Seaver (New York: Simon and Schuster, 1947), 217–24.[7]

"The Unacknowledged Champion of Everything," *The Noble Savage*, September 1960, 14–24; revised as "The Ryebread Trees of Spring," *The Last Carousel.*

"The Marquis of Kingsbury, You Could Have Him!" *The Gent*, February 1961, 48–49; reprinted as "July 9th: Concannon Gets the Ship in Trouble or Assy-end Up on Ho-Phang Road," *Notes from a Sea Diary: Hemingway All the Way.*

"They're Hiding the Ham on the Pinball King, or, Some Came Stumbling," *Contact*, 3, no. 1 (September 1961): 101–11; reprinted in *Who Lost an American?*

"The Peseta with the Hole in the Middle, Part II," *The Kenyon Review* 24, no. 1 (Winter 1962): 110–28; revised as "Seville: The Peseta with the Hole in the Middle," *Who Lost an American?*

"God Bless the Lonesome Gas Man," *The Dude*, March 1962, 11–12, 73; revised as "July 4th: East China Sea," *Notes from a Sea Diary: Hemingway All the Way;* revised as "Seven Feet Down and Creeping," *The New Orleans Review* 2, no. 1 (1970): 3–5; revised as "The Leak That Defied the Books," *The Last Carousel.*

"Early Chicago Journalism," *Chicago Free Press* 1, no. 3 (12 October 1970): 28–30, revised as "Different Clowns for Different Towns," *The Last Carousel.*

"The Last Carousel," *Playboy*, February 1972, 72–74+; reprinted in *The Last Carousel.*

MISCELLANEOUS

See also the following:

Nelson Algren, "A Walk on the Mild Side," *New York Times*, 20 April 1974, 31.

Henry Kisor, "Nelson Algren, That Hackensack Homebody," *Chicago Daily News Panorama*, 12–13 June 1976, 7.

Jan Herman, "Nelson Algren: The Angry Author," *Chicago Sun-Times Chicagostyle*, 21 January 1979, 8–11.

Arthur Shay, "Author on the Make: Nelson Algren's Bittersweet Affair with Chicago," *Chicago Tribune Magazine*, 14 September 1986, 10–12, 14–17, 32, 39.

Gambling Short Stories
and Other Works

Introduction

Mark Twain supposedly said, "Write what you know." It appears that Nelson Algren took this advice to heart. Algren spent much of his adult life gambling, and gambling (primarily poker) permeates many of his short stories. In addition, Algren often refers to gambling (again, primarily poker) in his other works.

Algren ran an "acey-deucy dice game" and also dealt blackjack when he was in the army. After the war, when he lived on West Wabansia Avenue on Chicago's West Side, he organized a weekly Saturday night poker game in his apartment. He was also a poker dealer at the Lucky Star Tavern, which was across the street from his apartment.[1]

During the early 1950s, Algren oversaw a poker game in the basement of a North Michigan Avenue mansion owned by Ellen Borden Stevenson, the heir to the Borden dairy fortune and the ex-wife of Illinois governor and presidential hopeful Adlai Stevenson. But in early 1955, *Time* magazine published an article called "How Writers Live," and it described Algren playing poker "in the basement of a North Michigan Avenue mansion." Although the article did not mention Ellen Stevenson by name, it must have hit her close to home, because she subsequently put an end to Algren's twice-a-week basement gambling activities. After that, he held weekly poker games in his Chicago apartment, which was then on West Evergreen Avenue. Studs Terkel reminisces about these games in his memoirs: "You go up to the third floor, and there's Nelson, with a visor on, as in the movies, and garters on his arms. He's got the table with the green felt, and several fresh decks of cards laid out."[2]

In 1965 Paul Engle, the director of the Iowa Writers' Workshop, a creative writing program at the University of Iowa in Iowa City, hired Algren as an instructor. A local shoe salesman hosted a weekly poker game in

Figure 32: In this 1973 photograph, Nelson Algren is standing on the back porch of his third-floor Chicago apartment at 1958 West Evergreen Avenue. Algren often threw parties in this apartment, where literary and media celebrities would mingle with ordinary Chicagoans. As many as thirty people would fill the apartment and spill out onto this porch, which would be festooned with Christmas lights. Studs Terkel recalled, "It was a crummy flat, but Nelson made it seem like the Dakota" (*Chicago Daily News*, Leon Lopez, photographer, courtesy of the *Chicago Sun-Times* and the Chicago History Museum).

his basement, and Algren started playing there. Unfortunately, Algren was a terrible player. Even worse, Algren thought that he was a great player. Burns Ellison was one of Algren's students and also one of the poker players, and he recalls that in one game Algren lost $1,200.00. Algren's wife, Betty Ann Jones, thought that while she and Algren were in Iowa, he lost $5,000. Ellison thought that it was closer to $10,000—and his annual salary was $12,000. And what did Algren think? Five months after he left the Workshop, he sent a Christmas card to a friend. On the bottom of the card, Algren scrawled, "My sole accomplishment at Iowa was to push a Taiwanese lady into the *Atlantic*. And to lose the bankroll I went there for. Ever best, ARM."[3]

All three of Algren's biographers comment about Algren's gambling. Bettina Drew believes that "certainly Algren could have answered yes to at least seven of the twenty questions Gamblers Anonymous asks new members; these seven alone indicate he had a serious problem." Mary Wisniewski writes that "it is not clear from Nelson's life if gambling was a

Figure 33: Nelson Algren in his second-floor apartment at 1523 West Wabansia Avenue in Chicago. The building across the street is the Lucky Star Tavern, 1528 West Wabansia Avenue. Algren's friend Art Shay claimed that this tavern was used as the model for the Tug & Maul Bar, the bar frequented by the principal figures in *The Man with the Golden Arm*. This is probably true; in a 1956 interview, Algren said that he used to deal a poker game in this tavern, and that "it was while running this game that I got the idea for 'Dealer,'" or Frankie Machine (Photograph by Robert McCullough, The Nelson Algren Collection belonging to Amanda Algren, the Rare Books and Manuscripts Library of the Ohio State University, Columbus, Ohio).

crippling addiction, or just an expensive way to relax—the degree of the problem varied over time." Colin Asher agrees, claiming that "it seems Nelson only gambled problematically during two distinct periods of his life."[4]

Ultimately, the opinions of his friends are not only the most pragmatic but also the most poignant. Art Shay and Herman Kogan maintained that

Algren's poker playing "had cost the world of literature perhaps four great novels."[5]

Algren's gambling short stories are listed below, together with other gambling-related works.

NOTES

1. George Murray, "His Old West Side Haunts," *Chicago American Pictorial Living*, 7 October 1956, 6; Bettina Drew, *Nelson Algren: A Life on the Wild Side* (Austin: University of Texas Press, 1991), 162.

2. Drew, *Nelson Algren*, 259–60; "How Writers Live, *Time*, 10 January 1955, 86; Mary Wisniewski, *Algren: A Life* (Chicago: Chicago Review Press, 2017), 214, 251–52; Colin Asher, *Never a Lovely So Real: The Life and Work of Nelson Algren* (New York: W.W. Norton, 2019), 325; Studs Terkel, *Touch and Go: A Memoir* (New York: The New Press, 2007), 194. *On the QT* was a 1950s and 1960s gossip magazine. Kermit Joyce wrote the following in a 1959 *On the QT* article about Algren: "The unwelcome glare of publicity shown on Algren a little later when he had a brief friendship with Ellen Borden Stevenson, Adlai's ex-wife. Daughter of wealthy socialites, Mrs. Stevenson was perfectly fascinated by Algren's guided tours of parts of the city she had never known. But her feelings changed when Algren told a national magazine that his sole income at that time came from dealing the poker game in a club for artists on Chicago's Gold Coast owned by Mrs. Stevenson." See Kermit Joyce, "Nelson Algren—The Unbeat Poet," *On the QT*, December 1959, 44.

3. Drew, *Nelson Algren*, 258, 325, 330, 331; Asher, *Never a Lovely So Real*, 422–25, 427–28; Burns Ellison, "The First Annual Nelson Algren Memorial Poker Game," *The Iowa Review* 18, no. 1 (Winter 1988): 68–71, 96; Art Shay, *Nelson Algren's Chicago* (Urbana: University of Illinois Press, 1988), xiv; John Clellon Holmes, "Arm: A Memoir," in *Representative Men: The Biographical Essays, Selected Essays by John Clellon Holmes*, vol. 2 (Fayetteville: University of Arkansas Press, 1988), 259. Not only was Algren a terrible poker player, he did not have a so-called "poker face." Mary Wisniewski writes that "[Algren's] friend Dave Peltz remembered that when a straight fell into his hands, Nelson's eyes shown 'like bright lights. He couldn't hide it.'" Wisniewski, *Algren*, 121.

4. Drew, *Nelson Algren*, 258; Wisniewski, *Algren*, 214; Asher, *Never a Lovely So Real*, 486. Asher refers to two periods of Algren's life during which he gambled "problematically." These were in 1953, after his passport application was denied, and in 1965–66, when he was teaching in Iowa. See Asher, *Never a Lovely So Real*, 359, 422–29.

5. Shay, *Nelson Algren's Chicago*, xiv.

6. See also Nelson Algren, "Home and Goodnight," in *Entrapment and other Writings*, eds. Brooke Horvath and Dan Simon (New York: Seven Stories Press, 2009), 55–56.

SHORT STORIES AND ARTICLES

"Katz," *The Neon Wilderness*.

"June 29th: East China Sea: We Didn't Come to Gamble," *Notes from a Sea Diary: Hemingway All the Way*.

"July 22nd: Arabian Sea," *Notes from a Sea Diary: Hemingway All the Way*.

"Stickman's Laughter," *Southern Review*, Spring 1942, 845–51; revised for *The Neon Wilderness*.

"Say a Prayer for the Guy," *Manhunt*, June 1958, 31–35.

"A Ticket on Skoronski," *Saturday Evening Post*, 5 November 1966, 48–49, 52–56; reprinted in *The Last Carousel*.

OTHER WORKS

References to gambling appear in the following works by Nelson Algren:

"Ballet for Opening Day: The Swede Was a Hard Guy," *The Last Carousel.*

"Come in If You Love Money," *The Last Carousel.*

"Home and Goodnight," *Poetry*, November 1939, 74–76.[6]

"June 21, 1962: Two Hours Out of the Port of Seattle," *Notes from a Sea Diary: Hemingway All the Way.*

"Epitaph: The Man with the Golden Arm," *Poetry*, September 1947, 316–17; reprinted in *The Man with the Golden Arm;* reprinted in *The Last Carousel.*

"The Unacknowledged Champion of Everything," *The Noble Savage*, September 1960, 14–24; reprinted in *Harlequin*, August 1963; revised as "The Ryebread Trees of Spring," *The Last Carousel.*

"Shlepker, or White Goddess Say You Not Go That Part of Forest," *Cavalier* (February 1963), 12–14, 84–89; see also "Kanani Mansions," *Notes from a Sea Diary: Hemingway All the Way.*

"Otto Preminger's Strange Suspenjers," in *Focus Media*, eds. Jess Ritter and Grover Lewis (San Francisco: Chandler Publishing Co., 1972), 10–18; reprinted in *The Last Carousel.*

"Blanche Sweet Under the Tapioca," *Chicago Tribune Magazine*, 30 April 1972, 42–45; revised as "Previous Days," *The Last Carousel.*

MISCELLANEOUS

See also the following books:

Martha Heasley Cox and Wayne Chatterton, *Nelson Algren* (Boston: Twayne, 1975).

Brooke Horvath, *Understanding Nelson Algren* (Columbia: University of South Carolina Press, 2005).

Horse Racing Short Stories
and Other Works

Introduction

Nelson Algren was an ardent horse racing fan and race track bettor. In 1958 *Sports Illustrated* invited him to spend a week in Louisville, Kentucky, attend the Kentucky Derby, and write an article about his experience. Unfortunately, although Algren wrote the article, the magazine never printed it. Years later, an editor for *Sports Illustrated* reminisced: "Possibly, in a different age of magazine writing, it might have been a prizewinner. But in 1958 what he wrote seemed a little too fractious, not to mention too fractured, for publication. Not a word by Nelson Algren appeared in *SI* that year."[1]

In 1966 Algren and a friend bought a race horse called Jealous Widow. Algren said that "she ran fourth in just about every race." His friend Art Shay was more blunt in his assessment, describing the horse as a "loser" and commenting that the horse was also known as "Algren's Folly." Algren owned the horse for a year, boarding it at Cahokia Downs racetrack in Southern Illinois until she became too expensive to keep.[2]

Algren never wrote a book about horse racing. He started writing a race track novel in 1964, but by 1967 his interest had waned. As shown below, however, he continued to write about the sport in the 1970s.[3]

Although Algren's work has been published in more than ninety anthologies (see Appendix A of this book), it appears that none of his horse racing and race track stories have ever appeared in a horse racing anthology.

Algren's horse racing short stories are listed below, together with other race track-related works.

Figure 34: In 1955 the editors of the then fledgling magazine, *Sports Illustrated*, asked William Faulkner to go to Louisville and write his impressions of the Kentucky Derby. In the following years, other writers were invited. *Sports Illustrated* asked Nelson Algren to attend the 1958 Kentucky Derby and write about his experiences. Although Algren wrote an article, the magazine did not print it, feeling that "what he wrote seemed a little too fractious, not to mention too fractured, for publication."

The April 28, 1986, issue of *Sports Illustrated* featured an article about Faulkner and the other so-called "literary notables" who had been assigned to write about the Kentucky Derby for the magazine during the latter half of the 1950s. This picture of Algren at the racetrack appeared in this retrospective *Sports Illustrated* article. (Illustration by Greg Spalenka)

NOTES

1. Whitney Tower, "Prose for the Roses," *Sports Illustrated*, 28 April 1986, 45; Bettina Drew, *Nelson Algren: A Life on the Wild Side* (Austin: University of Texas Press, 1991), 292–93; Michaela Tuohy, "A Day at the Races with Nelson Algren," *Chicago Tribune Magazine*, 30 June 1974, 18–19, 22; Simone de Beauvoir, *Force of Circumstance*, trans. Richard Howard (New York: G.P. Putnam's Sons, 1964), 229–30. Although *Sports Illustrated* did not print Algren's Kentucky Derby article in 1958, he was featured in the magazine a year later. See Nelson Algren, "Stoopers and Shoeboard Watchers," *Sports Illustrated*, 15 June 1959, E12, E14–16.

2. Drew, *Nelson Algren*, 332–33; Arthur Shay, "Author on the Make: Nelson Algren's Bittersweet Affair with Chicago," *Chicago Tribune Magazine*, 14 September 1986, 14; Mary Wisniewski, *Algren: A Life* (Chicago: Chicago Review Press, 2017), 277; Tuohy, "A Day at the Races with Nelson Algren," 19; Art Shay, *Nelson Algren's Chicago* (Urbana: University of Illinois Press, 1988), xiv; Art Shay, *Chicago's Nelson Algren* (Seven Stories Press: New York, 2007), xxi–xxii; Colin Asher, *Never a Lovely So Real: The Life and Work of Nelson Algren* (New York: W.W. Norton, 2019), 372, 438; Martha Heasley Cox and Wayne Chatterton, *Nelson Algren* (Boston: Twayne, 1975), [15]; Brooke Horvath, *Understanding Nelson Algren* (Columbia: University of South Carolina Press, 2005), 133.

Algren biographer Colin Asher refers to Algren's horse as "Jellious Widow" because the name is spelled that way in racetrack programs. On the other hand, perhaps this was merely a typographical error. Algren writes of being at the Cahokia Downs clubhouse, "studying the breeding of a seven-year-old mare named Jealous Widow" in his article, "Previous Days." Algren also calls a horse "Jealous Widow" in his story, "Moon of the Arfy Darfy." See Drew, Nelson Algren, 333; Asher, *Never a Lovely So Real*, 372, 438; Nelson Algren, "Previous Days," in *The Last Carousel* (New York: Seven Stories Press, 1997), 222, 223; Nelson Algren, "Moon of the Arfy Darfy," in *The Last Carousel*, 352.

3. Drew, *Nelson Algren*, 327, 333, 339; Cox and Chatterton, *Nelson Algren*, 56, 138; James R. Giles, *Confronting the Horror: The Novels of Nelson Algren* (Kent, Ohio: Kent State University Press, 1989), 85; "A Note on Our Contributors," *Zeitgeist* 1, no. 4 (Summer 1966): 94.

4. See also Nelson Algren, "Stoopers and Shoeboard Watchers," in *Entrapment*, 207–13.

5. See also Nelson Algren, "There Will Be No More Christmases, in *Entrapment and other Writings*, eds. Brooke Horvath and Dan Simon (New York: Seven Stories Press, 2009), 261–69.

SHORT STORIES AND ARTICLES

"Stoopers and Shoeboard Watchers," *Sports Illustrated*, 15 June 1959, E12, E14–16.[4]
"Moon of the Backstretch: Still and White," *Rogue*, August 1961, 12–16, 24.
"The Moon of the Arfy Darfy," *Saturday Evening Post*, 26 September 1964, 44–45, 48–49; reprinted in *The Last Carousel*.
"Get All the Money," *Playboy*, June 1970, 82, 84+; revised as "Bullring of the Summer Night," *The Last Carousel*; portion incorporated in "Moon of the Arfy Darfy," *The Last Carousel*.
"A Ticket to Biro-Bidjan," *Chicago Free Press* 1, no. 2 (5 October 1970): 37–38.
"I Never Hollered Cheezit the Cops," *The Atlantic Monthly*, October 1972, 93–96; reprinted in *The Last Carousel*.
"There Will Be No More Christmases," *Chicago*, July 1980, 132–34.[5]

OTHER WORKS

References to horse racing or the race track appear in the following works by Nelson Algren:

"Ballet for Opening Day: The Swede Was a Hard Guy," *The Last Carousel*.

"Come in If You Love Money," *The Last Carousel.*

"A Ticket on Skoronski," *Saturday Evening Post,* 5 November 1966, 48–49, 52–56; reprinted in *The Last Carousel.*

"I Know They'll Like Me in Cholon," *The Critic,* February–March 1969, 58–61; revised as "I Know They'll Like Me in Saigon," *The Last Carousel.*

"Previous Days," *Chicago Free Press* 1, no. 4 (19 October 1970): 30–31; revised as "Previous Days," *The Last Carousel.*

"Otto Preminger's Strange Suspenjers," in *Focus Media,* eds. Jess Ritter and Grover Lewis (San Francisco: Chandler Publishing Co., 1972), 10–18; reprinted in *The Last Carousel.*

"Blanche Sweet Under the Tapioca," *Chicago Tribune Magazine,* 30 April 1972, 42–45; revised as "Previous Days," *The Last Carousel.*

"Ode to an Absconding Bookie," *Chicago Tribune Magazine,* 8 October 1972, 29; reprinted in *The Last Carousel.*

MISCELLANEOUS

See also these newspaper articles:

Michaela Tuohy, "A Day at the Races with Nelson Algren," *Chicago Tribune Magazine,* 30 June 1974, 18–19, 22.

Henry Kisor, "Nelson Algren, That Hackensack Homebody," *Chicago Daily News Panorama,* 12–13 June 1976, 7.

Arthur Shay, "Author on the Make: Nelson Algren's Bittersweet Affair with Chicago," *Chicago Tribune Magazine,* 14 September 1986, 10–12, 14–17, 32, 39.

Epilogue

That boy Algren has really got it.
—Ernest Hemingway, interview with
Jackson Burke, circa 1953.[1]

Algren scholar James R. Giles comments in his book, *The Naturalistic Inner-City Novel in America* that "Algren has yet to be welcomed without reservation into the canon of twentieth-century American literature."[2]

Perhaps the following is why Nelson Algren is not yet in the canon.

After Algren's 1956 book, *A Walk on the Wild Side*, received mixed reviews, he walked away from working on another novel. In the 1960s he began calling himself a "freelance journalist," not a novelist. On occasion Algren would be asked about writing the "Big One"—his next novel. He would respond, "An awful lot of people would have to buy the little ones. But they don't." This may have prompted novelist Meyer Levin to snipe in 1973 that "Nelson Algren seems to be identified as *the* Chicago writer but—perhaps symbolically—doesn't write."[3]

Meyer Levin was wrong. Although Nelson Algren was not writing novels after 1956, he was still writing. He wrote articles and short stories, and much of his work was later reprinted in one of his "collection" books like *Who Lost an American?* (1963) and *Notes from a Sea Diary: Hemingway All the Way* (1965). But these books were met with indifferent reviews, and in 1969 Sheldon Norman Grebstein wrote: "Nelson Algren evokes little attention these days. Although he has published nine books, his last work of fiction, *A Walk on the Wild Side*, appeared in 1956, and the journalistic writing he has done in recent years hardly warrants our concern."[4]

Sheldon Norman Grebstein was also wrong. Unfortunately, Nelson Algren chose to hide his light under a bushel after *A Walk on the Wild Side* was published. He buried some of his best and most original work in men's magazines and specialty magazines. These stories and articles were often published once and then never again; they never made it into one of Algren's "collection" books. Harold Bloom, author of *The Western Canon*, writes of canonical literature as being immortal. That is, he describes a

Figure 35: Bill Targ and G.P. Putnam's Sons published *The Last Carousel* in 1973, and the publicity surrounding the book's release makes it clear that in Chicago, Nelson Algren was still a literary icon in the early 70s. *Panorama*, the *Chicago Daily News* weekend magazine, featured this Algren montage on its October 27–28 cover. Designed by Jack Bruza, the *Panorama* drawing measures eight and one-half inches by six and one-half inches, and it covers most of the front of the magazine. Letters three-quarters of an inch high proclaim "ALGREN'S WAY" above the drawing. Wrapped around its bottom edge are the words, "The Division St. Dostoevsky writes his best book in (*continued*)

canonical candidate as "a literary work that the world would not willingly let die." Meyer Levin thought that Algren "doesn't write." Perhaps book reviewers, college professors, book store owners, and even the general public thought so, too. Bloom's world, a world that "would not willingly let die" a canonical candidate, may not have even been aware of Nelson Algren's alternative universe of non-novels. Bloom's world did not "*willingly* let die" works like "Moon of the Backstretch, Still and White" (1961) and "Say a Prayer for the Guy" (1958); it never even knew that this article and story existed. This may be why Algren has not yet entered the canon of twentieth-century American literature.[5]

All of this might change, however, in the twenty-first century. New books have been written about Nelson Algren—books that reflect a new evaluation and appreciation of Algren and his writing. In addition, two documentaries have been released about the author. Finally, it is hoped that *The Short Writings of Nelson Algren* will help improve Algren's chances at canonical status by revealing the vast scope and richness of his short stories, poetry, and articles. If that happens, perhaps Giles' canon will eventually include a new member.[6]

NOTES

1. David M. Earle, *All Man! Hemingway, 1950s Men's Magazines, and the Masculine Persona* (Kent, Ohio: Kent State University Press, 2009), 58.

2. James R. Giles, *The Naturalistic Inner-City Novel in America: Encounters with the Fat Man* (Columbia: University of South Carolina Press, 1995), 96.

3. Cleveland Amory, "Could It Be That Midwesterners Are the Only Ones Alive?" *Chicago Tribune Book World*, 10 June 1973, 4; Leslie A. Fiedler, "The Noble Savages of Skid Row," review of *A Walk on the Wild Side*, by Nelson Algren, *The Reporter*, 12 July 1956, 43; Leslie A. Fiedler, "The Novel in the Post-Political World," review of *A Walk on the Wild Side*, by Nelson Algren, and other books, *Partisan Review* 23, no. 3 (Summer 1956): 360; Norman Podhoretz, "The Man with the Golden Beef," review of *A Walk on the Wild Side*, by Nelson Algren, *The New Yorker*, 2 June 1956, 132, 137; Alfred Kazin, "Some People Passing By," review of *A Walk on the Wild Side*, by Nelson Algren, *The New York Times Book Review*, 20 May 1956, 4; "Rough Stuff," review of *A Walk on the Wild Side*, by Nelson Algren, *Time*, 28 May 1956, 106; Bettina Drew, *Nelson Algren: A Life on the Wild Side* (Austin: University of Texas Press, 1991), 275–303 passim; Henry Kisor, "Nelson Algren, Hale and Salty at 64," *Chicago Daily News Panorama*, 27–28 October 1973, 2; Jimmy Breslin, "The Man in a $20 Hotel Room," in *The World According to Breslin*, 271; H.E.F. Donohue, *Conversations with Nelson Algren* (New York: Hill and Wang, 1964), 282; Jan Herman,

twenty years." Page two of *Panorama* features Henry Kisor's article, "Nelson Algren, Hale and Salty at 64." Van Allen Bradley's book review, "*Last Carousel*: His Best Book in 20 Years," is on page three. Bradley claims in this review that *The Last Carousel* is "the best book we have had from Algren since his magnificent prose poem *Chicago: City on the Make* (1951)" (illustration courtesy the *Chicago Sun-Times* and the Chicago History Museum).

"Nelson Algren: The Angry Author," *Chicago Sun-Times Chicagostyle*, 21 January 1979, 11; Irwin Saltz, "Nelson Algren on the Make," *Chicagoland Magazine*, May 1970, 26; Mary Wisniewski, *Algren: A Life* (Chicago: Chicago Review Press, 2017), 255; Burns Ellison, "The First Annual Nelson Algren Memorial Poker Game," *The Iowa Review* 18, no. 1 (Winter 1988): 71, 94; Martha Heasley Cox and Wayne Chatterton, *Nelson Algren* (Boston: Twayne Publishers, 1975), 134; Carlo Rotella, *October Cities: The Redevelopment of Urban Literature* (Berkeley: University of California Press, 1998), 330n31.

4. Sheldon Norman Grebstein, "Nelson Algren and the Whole Truth," in *The Forties: Fiction, Poetry, Drama*, ed. Warren French (DeLand, Fla.: Everett/Edwards, 1969), 299; Brooke Horvath, *Understanding Nelson Algren* (Columbia: University of South Carolina Press, 2005), 10.

5. Harold Bloom, *The Western Canon: The Books and School of the Ages* (New York: Harcourt Brace, 1994), 17, 19; Nelson Algren, *Entrapment and Other Writings*, eds. Brooke Horvath and Dan Simon (New York: Seven Stories Press, 2009), 15.

6. Examples of recent books about Nelson Algren include *Literary Legacies of the Federal Writers' Project: Voices of the Depression in the American Postwar Era* (2017), by Sara Rutkowski; *Algren: A Life* (2017), by Mary Wisniewski; and *Never a Lovely So Real: The Life and Work of Nelson Algren* (2019), by Colin Asher. Two documentaries—*Algren* and *Nelson Algren: The End is Nothing, the Road is All*—were released, respectively, in 2014 and 2015. In 2009 a group of actors and writers gathered in Chicago's Steppenwolf Theater for "an onstage reading and celebration of Algren's life and work in his own words." A DVD of the event, called "Nelson Algren Live," was released in 2020. See Rick Kogan, "2 Movies Try to Unravel the Mystery that is Algren," *Chicago Tribune*, 19 October 2014, sec. 4, 9; Tom Mullaney, "Rehabilitating Nelson Algren," *Chicago Tribune Printers Row Journal*, 29 March 2015, 21–22. See also Giles, *The Naturalistic Inner-City Novel in America*, 96, 117n3.

Appendix A: Anthologies

In 1952 Van Allen Bradley, literary editor of the *Chicago Daily News*, described Nelson Algren as "one of the most widely anthologized of contemporary writers." More than half a century later, is this still true? Brooke Horvath comments in his study of Algren's works, *Understanding Nelson Algren* (2005) that after *A Walk on the Wild Side* was published in 1956, there was a "gradual disappearance of his work from anthologies and textbooks." However, Horvath qualifies his statement, writing that "Algren still cannot be found in the standard anthologies used to teach American literature."[1]

Horvath is correct; Algren does not currently appear in those ubiquitous *Norton* school anthologies like *The Norton Anthology of Short Fiction*. However, Algren has consistently appeared in other anthologies, especially specialized anthologies, from the 1930s through and beyond the 1950s. Although the number of anthologies containing Algren's work (hereafter referred to as "Algren anthologies") peaked in the 1950s, he has still appeared in anthologies published in the twenty-first century.[2]

This appendix contains a comprehensive listing of ninety-seven Algren anthologies. I have chosen to define "anthology" as a collection of the *established* works of various authors. That is, I have deliberately omitted any collection of new writing, such as the stories found in *The American Mercury*, *The Penguin New Writing*, *Works in Progress*, or scholarly journals that refer to "new writers," "new writing," or "new literature." Because I have chosen to list anthologies of works that have stood the test of time, and not anthologies of works that are current at the time of the publication of the anthology, this collection may not include books that are noted in the "First Appearances in Books" section of Matthew J. Bruccoli's book, *Nelson Algren: A Descriptive Bibliography*. On the other hand, I have chosen to broadly define Algren's work. Thus, I have included not only traditional collections of short stories, but also a *Catch-22* casebook, a compilation of love letters, a book of "self-portraits," and a book containing "life lessons for success in the real world."[3]

I have deliberately listed the books chronologically. By doing so, one can look for trends or patterns—how do the number and type of Algren anthologies in the 1950s compare to anthologies in the 1960s and 1970s? Algren died in 1981. Anthologies did not stop printing his works after his death, but did the publication of post–1981 anthologies decrease in number? If so, how significant was the decrease?

By looking at the titles of the books, one can see how, especially in later years,

Algren's work has crossed over into many different types of anthologies. Martha Heasley Cox and Wayne Chatterton comment in their 1975 book, *Nelson Algren*, that "Algren's stories are highly homogeneous. As has been noted, his subjects are dope addiction, prostitution, incarceration, gambling, prize-fighting, horse racing, and army life, one or more of which predictably appears in most of his work." Algren's work is in specialized anthologies of all of these subjects except one—it appears that he has never been in a horse racing anthology, even though he has written several horse racing short stories.[4]

This listing begins in 1934 and ends in 2019. The number of anthologies published in each decade is shown below. This summary shows that Algren appeared in the most anthologies in the 1950s (twenty-one), he dropped to eighteen in the 1960s, and dropped two more in the 1970s. He died in 1981, and there were only five Algren anthologies in the 1980s. He then came back again, however, with fourteen anthologies in the 1990s, but down to ten in the first decade of the twenty-first century, then decreasing further to six in the second decade.[5]

My search for Algren anthologies has been exhaustive, but it is not over. It is likely that additional Algren anthologies have been published, still waiting to be discovered.[6]

Algren Anthologies, by Decade
1930–1939–2
1940–1949–5
1950–1959–21
1960–1969–18
1970–1979–16
1980–1989–5
1990–1999–14
2000–2009–10
2010–2020–6

Algren Anthologies: A Listing

"So Help Me." In *Story in America 1933–1934*, edited by Whit Burnett and Martha Foley, 42–53. New York: The Vanguard Press, 1934.

"The Brothers' House." In *O. Henry Memorial Award Prize Stories of 1935*, edited by Harry Hansen, 61–67. Garden City, N.Y.: Doubleday, Doran, 1935.

"A Bottle of Milk for Mother." In *O. Henry Memorial Award Prize Stories of 1941*, edited by Herschel Brickell, 69–89. New York: The Book League of America, 1941.

"How the Devil Came Down Division Street." In *The Best American Short Stories 1945*, edited by Martha Foley, 1–7. Cleveland: The World Publishing Co., 1946.

"The Heroes." In *Midland Humor: A Harvest of Fun and Folklore*, edited by Jack Conroy, 155–63. New York: Current Books, 1947.

"Single Exit." In *Cross Section 1947*, edited by Edwin Seaver, 217–224. New York: Simon and Schuster, 1947.

"How the Devil Came Down Division Street." In *U.S. Stories: Regional Stories from the Forty-Eight States*, edited by Martha Foley and Abraham Rothberg, 301–06. New York: Hendricks House–Farrar Straus, 1949.

"A Bottle of Milk for Mother." In *The Avon All-American Fiction Reader*, 549–64. New York: Avon Publishing, 1951.

"The Captain Is Impaled." In *Prize Stories of 1950: The O. Henry Awards*, edited by Herschel Brickell, 52–67. Garden City, N.Y.: Doubleday, 1951.

"How the Devil Came Down Division Street." In *The Best of the Best American Short Stories 1915–1950*, edited by Martha Foley, 1–6. Boston: Houghton Mifflin, 1952.

"How the Devil Came Down Division Street." In *This is Chicago: An Anthology*, edited by Albert Halper, 23–29. New York: Henry Holt, 1952.

"He Swung and He Missed." In *The World's Greatest Boxing Stories*, edited by Harold U. Ribalow, 14–20. New York: Twayne Publishers, 1952.

"So Help Me." In *These Your Children*, edited by Harold U. Ribalow, 187–202. New York: The Beechhurst Press, 1952.

"The Face on the Barroom Floor." In *Tales of Love and Fury*, 144–58. Avon Publications, no. A549, 1953.[7]

"Katz." In *The Stakes Are High*, edited by Brent Ashabranner, 67–71. New York: Pennant Books, 1954.

"Million Dollar Brainstorm." In *Champs and Bums*, edited by Bucklin Moon, 94–104. New York: Lion Books, 1954.

"How the Devil Came Down Division Street." In *Great Tales of City Dwellers*, edited by Alex Austin, 139–44. New York: Lion Library, 1955.

"Please Don't Talk about Me When I'm Gone." In *Stories of Scarlet Women*, 71–79. Avon Publications, no. T-113, 1955.

"Please Don't Talk about Me When I'm Gone." In *Stories of Scarlet Women*, 71–79. Avon Publications, no. G-112, 1955.

"The Silver-Colored Yesterday." In *The Fireside Book of Baseball*, 2–5. New York: Simon and Schuster, 1956.

"All Through the Night." In *Juvenile Jungle*, 120–34. New York: Berkley Publishing, no. G-86, 1957.

"Beasts of the Wild." In *The Best American Short Stories 1957*, edited by Martha Foley, 1–7. Boston: Houghton Mifflin, 1957.

"Depend on Aunt Elly." In *Women without Men*, 7–22. New York: Lion Library, no. LL141, 1957.

"The Face on the Barroom Floor." In *Tales of Midsummer Passion*, 144–58. New York: Avon Publications, no. 778, [1957].

"The Heroes." In *War!*, edited by Alex Austin, 126–34. New York: New American Library, 1957.

"The Captain Is a Card." In *The Armchair Esquire*, edited by Arnold Gingrich and L. Rust Hills, 161–171. New York: G.P. Putnam's Sons, 1958.

"So Help Me." In *A Treasury of American Jewish Stories*, edited by Harold U. Ribalow, 482–97. New York: Thomas Yoseloff, 1958.

"All Through the Night." In *The Permanent Playboy*, edited by Ray Russell, 419–29. New York: Crown Publishers, 1959.

"Chicago Is a Wose." In *The 1950's: America's "Placid" Decade*, edited by Joseph Satin, 177–78. Boston: Houghton Mifflin, 1960.

"How the Devil Came Down Division Street." In *Stories of Modern America*, edited by Herbert Gold, 221–227. New York: St. Martin's Press, 1961.

"How the Devil Came Down Division Street." In *A Doubleday Anthology*, edited by Bucklin Moon, 345–50. Garden City, N.Y.: Doubleday, 1962.

"So Help Me." In *Firsts of the Famous*, edited by Whit Burnett, 5–18. New York: Ballantine Books, 1962.

"Down with All Hands." In *First Person Singular: Essays for the Sixties*, edited by Herbert Gold, 15–26. New York: Dial Press, 1963.

"The Father and Son Cigar." In *The Bedside Playboy*, edited by Hugh M. Hefner, 97–111. Chicago: Playboy Press, 1963.

"How the Devil Came Down Division Street." In *Great Tales of City Dwellers*, edited by Alex Austin, 139–44. New York: Pyramid Books, 1963.

"The Monkey on the Back." In *Sociology Through Literature: An Introductory Reader*, edited by Lewis A. Coser, 373–76. Englewood Cliffs, N.J.: Prentice-Hall, 1963.

"The Weaker Sheep." In *The Addict*, edited by Dan Wakefield, 73–79. Greenwich, Conn.: Fawcett Publications, 1963.

"Ain't Nobody on My Side?" In *Crisis*, 23–28. Chicago: New Classics House, 1964.

"A Bottle of Milk for Mother." In *The Modern Talent: An Anthology of Short Stories*, edited by John Edward Hardy, 388–403. New York: Holt, Rinehart and Winston, 1964.

"The Daddy of Them All." In *Taboo*, 31–59. Chicago: New Classics House, 1964.

"A Bottle of Milk for Mother." In *The Short Story: Classic & Contemporary*, edited by R.W. Lid, 489–503. Philadelphia: J.B. Lippincott, 1966.

"A Lot You Got to Holler." In *National Book Award Reader*, edited by Robert J. Clements, Ph.D., 66–77. New York: Popular Library, 1966.

"Somebody in Boots." (excerpt) In *The American Writer and the Great Depression*, edited by Harvey Swados, 319–48. Indianapolis: Bobbs-Merrill, 1966.

"The Trouble with Daylight." In *Children of the Uprooted*, edited by Oscar Handlin, 343–54. New York: George Braziller, 1966.

"Mama and the Mammy-freak." In *Fille de Joie: The Book of Courtesans, Sporting Girls, Ladies of the Evening, Madams, a Few Occasionals & Some Royal Favorites*, 139–50. New York: Dorset Press, 1967.

"A Place to Lie Down." In *Years of Protest: A Collection of American Writings of the 1930's*, edited by Jack Salzman, 347–53. New York: Pegasus, 1967.

"Poor Man's Pennies." In *Love's Blues*, edited by James Olson and Laurence Swinburne, 21–31. New York: Noble and Noble, 1970.

"A Visit to the Playboy Key Club." In *Grooving the Symbol*, edited by Richard W. Lid, 342–50. Toronto: Collier-Macmillan Canada, 1970.

"The Captain Has Bad Dreams." In *Best Crime Stories 4*, edited by John Welcome, 177–91. London: Faber and Faber, 1971.

"A Lot You Got to Holler." In *Big City Stories by Modern American Writers*, edited by Tom and Susan Cahill, 85–96. New York: Bantam Books, 1971.

"He Couldn't Boogie-Woogie Worth a Damn." In *Travelers: Stories of Americans Abroad*, edited by L.M. Schulman, 124–38. New York: The MacMillan Co., 1972.

"He Swung and He Missed." In *75 Short Masterpieces: Stories from the World's Literature*, edited by Roger B. Goodman, 5–11. New York: Bantam Books, 1972.

"Otto Preminger's Strange Suspenjers." In *Focus Media*, edited by Jess Ritter and Grover Lewis, 10–18. San Francisco: Chandler Publishing Co., 1972.

"Remembering Richard Wright." In *Twentieth Century Interpretations of "Native Son": A Collection of Critical Essays*, edited by Houston A. Baker Jr., 115–16. Englewood Cliffs, N.J.: Prentice-Hall, 1972.

"The Catch." In *A "Catch-22" Casebook*, edited by Frederick Kiley and Walter McDonald, 3–5. New York: Thomas Y. Crowell, 1973.

"A Holiday in Texas." In *Writers in Revolt: The Anvil Anthology*, edited by Jack Conroy and Curt Johnson, 1–7. New York: Lawrence Hill, 1973.

"How the Devil Came Down Division Street." In *Stories of the American Experience*, edited by Leonard Kriegel and Abraham H. Lass, 312–316. New York: New American Library, 1973.

"Makers of Music." In *Writers in Revolt: The Anvil Anthology*, edited by Jack Conroy and Curt Johnson, 209. New York: Lawrence Hill, 1973.

"Program for Appeasement." In *Writers in Revolt: The Anvil Anthology*, edited by Jack Conroy and Curt Johnson, 210–11. New York: Lawrence Hill, 1973.

"Within the City." In *Writers in Revolt: The Anvil Anthology*, edited by Jack Conroy and Curt Johnson, 8–9. New York: Lawrence Hill, 1973.

"All Through the Night." In *All Through the Night: Stories of the World's Oldest Profession*, 177–90. Chicago: Playboy Press, 1975.

"Nelson Algren." *A Bibliographical Introduction to Seventy-Five Modern American Authors*, edited by Gary M. Lepper, 1–2. Berkeley, Calif.: Serendipity Books, 1976.[8]

(Drawing of a cat). *Self-Portrait: Book People Picture Themselves*, edited by Burt Britton, 10. New York: Random House, 1976.

"Dark Came Early in That Country." In *On the Job: Fiction About Work by Contemporary American Writers*, edited by William O'Rourke, 187–206. New York: Vintage Books, 1977.

"Dark Came Early in That Country." In *The Roar of the Sneakers*, edited by Robert S. Gold, 1–22. New York: Bantam Books, 1977.

"A Lot You Got to Holler." In *Stepping Stones: An Anthology*, edited by Robert S. Gold, 130–47. New York: Dell Publishing, 1981.

"A Bottle of Milk for Mother." In *Short Story Masterpieces*, edited by Robert Penn Warren and Albert Erskine, 14–31. New York: Dell Publishing, 1982.

"So Long, Swede Risberg." In *Best Sports Stories 1982*, edited by *The Sporting News* and Edward Ehre, 46–54. New York: E.P. Dutton, 1982.

"The Captain Is a Card." In *Great Esquire Fiction: The Finest Stories from the First Fifty Years*, edited by L. Rust Hills, 63–73. New York: The Viking Press, 1983.

"How the Devil Came Down Division Street." In *Chicago's Public Wits: A Chapter in the American Comic Spirit*, edited by Kenny J. Williams and Bernard Duffey, 267–74. Baton Rouge: Louisiana State University Press, 1983.

"American Christmas, 1952." In *"The Nation" 1865–1990: Selections from the Independent Magazine of Politics and Culture*, edited by Katrina Vanden Heuvel, 187–89. New York: Thunder's Mouth Press, 1990.

"The Silver-Colored Yesterday." In *The New Baseball Reader: More Favorites from The Fireside Books of Baseball*, edited by Charles Einstein, 1–7. New York: Viking, 1991.

"Nelson Algren to Simone de Beauvoir." In *The Book of Love: Writers and Their*

Love Letters, selected by Cathy N. Davidson, 228–230. New York: Pocket Books, 1992.[9]

"Chicago: City on the Make" (excerpt). In *Chicago Stories: Tales of the City*, edited by John Miller and Genevieve Anderson, 139–45. San Francisco: Chronicle Books, 1993.

"The Last Carrousel." In *Playboy Stories: The Best of Forty Years of Short Fiction*, edited by Alice K. Turner, 277–302. New York: Dutton, 1994.

"So Help Me." In *First Fiction: An Anthology of the First Published Stories by Famous Writers*, edited by Kathy Kiernan, 3–15. Boston: Little Brown, 1994.

"The Man with the Golden Arm" (excerpt). In *White Rabbit: A Psychedelic Reader*, edited by John Miller and Randall Koral, 7–14. San Francisco: Chronicle Books, 1995.

"Nobody Knows Where O'Connor Went." In *The Party Train: A Collection of North American Prose Poetry*, edited by Robert Alexander, Mark Vinz, and C.W. Truesdale, 47–50. Minneapolis: New Rivers Press, 1996.

"El Presidente de Méjico." In *Prison Writing in 20th-Century America*, edited by H. Bruce Franklin, 130–141. New York: Penguin Books, 1998.

"He Swung and He Missed" (excerpt). In *Boxers*, by Kurt Markus, 72. Santa Fe, N. Mex.: Twin Palms Publishers, 1998.

"Chicago: City on the Make" (excerpt). In *Smokestacks & Skyscrapers: An Anthology of Chicago Writing*, edited by David Starkey and Richard Guzman, 207–10. Chicago: Wild Onion Books, 1999.

"He Swung and He Missed." In *Boxing's Best Short Stories*, edited by Paul D. Staudohar, 199–206. Chicago: Chicago Review Press, 1999.

"The Man with the Golden Arm" (excerpt). In *Artificial Paradises: A Drugs Reader*, edited by Mike Jay, 273–74. London: Penguin Books, 1999.

"A Walk on the Wild Side" (excerpt). In *Rebel Yell: A Century of Underground Classics*, edited by Kevin Williamson, 15–22. Edinburgh, Scotland: Rebel Inc., 1999.

"Hollywood Djinn with a Dash of Bitters." In *Cinema Nation: The Best Writing on Film from "The Nation" 1913–2000*, edited by Carl Bromley, 91–95. New York: Thunder's Mouth Press, 2000.

"Dad Among the Troglodytes, or Show Me a Gypsy and I'll Show You a Nut." In *Editors: The Best from Five Decades*, edited by Saul Bellow and Keith Botsford, 761–766. London: The Toby Press, 2001.

"Stickman's Laughter." In *Life-Changing Stories of Forgiving and Being Forgiven*, edited by Thomas Dyja, 83–95. New York: Marlowe & Co., 2001.

"The Silver-Colored Yesterday." In *Baseball: A Literary Anthology*, edited by Nicholas Dawidoff, 227–33. New York: The Library of America, 2002.

"He Swung and He Missed." In *The Greatest Boxing Stories Ever Told*, edited by Jeff Silverman, 339–45. Guilford, Conn.: The Lyons Press, 2002.

"Chicago: City on the Make" (excerpt). In *Chicago Stories: Tales of the City*, edited by John Miller and Genevieve Anderson, 139–45. San Francisco: Chronicle Books, [2003].

"The Man with the Golden Arm" (excerpt). In *The Outlaw Bible of American Literature*, edited by Alan Kaufman, Neil Ortenberg, and Barney Rosset, 457–61. New York: Thunder's Mouth Press, 2004.

"The Man with the Golden Arm" (excerpt). In *Read 'Em and Weep: A Bedside Poker Companion*, edited by John Stravinsky, 1–8. New York: HarperCollins, 2004.

"Nelson Algren." In *Writers*, by Nancy Crampton, 14–15. New York: The Quantuck Lane Press, 2005.[10]

(Excerpt from *A Walk on the Wild Side*.) In *The Best Advice Ever Given*, edited by Steven D. Price, 111. Guilford, Conn.: The Lyons Press, 2006.[11]

"Surrealism? In Chicago?: Talks with Nelson Algren, 1975." In *Armitage Avenue Transcendentalists*, edited by Janina Ciezadlo and Penelope Rosemont, 95–99. Chicago: Charles H. Kerr Publishing, 2010.

"A Bottle of Milk for Mother." In *The Oxford Book of American Short Stories*, 2nd edition, edited by Joyce Carol Oates, 380–94. New York: Oxford University Press, 2013.

"The Man with the Golden Arm" (excerpt). In *The Graphic Canon, Volume Three: From Heart of Darkness to Hemingway to Infinite Jest*, edited by Russ Kick, 390–97. New York: Seven Stories Press, 2013.[12]

"He Swung and He Missed." In *Chicago Noir: The Classics*, edited by Joe Meno, 93–101. N.p.: Akashic Books, 2015.

"A Bottle of Milk for Mother." In *Chicago Stories*, edited by James Daley, 154–68. Mineola, N.Y.: Dover Publications, 2016.

"Say a Prayer for the Guy." In *The Best of "Manhunt": A Collection of the Best Stories from "Manhunt" Magazine*, edited by Jeff Vorzimmer, 369–72. Eureka, Calif.: Stark House Press, 2019.

NOTES

1. "This is Algren," *Chicago Daily News*, 3 December 1952, 44; Brooke Horvath, *Understanding Nelson Algren* (Columbia: University of South Carolina Press, 2005), 9, 151. For additional comments about Algren's disappearance from standard anthologies, see James A. Lewin, "Algren's Outcasts: Shakespearean Fools and the Prophet in a Neon Wilderness," in *MidAmerica XVIII: The Yearbook of the Society for the Study of Midwestern Literature*, ed. David D. Anderson (East Lansing: The Midwestern Press, Michigan State University, 1991), 112. Note that Algren has not *completely* disappeared from general anthologies. See Nelson Algren, "A Bottle of Milk for Mother," in *The Oxford Book of American Short Stories*, 2nd ed., ed. Joyce Carol Oates (New York: Oxford University Press, 2013), 380–94. Oates writes of the continuing significance of Algren in the preface to this second edition: "Within a literary culture so shifting, as the larger culture is continually shifting, it seems necessary to look both forward and back, to include new work by young and emerging writers like those mentioned above, but also to retrieve from the past writers who were not, for one reason or another, included in the original *Oxford Book of American Short Stories*, whose work has endured through the decades: H.P. Lovecraft, whose influence upon 'gothic' fiction and film has been inestimable; Nelson Algren, poet of Chicago slum-life; Shirley Jackson...." Oates, *The Oxford Book of American Short Stories*, 2nd edition, xix.

2. *The Norton Anthology of Short Fiction*, 7th edition, ed. Richard Bausch and R.V. Cassill (New York: W.W. Norton, 2006). Algren appeared in twenty-one anthologies in the 1950s, the most in any decade.

3. Matthew J. Bruccoli, *Nelson Algren: A Descriptive Bibliography* (Pittsburgh: University of Pittsburgh Press, 1985), [93]–104.

4. Martha Heasley Cox and Wayne Chatterton, *Nelson Algren* (Boston: Twayne, 1975), 49.

‖‖‖

This Is Algren

Chicagoan Nelson Algren is the author of "The Man with the Golden Arm," the first novel to win the National Book Award. One of the most widely anthologized of contemporary writers, he is hailed in many quarters as a major talent. He is studied, along

NELSON ALGREN

with Faulkner and Hemingway, at our major universities.

The editor of these pages asked Mr. Algren for his comments on the state of American writing today. This article is his reply. The opinions expressed are Mr. Algren's and not necessarily those of the Daily News or its literary editor.

‖‖‖

Figure 36: In the summer of 1952, Van Allen Bradley, literary editor of the *Chicago Daily News*, asked Nelson Algren to write an article for the newspaper's Christmas book section. Algren's article, "The State of Literature," appeared in the December 3, 1952, issue of the newspaper.

"The State of Literature" included a photograph of Algren and a short sidebar article (two paragraphs) entitled, "This Is Algren." It appears that Van Allen Bradley wrote these two paragraphs. Kate Bales and artist Marshall Philyaw took a scratched and blurry microfilmed copy of the newspaper page and recreated both the picture and the sidebar article, exactly as it appeared in the *Daily News* in 1952. These two paragraphs read as follows:

"Chicagoan Nelson Algren is the author of *The Man with the Golden Arm*, the first novel to win the National Book Award. One of the most widely anthologized of contemporary writers, he is hailed in many quarters as a major talent. He is studied, along with Faulkner and Hemingway, at our major universities."

"The editor of these pages asked Mr. Algren for his comments on the state of American writing today. This article is his reply. The opinions expressed are Mr. Algren's and not necessarily those of the *Daily News* or its literary editor" (illustration courtesy the *Chicago Sun-Times* and the Chicago History Museum).

5. Although four of Algren's works appeared in the 1973 collection, *Writers in Revolt: The Anvil Anthology*, this book is counted only once in the compilation of 1970 anthologies.

6. "Hank, the Free Wheeler" appears in *A Treasury of American Folklore* under Algren's name. However, it is not listed in this appendix of anthologies, as authorship of this story has been attributed to Jack Conroy and not Nelson Algren. See Nelson Algren, "Hank, the Free Wheeler," in B.A. Botkin, ed., *A Treasury of American Folklore: Stories, Ballads, and Traditions of the People* (New York: Crown Publishers, 1944), 540–42; Douglas Wixson, *Worker-Writer in America: Jack Conroy and the Tradition of Midwestern Literary Radicalism, 1898–1990* (Urbana: University of Illinois Press, 1994), 439. Similarly, Algren is

Figure 37: During the 1950s, paperback book publishers used sex indiscriminately to sell Nelson Algren's short stories. Consider the titles of these four anthologies; each book contains an Algren story: *Tales of Love and Fury* (1953), *Stories of Scarlet Women* (1955), *Women without Men* (1957), and *Tales of Midsummer Passion* (1957). The cover of *Tales of Midsummer Passion* depicts a man leering at a woman falling out of her dress, yet this book incongruously includes "The Face on the Barroom Floor," Algren's horrific story of a legless man who savagely beats a bartender.

listed as the author of "Highpockets" in the book, *First-Person America*. That story was also written by Jack Conroy and not Algren. See Ann Banks, *First-Person America* (New York: Alfred A. Knopf, 1980), 90–92; Wixson, *Worker-Writer in America*, 439, 570n63.

7. Publishers of paperback anthologies were not adverse to using sex to sell books during the 1950s, and perhaps this is why the 1950s featured the most Algren anthologies. The books had titles like *Tales of Love and Fury* and *Tales of Midsummer Passion*. As shown in Figure 37, The front cover of *Tales of Love and Fury* shows an older woman, her eyes closed, head raised, cradling the head of a young man in her lap. The back cover suggestively refers to Algren's story as, "Nelson Algren, vividly describing the animal-like actions of men and women in a private club." But the book features, "The Face on the Barroom Floor," Algren's grim and graphic story of a legless man who mercilessly beats a bartender until "the face on the floor was a scarlet sponge." See Bill Savage, "'It Was Dope!' The Paperback Revolution and the Literary Reputation of Nelson Algren," in *Nelson Algren: A Collection of Critical Essays*, ed. Robert Ward (Madison, N.J.: Fairleigh Dickinson University Press, 2007), 141–61; Kenneth C. Davis, *Two-Bit Culture: The Paperbacking of America* (Boston: Houghton Mifflin, 1984), 135–41; Nelson Algren, "The Face on the Barroom Floor," in *Tales of Love and Fury* (New York: Avon Publications, #A549, [1953]), 157.

8. The introduction to *A Bibliographical Introduction to Seventy-Five Modern American Authors* states: "This book is a compendium of checklists of the writings of seventy-five American poets and novelists who have achieved literary prominence since 1945."

9. See also ["Simone de Beauvoir to Nelson Algren"] in *Hell Hath No Fury: Women's Letters from the End of the Affair*, ed. Anna Holmes (New York: Carroll & Graf, 2002), 86–88; "Simone de Beauvoir to Nelson Algren," in *The 50 Greatest Love Letters of All Time*, ed. David H. Lowenherz (New York: Gramercy Books, 2002), 139–41.

10. The dust jacket of *Writers* states: "Here are more than a hundred wonderful and sensitive duotone portraits of our major novelists, poets, and playwrights. Paired with the photographs are fascinating texts from each writer on writing."

11. The title of this book is, *The Best Advice Ever Given*. Nelson Algren's advice consists of his famous lines from *A Walk on the Wild Side*: "Never play cards with a man called Doc. Never eat at a place called Mom's. Never sleep with a woman whose troubles are worse than your own." See Nelson Algren, *A Walk on the Wild Side* (N.p.: Thunder's Mouth Press, 1990), 312.

12. A statement on the front cover of *The Graphic Canon* describes the book: "The world's great literature as comics and visuals."

Appendix B:
"The World's Busiest Police Station": A Lost Masterpiece on Race Relations

Introduction

During the 1940s and the 1950s, Nelson Algren fought tirelessly against injustice. In the late 1940s he helped head the Chicago Committee for the Hollywood Ten, a group of screenwriters and directors who refused to testify about their political affiliations when subpoenaed by the House Un-American Activities Committee, or HUAC. In the early 1950s he joined an anti-war group. In 1951 he signed a public statement denouncing loyalty oaths, job terminations without cause, and the imprisonment of people (including the Hollywood Ten) for refusing to testify as to their political beliefs. As shown in Figure 38, this statement was published in the *New York Times*. After Julius and Ethel Rosenberg were convicted of conspiracy to commit espionage in 1951, he became the honorary chairman of the Chicago Committee to Secure Justice in the Rosenberg Case.[1]

Algren's profound and prescient essay, "The World's Busiest Police Station," was featured in the January 1950 issue of *Negro Digest*. In this article, written years before even the parents of the founders of the Black Lives Matter movement were born, Algren asks the question, "Where does the Negro hoodlum, stickup man, rapist, come from?" He then answers the question with another question: "Is it possible that there would be fewer of these if more Negro youth had better chances at living clean, at getting jobs that are not dead-end, at living just a little more free from discrimination and hate."[2]

The essay is virtually unknown; it is not listed in Matthew Bruccoli's bibliography, nor is it mentioned in any of the scholarly books about Algren, such as *Understanding Nelson Algren*, by Brooke Horvath. It is not listed in the online catalogue of the Nelson Algren Collection at the Rare Books and Manuscripts Library of the Ohio State University. Algren never revised or recycled it into one of his later books. It is truly a lost masterpiece on race relations.[3]

It is possible that comparatively few people even read this remarkable Algren article when it was published. It appears that in 1950 *Negro Digest* had very low

What are you doing out there?

Figure 38: Nelson Algren and sixteen other intellectuals paid for and added their names to a one-third page advertisement entitled "What are you doing out there?" that appeared in the January 15, 1951, issue of the *New York Times*. The advertisement includes this drawing by artist Ben Shahn of a man look-ing out through the bars of a jail. Below the drawing are several *(continued)*

circulation numbers. Described as "unprofitable," the magazine ceased publication a year later.[4]

"The World's Busiest Police Station" is reprinted below courtesy of Bernice S. Behar of the Nelson Algren estate.[5]

* * *

"The World's Busiest Police Station" by Nelson Algren

In the ceaseless city-wide warfare waged between the law and the criminal, every Chicago ward and suburb has a daily skirmish or two: but on the South Side both sides multiply their mercenaries and the battle is truly joined.

On the walls of the Wabash Avenue Station hang pictures of patrolmen killed in the line of duty; and in the lockup below the captured wait: the strayed, the lost and the fallen of a captured race.

Poolroom punks on the muscle and old rogues with records that read like a Southern Pacific timetable; boosters and forgers, mush-workers and lush-workers, square-johns and copper-johns, hallroom boys and lamisters, bail-jumpers and parolees, peeping toms and firebox-pullers, old cold-deckers doing life on the installment plan and the Indiana Avenue torpedoes coming on faster than they can be picked up: the unlucky brothers with the hustlers' hearts, the afternoon prowlers and the midnight creepers. The strongarm wonders and the weaker sheep.

"Why'd you tear up your coat in the wagon on the way to the station?" a disappointed soft-clothesman wants to know of a shirtsleeved sprout holding onto the bars with hands like an outfielder's.

"It was full of bedbugs."

"Full of hand-ground gauge you mean. Where'd you get it?"

"Found it."

"Go down to State 'n' Madison Christmas Eve, maybe you'll find a piano."

They come in cuffed and they come in bandaged. Down-and-out cotton-shooters who'd give a gold tooth out of the mouth for a single cap of cocaine and the well-groomed policy-boy telling his lawyer just what to do next.

paragraphs of text. The first paragraph recounts the story of Henry David Thoreau being jailed in Concord, Massachusetts, for refusing to pay a poll tax, or head tax, as a protest against slavery. According to this story, when Ralph Waldo Emerson visited Thoreau in jail and asked him, "What are you doing in there?" Thoreau replied, "What are you doing out there?"

The advertisement makes and discusses three observations: American artists are being judged, convicted, and fired solely on charges of professional informers; American writers have been forced to choose jail rather than the betrayal of their beliefs; and American scholars are losing their posts as a result of the imposition of loyalty oaths that have nothing to do with their competence as free and honest teachers.

The advertisement ends with the plea: "Speak up for freedom!" (Art © 2021 Estate of Ben Shahn/Licensed by VAGA at Artists Rights Society [ARS], NY).

They come in drunked-up and hopped-up and cocky as roosters or beat clear into the ground. Every hue and shade of Negro, from every corner of Chicago's narrow black ghetto: out of the dimlit sidestreets and out of dimlit lives: the ones for whom civilization has hung out so many warning-signs, on apartments, schools and jobs: No Colored Need Apply.

With 39 police districts in the city, the Wabash Avenue District accounted for over 21 per cent of the city's murders, 12.3 per cent of all robberies and 24.9 per cent of rape incidence in 1945. In the preceding year one fourth of the city's murders were committed in the same district, and in 1943 the percentage of the city's murders was even higher for the same area. The law is called upon to investigate more instances of juvenile delinquency here than in any other police district.

And yet the crimes of Negroes are not crimes of their race: they are the crimes of the race that has segregated them and kept them impoverished. Negroes constitute the least-privileged, most untaught, unemployed, underfed and underpaid American minority. Yet they pay proportionately higher prices for rent, food and clothing. It costs the Negro who cleans the barber-shop cuspidors as much to live as it does the master-barber who owns the chairs. The Negro who has to depend on the tips offered for giving an overcoat an unnecessary brushing gets just as cold, without an overcoat, as does the overcoat's owner. And it costs society as much to restore a sick Negro to health at the County Hospital as it would have to give him a job at which he could have kept his health in the first place.

And when a Negro supplements his income by gambling or robbery or vice, society makes up the loss by building a new jail. Thus prejudice has its price. And racism isn't had for nothing.

Force a man to earn his living down a dead-end street and he'll be the first to drag you down it and latch onto your gold: both of you would have been better off had you given him a larger chance in the first place. And when you con a woman out of her chance to live like a woman, because of the color of her skin, she'll con you out of your very pants the first chance that's offered.

"Tell us what you told your mother when we picked you up," the soft-clothesman asks the bull-throated boy in the faded hard-straw kelly.

"I told her, 'Mother dear, you've worked for me for twenty-two years. Now go out 'n' get a job for yourself.'"

"Hold him for Central," the soft-clothesman advises the lockup-keeper.

For the Central Police lineup, that is, at Eleventh and State. Where a couple hundred victims and witnesses will sit restlessly in the hope of identifying the man who slugged the phone collector: "Phone company's always collectin', I decided to do a little collectin' from the phone company." For the platform punk who snatched the purse from the moving El; for the lush who ran somebody's favorite aunt down a blind alley; or forged his boss's signature or kidnapped a night-watchman, slit the janitor's throat in the coal-bin or performed a casual abortion on the janitor's wife. The little things done in simple fun and the big things done for love.

The aging jitterbug in the neat trenchcoat and patent-leather pumps that catch the yellowish lockup light in their pointed toes sums up his own case indifferently: "For arsony 'r somethin'."

"You mean larceny."

"I don't mean 'larceny.' I mean 'arsony.' Burned down the place I works to show 'em I was quittin'."

"The slums take their revenge," a Chicago poet has told us, "always somehow or other their retribution can be figured in any community. Where does the Negro hoodlum, stickup man, rapist, come from? Is it possible that there would be fewer of these if more Negro youth had better chances at living clean, at getting jobs that are not dead-end, at living just a little more free from discrimination and hate?"

The slums take their revenge—and you can take your pick of the avengers among the fast Saturday night set at 48th and Wabash. The station is always open and there are always new faces. Always someone you never met before, up against the same walls that prejudice and fear have raised; so high that the white man's voice and the Negro's voice come only faintly across the barrier to each other, like alien tongues. And behind the barrier of the Wabash Avenue bars the muted voices come on and come on. And where they come from no one says and where they go to no one cares.

And much of the Negroes' undoing must be laid at the door of organized labor, backed by hostile State and Federal statutes. Since the Negro is forbidden to rise above actual want, he is not above committing those misdemeanors which compensate him for the money he is not allowed to make the legal way. When a Negro is arrested for stealing sheets and pillow-cases belonging to the Pullman Company, the source of his crime is not in the color of his skin, but in the color of the official charter of the unions of railway car men, dining car conductors, sleeping car conductors, railway conductors; boilermakers, machinists, firemen, engineers, switchmen, telegraphers, train dispatchers, train-men, yard-masters, railroad workers, wire weavers, clerks, freight handlers, express and station employees, masters, mates and pilots. These are the chief trade-unions which have locked their doors to Negro workers.

The most sorrowful aspect of the whole sorry picture being that these unions, by binding the Negroes' arms, bind themselves with the same taut rope. With legislation like the Taft-Hartley Law on the books, these unions need the Negro as much as the Negro needs them. It is as if a man with two good arms, one black and one brown, refuses to use the darker one and thinks, therefore, that the arm is the loser.

While a lowering evening light casts a wan and whitish glare upon the youthful junkee's face. As though he had lived all his life in such a glare, wearing the same frayed jacket with the Pfc. stripe and two overseas bars on the left sleeve.

"Bond me out!" The Pfc. wants a bondsman, though he doesn't own penny-one. His bonus is down to a pin-point and the pupils of his eyes are drawn even tighter: nothing is reflected in them except a capsule of light the size of a quarter-grain of morphine. He has scaled the walls of his personal ghetto with no other help than that contained in a little brown drugstore-bottle filled with fuzzy white caps. A self-made man: he has freed himself single-handed, with no Lincoln to speak for him at all.

But all the drugstores are closed tonight and the cold blue bars keep getting in the way.

"Bond me out! Bond me out!"

"That one'll holler all night," the soft-clothesman decided wearily: always some junkee hollering all night. So you know that here is one G.I. who lost the war. And loses it anew every time the drugstores close.

Upstairs, in the women's tier, a slight girl in plaid slacks sits, waiting for nothing, alone in high-walled cell. When the soft-clothesman calls her to the bars she comes forward with the arched black arrows of her lashes dipped in two fresh tears.

"Save it for the jury, Roberta," Soft-Clothes advises her; and offers a policeman's version: "This is the slickest little knockout broad on South State. How come you always pick on white married men, Honey-Hush?"

Honey-Hush raises the lashes: her eyes hold a wry and mocking light belying anyone's tears.

"They're the ones who don't sign complaints," she explains softly; and gives Soft-Clothes a hard profile.

Well, anybody's daughter can grow weary of scrubbing other people's toilets. White, black or brown, there's always a world of lost pride at the bottom of a whiskey glass. There's one world, at least, where color doesn't count at all: the world at the bottom of any cheap gin bottle.

"Of these 12,000,000 Americans," a white bishop informs us, "a disproportionate number have translated a deep inner frustration into an external attitude that is completely anti-social."

And it was only when the gin gave out that the girl in the plaid slacks broke at last, to cry out to the scarred walls all around:

"Ain't *any*body on *my* side?"

"I picked up a boy of twelve, sleepin' in a doorway," Soft-Clothes tells us, with some bewilderment still in his voice. "He said he had slept there five nights. I asked him why he didn't go home. He said 'Did you ever see my home? Five people sleep in one bed. It's better in the doorway.'"

The Chicago Crime Commission concludes that "undesirable living conditions in the area contribute materially to a high incidence of criminality.

"Every available facility for housing is utilized to provide sleeping and living quarters for a huge population that is crowded into the small geographical area comprising the 5th Police District.... After the outbreak of the war the population increased tremendously and overcrowded living conditions became more aggravated.... It was not infrequent that relatives who arrived in Chicago to engage in war work moved in with large families because of inability to find any other place to live.

"Crowded conditions result in family arguments. In many instances community bathroom and cooking facilities are used by several families. Disputes arising over the use of such facilities many times end in acts of violence. Cuttings and shootings have followed arguments over the time required to cook a piece of meat. It is very common for entire floors in residence buildings to be equipped with only one bathroom which accommodates several families. Men and women are thus thrown into close contact with one another resulting in quarrels and immorality. Crowded sleeping quarters make it necessary in many instances for as many as four people to sleep in one bed ... people sleep in hallways on newspapers, thus creating a fire hazard."

Such conditions also account for the high incidence of delinquency among Negro juveniles. It is a common circumstance that parents live at one address and the children at another. Children of such conditions are those who get into trouble almost as soon as they can walk around the block by themselves. Their graduation cry, too, is that bewildered one of the girl in the Wabash lockup:

"Ain't *any*body on *my* side?"

"What you cuffed for?" Soft-Clothes want to know of one of the boys who's so tough he drinks razor-soup for breakfast; with his left sleeve slit to the shoulder.

As if his life, like his knife, had been turned upon himself at last.

"I come in contact with a grey-boy," he explains; meaning any white man at all.

"You took forty-six cents off him."

"I didn't *take* it. It drop out of his pocket when I hit him."

"Why'd you hit him?"

"For good luck."

Negroes like to change their luck too.

And down in the lockup are the ones who've pressed their luck too long: there wait the pickpocket's deadpan mask and the shoplifter's measured manner; here the brutal lines of the paid-in-full premeditated murderer and there the coneroo's cynical leer.

Yet the man behind the murderer's mask is behind bars for stealing a bushel of mustard greens from an aunt and the coneroo's leer has been picked up for sleeping in a 47th Street hallway.

"What you here for, Boy?"

"For standin' by watchin'."

"Watchin' what?"

"The officers linin' up the boys on 39th Street—one of the officers called me 'boy' 'n' I told him I was a man so I had to come along too."

"If the Negro is worthy to die with the white man," the white bishop concludes, "he is worthy to live with him on terms of honest, objective equality. He fought for the liberty to speak, think and worship as conscience dictates, free from the specter of unemployment and enforced poverty, the opportunity for education, for the normal fulfillment of those human desires which spell human happiness."

And out of the curtained corners of the Negro slums a pall—the pall of human beings living in misery—creeps out of the city's farthest suburb and over the land like an unseen fog.

For no slum is an island. Chicago is tied together like the body of a man and we cannot ignore a great sore in one part and yet not expect other parts to be affected.

"Your Honor," the defense was made to plead in Richard Wright's *Native Son*, "Your Honor, there are four times as many Negroes in America today as there were people in the original thirteen colonies when they struck for their freedom. These twelve million Negroes, conditioned broadly by our own notions as we were by European ones when we first came here, are struggling within unbelievably narrow limits to achieve that feeling of at-home-ness for which we once strove so ardently. And, compared with our own struggle, they are striving under conditions far more difficult. If anybody, surely we ought to be able to understand what these people are after. This vast stream of life, dammed and muddied, is trying to sweep toward that fulfillment which all of us seek so fondly, but find so impossible to put into words. When we said that men are 'endowed with certain inalienable rights, among these are life, liberty and the pursuit of happiness,' we did not pause to define 'happiness.' That is the unexpressed quality in our quest, and we have never tried to put it into words. That is why we say, 'Let each serve God in his own fashion....'

"Your Honor, remember that men can starve from lack of self-realization as much as they can from lack of bread! Did we not build a nation, did we not wage war and conquer in the name of a dream to realize our personalities and to make those realized personalities secure.

"There are others, Your Honor, millions of others, Negro and white, and that is what makes our future seem a looming image of violence."

"I snatched a purse at a show where Sinatra was singin'," one of the Wabash Avenue Bigger Thomases confesses.

"Do you swoon too?" Soft-Clothes asks ever so softly.

And doesn't wait for an answer at all.

NOTES

1. "What Are You Doing Out There?," *New York Times*, 15 January 1951, 9; Bettina Drew, *Nelson Algren: A Life on the Wild Side* (Austin: University of Texas Press, 1991), 215, 237; Colin Asher, *Never a Lovely So Real: The Life and Work of Nelson Algren* (New York: W.W. Norton, 2019), 248–49, 303; Ellen Schrecker, *Many Are the Crimes: McCarthyism in America* (Princeton, N.J.: Princeton University Press, 1998), 178, 319–30.

2. Nelson Algren, "The World's Busiest Police Station," *Negro Digest*, January 1950, 5.

3. Algren, "The World's Busiest Police Station," 3; Brooke Horvath, *Understanding Nelson Algren* (Columbia: University of South Carolina Press, 2005).

4. James A. Miller, "*Black World/Negro Digest*," in *Encyclopedia of African-American Culture and History*, 2nd ed., ed. Colin A. Palmer (Farmington Hills, Mich.: Thomson Gale, 2006), 1: 287; C. Gerald Fraser, "Hoyt W. Fuller, a Literary Critic and Editor of Black Publications," *New York Times*, 13 May 1981, A32.

5. All of the ellipses in the text are in the original.

Appendix C:
Bibliography for Captions
to Illustrations

Some of the captions to the illustrations in this book contain information that does appear in the text and therefore is not cited in the endnotes. In those instances, bibliographic citations relating to this additional material that is contained in the captions appear below.

Figure 1
Nelson Algren at Marina City.
Michael Phillips, "The Stunt that Made Marina City Immortal," *Chicago Tribune*, 15 September 2019, sec. 1, 21.

Figure 4
Front cover of *Manhunt*, June 1958.
Jeff Vorzimmer, "Introduction: The Tortured History of *Manhunt*," Introduction to *The Best of "Manhunt*," ed. Jeff Vorzimmer (Eureka, Calif.: Stark House Press, 2019), 9; Earl Kemp and Luis Ortiz, eds., *Cult Magazines A to Z* (New York: Nonstop Press, 2009), s.v. "Manhunt."

Figure 5
Nelson Algren's 1931 University of Illinois yearbook picture.
H.E.F. Donohue, *Conversations with Nelson Algren* (New York: Hill and Wang, 1964), 11; Bettina Drew, *Nelson Algren: A Life on the Wild Side* (Austin: University of Texas Press, 1991), 11–13, 25; Nelson Algren to Ken McCollum, 9 January 1973, photocopy, author's collection, courtesy of Ken McCollum.

Figure 6
Front cover of *The Ring* magazine, May 1934.
"Dempsey v. Fish," *Time*, 29 February 1932, 39; J.J. Johnston and Sean Curtin, *Chicago Boxing* (Charleston, S.C.: Arcadia, 2005), 62; Nelson Algren, "A Ticket to Biro-Bidjan," *Chicago Free Press* 1, no. 2 (5 October 1970): 37–38.

Figure 8
Nelson Algren standing next to a table on moving day, 1975.
Bettina Drew, *Nelson Algren: A Life on the Wild Side* (Austin: University of Texas Press, 1991), 353; Trunk Line, undated advertisement, author's collection; *Chicago Sun-Times* photographs, author's collection; Eleanor Randolph, "Algren's

House Sale Not Quite a Best Seller," *Chicago Tribune*, 9 March 1975, sec. 1, 10; Henry Kisor, "Algren: First, He Was a Poet," *Chicago Sun-Times*, 10 May 1981, 20; https://www.chicagoreader.com/Bleader/archives/2009/04/01/nelson-algren (accessed January 11, 2021).

Figure 9

Nelson Algren sitting under a bridge, 1949.

Simone de Beauvoir, *A Transatlantic Love Affair: Letters to Nelson Algren*, comp. and annot. by Sylvie Le Bon de Beauvoir (New York: New Press, 1998), dust jacket, 9–10, 301, 355, 508; Art Shay, *Chicago's Nelson Algren* (New York: Seven Stories Press, 2007), xiv–xv.

Figure 11

The Arcade (Rat Alley), 1940.

Jack Conroy, "On Anvil," in *TriQuarterly* 43 (Fall 1978), 116; Jack Conroy, "On Anvil," in *The Little Magazine in America: A Modern Documentary History*, eds. Elliott Anderson and Mary Kinzie (Yonkers, N.Y.: Pushcart Book Press, 1978), 116; Nelson Algren to Ken McCollum, 21 April [1973], photocopy, author's collection, courtesy of Ken McCollum.

Figure 12

Advertisement, "How Long—How Long Blues."

"How Long—How Long Blues," *The Chicago Defender*, 8 September 1928, 8; David Leander Williams, *Indianapolis Jazz: The Masters, Legends and Legacy of Indiana Avenue* (Charleston, S.C.: History Press, 2014), 47–50; Elijah Wald, *Escaping the Delta: Robert Johnson and the Invention of the Blues* (New York: Amistad, 2004), 36–36.

Figure 14

Nelson Algren's bookplate.

Matthew J. Bruccoli, *Nelson Algren: A Descriptive Bibliography* (Pittsburgh: University of Pittsburgh Press, 1985), [92]; Art Shay, *Chicago's Nelson Algren* (Seven Stories Press: New York, 2007), xvii, xx; Deirdre Bair, *Simone de Beauvoir: A Biography* (New York: Summit Books, 1990), 501; Burt Britton, *Self-Portrait: Book People Picture Themselves* (New York: Random House, 1976), 10; Nelson Algren, *The Devil's Stocking* (New York: Arbor House, 1983), [309].

Figure 15

Draft book review.

Nelson Algren, "The Radical Innocent," *The Nation*, 21 September 1964, 142–43; Nelson Algren, "The Donkeyman by Twilight," *The Nation*, 18 May 1964, 509–12; Rick Soll, "Nelson Algren Bids Final Farewell," *Chicago Tribune*, 10 March 1975, sec. 1, 2; Eleanor Randolph, "Algren's House Sale Not Quite a Best Seller," *Chicago Tribune*, 9 March 1975, sec. 1, 10; Nelson Algren, *America Eats* (Iowa City: University of Iowa Press, 1992), xii–xiii; Undated book catalog, circa 2015, Bibliodisia Books, Chicago, Illinois; Ikumi Crocoll, formerly of the Newberry Library, to Richard F. Bales, 19 March 2016; Brooke Horvath, *Understanding Nelson Algren* (Columbia: University of South Carolina Press, 2005), [iv], 13*n*168–69.

Figure 16

James Blake, circa 1971.

James Blake, "Day of the Alligator," in *Nelson Algren's Own Book of Lonesome Monsters*, ed. Nelson Algren (New York: Lancer, 1962), 120–35.

Figure 18

Jack Conroy, circa 1936.

Douglas Wixson, *Worker-Writer in America: Jack Conroy and the Tradition of Midwestern Literary Radicalism, 1898–1990* (Urbana: University of Illinois Press, 1994), 411, 424; *New Letters* 57, no. 4 (Summer 1991): 73.

Figure 19

Nelson Algren's birthday party, circa 1947.

Stuart Brent, *The Seven Stairs* (New York: Simon & Schuster, 1962), 37, 59, between pages 128 and 129.

Figure 21

Nelson Algren at his typewriter.

George Murray, "His Old West Side Haunts," *Chicago American Pictorial Living*, 7 October 1956, 6; Art Shay, *Chicago's Nelson Algren* (Seven Stories Press: New York, 2007), xv, 2–[3]; Nelson Algren, *The Man with the Golden Arm*, eds. William J. Savage, Jr., and Daniel Simon, 50th Anniversary Critical Edition (New York: Seven Stories Press, [1999]), 11–13, 17, 33–36.

Figure 22

"Shoeless" Joe Jackson baseball card.

Nelson Algren, "A Lot You Got to Holler," in *The Neon Wilderness* (New York: Seven Stories Press, 1986), 110; Ted Golden, "Historic 1920–1921 W514s: The 'T206' of Strip-Card Sets," *Old Cardboard*, no. 11 (Spring 2007): 14–20.

Figure 23

Strip of five baseball cards.

Nelson Algren, *Chicago: City on the Make*, 60th anniversary edition (Chicago: University of Chicago Press, 2011), 37; Nelson Algren, "A Lot You Got to Holler," in *The Neon Wilderness* (New York: Seven Stories Press, 1986), 110; Ted Golden, "Historic 1920–1921 W514s: The 'T206' of Strip-Card Sets," *Old Cardboard*, no. 11 (Spring 2007): 14–18.

Figure 24

Swede Risberg baseball card.

Nelson Algren, *Chicago: City on the Make*, 60th anniversary edition (Chicago: University of Chicago Press, 2011), 34, 37; Ted Golden, "Historic 1920–1921 W514s: The 'T206' of Strip-Card Sets," *Old Cardboard*, no. 11 (Spring 2007): 14, 18.

Figure 25

The Black Sox, *Sporting News*, October 7, 1920.

Gene Carney, *Burying the Black Sox: How Baseball's Cover-Up of the 1919 World Series Fix Almost Succeeded* (Washington, D.C.: Potomac Books, 2006), 145, 147.

Figure 26

Studs Terkel, circa 1960.

Douglas Wixson, *Worker-Writer in America: Jack Conroy and the Tradition of Midwestern Literary Radicalism, 1898–1990* (Urbana: University of Illinois Press, 1994), 470–71; Bettina Drew, *Nelson Algren: A Life on the Wild Side* (Austin: University of Texas Press, 1991), 324, 400.

Figure 27
Nelson Algren's cottage, Miller Beach, Indiana.
Art Shay, *Nelson Algren's Chicago* (Urbana: University of Illinois Press, 1988), xvi.

Figure 29
James T. McCutcheon cartoon, *Chicago Tribune*, July 29, 1919.
James R. Grossman, Ann Durkin Keating, and Janice L. Reiff, eds., *The Encyclopedia of Chicago* (Chicago: University of Chicago Press, 2004), s.v. "Great Migration"; *Chicago Tribune*, 29 July 1919, "City Problems," 1; Carl Sandburg, *The
Chicago Race Riots July, 1919* (New York: Harcourt, Brace and World, 1969), ix–
xvii passim, 12–16.

Figure 31
Nelson Algren's book inscription to Richard Merkin.
William Grimes, "Richard Merkin, 70, Painter, Illustrator and Fashion Plate,"
New York Times, 13 September 2009, sec. 1, A38; Richard Merkin, "Nelson
Algren: A Fan's Notes," introduction to *The Neon Wilderness, The Man with
the Golden Arm, A Walk on the Wild Side*, by Nelson Algren (New York: Quality Paperback Book Club, 1993), viii; Mike McInnerney, Bill DeMain, and Gillian G. Gaar, *Sgt Pepper at Fifty: The Mood, the Look, the Sound, the Legacy of
the Beatles' Great Masterpiece* (New York: Sterling, 2017), 72, 73, 75, 76, 78–83.

Figure 32
Nelson Algren on his back porch, 1973.
Bettina Drew, *Nelson Algren: A Life on the Wild Side* (Austin: University of Texas
Press, 1991), 296, 311, 343, 402; Henry Kisor, "Nelson Algren, Hale and Salty
at 64," *Chicago Daily News Panorama*, 27–28 October 1973, 2–3; Jeff Huebner,
"Full Nelson," *Reader* 28, no. 8 (20 November 1998): 30.

Figure 33
Nelson Algren standing in his apartment.
George Murray, "His Old West Side Haunts," *Chicago American Pictorial Living*,
7 October 1956, 6; Art Shay, *Chicago's Nelson Algren* (Seven Stories Press: New
York, 2007), xv, 2–[3]; Nelson Algren, *The Man with the Golden Arm*, eds. Wil-
liam J. Savage, Jr., and Daniel Simon, 50th Anniversary Critical Edition (New
York: Seven Stories Press, [1999]), 17, 44, 57.

Figure 34
Sports Illustrated drawing of Nelson Algren at the Kentucky Derby, 1958.
Whitney Tower, "Prose for the Roses," *Sports Illustrated*, 28 April 1986, 38–40, 42,
45.

Figure 36
Chicago Daily News drawing of Nelson Algren, circa 1952.
"This is Algren," *Chicago Daily News*, 3 December 1952, 44.

Figure 38
Ben Shahn drawing of a man in jail.
"What Are You Doing Out There?," *New York Times*, 15 January 1951, 9; Walter
Harding, "Was It Legal? Thoreau in Jail," *American Heritage*, August 1975, 36.

Index